THE

ANTI-SLAVERY CRUSADE

IN AMERICA

THE LIBERTY AND
FREE SOIL PARTIES
IN THE NORTHWEST

Theodore Clarke Smith

ARNO PRESS
&
THE NEW YORK TIMES
NEW YORK 1969

Reprint edition 1969 by Arno Press, Inc.

*

Library of Congress Catalog Card No. 76–28555

*

Reprinted from a copy in
The New York State Library

*

Manufactured in the United States of America

THE LIBERTY AND FREE SOIL PARTIES
IN THE NORTHWEST

THE

LIBERTY AND FREE SOIL PARTIES

IN

THE NORTHWEST

TOPPAN PRIZE ESSAY OF 1896

BY

THEODORE CLARKE SMITH, PH.D.

SOMETIME OZIAS GOODWIN MEMORIAL FELLOW OF HARVARD UNIVERSITY
INSTRUCTOR IN THE UNIVERSITY OF MICHIGAN

NEW YORK
LONGMANS, GREEN, AND CO.
LONDON AND BOMBAY
1897

University Press:

John Wilson and Son, Cambridge, U.S.A.

PREFACE.

———◆———

THE history of the anti-slavery controversy in Congress
and in national politics is the subject of a vast and increasing number of writings ranging from monographs
to large volumes, but the local history of this great
struggle has received little or no attention. Believing,
with many students of recent years, that national and
State politics are too closely related, logically to admit
of such absolute separation, I have endeavored in this
monograph, by a study of the political anti-slavery
parties in the Old Northwest, to work out the local
history of that great movement in a region of which the
importance in our national development has not always
been adequately recognized. Combined with this main
object — and in my mind scarcely less important — has
been the effort to add to the knowledge of the growth
of the American party system.

This work has occupied much of my time during three
years spent in the Seminary of American History and
Institutions of Harvard University, and one year in the
University of Wisconsin. The authorities used are
stated and explained in an Appendix below : they have
been found by search in the great libraries of Boston,

Cambridge, and Madison, Wisconsin, by visits to many places in the various Northwestern States, and by correspondence with survivors of the period studied and their descendants. Yet the diaries and letters of the anti-slavery leaders, the reminiscences and biographies, have furnished but a small part of the material. The recollections of living men, communicated in person or by letters, have been suggestive, but have been used as authorities only to explain facts already learned from contemporary material. The most valuable group of sources has therefore been the newspapers of the time, and especially the Liberty and Free Soil press.

In reaching, studying, and arranging this large and confused mass of material, I have received indispensable assistance and kindness in every quarter. I desire to express a special obligation to the following gentlemen: Prof. Frederick J. Turner of the University of Wisconsin; Mr. Reuben G. Thwaites, Secretary of the Wisconsin Historical Society; Mr. Warren Upham, Secretary of the Western Reserve Historical Society; Hon. Edward L. Pierce, Milton, Massachusetts; Hon. Samuel D. Hastings, Madison, Wisconsin; Prof. W. P. Howe, Mt. Pleasant, Iowa; Mr. Charles M. Zug, Rev. George W. Clark, and Rev. J. F. Conover, Detroit, Michigan; Hon. Albert G. Riddle and Gen. William Birney, Washington, D. C.; Hon. George Hoadly, New York; and Mr. Sherman M. Booth, Chicago. I also wish to record the kindness of Mr. Herbert Putnam of the Boston Public Library, who gave me access to the newspapers of that institution while as yet unclassified and unarranged; and the courtesy of the editorial staffs of the *Chicago Journal* and *Cleveland Leader* who have given me every facility to examine the valuable files of these papers.

Especially do I wish to thank the Hon. George W. Julian, of Irvington, Indiana, for the unfailing kindness and courtesy with which on very many occasions he has aided me by his manuscript records and his own accurate memory. Finally, and above all, I wish to express my indebtedness to Prof. Albert Bushnell Hart, of Harvard University, at whose suggestion and under whose guidance the work was begun, and from whom at every stage I have received invaluable advice and assistance.

THEODORE CLARKE SMITH.

ANN ARBOR, *November, 1897.*

CONTENTS.

CHAPTER VIII.

CHAPTER IX.

CHAPTER X.

CHAPTER XI.

CHAPTER XII.

CHAPTER XIII.

CHAPTER XIV.

CHAPTER XV.

CHAPTER XVI.

THE

LIBERTY AND FREE SOIL PARTIES.

CHAPTER I.

THE NORTHWEST IN THE ANTI-SLAVERY STRUGGLE.

1830–1861.

THE years 1854–56 saw the creation of a new party out of fragments of the Whig organization combined with anti-slavery Democrats, Free Soilers, Temperance men, Abolitionists, and Know Nothings. Great, however, as was the popular upheaval at this time, the platform and programme of the party were by no means new; for its opposition to the extension of slavery had long been the basis of certain political organizations, in which, moreover, many of the ablest men in the Republican party had gained that experience and prominence which gave them their leadership. In fact, to their thirteen years of activity may justly be ascribed, in no small degree, the growth of that Northern anti-slavery sentiment which in 1854, by the formation of the new party, took the first political step toward civil war; yet notwithstanding these well-known facts, there has so far been no adequate study of the development and achievements of the Liberty and Free Soil parties.

In political matters the "Old Northwest," maintaining in most respects the characteristics of a frontier region down to the middle of the century, presents features of peculiar interest. Organization was incomplete, personalities counted for more than principles, and eloquence and combativeness for more than

social culture and wealth: hence there was an unsteadiness in
party fortunes and, particularly in anti-slavery matters, a vari-
ableness in political opinion far exceeding similar phenomena in
New England and in the Middle States.   Hence, in the West
began the uprising of 1854, which in one year accomplished
the creation of a new party and the complete overthrow in most
of the Western States of the hitherto victorious Democracy.

It is this last feature which gives to the anti-slavery movement in the Northwest its peculiar significance.   Had not the
Republican party been born in the Northwest, had not this section as a unit taken the lead in the movement, the history of
the country would probably have been altogether different.   The
Middle and Eastern States, slow as they were to change front,
might have been expected eventually to oppose the spread of
slavery; but had not the Northwest also proved anti-slavery in
character, the action of the East might have had more resemblance to the Hartford Convention of 1814 than to the Republican Convention of 1860; and the war which followed might
have been directed, not against Southern, but against Northern
secession.

The new States, then, eventually turned the scale in favor of
freedom; but what determined their action?   Any Northwest-
erner during the years 1840 to 1860 would have said without
hesitation that the anti-slavery clause of the Northwest Ordinance, by excluding slaves and slave-holders, had settled the
question from the outset.   Modern opinion, however, suspicious
of such generalizations, and inclined to look for something more
deep-seated than "mere legislation" to account for the social
and political characteristics of a vast region, inclines to believe
that the result would have been the same, even had there been
no prohibition of slavery in 1787; that it was the stream of emi-
grants from New England, New York, and Pennsylvania, pouring
first into Ohio, then Michigan and Indiana, and lastly Illinois,
Wisconsin, and Iowa, who inevitably preserved the Northwestern
States for freedom, in spite of a large immigration from Virginia, Maryland, and Kentucky.   It was, according to this view,
a mere question of physiography, the slave-holding States naturally pouring their surplus population into the neighboring

Southwest, the free States into the Northwest, each seeking physical conditions similar to those of the parent communities.

In the case of Michigan and Wisconsin, we may at the outset admit the truth of this explanation, for these regions were too far north to be easily accessible to Southern immigration or to furnish profitable fields for slave labor; but in regard to the southern tier of free States something may be said in favor of the old view. Nearly half of Indiana and Illinois, and a large part of Ohio, lay to the south of Mason and Dixon's line, in immediate contact with slave territory. In this region slavery was just as likely to be profitable as in Missouri, Kentucky, Virginia, and Maryland; and, as a matter of fact, these sections actually were settled by people from the South, so that each of these three Ohio River States — Ohio, Indiana, and Illinois — repeated in miniature the political condition of the nation during the first half of the century. Men of Southern birth or descent led parties, directed the State policy, and furnished the great majority of governors, judges, senators, and State officials of all kinds, until the Republican outburst drove them from power. The influx from New England, New York, and Pennsylvania was very large in these States, and played a very important part in preparing the way for the Republican movement; but until very late it had little more effect in directing State sentiment than had New England in influencing Federal policy toward slavery. Having the power, then, why did not the Southern-born leaders of these States admit slavery? What was the cause of the failure of the efforts made in all three States? The reason, it would seem, must lie in the fact that the prohibition of slavery had kept people who lived by the institution from coming into these States, so that in the years 1800 to 1830 the majority of Southerners in the Northwest, although sympathizing in most respects with the Southern point of view, had never held slaves themselves, were personally indifferent to the system of slavery, and cared nothing for its introduction.

The Ordinance of 1787, therefore, by determining the character of the settlers during the territorial period, did fulfil its purpose of keeping slavery out of the Northwest; but no legislation could or did make anti-slavery a dominant political force in that region. Over half a century was to pass before the rule of Southern sympathizers was repudiated by the Northwest, and before the States subject to the Ordinance of 1787 — together with Iowa, first fruits for the North of the Louisiana Purchase and the Missouri Compromise — determined to throw their weight against Southern domination at Washington and in the State capitals.

In bringing about this result, political agitation played a prominent part; and it is this phase of the anti-slavery movement with which the present monograph is concerned. That no attempt is here made to cover the entire field of anti-slavery action, but mainly its political aspects, must not be understood to imply that political anti-slavery agitation was more important than purely moral and religious action; for the appeal to the conscience was in fact the cause and condition of the existence of anti-slavery sentiment, and continued steadily in operation during the entire course of the Liberty, Free Soil, and Republican parties. " There can be no doubt but that the teachings of the Gospel were decisive influences in thousands of individual cases in the United States in creating a public opinion against slavery before the civil war; but it would be far more difficult to write the history of their action than to write the history of the political influences which combined with them." [1]

The mistake is often made of failing to distinguish between the different forms of anti-slavery agitation, and confusing the terms "anti-slavery" and "abolition." [2]   Only before 1840 did " abolitionist " and " anti-slavery man " mean the same thing. From 1840 to 1848 the name of " abolitionist " was accepted by such men only as sought anti-slavery ends outside the long established political and moral agencies; it included not only the Garrisonians, but also Liberty men of all shades. After 1848 the term, although often used as equivalent to " Free Soil " or " Republican," was generally avoided by those parties;

---

[1] G. B. Adams, *Civilization during the Middle Ages*, 51.

[2] See, for example, the hopeless vagueness of the use of the words in J. T. Morse's *Abraham Lincoln*, I. 176–7, where Giddings and Garrison are classed together.

but it remained the appellative of two groups, — the Garriso-nians, and the followers of Gerrit Smith and William Goodell. Nevertheless, the two men commonly referred to as the personi-fication of abolitionism are William Lloyd Garrison and Wendell Phillips, whose striking personality causes the fact to be for-gotten that after 1840 their followers in the whole United States numbered at the most a few thousands, and that their leadership was expressly repudiated by the majority of actual "abolition-ists." In the Northwest there was, after 1840, very little knowl-edge of Garrison and his methods, the main interest of Western anti-slavery men finding its outlet in political action rather than in demands for disunion.

To separate out the political from the moral movement is, therefore, possible. It is the aim of this monograph to describe that political activity which was most characteristic of the Western movement, and to trace the growth of anti-slavery political parties in the several Northwestern States, from their beginnings to the time when the public sentiment which they had assisted so powerfully to create resulted in the formation of the Republican party, in the year 1854. It does not treat of the Whig and Democratic parties, except when directly concerned with anti-slavery questions or with the Liberty and Free Soil organizations; nor does it include, except for pur-poses of illustration or explanation, any consideration of the Congressional action of Northwestern men, whether as members of the old parties or of the distinctively anti-slavery bodies.

CHAPTER II.

ANTI-SLAVERY BEGINNINGS IN THE NORTHWEST.

1830–1838.

In 1830 the conception that slavery was "a problem" was little known in the Northwest; still less the idea that it was a national sin or a crime. Neither the Virginia immigrant nor his neighbor from New England had any particular fondness for the institution; but the thought that it bore any different relation to them than did poverty, crime, or evil in the abstract scarcely entered their minds. That there could be any remedy for it seemed never to occur to either group.

Certain movements of an anti-slavery character with which the Northwest was not wholly unacquainted had, it is true, taken place in the preceding decade; but these were not of a kind to disturb the general indifference, nor were they in fact on the same basis as the later anti-slavery agitation. An emancipation propaganda, mainly in the Southern States, had been in existence for a score of years, and since 1814 had gone so far as to bring about national conventions, representing in all over a hundred local societies. There had been a few societies in Ohio, and one or two abolition newspapers had sprung up, notably Benjamin Lundy's *Genius of Universal Emancipation*, and Charles Osborn's *Philanthropist;* and in 1824 the Ohio legislature had adopted resolutions favoring gradual emancipation; [1] but the whole movement was so purely moral and unaggressive, and its activity was so largely confined to the slave States, that upon the Northwest it made little general impression. By 1830 these societies had begun to decay rapidly in the South, and,

[1] *Senate Journal,* 18 Cong., 1 sess. 245 (March 23, 1824).

although some of them still existed in Ohio, they were without vigor, and attracted no attention whatever.[1]

There had been two controversies which brought slavery into politics: the national struggle leading to the Missouri Compromise, and the local attempts to introduce slavery into the Northwestern States;[2] but by 1830 both of them were passing into oblivion, almost forgotten in the rush of tariff and financial controversy, and the results of both were so thoroughly acquiesced in that revival seemed impossible. Both of these struggles, moreover, were too purely defensive on the part of the free States to suggest any aggressive conflict with slavery where it already existed.

Colonization, the only philanthropic movement which at this time concerned the negroes as such, was not in any sense anti-slavery: it had for its basis the inferiority of negroes and their incompatibility with whites; it was therefore, at its best, only an attempt to better the lot of free blacks, while in the South it was looked upon chiefly as a means of removing a class whose existence in a slave-holding community was an anomaly and a possible danger. In 1830, however, the activity of this movement in the North seemed justified, in the minds of benevolent people, by the apparently hopeless degradation in which free blacks were condemned to live; for in every free State "Black Laws," of varying degrees of rigor, segregated them as an inferior class under grave social, civil, and political disabilities.[3] Without going into all the details, it may be said that in the Northwest free negroes could not testify against a white, serve on juries, vote, or send their children to public schools; they were forbidden, in some cases, to enter the State without giving bonds not to become paupers; and if

---

[1] For the emancipation movement before 1830, see Henry Wilson, *Slave Power*, I. chs. ii, xiii, xiv, and William Birney, *J. G. Birney and his Times*, 74–86, 169, 382–412.

[2] On the efforts to introduce slavery into the Northwest, see B. A. Hinsdale, *The Old Northwest*, 351–67.

[3] Ohio laws of Jan. 5, 1804; Jan. 5, 1807; Feb. 9, March 14, 1831. Indiana laws of Dec. 30, 1816; Jan. 28, 1818; Jan. 22, 1824. Illinois laws of March 22, 1819; Jan. 3, 17, 1825; Jan. 17, 1829; Feb. 1, 1831. Iowa law of Jan. 21, 1839.

they were claimed as slaves, they were obliged, under the national Fugitive Slave Law, or under special State laws, to prove their title to freedom before a magistrate alone, without the privilege of a jury. That any incongruity existed between these Black Laws and the long Bills of Rights prefixed to the various State constitutions, scarcely occurred to any one. The negro disabilities were considered fit and necessary; they merely proved how much it was for the interest of the free blacks to go to Liberia under the auspices of the Colonization Society.

Some scattered individuals could be found, however, to whom the system of negro bondage appeared something else than merely a regrettable necessity. Many of these were anti-slavery Quakers, whose conscientious scruples are shown, for example, by the fact that a dry-goods store in Philadelphia kept by Lydia White, a Quakeress, whose wares were made entirely by free labor, received orders from far-off Ohio and Indiana.[1] There were others whose sensibilities had been roused by the sight of a fugitive-slave chase, or by the kidnapping of a free black; and there were still more who from religious logic found themselves unable to reconcile slavery and Christianity. Many of the last-mentioned were Southern men, who had become convinced of the iniquity of the slave system, and had removed to the North to escape from contact with it. Some of these had been active in the earlier emancipation movement, and still continued to assert the sinfulness of slavery,[2] and without doubt to assist fugitives with all possible zeal.[3]

Thus, while on the whole Northwestern popular feeling was utterly indifferent, anti-slavery elements were slowly growing. What was needed was some stimulus to rouse them into activity. Vague dislikes, religious scruples, sentimental and emotional

---

[1] *Liberator*, May 28, 1831.

[2] See, for example, W. Birney, *J. G. Birney and his Times*, 382 *seq.*, and G. W. Julian, *The Genesis of Modern Abolitionism*, in the *International Review*, June, 1882.

[3] For details, see W. F. Siebert, *Underground Railroad* (in preparation, 1897).

objections, must be united in pursuit of some tangible end before the popular indifference could be pierced. This stimulus, this direction, was undoubtedly furnished in the years 1831–35 by William Lloyd Garrison's *Liberator*, whose eloquent, uncompromising, even violent utterances, demanding immediate, unconditional emancipation, fell with thrilling effect upon the nascent anti-slavery sentiment in the Northwest. The man into whose hands a copy came could no longer maintain a careless indifference on the subject; he might be alarmed or indignant, but he was forced to think, and with many men there could be but one outcome. The paper made converts from the very start; to the old-time emancipationists it came like a draught of fire reviving their enthusiasm and redoubling their energies. Still better, the *Liberator* served as an outlet to sentiments that had hitherto been suppressed; it put Western and Eastern anti-slavery men into communication with each other; and, from its unique position as the only aggressive abolition paper in the country, it served as a national organ. It must always be remembered that Western abolitionism had an independent beginning; but while credit for independent action must be given to President Storrs of Western Reserve College; to Asa Mahan, John Rankin, Elizur Wright, Jr., Beriah Green, Theodore D. Weld, and Samuel Crothers in Ohio; to Charles Osborne in Indiana; and to James G. Birney in Kentucky, nevertheless the establishment of the *Liberator* gave the abolition cause its first real impetus in the West as well as in the East.

The smouldering flames thus fanned by Garrison spread in all directions, and within a year from the foundation of the paper an agitation of a kind as yet unknown had begun in the Northwest. Some clergymen early in 1831 wrote letters to the *Liberator*, or rushed into print in the local papers, to the amazement of all and to the disgust of most quiet-minded, conservative men. Then, after the moral indignation of the new reformers had expressed itself in condemnation of slaveholding on religious grounds, their practical natures led them to fall foul of the only movement wherein negro philanthropy had at the time any outlet, namely, colonization. As early as 1831 the free blacks of Cincinnati, Columbus, and other places

in Ohio had been protesting against the project;[1] and this circumstance, joined with the relentless logic of the *Liberator*, at
once led anti-slavery men to appreciate the fact that colonization was not in reality a scheme to benefit the negroes, even
the freed men, but simply to get rid of them.   The negroes
themselves might have protested against colonization until the
end of time, without attracting any notice; but this attack from
a new quarter aroused the liveliest indignation.   Controversy
immediately began, and after 1832 a war of biblical texts broke
out in Ohio, and to a much less extent in Indiana and Michigan.
Nowhere was the attack upon colonization more active than in
Western Reserve College, from which, until the death of its
anti-slavery president, C. B. Storrs, and the subsequent departure of the anti-slavery professors, Elizur Wright, Jr., and
Beriah Green, there poured forth a constant succession of
lectures, sermons, pamphlets, newspaper articles, and letters.

Organization began almost simultaneously with the movement
in the East.   As early as the fall of 1832 an anti-slavery society
was projected in Western Reserve College; but the first actual
organization on record was that of the Tallmadge Anti-Slavery
Society, founded April 10, 1833, by thirty-two persons under
the leadership of two clergymen.[2]   After this speedily followed the Paint Valley Abolition Society under the lead of
Rev. Samuel Crothers, the Gustavus Anti-Slavery Society, the
Western Reserve College Anti-Slavery Society, and others,
until by the end of 1833 there were as many as seven or eight.[3]

---

[1] *Liberator*, July 30, Sept. 10, 1831 ; Jan. 28, 1832.

[2] General William Birney, in his life of his father (p. 164 *seq.*), shows that
several old societies dating from the emancipation movement were still in
existence at Ripley in Monroe County, at Mt. Pleasant, West Union, Zanes-
ville, and Columbiana, most of which in the years following 1833 joined in
the new movement.   They were, it seems, in a state of inaction after
1828–29, and played no formative part in the later organization.   Indeed,
they seem hardly to have been known, although signs of them appear from
time to time.   For a mention of the Putnam Society, see *Liberator*, Aug. 17,
1833, p. 131.

[3] From the *Liberator*, Sept. 7, 1833, we learn that there existed at this
time a State organization of "abolition societies"; but it seems to have had
no influence on later events.   The history of these societies is very obscure.

The relation of this movement to that in the East was shown when, on December 4, 1832, the American Anti-Slavery Society was formed at Philadelphia, at a convention presided over by Beriah Green, of Western Reserve College. Yet the only other Western members present were Elizur Wright, Jr., Rev. Samuel Crothers, J. M. Stirling of Cuyahoga County, and the Sutliff brothers of Ashtabula County: no one came from any State west of Ohio, nor were any managers appointed for any other Northwestern State, — facts clearly indicating how far Ohio was at this time in advance of its neighbors in anti-slavery sentiment.

So far the movement had met no opposition other than colonizationist criticism; but in the year 1834 a conflict occurred which had far-reaching effects. Lane Seminary, a theological school at Cincinnati under the presidency of Lyman Beecher, was the leading institution of its kind in the Northwest. Theodore D. Weld, one of the instructors, a man whom Dr. Beecher called " eloquent as an angel and powerful as thunder," became interested in anti-slavery matters, and at the formation of the American Anti-Slavery Society was appointed a manager for that body. In the following spring the issue between colonization and abolition came up sharply in the Seminary, and to settle the question a two days' debate was held. Although a majority of the students came from the South, Mr. Weld's eloquence and the testimony of an emancipated slave carried the day in favor of the new movement, and with the utmost enthusiasm an anti-slavery society for active agitation was organized on the spot. Turning their hands to the nearest work, some members began to aid free blacks in Cincinnati; others went on lecturing tours in the surrounding country, or appeared in the East as delegates to the American Anti-Slavery Meeting. In August, however, an unexpected blow fell upon the new society; the trustees, in the absence of Dr. Beecher, voted that anti-slavery agitation being " political in character," was improper in a theological school, and that all organization, discussion, or even conversation in public places on the subject should henceforth be forbidden. The Southern blood of the young men of the institution

revolted at such dictation, and under the lead of Theodore
Weld fifty-one of the students — two-thirds of the whole num-
ber — instantly asked for dismissal. Just at this time, in the
woods of Lorain County, Rev. John Shipherd was founding
"Oberlin Collegiate Institute" as an evangelical anti-slavery
institution, under the presidency of Rev. Asa Mahan, with
Charles G. Finney, already noted as a revivalist, as a professor.
Here most of the seceders found a refuge ; and, when Western
Reserve College lost its anti-slavery professors, Oberlin, led by
its vigorous faculty and inspired by the accession of the Lane
Seminary students, soon became the centre of religious anti-
slavery propagandism in Ohio, and in fact in the whole
Northwest.[1]

This Lane Seminary incident made a profound impression
upon public sentiment. It was the first action in the Northwest which looked like persecution, and as such it thrilled all
anti-slavery workers with a new sense of the importance of
their cause; yet still more it emphasized what as yet abolitionists had hardly realized, the supreme indifference which
many deeply religious men felt toward slavery. The stir which
it had created was not soon allowed to die down; for some
of the seceders, burning with a sense of their wrongs, and not
content to settle quietly at Oberlin, began an active anti-slavery
agitation. H. B. Stanton, J. A. Thome, M. R. Robinson, and,
most eloquent of all, Theodore D. Weld, may fairly be said to
have done more to advance the anti-slavery movement in Ohio
than any other body of men. From town to town they went
preaching, lecturing, talking; in churches, in school-houses
when churches were shut to them, in private houses, barns, or,
as a last resort, in the open air; to audiences large or small,
friendly or contemptuous. Not content with mere denunciation, they tried in every town to found an anti-slavery society
and to start anti-slavery petitions; and thus they prepared the
way for the growth of a general anti-slavery feeling. In no

---

[1] For the Lane Seminary affair and its connection with Oberlin, see J.
H. Fairchild, *Oberlin Colony and College*, 50–77 ; L. Tappan, *Life of Arthur
Tappan*, 229–242 ; Asa Mahan, *Autobiography*. There is also an account in
Henry Wilson, *Slave Power*, I., ch. xix.

part of Ohio did the lecturing of Mr. Weld make a deeper impression than on the Western Reserve, a region more like the New England of the preceding century than was the original New England itself in 1835. There the Puritan element proved such fertile ground for the sowing of abolition doctrine, that, after Weld's tour in 1835–36, popular sentiment became antislavery with a nearness to unanimity probably unequalled in any similar area in the United States. When, after a year's campaign, most of the young agitators settled down as clergymen, or turned Eastward, their work had been well done in Ohio; but Michigan and Indiana had experienced little of the impetus, and Illinois and the outlying Territories none at all. In view of the results attained in Ohio, where, until 1830, popular sentiment had been no farther advanced than in its Western neighbors, it seems possible that, had Weld, Stanton, Thome, and the rest extended their work, those other States might have developed an anti-slavery sentiment commensurate with that of Ohio.

After 1834–35, anti-slavery societies gradually overspread the Northwest, their aims for the most part moral and religious, and their activity still confined to protests against slavery rather than to aggressive attacks upon it. A typical plan of action is that of the Ohio State Anti-Slavery Society, as stated by J. G. Birney in 1835: "We shall seek to effect the destruction of slavery, not by exciting discontent in the minds of the slaves — not by the physical force of the free States, not by the interference of Congress with State Rights; but . . . by ceaseless proclamation of the truth upon the whole subject, by urging upon slave-holders and the whole community the flagrant enormity of slavery as a sin against God and man, by demonstrating the safety of immediate abolition, by presenting facts, . . . by correcting the public sentiment of the free States. We shall absolve ourselves from political responsibility by petitioning Congress to abolish slavery and the slave trade wherever it exercises constitutional jurisdiction." [1]

In Ohio the number of societies increased from a dozen or more in 1834, to over three hundred in 1838, and to a consider-

[1] *Liberator,* May 9, 1835.

ably greater number in 1840. After that year the anti-slavery
sentiment of Ohio took a new direction, and the societies tended
to disappear; yet many continued, particularly on the Western
Reserve, until the Civil War. In Indiana the first societies did
not appear until 1836, and their growth was slow. In 1838 only
eight reported to the American Anti-Slavery Society; nor was it
until the end of 1839 and the beginning of 1840 that the energetic but single-handed work of Arnold Buffum succeeded in
causing a marked increase. The names of only a score of
these societies are known, and in all probability most of them
were ephemeral. It is certain that in Indiana anti-slavery sentiment was less organized and feebler than in any other of the
Northwestern States except Iowa: this may be accounted for
by the comparatively small proportion of Northern-born settlers, and by the lack of agitation, of which, except at rare
intervals, Indiana had little experience.

In Michigan societies were formed in 1834, and by the spring
of 1838 nineteen were reported. After this time, as the agitation went on, the number must have increased rapidly,
although we have no full statistics. The centre of the movement was in Lenawee County, in which alone, in 1839, there
were fifteen societies. Illinois's first society was that of Putnam
County, formed in 1835. By 1838 thirteen had reported to the
National Anti-Slavery Convention, a number which must have
been very greatly increased by 1840. They were scattered over
the northern and northwestern parts of the State, the strongest
region being the seven or eight northeastern counties, which
stood in relation to the rest of the State much as the Western
Reserve did to Ohio. In Wisconsin and Iowa at this time
scarcely any attention was given to anti-slavery agitation; it
was not until 1840–41, when elsewhere in the country the
formation of societies had practically ceased, that a few individuals in these frontier Territories began the work of
organization.[1]

As might be expected from the religious character of the
early anti-slavery movement, church action on the subject was

[1] For statistics of anti-slavery societies at this time, see the annual reports
of the American Anti-Slavery Society from 1835 to 1838.

promptly invoked by zealous clergymen. In 1834 individual congregations adopted resolutions deploring slavery as an evil; and later in the year a long, ably written declaration in favor of immediate emancipation was published, signed by sixteen Ohio clergymen, nearly all Presbyterians. Within a year from this time the subject was fairly placed before the larger church bodies, where it caused hot debate. The Synod of Illinois passed resolutions condemning slavery, at a time when abolitionism, properly so called, was hardly known in the State. Throughout the Northwest, Presbyterian Synods, Baptist Associations, Methodist Conferences, and Friends' Yearly Meetings were shaken out of their customary composure, and by 1838 the condition of things in the churches was suggestive of nothing so much as of civil war. All the forces of conservatism united to suppress anti-slavery discussion and to reject anti-slavery principles as in any way a suitable test for church fellowship; while from the Southern branches of each denomination came bitter remonstrances against agitation, with eager and plausible defences of the institution quoted from the Bible. The anti-slavery clergymen, on their part, cried aloud and spared not, including the slave-holder, his apologist, and even his fellow-communicant, in the same bitter condemnation. Thus the struggle went on with increasing violence until it resulted, in several of the Christian denominations, in a split on anti-slavery lines.[1] In these internal controversies the clerical element, hitherto predominant in general anti-slavery work, found a field of occupation, and tended to withdraw from the lead in anti-slavery societies; leadership thus fell to laymen, under whose management anti-slavery agitation in the years after 1838 took a new trend.

Thus the new movement was started by moral and religious agitation; but without the powerful aid of another factor it could never have made such gains after 1835. In its early years in the Northwest it made little stir in the community at large, but by 1835 the number of anti-slavery societies had grown to be so considerable, the churches were so convulsed, and the outcries

---

[1] Von Holst has a lucid discussion of the status of the churches on slavery in his *Constitutional History*, II. 226 *seq.*

of the agitators were so continuous, that the ultra-conservative and the pro-slavery elements of society took alarm, particularly since the insurrection of Nat Turner in Virginia in 1831 had given a fatal blow to negro philanthropy in the South. This tragedy, although entirely unconnected with the agitation described above, had naturally given Southerners so great a fear and horror of abolition, that by 1835 it was a settled conviction that the one unpardonable crime was to tamper with the lot of slaves or to try to alter it in any way whatever. The result was persecution, the one thing necessary to give the cause an immense impulse.

In the autumn of 1834 mobs began to appear, but only here and there, and they met with little popular support. The next year, however, some Kentuckians caught Amos Dresser, one of the Lane Seminary students, distributing abolition books; and they furnished an example for their sympathizers north of the Ohio River by stripping and lashing him in public, with threats of worse treatment if he repeated his offence. After this, mob violence became increasingly common. Weld on his journeys met with uproars, insults, and at last with rotten eggs and filth, a kind of treatment which resulted only in increasing his fervor without in the least restraining him. In the next year it seemed as if the lower elements of society all over the North were leagued together to suppress free speech, while respectable people and municipal officials looked on with indifference or with active approval. In every part of Ohio, even on the Western Reserve, each new society was formed amid the crashing of stones against doors and windows, and the hootings of a mob. That all who assailed the abolitionists had any clear idea why they were doing it, is altogether unlikely. Some of them regarded the reformers as upsetters of society, deniers of the Bible, "amalgamationists," — in short, as anarchists; others considered them as emissaries of British enemies to Republican institutions, corrupted by British gold;[1] but many others, no doubt, knew them merely as unpopular persons, and therefore as fair marks for rotten eggs and decayed vegetables.

Missouri and Kentucky now proceeded to eject from within

[1] *Philanthropist*, April 21, 1837.

their borders all men suspected of abolition leanings. From Kentucky came James G. Birney, largely influenced by Theodore Weld, escaping a threatened persecution only to fall into an actual one; for in 1836 the office in Cincinnati where he printed the *Philanthropist*, the first Western anti-slavery organ, was twice sacked and his press destroyed. From Missouri were driven Elijah P. Lovejoy, like Birney, the publisher of an anti-slavery newspaper, which he now issued at Alton, Illinois ; and Dr. David Nelson, formerly an army surgeon, now an anti-slavery schoolmaster.

In 1836 anti-abolition meetings in Cincinnati and elsewhere served to give some sort of respectability to the attack; but in 1837 the more law-abiding elements of society were willing to cease opposition, for the popular opponents of the new movement had, by their reckless violence, overshot the mark. Tar and feathers were freely applied in Indiana ; pistol shots were used to intimidate in Ohio; and finally, in November of that year, mob rule culminated in Illinois, where Lovejoy, who had refused to give way to repeated attacks, perished gun in hand while defending his printing-office against an armed mob. It is needless to say that the anti-slavery movement flourished under this persecution as never before. Men of a Puritan cast of mind were forced to think, and found themselves at one with the abolitionists ; fair-minded people, indignant at the oppression of a minority, sided with them; notoriety seekers and lovers of excitement, fanatics and cranks of every sort, side by side with earnest, devoted men and women, rushed into the anti-slavery ranks; and in the track of every mob societies sprang up like mushrooms. After 1839 outbreaks of violence became infrequent, and although in pro-slavery sections of the Northwestern States there were occasional mobs down to the time of the Civil War, general persecution was at an end. The abolitionists had grown to be too many and too respectable to be thus put down.[1]

[1] On anti-slavery mobs, see Henry Wilson, *Slave Power*, I. ch. xx, xxi, xxvii ; *Life of W. L. Garrison*, by his children ; *Liberator*, and *Emancipator*, 1836–39, *passim ;* H. B. Stanton, *Random Recollections*, 32–5. Compare, however, W. Birney, *J. G. Birney and his Times*, 250 seq.

Thus events from 1835 to 1839 had caused the anti-slavery propaganda to increase, but more and more clearly had brought into prominence the fact that moral suasion alone was inadequate to effect the desired result. Moreover, now that the clerical anti-slavery forces were becoming involved in their sectarian troubles, the laymen, — lawyers, physicians, farmers, — into whose hands the management of the cause came, tended to look at their work from a more practical point of view. Since moral suasion as an agent to effect an immediate reform had by 1838 proved a failure, the American man of affairs began to think that, if he could not persuade, he could enforce. The time had come for the anti-slavery cause to enter politics.

CHAPTER III.

ABOLITION IN WESTERN POLITICS.

1836–1839.

THE earliest anti-slavery societies, although depending for success mainly on moral suasion, did not fail to give attention sometimes to the political duties of abolitionists. In answer to the charge of the South that they were trying to interfere with slavery in the States, they uniformly admitted the dependence of slavery on State law alone, and the consequent inability of Congress or the free States to carry out their desire for immediate emancipation. There remained two points at which the North could attack slavery, namely, the District of Columbia and the Territories; and accordingly from an early date we find resolutions like those of the Portage County (Ohio) Society, of November 30, 1834: " While we believe that we ought to use all moral means for the universal abolition of slavery, we also hold that the free States are peculiarly responsible for slavery in all Territories subject to the legislative control of Congress ; and that they are under the most special and solemn obligations to use every means, moral or political, to give freedom to those of our fellow-citizens now held in slavery under the laws of Congress." [1]

To induce Congress to take such action, the societies resolved, in the words of the Ohio Anti-Slavery Society in 1835, " to absolve themselves from the political responsibility by petitioning Congress to abolish slavery and the slave trade wherever it exercises constitutional jurisdiction " ; and the result was a steady stream of petitions from Ohio, Michigan, and

[1] *Emancipator*, Dec. 23, 1834.

later from Indiana and Illinois.   Of the strenuous Congressional struggle over the question of their reception, it is not necessary to speak here, except to say that it played a considerable part in increasing anti-slavery interest in the Northwest during the years 1836–42, and furnished to the later political anti-slavery struggle two men, Thomas Morris and Joshua R. Giddings, both of whom took distinct anti-slavery ground in regard to petitions.   Another stream of petitions directed to several of the Western State legislatures, asking for the repeal of the Black Laws, fared little or no better than did the national petitions at Washington, except that none of the legislatures ventured to adopt a "gag-rule."   Finding petition an effective method of agitation, the societies kept it up with vigor, and as their num- bers increased greatly during the years of persecution, so the size and number of the petitions increased, until men willing to present them, like John Quincy Adams, Giddings, and Morris, found themselves involved in a heavy task.

In the Northwestern State legislatures, where the Southern- born element was preponderant, we find at this time a series of remarkable legislative acts called forth by the continual influx of these petitions.   Even in Michigan, where the population was mainly from the Eastern States, and where there were no severe Black Laws, a conservative spirit prevailed, and in 1838 the legislature refused to consider a proposition to secure the right of jury trial to fugitive slaves,[1] and declared it " unneces- sary and inexpedient" to express any opinion as to the power of Congress over slavery in the District of Columbia and the Territories, and over the interstate slave trade.   In Illinois, the legislature in 1837 adopted a long series of resolutions to the fol- lowing general effect: It "fully appreciated and shared the feelings of alarm caused by the misguided abolitionists, whose end, even if attained peaceably, would bring disaster."   Though it deplored the existence of slavery, it believed that the general government had no power to free the slaves, and it therefore resolved (1) That it deplored abolition societies and considered that they did more harm than good; (2) "That the right of property in slaves could not be interfered with by the general

[1] *Philanthropist*, Feb. 13, 1838.

government or any power outside the separate slave-holding States," and that "abolition in the District of Columbia would be highly inexpedient and injudicious." [1] Two years later the Indiana legislature adopted a somewhat similar vote: "*Resolved,* That any interference in the domestic institutions of the slave-holding States—either by Congress or the State legislatures—is contrary to the compact by which those States became members of the Union, and that any such interference is highly reprehensible, unpatriotic, and injurious to the peace and stability of the Union of the States." [2] It is to be noted that both these sets of resolutions asserted triumphantly what no abolitionist at that time denied: that Congress had no power over slavery in the States.

In Ohio the first legislative expression on the subject of negroes after 1831 was a report of a select committee, in 1832, on the condition of the free blacks. The language used gives an idea of the public attitude toward that unfortunate class, which the committee considered to form a " distinct and degraded caste forever excluded by the fiat of society and the laws of the land from all hopes of equality in social intercourse and political privileges," and " a blotch upon the body politic." The committee concluded that no legislation could improve their condition. [3] Two years later petitioning began, and in 1834 appeared the first of a series of reports from the Judiciary Committee adverse to the petitions for the repeal of the Black Laws. A second adverse report was rendered in 1835, and another in 1837. In 1836 a motion made in the Senate to repeal the Black Laws was rejected, 33 to 1, the mover, Leicester King, giving the only affirmative vote. In 1838 some petitions were referred to a friendly select committee, who reported strongly through the same Mr. King in favor of the complete repeal of all laws discriminating on account of color; but the bill thereupon introduced was killed by postponement. In this year petitions asking for a legislative protest against the Congressional " gag-rule " were referred to a select committee, headed by B. F. Wade; they received a strong favorable report,

---

[1] *Liberator*, May 19, 1837.   [2] *Philanthropist*, Jan. 22, 1839.
[3] *Liberator*, Feb. 4, 1832.

but a resolution introduced by the chairman was indefinitely postponed.

In the next year, 1839, the Ohio legislature proceeded to surpass Indiana and Illinois in its anxiety to please the slave-holding States. On January 12 a series of resolutions passed the House, to the following general effect : —

1. Congress has no jurisdiction over slavery in the States.

2. Agitation against slavery is attended with no good results.

3. The schemes of abolitionists are wild and delusive and tend to disrupt the Union.

4. Any attempt by Congress to interfere with slavery is in violation of the Constitution.

5. The repeal of the Black Laws is impolitic and inexpedient.

6. "That the blacks and mulattoes who may be residents within this State have no constitutional right to present their petitions to the general Assembly for any purpose whatsoever." [1]

This measure was followed by one even more galling to the abolitionists. In the middle of January arrived two commissioners from the Kentucky legislature, Morehead, a Whig, and Speed-Smith, a Democrat, charged with the duty of asking Ohio for a fugitive-slave law to assist Kentucky masters in reclaiming those slaves whom the rapidly growing Underground Railway kept transporting in increasing numbers. On February 12 the request of the commissioners, sent to the legislature by the governor, was referred to the Judiciary Committee with favorable instructions; and a bill framed to suit the Kentuckians passed the House, 54–15, on February 19. In the Senate, B. F. Wade made a vigorous fight, delivering a speech which was printed in anti-slavery papers all over the country; but the bill passed, 26–10, on February 22, and thus became law. A public dinner was given to the commissioners, who, after the festivities, finally returned home, in March, to report their success. The main points of the bill were, that a pursuer of a fugitive slave could upon affidavit have a warrant made out; and that upon proof to the satisfaction of a justice of the peace, the " person seized " should be returned to the State whence he had

[1] *Emancipator*, Feb. 7, 1839.

fled; in case the agent could not swear to the fugitive's identity, the latter was to be committed to jail to await trial; any person hindering a sheriff or an agent, or assisting a fugitive, was to be fined not over five hundred dollars.[1]

Since abolition efforts had gained from the South nothing but abuse, from Congress only the " gag-rule," and from the North only mobs and more stringent anti-negro laws, it was evident that moral suasion and petitioning were inadequate. The possibility and desirability of political action at the polls were thus suggested by numerous considerations: rigid religious convictions called for anti-slavery protest by voting; expediency saw in such action a way to impress obdurate politicians; impatience expected in this course a shorter road to abolition than through mere moral protest; and anti-slavery men of all kinds realized from the effectiveness of the few abolitionists in public life how much the cause might gain by having representatives in State and national legislatures.

Four men of the Northwest had produced a profound effect upon anti-slavery sentiment. Leicester King, a Whig lawyer and judge, active in philanthropy of all kinds, and president of the Ohio Anti-Slavery Society, sat in the Ohio Senate from 1833 to 1838, for the district comprising the eastern end of the Western Reserve. Throughout his term he was a consistent worker for anti-slavery ends. B. F. Wade, of Ashtabula County, on the Reserve, a self-made lawyer, in 1833 for a time a member of the local Anti-Slavery Society, served from 1835 to 1839 in the State Senate. His action during his term of office, and especially his speech in 1839 against the Fugitive Slave Bill, raised him to a high position in the esteem of Ohio abolitionists. Joshua R. Giddings, at one time Wade's law partner, was in 1838 elected to Congress as a Whig from the Western Reserve. He was one of Theodore D. Weld's converts, and in 1836 had served as one of the local managers of the Ohio Anti-Slavery Society. No sooner had Giddings taken his seat in Congress in 1839 than he placed himself beside John Quincy Adams as a consistent opponent of the " gag-rule " ; and soon made himself the abolitionist champion in the House.

[1] For this fugitive slave law, see *Philanthropist*, Jan. 22–March 26, 1839.

More impressive, probably, to the Ohio mind than any of the foregoing was Thomas Morris, the first abolition senator of the United States.   He was born of New England ancestry in Pennsylvania in 1778, and moved into Ohio when most of the State was still a wilderness.   Working with head and hands like many another poor frontier boy, he made a living, gained a fragmentary education, read law, and worked his way up from the very bottom to a considerable practice.   Entering politics early, he served from 1806 to 1832 in the legislature, and later was chosen to the United States Senate, where he took his seat in the session of 1833–34.   Up to this time Morris had been a Jeffersonian Democrat, a rather rugged speaker, but a hard worker, a clear thinker, and a reliable party man.   He had shown no signs whatever of being in advance of his constituents on the slavery question, nor did he in the Senate say anything on the topic during the first half of his term, although petitions kept coming in, which his Whig colleague, Thomas Ewing, presented from time to time.   In 1836, however, he became acquainted with J. G. Birney, who had just removed to Ohio and was publishing the *Philanthropist;* and there is a strong probability that Birney's logic opened Morris's eyes.   At any rate, he suddenly began to take part in affairs in the Senate, of which he had hitherto been a silent member; he introduced abolition petitions, spoke in favor of the right to present them, and condemned on anti-slavery grounds the new constitution of Arkansas and the proposed annexation of Texas.   In November, 1836, he still more clearly showed his sympathies by making a speech at a meeting of the Clermont County Anti-Slavery Society; but it was not until 1838 that he attracted general attention.   In that year, on Calhoun's introduction of certain resolutions touching the constitutional status of slavery, Morris entered the lists with an alternative series of resolutions, which he upheld at length, incidentally defending the rights of free speech and petition, and the cause of the abolitionists.

This speech produced an instant effect; every anti-slavery paper in the country rejoiced, and the rapidly growing anti-slavery sentiment of Ohio in particular prided itself upon possessing such a representative; but the old parties scented

mischief; and the Whigs, eager to fasten the odium of " abolitionism " upon the Democratic party, proceeded to pass
resolutions in their State Convention censuring Morris as
misrepresenting the State.   He replied in a letter as follows: —

"I have opposed and voted against the further extension of
slavery in every case in which I was permitted to do so by the
Constitution.   The Whig convention most undoubtedly have
viewed slavery with a very favorable eye and felt willing for its
extension into every State in the Union. . . . I have opposed
the slave trade between the different States and with the Republic of Texas.   The Whig convention probably thought this
trade an honest mode of turning a penny. . . . I have con-
tended that all men were born equally free and independent,
and have an indisputable right to life, liberty and the pursuit of
happiness.   In this particular I have no doubt I am entirely antipode to the Whig convention." [1]

In November, 1838, the Democrats in the Ohio Legislature,
with whom lay the power to elect Morris's successor, addressed
to him three questions, on the bank, the tariff, and on slavery.
The first two he answered according to the party creed, but as
to the third he gave a full exposition of his abolition principles,
which, he claimed, were pure Democratic doctrine.   The Democratic caucus thought otherwise, and discarded him for Benjamin
Tappan.   Morris felt this blow keenly; but its only effect was
to drive him still farther along the abolition road.   He had
already, in 1838, written a letter to the Liberty Committee, who
were building Pennsylvania Hall in Philadelphia; now in every
way he identified himself with the movement, and in the Senate,
in the short session of 1838–39, he made the effort of his life.
He had already dared to encounter Calhoun; now he ventured
to match himself with Clay, speaking at great length, justifying
himself and the abolitionists, and predicting the final extinction
of slavery through political action.

Morris's " martyrdom " at the hands of his party, as it was
called, and this speech in reply to Clay, raised him to the highest pinnacle in the esteem of anti-slavery men; but upon the
public at large the episode made little impression.   Morris

[1] *Philanthropist*, July 24, 1838.

was a clear thinker; his resolutions on the constitutional position of slavery might have stood for the basis of all political
action from that time until 1860; his speech against Clay was
sound in reasoning, moderate in temper, and uncompromising
enough for any one. He was not, however, an impressive
speaker, for his delivery was poor and his style often heavy;
and he failed to gain due recognition at a time when eloquence
was thought indispensable for a leading public man.[1]

[1] See B. F. Morris, *Life of Thomas Morris.*

CHAPTER IV.

BEGINNINGS OF THE THIRD PARTY.

1836–1840.

ONE of the first attempts to define the political duties of abolitionists was made by Birney in the *Philanthropist* of September 23, 1836, when he declared that there was not much to choose between the two candidates for the Presidency, Harrison and Van Buren. "If abolitionists unite themselves to either of the existing parties they will weaken their influence. Let our votes be given, where we can vote at all, to the most worthy without partisan distinction." A few days later the *Philanthropist* gave more specific advice, by suggesting that abolitionists ought not to vote for Mr. Storer, the Democratic candidate for Congress, who was a declared opponent of abolition in the District of Columbia.[1] If, as asserted at the time, this advice turned the scale against Storer, it was the first political success attained by abolitionists in the Northwest.

At about the same time anti-slavery men in the northern section of the State were considering the same question. The Columbiana County Anti-Slavery Society voted, on October 24, 1836, "not to aid in elevating to office any one who gives reason to suspect that he would deprive us of our constitutional rights to publish throughout the land our opinions."[2] This was aimed at sympathizers with mobs. In March, 1837, there appeared in the *Philanthropist* a call for abolitionists to oppose the Democratic candidates for city offices, because

[1] *Philanthropist*, Oct. 28, 1836; W. Birney, *J. G. Birney and his Times*, 232.

[2] *Philanthropist*, Nov. 18, 1836.

Van Buren, the head of that party, was pledged not to allow the abolition of slavery in the District of Columbia. " The success of our principles demands of us," it said, "that discarding every name of party, we vote for men of principle, the friends of Liberty, of Law, of Order. If such cannot be found let us not vote at all. In this way and in this alone shall we be felt." Whether any results followed from this appeal is not known; but it became manifest, when the State Society met in April, that the question of the exercise of the suffrage had grown in importance. Feeling that an authoritative statement of opinion was called for, the Society resolved: " That it is time for the abolitionists of Ohio to relinquish all party attachments and act with a single view to the supremacy of the law, the inviolability of constitutional privileges and the rights of all "; [1] and in order to make this resolution effectual, it advised abolitionists to interrogate candidates and to vote for those only who agreed with their principles. In the East, interrogation of candidates had already been common for some time; but it must be borne in mind that until this time, in Ohio, the clerical element had continued predominant, and had but just begun to relinquish the leadership to such men as Birney and King.

During 1837 the outcries from the South, that the abolitionists were forming a new party, met with repeated denials from Ohio as well as from the East. The *Philanthropist* said, on May 19: "Abolitionists have never organized; they never will organize as a political party for the purpose of accomplishing the great object of their desires." On September 8, it said that a third party for abolitionists was unnecessary and inexpedient: " Let them attempt a regular political organization, and who does not see that . . . zeal for human rights would be smothered in the dust of party conflict ? . . . We have been thus explicit, not because we apprehend abolitionists will ever become so imprudent as to pursue the course animadverted on, but to convince our adversaries . . . how impossible it is that abolitionists, men of all politics and religions, should ever organize as a distinct, regular and political party."

In spite of these disclaimers, however, the tide had evidently

[1] *Emancipator*, Sept. 21, 1837.

begun to run toward politics and away from Biblical discussion and moral work.   Lloydsville, Belmont, Hamilton, Clermont, Ashtabula, and Geauga abolitionists passed resolutions not to support any but anti-slavery men for office, and to propound to all candidates searching questions covering the power of Congress over slavery and the slave-trade, and the position of the candidate himself with regard to slavery in the District of Columbia, to the annexation of Texas, and to the Black Laws. Such action led to a dilemma whenever both candidates were unsatisfactory.   Unless the abolitionists chose to run a separate ticket, they could show disapproval only by refraining from voting or by scattering their votes, both courses irritatingly impotent, and unpractical except where parties were nearly equal.

Although the abolitionists still entirely failed to foresee the outcome, and continued to disclaim any intention to form a new party, the Ohio men, in 1838, continued to go farther toward a political organization.   The State Society, and the county and local societies, in increasing numbers, abjured party action and demanded anti-slavery principles as a prerequisite for gaining their support.   The system of questioning candidates, which in 1837 had proved hardly as successful as had been hoped, was now resumed with the utmost vigor in most of the Western Reserve and in many other counties scattered over the State. When Vance and Shannon, the Whig and Democratic candidates for governor, were both formally interrogated by the officials of the State Society, and refused to reply, an enthusiast suggested L. P. Whipple as an independent anti-slavery nomination. The proposal was instantly frowned down.   "We are utterly opposed to every measure that looks toward a separate political organization," said the *Philanthropist.*   "The cause of anti-slavery belongs to all parties and all sects, and we should as much regret to see abolitionists drawing off from the parties to which they belong as we should to see them leaving the churches of which they are members to build up a separate anti-slavery church . . . All that can safely be done in a political way is to be done by questioning candidates . . . We believe these are the sentiments of nineteen twentieths of abolitionists throughout

Ohio." [1]   Meanwhile, in Indiana the State Anti-Slavery Society passed resolutions in favor of political independence, and in Michigan the questioning of candidates was actively prosecuted. Evidently the abolitionists were glad to find some tangible way of showing their anti-slavery feelings.

In Ohio special circumstances rendered the fall election of 1838 interesting; a desire to secure the re-election of Thomas Morris to the Senate brought many anti-slavery men to the polls with Democratic tickets.   Moreover, just before the election, an event took place which could not have been better calculated to work against the Whigs; an indictment having been brought by a Kentucky jury against J. B. Mahan for assisting a runaway slave, Governor Vance, the Whig candidate for re-election, proceeded to arrest Mahan and deliver him to the Kentucky authorities.   The news of this, as the *Philanthropist* said, thrilled through Ohio like an electric shock, and wrought every abolitionist to a high pitch of excitement.   When the election occurred, the Whig defeat was decisive.   Vance, elected in 1837 by 6,000 majority, was now beaten by 5,000; and Whig members of the legislature, and Congressional candidates in every section, were either defeated or elected by reduced majorities.   That this result was due entirely to abolition votes, no one seemed inclined to doubt; even Whig papers asserted it as an undeniable fact. The *Philanthropist* exulted over the first real demonstration of abolition strength, of which the transfer of 5,500 votes on the governorship seemed a fair measure.   The result in the legislature was universally ascribed to the popular desire to secure the senatorship for Morris and to rebuke the Whig convention for censuring him.   In Belmont County the Whigs stayed at home, "from their high respect for Morris"; in Fayette County from the same cause the Whig majority dropped from 500 to 6. The *Emancipator*, of New York, estimated the change in the popular vote for the legislature as 20,000, due to Morris's popularity.

Besides their direct influence in the election, the abolitionists had gained a triumph in the choice of J. R. Giddings to Congress; his nomination is said to have been brought about by

[1] *Philanthropist*, March 27, 1838.

some timely letters of J. G. Birney to the local Whig managers on the Reserve.[1]   On the whole, the election of 1838 was an intoxicating draught for the abolitionists of Ohio.   The widespread reports of their political doings, the congratulations heaped upon them by Eastern anti-slavery papers, and the half-dazed admission of their power by the local Whig party, led them to feel that the liberties of the country were now assured, and that merely by the questioning of candidates they had succeeded in gaining all they could wish.

When the results of this election were tested in 1839, the political abolitionists experienced nothing but perplexity and disappointment.   In the first place, Thomas Morris, to secure whose re-election anti-slavery men had voted the Democratic ticket, was thrown over by his party, obviously on account of those very principles for which abolitionists had honored him. Then, in January, 1839, came the series of State resolutions condemning abolition, and in February, most humiliating of all, the passage of the Fugitive Slave Law at the request of two Kentucky slave-holders.   Men who had been elected as opponents of slavery found nothing incongruous between their professions in October, 1838, and their votes for these drastic measures; and the faith of Ohio reformers in the efficacy of questioning candidates received a severe blow.   Still, in default of any better way of getting what they wanted, they were obliged to continue the system, except in cases where the behavior of the candidates in the legislature or elsewhere rendered interrogation superfluous.   The State Society said somewhat gloomily in its annual report: " We can see no other course for abolitionists to pursue." [2]

On the Western Reserve so great was the general indignation against the new Fugitive Slave Law, that the local Whig conventions found it advisable to discard all members of the legislature who had voted for the bill, and to nominate new can-

---

[1] W. Birney, *J. G. Birney and his Times*, 341.   General Birney sees his father's influence in every event of abolitionist history.   If Birney really secured Giddings' nomination, his diplomacy has not been recognized by other writers.   See G. W. Julian, *Life of Joshua R. Giddings*.

[2] *Philanthropist*, June 11, 1839.

didates. The renomination of B. F. Wade, who had won the approbation of anti-slavery men by his resistance to the bill, was opposed by a large number of local Whigs; but the anti-slavery elements of the party forced it through. In Geauga County, where the Whig majority was very large, the party convention braved anti-slavery wrath by selecting men of thoroughly unsatisfactory views; and as the Democratic nominees were no better, a dilemma presented itself. The Geauga abolitionists solved it by making an independent nomination, the first in the Northwest; although the same men, two years earlier, had resolved in their county anti-slavery society: "We will never countenance the organization of abolitionists into a distinct political body." [1]

When the election of 1839 came, it resulted in another Democratic victory even more sweeping than the preceding; but the abolitionists could not claim, as in 1838, that they were the sole cause; for their votes had been either divided between the two parties, or withheld, with no sort of common action. The Whigs had done nothing to gain their regard, nor had the Democrats any claim to their support after their treatment of Morris. In Wade's district the disaffection of some of his party over his abolitionism resulted in his defeat by a very narrow majority. [2] In Indiana and Illinois anti-slavery men were too few and scattered to think of independent action; so that Michigan was the only other Northwestern State in which the abolitionists played any considerable part in the election. Here the system of questioning was thoroughly applied. In Jackson County it resulted in the usual dilemma; whereupon the abolitionists proceeded to make independent nominations. In alarm at this unseasonable action, the president and officers of the State Anti-Slavery Society felt called upon to issue a manifesto denying any complicity in it or sympathy with it.

The elections of 1839 taught once more the lesson of the futility of the mere interrogation of candidates, and showed

---

[1] *Philanthropist*, Oct. 13, 1837.

[2] *Emancipator*, Oct. 24, 1839. In Geauga County, where the first third-party ticket was run, the vote stood: Democratic, 1,439; Whig, 1,630; Anti-slavery, 432; and some 300 abstained from voting.

also that some abolitionists were ready for the next step — separate party action. Nevertheless, that the body of Western anti-slavery men were not prepared in 1839 for such an innovation, is shown conclusively by their action during this year and the next. Since the spring of 1839 a movement in favor of a new party had been rapidly taking shape in the minds of a few men. In western New York, Myron Holley, in eastern New York and in New England, C. T. Torrey, were agitating the same question; and the *Emancipator*, the organ of the American Anti-Slavery Society, now gave its support to the new view. The questions before abolitionists this year were three: should they vote at all; if they did, should they insist on a full confession of anti-slavery faith from a candidate; and what should they do in case there were no fit nominations by either party?

In regard to the first question, there was little difference of opinion in the Northwest; but in the older States it roused the bitterest possible controversy between the practical anti-slavery men on one side, and W. L. Garrison and his followers on the other. The latter had adopted the Quaker doctrine of non-resistance, and had carried it to its logical result in a sort of theoretical Christian anarchism. So generally was the duty of voting taken for granted by Western abolitionists at this time, that it was seldom discussed, and such individuals and societies as did mention the matter almost invariably went contrary to the Garrisonian position. The Lorain County (Ohio) Anti-Slavery Society voted: "That it is the duty of abolitionists to use their influence to secure the nomination for office of men who are the friends of equal rights. That it is their duty to attend the polls and vote for such men." [1] A convention at Oakland, Clinton County, Ohio, on September 7, voted: "That all abolitionists who deem it their privilege to go to the polls are bound by their duty to God . . . to make their votes tell for the slave." [2] The Illinois Anti-Slavery Society voted on September 25: "That every abolitionist who has a right to vote be earnestly entreated to lose no opportunity to carry his abolition principles to the polls"; [3] and again, on December 11: "We

[1] *Emancipator*, July 25, 1839.   [2] *Liberator*, Nov. 15, 1839.
[3] *Philanthropist*, Nov. 26, 1839.

regard the elective franchise as a boon from the Great Author of every . . . perfect gift, . . . and those who neglect to use it at all as false to the solemn trust committed to them." [1]   When, in July, 1839, a national anti-slavery convention at Albany voted, " That every abolitionist who has the right to vote be earnestly entreated to use his right," its action met with nothing but approval in the Northwest; nor did the people in that section regard with much interest the controversy between Garrison and his opponents over the matter.

Expecting to vote somehow, the Northwestern anti-slavery men faced the remaining two questions, that were now forced on them by the approaching Presidential election.   Could an abolitionist vote for any one but an abolitionist?   The conclusion toward which the minds of hundreds of men were gradually tending was that he could not.   In that case, what was to be done if Van Buren were the Presidential candidate against Clay or Harrison?   Torrey, Elizur Wright, Holley, Stanton, and their followers felt that the only solution of the question lay in the support by abolitionists of a separate independent candidate; but from this step all save the most radical recoiled.   During the summer of 1839 the pages of anti-slavery papers were filled with controversy, steadily increasing in bitterness as the year advanced.   In the Northwest the extreme position of Holley found as little favor as did that of Garrison.   Societies and newspapers had repeatedly denied the advisability, or even possibility, of an anti-slavery political party; and now in 1839 they held to the same position.   Questioning, futile as it had proved, seemed preferable to organizing a forlorn-hope party; and even the dismal prospect of two pro-slavery Presidential candidates failed to convince abolitionists of the practicability of such a mode of action.   "Let us retire from the contest," said the *Philanthropist,* "and leave the dough-faced politicians to fight their own battles." [2]

In July an attempt to clear the air was made at a national convention at Albany, called to discuss particularly " the questions which relate to the proper exercise of the suffrage by citizens of the free States."   After a long and animated debate

[1] *Emancipator*, Jan. 2, 1840.   [2] April 30, 1839.

the assembly resolved not to vote for any one not an abolitionist, and to leave the matter of nominating independent anti-
slavery candidates to the discretion of anti-slavery men in
different localities.[1] Against the first resolution the *Philanthropist*, speaking for the majority of Ohio anti-slavery men, protested, as " wrong in principle and inexpedient"; as demanding
from a candidate entirely arbitrary qualifications, whereas
" requirements should be limited by the constitutional respon-
sibilities of the office they seek"; as tending to confirm the
slave-holder in his suspicions that abolitionists had unconstitutional designs ; and, lastly, as tending " to disfranchise the anti-
slavery people of the United States."[2] Most of the Ohio
societies adopted this position, and demanded from candidates
only such pledges as they could reasonably be required to
give. The conventions of Huron, Lorain, Cuyahoga, Geauga,
Ashtabula, Portage, and Clinton counties, and, on September
11, a general Western Reserve convention, resolved: " That
abolitionists ought not, and we *will not*, vote for any man for
any legislative or executive office who is not heartily opposed
to slavery and who will not openly meet and honestly sustain
all constitutional measures calculated immediately to restore
to the oppressed their rights."[3] Some of these conventions
formally rejected the Albany resolution. The Michigan abolitionists, as represented by the *Michigan Freeman*, agreed with
the Reserve; but in Illinois the extreme position met with a
partial acceptance. On September 25 the State Anti-Slavery
Society voted: " That we will neither vote for nor support
the election of any man . . . who is not in favor of the immediate abolition of slavery";[4] and, on December 4, a convention
at Canton resolved: " That while we are averse to the organization of an anti-slavery party for political action, we believe it to
be the duty of all friendly to the cause of human Liberty to
cast their votes for men favorable to the abolition of slavery."[5]

But whether abolitionists demanded abolitionism in a candidate
or were satisfied with pledges, the dilemma where there were

---

[1] *Emancipator*, Aug. 8, 1839.   [2] *Philanthropist*, Sept. 3, 1839.
[3] *Ibid.*, Oct. 8, 1839.   [4] *Ibid.*, Nov. 26, 1839.
[5] *Emancipator*, Jan. 2, 1840.

two unsuitable candidates could not be escaped.   Every month
the movement for independent action grew stronger, its drift
being evident in such events as the anti-slavery nominations in
Geauga County, Ohio, and in Jackson County, Michigan.   On
October 23, at a special meeting of the American Anti-Slavery
Society at Cleveland, the exciting political question came
up for consideration by a body of four hundred abolitionists,
almost exclusively from Ohio.   Two resolutions were offered:
first, to vote for no opponents of abolitionism; second, to
"neglect no opportunity to record their votes against slavery
when proper candidates in all respects are put up for office."
To the radical element these resolutions seemed absurdly timid
and inconclusive.   Blodgett, of Cuyahoga County, at once
moved an amendment sanctioning independent nomination in
cases where neither candidate was satisfactory ; this was rejected.   Myron Holley then introduced a more radical resolution: "That when existing parties directly oppose or purposely
overlook the rights of the slave it is time to form a *new political
party*," concluding with the still more daring proposition to
appoint a committee to nominate candidates for President and
Vice-President.   Blodgett tried so to amend the latter suggestion that it should authorize the calling of a nominating convention, "provided neither of the existing candidates proved
suitable "; but after a prolonged and exciting debate, occupying
nearly a whole day, the resolutions and amendments were all
rejected, and the attempt to turn the American Anti-Slavery
Society into a political party was given up.[1]

This episode gave rise to violent recriminations in the East
between the third-party faction and the Garrisonian wing, the
latter of whom charged the former with attempting a trick.   In
the West, Holley's attempt was generally condemned.   The
Oberlin Evangelist said: "Such a measure will meet with no
favor, we trust, among Western abolitionists."[2]   The *Philanthro-*

[1] On the Cleveland Convention, see *Emancipator*, Nov. 17–24, 1839;
Liberator, Nov. 15–22, 1839; *Philanthropist*, Oct. 29–Nov. 19, 1839; Elizur
Wright, *Life of Myron Holley*, 252 *seq.*; W. P. and F. J. Garrison, *Life of
W. L. Garrison*, II. 314 *seq.* ; W. Birney, *J. G. Birney and his Times*, 348.

[2] Quoted in *Liberator*, Nov. 29, 1839.

pist remarked: "To us it seems unreasonable to project the organization of a party on the basis of exclusive attention to any single interest, however important"; and pointed out that the change of the existing organization into a political party was impossible. "The primary object of the American Anti-Slavery Society was declared to be the abolition of slavery in the States. . . . A political party contemplating as its object the extinction of State slavery is manifestly an absurdity, for it can act by no political means. . . . The attempt to convert our organization into a political one we regard as a violation of good faith, and, if persisted in, it must end in division."[1] The Anti-Slavery Society of Salem, Columbiana County, Ohio, resolved, that "we deprecate the foundation of a third political party as exceedingly injudicious, dangerous to the success of our enterprise and a violation of good faith."[2] The Niels Creek (Indiana) Anti-Slavery Society resolved, that "we view with mournful and sincere regret the attempt made at the late special meeting of the American Anti-Slavery Society at Cleveland, Ohio, to organize a distinct anti-slavery political party, believing as we do that such a party would prove injurious if not fatal to the cause in which abolitionists are engaged."[3]

Nevertheless, the *Philanthropist,* the *Michigan Freeman,* and all the societies in the Northwest could neither escape the dilemma nor prevent the more radical from acting. On November 13, a convention at Warsaw, Genesee County, New York, led by Myron Holley, nominated J. G. Birney, and F. J. Lemoyne of Pennsylvania, for President and Vice-President respectively. Birney, who had turned over the *Philanthropist* to Dr. Gamaliel Bailey in 1838, and since then had been in New York, was as widely known and generally respected as any abolitionist, and Lemoyne was prominent in Pennsylvania. Both declined the nomination, Lemoyne not seeing any necessity for a third party, and Birney saying: "While I agree with you fully in the opinion that the great anti-slavery enterprise can never succeed without independent nominations, I feel assured that the views of aboli-

---

[1] *Philanthropist,* Dec. 10, 1839.   [2] *Liberator,* Feb. 7, 1840.
[3] *Philanthropist,* Feb. 4, 1840.

tionists as a body do not enough harmonize to make such a
measure advisable now."[1]

For the time being the third-party men seemed to have been
rebuffed on all sides ; but, as the winter passed, the spectacle of
Harrison as the Whig candidate, opposed to Van Buren, whose
renomination was certain, began to make many who had hitherto been lukewarm feel that a third party might not be wholly
unnecessary.   Letters from Western men favoring independent
action began to appear from time to time in the *Emancipator*
and the *Philanthropist.*[2]   Dr. Bailey, of the last-named paper,
at this time rather favored the Whigs; he published some evidence to show that Harrison was not pro-slavery,[3] and on January 15 wrote to J. R. Giddings that he thought a "tolerably fair
case might be made out for the General."[4]   Throughout the
winter of 1840 the debate continued, although the first murmurs
of the "hard cider" campaign for Harrison were beginning to
distract the attention of abolitionists.   Early in February appeared a call from Holley's county convention for a "National
Third-Party Anti-Slavery Convention" to meet at Albany on
April 1, to discuss the question of an independent Presidential
nomination.   The controversy grew hotter.   The *Philanthropist*
printed long and frequent editorials condemning the new movement from every point of view; and the Trumbull County (Ohio)
Anti-Slavery Society uttered a "*Solemn Protest* against the proposed convention as uncalled for."[5]   On the other hand, the
Bellefontaine society resolved : "That our righteous cause calls
us to come out from among the present political parties, and be
separated, that we may get rid of the unclean thing and escape
its plagues."[6]   Letters representing all degrees of approval and
condemnation poured in upon anti-slavery newspapers.

On April 1, the Liberty convention at Albany met, without a
single member from the Northwest.   It nominated J. G. Birney
and Thomas Earle of Pennsylvania, and thus forced the abolitionists of Ohio and the Northwest to decide whether they would re-

---

[1] *Philanthropist*, Jan. 21, 1840.

[2] *Ibid.*, Jan. 21, Feb. 25, April 14, 1840.   [3] *Ibid.*, Feb. 4, 1840.

[4] G. W. Julian, *Life of J. R. Giddings*, 88.

[5] *Emancipator*, April 2, 1840.   [6] *Philanthropist*, April 14, 1840.

fuse to support a thoroughly anti-slavery nomination now that it was practically forced upon them. A majority of anti-slavery men in the Northwest were without doubt Whigs; for among the New England and New York elements of population, which furnished the body of that party, anti-slavery principles naturally gained their earliest foothold. To such it was a trying time; for the "Tippecanoe and Tyler too" craze was swelling from week to week, intoxicating all with its presage of victory. When the prospect of demolishing Van Buren, crushing the sub-treasury, and restoring the bank and the tariff loomed shining in the near distance, it required a painful effort to leave their organization in full career, and out of conscientious scruples to vote for a man nominated by a corporal's guard as a forlorn hope.

As the spring advanced, the machinery of abolitionism, which, by nine years of incessant work, privation, self-sacrifice, danger from mobs, and ridicule from friends, had been built up into what seemed a strong and permanent system, seemed to crumble into atoms. In May, at the annual meeting of the American Anti-Slavery Society, a violent outbreak occurred between the Garrisonian wing and the third-party sympathizers. Garrison's followers came in great numbers from Boston, completely out-voted the other side, and after a stormy controversy, nominally on the position of women in the movement, the third-party men were defeated, retired, and formed a new organization under the name of "The American and Foreign Anti-Slavery Society." The *Emancipator*, hitherto the official paper of the National Society, was taken over by the new body, and acted as its organ in the contest of recrimination and abuse which broke forth. Charges of unfair, hypocritical, and even criminal conduct were freely made by each wing against the other. In the Northwest, however, this split produced no immediate effect other than seriously to injure common feeling and to make it easier for Whig or Democratic abolitionists to decline to follow Birney and the rest into the new party.

In Ohio the struggle began with the annual meeting of the State society on May 27, 1840, to which came fully five hundred delegates, many of them instructed to oppose the formation of

a third party.[1] After two days of heated debate, the society
decided to stand neutral on every question.   To avoid taking
sides in the quarrel between the old and the new national organization, it withdrew from being auxiliary to the one without
committing itself to the other.   It resolved that abolitionists
ought to vote so as to aid the cause, but that it would not pre-
tend to decide which was the most efficient method, whether
by staying away from the polls, by scattering votes, or by forming a third party; that it was an organization for moral purposes; that servility to slave-holders disqualified a candidate
from receiving the suffrages of a free people.   The radicals held
several caucuses, and tried to get the society to resolve at least
that Harrison and Van Buren were both disqualified for the
Presidency by reason of their disregard of human rights; but
they were outvoted.[2]

Rising from this first rebuff, the third-party men resumed the
struggle in local societies.   In the last week of July some men
of Harrison County took the first definite step by nominating
R. Hammond as a district Presidential elector.   A week later
L. Bissel was similarly nominated as elector for the Sixteenth
Congressional District, and calls appeared for a dozen independent political anti-slavery meetings.   A call for a convention for
Hamilton County was finally enlarged so as to cover the whole
State; and on September 1 there met, accordingly, the first
Liberty Party convention in Ohio.   Like its prototype at
Albany, it was neither a large nor a very representative body;
but, unlike that meeting, its scanty membership was not reinforced by the strength of its leaders.   The uproar of " Tippecanoe and Tyler too," Hard Cider, Coons, and Log Cabins was
carrying the Ohio Whig abolitionists fairly along with it; and
with few exceptions, the very men who in later years were regarded as the personification of political abolitionism were now
in the Whig ranks.   Joshua R. Giddings, B. F. Wade and his
brother Edward Wade, Leicester King, Samuel Lewis, and Salmon P. Chase were among those who followed the triumphal
Whig car in this year.

In this convention, accordingly, the leadership fell to two men,

---

[1] *Emancipator*, June 18, 1840.   [2] *Ibid.*, June 11, 1840.

Dr. Gamaliel Bailey and Ex-Senator Thomas Morris. The former, as has been said, at first favored Harrison; but in the summer of 1840 he gradually turned the influence of the *Philanthropist* in favor of Birney and Earle. The cause could not have gained a more valuable acquisition in all the Northwest than this clear-headed, energetic organizer and journalist. Thomas Morris, in spite of his rejection by the Ohio Democratic caucus in 1838, had maintained his connection with the party. His interest, however, was wholly in anti-slavery political action, and among the advocates of that movement none spoke or wrote with greater effect. In May, 1839, at a public meeting in Cincinnati, he vigorously condemned the Fugitive Slave Law, just passed. In July he wrote to the Albany National Anti-Slavery Convention a letter strongly commending political action. " Moral power," he said, " is sufficient for this work, but that moral power must operate by means to make it effectual. Political action is necessary, and that action can only be effectually exercised through the Ballot-Box. And surely the Ballot-Box can never be used for a more noble purpose than to restore and secure to any man his inalienable rights." [1] In the fall of that year he lectured repeatedly against slavery, and at one time held a joint debate for a week with two Democratic politicians who favored the Black Laws. In January, 1840, Morris went as a delegate to the Ohio Democratic State Convention, where as usual he kept quiet on matters unconnected with slavery. A series of resolutions violently condemning anti-slavery societies having been reported, however, he rose to protest. At once a pandemonium of hissing and confusion broke out; in spite of the uproar, and cries of "Turn him out of the party, and all abolitionists with him!" Morris stubbornly refused to yield, and, with one supporter only, persisted until he had said his say. After he had finished, some one rose, and amid general applause described him as a " rotten branch that ought to be lopped off." [2] In view of these facts, it is not surprising that Morris, with Democratic insults and proscription still burning within him, appeared in September at the Anti-

---

[1] B. F. Morris, *Life of Thomas Morris*, 230.
[2] *Ibid.*, 191; *Philanthropist*, Jan. 28, Aug. 11, 1840.

Slavery Nominating Convention, and in an impassioned speech renounced Van Buren and his policy, and threw himself heart and soul into the new movement. Spurred on by his fervor, the convention, not without considerable opposition from among its own members, proceeded to nominate a full electoral ticket.

In the local conventions that followed in several of the Western Reserve counties and elsewhere, there were sharp contests. In some places the policy of questioning was continued, as in the Nineteenth Congressional District convention at Akron, which also supported Birney. In Portage County the convention resolved to support three of the Whig candidates, and to oppose another on the ground " that both the honor and the interests of the anti-slavery enterprise are pledged against the nomination of separate candidates when the existing parties offer such as abolitionists can consistently vote for." In this case the third-party men were not suppressed; they reassembled after the convention adjourned and nominated some anti-slavery men of their own.[1] In Ashtabula County a two days' convention rejected a third-party proposal; whereupon the defeated section, under the leadership of General J. H. Paine, withdrew and set up for themselves. In some places third-party tickets were run more successfully; but as a general rule local organization hardly existed, and in the State election in October there were scarcely any third-party votes.

Meanwhile the other Northwestern States had been undergoing experiences similar to that of Ohio. Illinois was first in the field, its anti-slavery society meeting on July 4 at Princeton, Bureau County. Like the Ohio Society, it adopted a policy of neutrality, ceasing to be auxiliary to the American Anti-Slavery Society, and also refusing to take any definite stand on voting. Thereupon a separate meeting of third-party men was called at the same place, and on July 5 the first Northwestern electoral ticket was put forth, with a series of resolutions supporting Birney and Earle, and promising votes for none but abolitionists. Among the officers of this convention was David Nelson, who, like Birney, had been persecuted out of Missouri into Illinois, and was found among those willing to go farther

[1] *Philanthropist*, Oct. 2, 1840.

in opposing slavery. So small was the band of third-party men in this State that no local organization was attempted.

After Illinois came Michigan. Here anti-slavery action had been wide-spread for several years, and the condition of things was more like that in Ohio. Up to the time of the Birney nomination none of the leading men in the State had favored a third party; but in the spring of 1840 the current began to set that way, and S. B. Treadwell, of the *Michigan Freeman*, gradually came to approve the "Liberty" nomination. In July appeared a call, signed by seventy voters, for a State Nominating Convention on August 5. Among the signers were Dr. Porter, one of the most active abolitionists, and T. McGee, who less than a year before, when president of the Michigan Anti-Slavery Society, had issued a manifesto condemning the third-party nominations in Jackson County. When the convention met, some confusion was caused by an attempt to prevent nomination; but the recalcitrant members were eventually silenced, and an electoral ticket was selected. After this followed local nominations in Jackson and Calhoun counties and in the Fifth Senatorial District. The opponents of a third party did not in Michigan, any more than in Ohio, fail to express their disgust at the course of events. Some of those who had withdrawn from the nominating convention issued an address in the *State Gazette*, complaining of the tyranny of the third-party men in not allowing the expediency of separate nominations to be debated; but, according to the *Freeman*, nearly all of the signers of the card were Whig office-holders. Some members of the executive committee of the State Anti-Slavery Society followed with a resolution declaring the *Freeman*, on account of its political action, to be no longer the official organ of the society; but, although recriminations were caused by these measures, they did not prevent the formation of the new party.

Indiana was the third State in which the question of a third party came up for decision. A meeting of abolitionists on July 20, at Newport, Wayne County, invited the friends of anti-slavery to assemble in a general State Convention at that place on August 24, " to consider what measures are necessary to be adopted to effect the desired reform." Indiana was the most backward of all the Northwestern States in anti-slavery matters. Not until the years 1839–40, when the growth of societies in Ohio and Michigan had come to a standstill, was Arnold Buffum able to achieve much success in forming them in Indiana. Consequently, of the several hundred members present in the convention, few were abolitionists of long standing, and scarcely any were ready for radical measures. In the opinion of Arnold Buffum, fresh from working among the people, anti-slavery sentiment ran so strongly against separate nominations that he judged it unwise to try to force matters. Others thought differently, and introduced a series of resolutions ratifying the nomination of Birney and Earle, and selecting an electoral ticket. As Buffum had predicted, this proposal aroused great opposition. Mr. Rariden, a Whig member of Congress, spoke strongly against it; the resolutions were rejected by a great majority, and another set was adopted, condemning both the great parties for their subservience to slavery, and postponing separate action until 1844. Thus Indiana refused to join the new movement.[1]

Considerable as were the political changes in the summer of 1840 among anti-slavery men and measures, and bitter as were the feelings aroused, they attracted very little general attention ; for the Tippecanoe campaign was now at its height, its uproar completely drowning the lesser discords of quarrelling abolitionists. When the party conventions or newspapers did turn aside from the main battle to glance at abolitionist movements, they generally condemned them, and did their best to free their own skirts and inculpate the other party. The Ohio Democratic Convention of January 8, after condemning abolition in general, resolved that Congress ought not to abolish slavery in the District of Columbia without the consent of the people of Virginia; " that the efforts now making for that purpose by organized societies in the free States are hostile to the spirit of the Constitution "; and " that political abolition is but ancient federalism under a new guise, and that the political action of anti-slavery societies is only a device for the overthrow of democracy." [2] The *Indian-*

---

[1] *Emancipator*, Sept. 24, Nov. 12, 1840.
[2] *Philanthropist*, Jan. 28, 1840.

apolis Democrat, which had at one time " admired the courage
and firmness of this singular party," later said : " We now believe that the abolitionists are but a branch of the federal Whig
party . . . we believe that Harrison is the Northern Abolitionist
candidate."[1] The Michigan *Monroe Times* asked : " Is not
the whole movement in fact another of those cowardly tricks
resorted to by the party in order to deceive the people, . . . to
pacify the Southern Whigs ? "[2] Whig papers, of course, adopted
the same strain, charging the abolitionists with virtually trying
to elect Van Buren ; but their interest in this campaign was not
so lively as it became later, for they did not feel any especial
danger from the " mad folly " of Birney and his followers.[3]

Of any campaign on the part of the newly-born third party
there are few traces. Without organization, at swords' points
with those hitherto their strongest allies, despised by the regular
parties, and deafened and overborne by the tremendous cry of
" Tippecanoe and Tyler too," the political abolitionists could
do little but play their part in silence.   " So strong has been the
political excitement," wrote a correspondent from the Western
Reserve to the *Philanthropist*, " that for all the good to be accomplished it seemed like sailing against the wind. . . . The
Whig candidates for Congress did us more harm than any other
men on the Reserve. They had nothing to fear for themselves, and stumped it for Harrison, for weeks throwing out in-
sinuations against the third party as an affair got up to help Van
Buren."[4] From Illinois came a similar tale : " Many who in

---

[1] Quoted, *Philanthropist*, Sept. 29, 1840.

[2] Quoted, *ibid.*, Aug. 18, 1840.

[3] The *Philanthropist* (Aug. 18, Sept. 29, 1840) collected the following
remarks : the *Urbana Citizen* asked, " Have the Locofocos and the ultra
abolitionists of Ohio formed a coalition ? "; the *Conneaut Gazette* queried,
" Can any man doubt that this is a Loco-Foco move from the foundation ? ";
the *Marietta Intelligencer* said, " The editor of the *Philanthropist* may talk
of his indifference, but we imagine he can hardly make any man believe
that his influence is not subservient to the interests of Van Buren "; and the
Medina Constitutionalist remarked, " The leaders in this scheme are more
desirous to secure the re-election of Van Buren . . . than to ameliorate the
condition of the slave." See *Emancipator*, Aug. 18, 1840.

[4] *Ibid.*, Dec. 9, 1840.

times more perilous, when Lovejoy fell, remained unshaken by the threats and howlings of mob fury, were borne headlong by the shout of 'Tip and Tyler.' Prominent members and officers of the State Society, and men in the garb of the Christian ministry even, voted for Harrison." [1]

When election day came, very many waverers finally went with their party " once more "; many others, prepared to vote for Birney, could find no ballots, and did not know the names of the third-party electors; and some stayed away from the polls. It was not until weeks after the result of the contest was known that, in the few insignificant returns of scattering votes, the new party recognized itself. [2] Only in Massachusetts was the third-party vote one per cent of the total; and in Ohio, where the anti-slavery movement had been extremely active, the vote was less than half as numerous proportionally as that of Michigan. It is not at all certain, however, that the figures given below are correct. In all probability a good many more anti-slavery votes were cast in scattered places, but, through the carelessness or the indifference of election officials, were not returned. Nevertheless, whatever additions be made on this score, the fact remains that the Birney ticket failed completely to attract any large proportion of even the professed abolitionists. Elizur Wright, in his life of Myron Holley, estimates the number of voting members of anti-slavery societies as not less than 70,000. [3] If we

[1] *Emancipator*, June 10, 1841.

[2] The Northern vote by States was as follows: —

	Democratic.	Whig.	Abolitionist.	Per cent.
Maine	46,201	46,612	194	.002
New Hampshire	32,761	26,158	111	.001
Vermont . . .	18,018	32,440	319	.006
Massachusetts .	51,944	72,874	1,415	.011
Rhode Island .	3,301	5,278	(42)	.004
Connecticut .	25,296	31,601	174	.003
New York . .	212,527	225,817	2,798	.006
Pennsylvania .	143,672	144,021	343	.001
Ohio	124,982	148,157	903	.003
Michigan . . .	21,131	22,933	328	.007
Illinois . . .	47,496	45,558	157	.001
	727,329	801,449	6,784	

[3] Elizur Wright, *Life of Myron Holley*, 235.

consider that, in 1837, 607 societies out of a total of 1,006 reported 55,790 members, and that in 1840 there were many more societies, this seems a conservative estimate. It is safe to say that in 1840 not one in ten of the thousands of abolitionists who had resolved to act without regard to party ties, and with a sole purpose of aiding the cause of liberty, felt called upon to leave the party with which he had hitherto voted.

From the Northwest we have a few returns by counties, the distribution of which is not without significance. In Ohio seventeen counties out of seventy-eight return 550 votes, Ashtabula leading the list with 95 votes, Trumbull and Lorain having each 52; and the ten counties of the Western Reserve cast nearly half of the total State vote. The contrast, however, between the 425 from the Western Reserve and the 432 which Geauga County alone cast in 1839, is significant. Outside the Reserve the most votes appear to have been cast near Cincinnati, which, like the Western Reserve, had many New England settlers. Since both these sections were later the strongholds of Liberty and Free Soil parties, this vote of 1840, meagre as it was, really indicated the future course of anti-slavery political growth in Ohio.[1]

In Illinois, on the contrary, almost nothing of the sort is visible; for the seven northeastern counties, later to become the rivals of the Ohio Western Reserve, gave barely 20 votes to the diminutive total of 157. The centre of Illinois political abolitionism, in 1840, was Adams County on the Mississippi, which gave 42 votes. The only facts brought out by the Illinois vote were that "Egypt," the southern half of the State, would give no abolition votes, and that the influence of Lovejoy's murder still lingered to make the region near Alton more radical than the northern part of the State.[2]

[1] For the Ohio vote, collected from scattered returns, see *Emancipator*, Nov., 1840–Jan., 1841.

[2] For the Illinois vote, see *Emancipator*, Dec. 10, 1841.

CHAPTER V.

ORGANIZATION OF THE LIBERTY PARTY.

1840–1843.

At the end of 1840 the new abolition movement had completed ten years of its course; and the fruit of its agitation was seen in the general development of a distinctly Northern anti-slavery sentiment. In the Northwest, even where indifference had been most marked and had proved hardest to overcome, the growth of anti-slavery societies had steadily gone on. Ohio and Michigan were covered with them; Illinois and Indiana contained clusters of anti-slavery communities; and even the two frontier Territories, hitherto entirely under the influence of Mississippi River traffic and connections, were beginning to feel the new anti-slavery influence. In 1840–41 societies started up in the southeastern counties of Wisconsin adjacent to the anti-slavery region of Illinois, and in 1841 the first society in Iowa was formed. Wherever these organizations had worked, came a change in public sentiment. It was no longer fashionable among Whig papers entirely to condemn agitation, nor did any but the hardiest Democratic sheets continue in the contemptuous strain which was common a decade earlier.

Of this growth of anti-slavery sentiment the legislative action of the Northwestern States, as we have seen, gives almost no reflex. On the contrary, the years 1834–40 saw a series of resolutions and enactments condemning abolition, and rendering harsher the burdens already oppressing the free blacks in the Northwest; for the Southern-born elements of population in the southern and western halves of all the States except Michigan controlled local politics, and it was not among these people,

nor among professional politicians of any locality, that abolitionists could expect to make converts.

There was, however, one point in which the rudiments of a
distinctly Northern feeling were evident: namely, in the opposition which some of the Northwestern States manifested toward
the proposed annexation of Texas. This matter will be considered at greater length in another place.[1] It is enough to say
here that the legislatures of Indiana, Ohio, and Michigan took
action in this direction in 1836–38, and that there were
occasional public meetings condemning the annexation of any
new slave territory. Since these were the very years in which
the same legislatures poured out disapproval on abolitionists
and increased the severity of Black Laws, it is evident that too
much weight must not be attached to their anti-Texas action.
The political managers in the Northwest were not yet abolition-
ized, nor were they to become so for a score of years; but they
had no love for slavery, and felt the danger of having a prepon-
derance of slave States. All they wanted was to preserve the
status quo. Whatever section seemed to be altering or trying
to alter the existing balance would meet with their opposition.

Scarcely any of the abolitionists themselves realized the difficulties lying in their way. So little did they appreciate the
motives that sway the politician's mind, that such an acute
observer as Birney in 1838 claimed anti-Texas resolutions of
State legislatures as abolition victories; and Garrison and his
followers actually thought that a scattering of votes, or a refusal
to vote at all unless some one of the old parties should nominate
an abolitionist, would inevitably and speedily bring politicians
to the feet of the new party, and thus, as the Michigan Anti-
Slavery Society said in 1839, " accomplish the universal triumph
of liberty." [2] This expectation proved futile in 1839, and now
abolitionists were turning strongly toward a new party.

After the delirium of 1840 followed a general reaction, from
which the political abolitionists profited. Numbers of Whig
members of anti-slavery societies, who had been carried away in
the excitement of the Presidential campaign, felt a desire when

[1] Chapter VIII.
[2] *Michigan Freeman*, Oct. 23, 1839; quoted in *Liberator*, Nov. 15, 1839.

it had passed to resume anti-slavery work. When Tyler succeeded Harrison, very many Whigs in the Northwest lost all
personal interest in the administration; and later, when the
accidental President became embroiled with his party in Congress, their disgust made them turn for relief to the anti-slavery
organizations. Now, after 1840, although the old State and
local anti-slavery societies existed, the strength of the movement
no longer resided in them, but in the new " Liberty Party," as
it had begun to style itself. If the Birney nomination for a time
was regarded as merely sporadic, the action of State and local
conventions in the free States in 1841 dispelled this idea.
Almost immediately after the election a movement began, from
Maine to Illinois, for a national and local reorganization of the
political abolitionists for distinct party action.

In Ohio the call for a convention said somewhat timidly : " It
will not be a third-party or anti-third-party convention. . . . It
is not called with a view of deciding upon this question . . .
but to re-establish harmony and to agree upon some rational,
effective plan of anti-slavery political organization." [1] Before
this State Convention met, the Western Reserve third-party
men were in the field with a convention for northern Ohio, at
Akron, on October 23–24, which resolved that " it was expedient
for the Liberty party to continue the nomination of men true to
the principles of equal rights "; and it nominated Thomas Morris
for Governor in 1842, subject to the decision of the State Convention. Committees were also appointed and lectures arranged.[2]
The State Convention, on January 20–21, in spite of the deprecating language of its call, proved no less in favor of the
" Liberty Party." Having defined the formal anti-slavery societies as purely moral agencies, the two hundred and eight
delegates from thirty-six counties wrestled for two days with
the problem of political action; and finally, late in the night,
by a vote of 87 to 30, rejected the old policy of questioning. A resolution was then passed, " that it be recommended
to the voting anti-slavery citizens of Ohio to adopt the policy
of previous independent nominations in all cases where they
are not perfectly assured that men in whom they can confide

[1] *Philanthropist*, Dec. 16, 1840.   [2] *Ibid.*, Jan. 13, 1841.

will be presented by one or both of the existing political parties."[1] In this convention, which definitely established the Liberty party in Ohio, Thomas Morris and Dr. Bailey were again the leading spirits.   Purdy, of the *Xenia Free Press*, a "Whig abolitionist," led the opposition with great pertinacity, but was voted down; and he finally separated from his old colleagues. From this time, although there were still occasional protests and complaints from disappointed Whig or Democratic abolitionists, predicting total failure and fearing that the attempt to run a third ticket would "make a laughing-stock of our holy cause," the Liberty party was established beyond dispute.

In Indiana the reaction was still sharper.   A meeting of independent abolitionists for the First Congressional District, at Economy, Wayne County, began a movement for third-party action in December, 1840, and recommended the nomination of independent candidates for executive, legislative, and judicial offices. The president of this meeting was Isaiah Osborne, a son of the Quaker, Charles Osborne, who had been the predecessor of Lundy and Garrison in advocating immediate emancipation;[2] his selection shows how the old emancipationist movement, as well as the later abolitionism, was swallowed up by the new political agitation. A convention for the Third Congressional District, January 1, 1841, resolved "that to oppose slavery morally by speaking against it as a sin while we sustain it politically . . . is a gross inconsistency and paralyzing to our moral influence."[3]   A call was finally issued for a State Convention of the friends of independent political action to meet at the same time with the State Anti-Slavery Society, to consider the subject of nominating for Congress and for the legislature. On February 8 the convention met, resolved almost unanimously to support Liberty candidates, and thereby reversed completely the action of that State Convention which six months before had resolved to adhere to the old methods. The true explanation

[1] *Philanthropist*, Jan. 27, Feb. 3, 1841.
[2] Correspondence of writer with G. W. Julian, 1895. See also *Philanthropist*, Dec. 23, 1840.
[3] *Philanthropist*, Jan. 27, 1841.

of this change is that abolitionists who favored acting with the old parties no longer attended abolitionist conventions; and those present, finding no opposition, gained courage to go on by themselves.

Michigan followed Indiana. After the meeting of the State Anti-Slavery Society at Jackson, on February 10–11, a Liberty convention organized, with Thomas McGee as president. Ohio and Indiana had been content merely to record their opinion in favor of independent action and to begin preparations; but Michigan far outstripped them by selecting a State Central Committee, and nominating Jabez S. Fitch, of Calhoun County, and N. Power, of Oakland County, for Governor and Lieutenant-Governor respectively: this was the first Liberty State ticket in the Northwest. Furthermore, a ballot was taken on the preferences for Liberty candidates for President and Vice-President.[1] There is no doubt that at this time Michigan abolitionists were much better organized and more united in sentiment than those of any other Northwestern State; but we shall see that this superiority was held for a few years only, and that after 1844 anti-slavery political sentiment in that State rapidly lost its coherence.

Illinois followed close after her sister States. On February 25 a State Anti-Slavery Convention met at Lowell and adopted a series of resolutions commenting on national affairs, urging a National Liberty Presidential Nominating Convention, and recommending abolitionists in Illinois to make nominations for Congress, on the ground that " efficient political action can be produced only by independent and united effort," and that " the right of suffrage includes the right of nomination." A letter from J. Cross describing this convention in the *Emancipator* said: " The rallying shout of ' Hard cider' has lost its power. A log cabin no longer has the charm of novelty. Many, very many who voted with the prominent parties at the Presidential election have seen their error and repented. . . . The plan of

---

[1] The ballot resulted as follows:—

President: J. G. Birney, 49.   Vice-President: T. Earle, 48.
        T. Morris, 1.   A. Stewart, 1.
See *Emancipator*, June 3, 1841.

independent nominations is rising rapidly in the estimation of the more efficient abolitionists." [1]

Definitely to establish the new party, there met in New York on May 12 the first really national Liberty convention. Delegates were present from all the New England States, from New York, Pennsylvania, and New Jersey, three from Ohio, and two from Indiana; the delegates chosen by Michigan seem not to have come. The composition of the meeting and the proceedings show that as yet the centre of gravity of the political anti-slavery movement was in the East, and that the Northwest was content to follow the leadership of such men as Joshua Leavitt, William Goodell, and James G. Birney. On the first day it was resolved to nominate candidates for President and Vice-President in 1844, and on the first ballot Birney and Morris were selected.[2] On the second day the convention discussed the question of organization. It was resolved " that the friends of Liberty throughout the nation be requested to nominate and to vote for township, county, and all other officers favorable to the immediate emancipation of slavery "; and in furtherance of this comprehensive scheme it was resolved to have State, county, town, ward, and district committees, auxiliary to a National Committee. These were to canvass every town and ward in the free States, keeping a roll of Liberty voters and reporting the same to the National Committee.[3] The convention then adjourned, to meet again in two years at the call of the Central Committee. It had pledged the political abolitionists to the policy of building up from the start a new political party, a plan involving labors to which all previous work was merely preliminary, but into which all the Liberty men of the country now threw themselves with enthusiasm, high hopes, and complete lack of comprehension of the difficulties of the task before them. Probably half of the delegates expected the Lib-

[1] *Emancipator*, June 10, 1841.
[2] The vote was as follows : —

President : J. G. Birney, 108.	Vice-President : Thomas Morris, 83.
Thomas Morris, 2.	Thomas Earle, 18.
Gerrit Smith, 1.	Gerrit Smith, 2.
William Jay, 1.	A. Stewart, 1.

[3] *Emancipator*, May 20, 1841.

erty party to carry the election of 1844; and even the mos
cautious felt that by 1848 their party would be dominant in th
North. Yet nineteen years were to pass before a party in any
sense a descendant of the Liberty organization was to carry a
national election, and that by a minority vote.

In the spring of 1841, then, the Liberty party was placed on
its feet in all the Northern States. The system of questioning
candidates, and of waiting for favorable action on the part o
the old parties, were things of the past; and a new organization
had begun its attempt to absorb all radical anti-slavery feeling
except that which still clung to the tenets of Garrison, Henry C
Wright, and the other "Non-Resistants." The next three year
were a period of intense activity in the Northwest. To treat th
details fully, however, would be neither interesting nor profit
able, since it would be nothing more than to give a list c
conventions, nominations, and votes cast. In no State of th
Northwest did the Liberty men succeed in electing any one; no
in these three years did their organizations succeed in produc
ing any visible effect on the policy of the older parties. Thei
activity was directed to agitation and protest, and not to legi
lative action or questions of policy; it was, as the *Emanc
pator* said, practically a continuation of the anti-slavery societ
methods under a new organization, with some addition
principles of action.

In Ohio several local conventions were held, mostly o
the Western Reserve and in the territory near Cincinnati
but the process of disentanglement between Liberty and Whi
abolitionists was slow. At a political convention held aft
the State Anti-Slavery convention, a last effort was made
commit the party in favor of withdrawing its candidates in ca
the other parties offered suitable nominations; but, thoug
strongly supported, it met defeat. Still the Clinton Count
convention resolved not to nominate, unless no sound cand
dates were put up by the other parties; and in Lorain an
Trumbull counties the fact that the Whig nominees were m
hitherto known as "abolitionists" prevented the Liberty tick
from achieving much success. In some places nominatio
were made too late to be widely known; but, in spite of

drawbacks, the Ohio Liberty men succeeded in casting over 2,000 votes.[1]

In Indiana there were not the same difficulties as in Ohio, for here was no large class of abolitionists in the old organizations to distract third-party men by claiming to be more anti-slavery than they. The scanty numbers and scattered condition of Liberty sympathizers, however, made concerted action very difficult. In a few places county nominations were made for the August election; but how large a vote the Liberty party cast is not known. There are returns of 594 votes from two counties.[2]

In the spring of 1841, Michigan anti-slavery men opened the campaign by running third-party tickets in town elections; and in April the State Anti-Slavery Society declared itself in favor of political action, condemned scattering votes — a favorite Garrisonian device — as " a species of duplicity," and separated from the American Anti-Slavery Society. Following this action, the third-party men made vigorous efforts at organization. Besides the candidates for Governor and Lieutenant-Governor, there were three nominations for the Senate and at least twenty-five for the House. Conventions were held in a large number of counties; and Birney, now a resident of the State, took the stump for a part of the fall, Michigan being the first Northwestern State to organize a distinct campaign. The vote was as follows: Democratic — Barry, 20,975; Whig — Fuller, 15,469; Liberty — Fitch, 1,214.[3]

In Illinois the Liberty men made only one nomination, that of F. Collins for Congress in the Third District. There was some agitation, but nothing like a campaign. The Liberty

---

[1] For the Liberty campaign in Ohio, see *Philanthropist*, May 26–Oct. 27, 1841; for the vote, see *Emancipator*, Nov.–Dec., 1841, and *American Liberty Almanac*, 1844. We have separate returns for twenty-one counties, which amount to 1,782. The total was claimed to be 2,848, three times as large as the vote of the preceding year.

[2] *Emancipator*, Sept. 9, 1841.

[3] *Ibid.*, June 3, Aug. 5, Sept. 23, 1841. For the vote, see *Ibid.*, Dec. 10, 1841, and *Detroit Advertiser*, Dec. 9, 1841, Dec. 4, 1843. There are separate returns from eight counties.

vote, for which we have full returns, amounted to 527, a considerable increase over the 157 of the year before.[1]

In 1842 much the same programme was continued. In Ohio a State Convention, on December 29, 1841, nominated Leicester King for Governor, thereby showing the thoroughly practical character of the Ohio leaders; for King was a member of the State bench, and had served two terms as State Senator. Wholly in sympathy with the cause, and yet an experienced politician, he was an eminently fit candidate. It would be easy to fill pages with accounts of local conventions, with the labors of King, Morris, and others, and with the signs of the growth of anti-slavery feeling in portions of the State outside the Reserve and the Cincinnati district; but it suffices to say that the Liberty men made a more thorough canvass than had before been attempted, and in October almost doubled their vote.[2] The election returns are: Democratic — Shannon, 129,064; Whig — Corwin, 125,621; Liberty — King, 5,405. Of the Liberty vote the eleven Western Reserve counties cast 2,433; the sixty-seven others, 2,972.[3] For the first time the Liberty men appeared to have the balance of power.

Indiana continued the same course as before, making several local nominations, but having little or no State organization. There was still so much timidity among professed anti-slavery men about joining the Liberty party, that the *Free Labor Advocate* felt obliged to adopt a somewhat apologetic air, saying, as a justification for its course in advocating political anti-slavery action: " We think the abolitionists of the West very generally believe in the propriety of the measures mentioned." Of the vote, no exact returns are known, but it was claimed to be between 800 and 900.[5] In Michigan the activity of the preceding year was continued, largely owing to the influence of Birney, who travelled and spoke indefatigably. Local and legislative nominations received in the fall the support of a

---

[1] *Emancipator*, Aug. 5, 1841.   For the vote, see *Ibid.*, Dec. 10, 1841.
[2] For this campaign, see *Philanthropist, passim.*
[3] Vote in *Whig Almanac*, 1843.
[4] *Free Labor Advocate*, Sept. 24, 1842.
[5] *Emancipator*, Sept. 1, 1842; *Liberty Almanac*, 1844.

least 1,665 votes.[1] Illinois took a decided step in advance. A State convention in May nominated C. W. Hunter, of Madison County, and F. Collins, of Adams County, for Governor and Lieutenant-Governor respectively; and regular Liberty nominations were made in twenty counties. In August the vote stood: Democratic — Ford, 45,608; Whig — Duncan, 38,304; Liberty — Hunter, 909.[2]

The opening of the year 1843 found the Liberty party established and, although still very diminutive, apparently growing at a rate to render it important in the near future. In Ohio the activity of the Liberty men was unceasing; convention followed convention in a majority of the senatorial districts of the State, and the leaders of the cause lectured from spring until the election. In spite of the facts that it was an " off year," with no State ticket, and that the Whigs made urgent efforts to get the Liberty abolitionists to support their nominees, the official returns gave the Liberty vote a considerable increase in eighteen out of twenty-one districts, as follows: Democratic, 102,335; Whig, 107,249; Liberty, 6,552. The *Philanthropist* was dissatisfied with these figures and charged fraud, claiming to have returns amounting to 7,466.[3]

In Indiana, at the same time, a vigorous effort was made. In September, 1842, a State Convention nominated the first ticket for Governor and Lieutenant-Governor, naming E. Deming and S. S. Harding respectively. Attempts were made to carry on a regular campaign with the help of speakers from Ohio; and in August of 1843 the vote stood: Democratic — Whitcomb, 60,714; Whig — Bigger, 58,701; Liberty — Deming, 1,684. Of the Liberty vote, Wayne, Randolph, and Henry counties gave 792, almost half.[4] Wayne County, with a large Quaker population, was the centre of activity, its convention

---

[1] *Emancipator*, Sept. 1, Nov. 17, 1842; *Detroit Advertiser*, Dec. 15, 1842; *Liberty Almanac*, 1844. Probably there were more votes.

[2] Vote in *Whig Almanac*, 1843. See *Philanthropist*, April 20, 1842; *Emancipator*, Aug. 25, 1842.

[3] Official returns in *Whig Almanac*, 1844. See *Philanthropist*, quoted in *Emancipator*, Dec. 14, 1843.

[4] Official returns in *Whig Almanac*, 1844.

resolving to form Liberty associations in every township, which should pledge their members in writing to vote only Liberty tickets.[1]

The Michigan Liberty men were also in the field with a State ticket, nominating J. G. Birney and L. F. Stevens for Governor and Lieutenant-Governor respectively, at a convention in February. Besides these, there were candidates for Congress in all the three districts, six candidates for State Senators, and nominations for the Assembly in a dozen counties. At the State Convention a ludicrous incident occurred: two colored delegates were not allowed to participate in nominating because they were not legal voters. This delightful inconsistency in an abolitionist convention served to furnish Democratic papers with endless amusement; and the *Signal of Liberty* felt ill-concealed mortification.[2] Birney was again the life of the cause, and in September drew a greatly increased vote. It stood: Democratic — Barry, 21,414; Whig — Pitcher, 15,007; Liberty — Birney, 2,775. This proportion showed Michigan to be one of the strongest Liberty States in the country.[3]

In Illinois, in this year (1843), the Liberty party made great gains. State conventions planned for organization; local conventions made nominations; and before the election there were Liberty candidates for Congress in every district except the two in the southeast, called "Egypt," where, among former slave holders and the descendants of immigrants from Kentucky and Tennessee, abolitionism found barren soil. In August the vote stood at a figure more than twice as large as ever before — 1,954, of which the Fourth District, in the northeastern corner, gave 1,174.[4]

In this year a new member joined the Liberty ranks, the Territory of Wisconsin, hitherto hardly touched by the anti-

---

[1] *Free Labor Advocate*, May 20, 1843.

[2] Ann Arbor *Michigan Argus*, Feb. 13, July 26, Aug. 2, 1843.

[3] Official returns in *Whig Almanac*, 1844.

[4] *Emancipator*, Aug. 31, 1843; *Albany Patriot*, Aug. 22, Oct. 3, 1843. The *Western Citizen* claimed a total of 2,171, and in all probability the vote was larger than the official returns; for the figures indicate in some counties a suppression or an omission of Liberty votes.

slavery movement, but destined to surpass all the other North-western States in the vigorous growth of its anti-slavery principles. In 1838–40 had begun the invasion of this outlying Territory by Eastern immigrants, many of whom, coming from New England and New York, brought with them anti-slavery principles and habits. Occupied as these people were, however, in frontier pursuits, it was not until 1842 that a Territorial Anti-Slavery Convention was held and a society organized. In 1843 the Wisconsin abolitionists, in spite of the fact that their agitation had hardly begun, were too impatient to join the Liberty party to wait any longer, and accordingly called a Territorial conven-tion to nominate a candidate for delegate to Congress. The movement ended in almost a complete fiasco; for the candidate elected, a strong Whig, proceeded to advise people not to vote for him, with the result that at the election there was only a handful of Liberty votes, the ticket receiving almost no sup-port in counties where anti-slavery sentiment was most prevalent. The vote stood: Democratic — Dodge, 4,685; Whig — Hickox, 3,184; Liberty — Spooner, 152.[1]

Thus by the end of the fourth year of the Liberty party's existence its vote had increased practically ten times since 1840;[2] but it fell far short of the Liberty hopes of 1841. In none of the States was it yet over ten per cent; and in Ohio, where for ten years abolitionist agitation had been active, it was only three per cent. The reason was, that in this period the Liberty party, gain as it might, entirely failed to convince the public that it was called for by the national political situation. This failure was not due to lack of leadership, or of adequate effort; for among the most active agitators were men who were to become founders of a successful anti-slavery party.

[1] *Emancipator*, April 6, Sept. 28, Oct. 26, 1843; *Milwaukee Sentinel*, Sept. 23, 1843. For Spooner's action, see *Milwaukee Democrat*, Nov. 17, 1843.

[2] This increase is shown by the following comparison : —

	Ohio.	Indiana.	Michigan.	Illinois.	Wisconsin.
1840 . . .	903	—	328	157	—
1841 . . .	2,800 (?)	599	1,214	527	—
1842 . . .	5,405	900 (?)	1,665	909	—
1843 . . .	6,552	1,684	2,775	1,954	152

In Ohio the ebb tide after 1840 brought a number of brilliant men into the Liberty ranks to aid Dr. Gamaliel Bailey, General J. H. Paine, and the indefatigable Thomas Morris. Salmon P. Chase had lived in Cincinnati for ten years without taking part in politics. Falling in with J. G. Birney in 1835–36, he, like Thomas Morris, was converted into a strong opponent of slavery. He bore a creditable part in the events connected with the mobbing of Birney's press; but he did not identify himself with the anti-slavery cause until, in May, 1841, he joined the Hamilton County convention, and at once by his ability, personal impressiveness, eloquence, and remarkable power in constitutional argument stepped into the lead.[1] Fully as valuable an accession was Samuel Lewis, also of Hamilton County. He was a native of Massachusetts, a man of the most fiery eloquence heard in behalf of the anti-slavery cause in Ohio since the days of Theodore Weld. Lewis had served a term as Superintendent of Public Instruction, and in this capacity had carried on a systematic educational propaganda, travelling the State from end to end, stirring the people of backwoods counties into an appreciation of education, so that wherever he passed schools sprang up and flourished. Into the anti-slavery cause he now brought his zeal, his talents as a public speaker, and a devotion and self-sacrifice unsurpassed by those of any other man in Ohio.

With Morris, Bailey, Chase, and Lewis, there labored at this time in the southern part of the State a number of men well worthy of more extended notice than can be given here. Such were Rev. W. H. Brisbane, formerly of North Carolina, now an ardent radical Liberty man; G. W. Ells, who had been Morris's only supporter in the Democratic State Convention of 1840, and who like him had been "kicked out of the party"; and William Birney, the son of J. G. Birney, showing already his father's talent for organization. In the Western Reserve General J. H. Paine, of Painesville, a vehement speaker and a practical worker, who had been for a time the only prominent

[1] See R. B. Warden, *Private Life and Public Services of Salmon Portland Chase;* J. W. Schuckers, *Life and Public Services of Salmon P. Chase;* W. Birney, *J. G. Birney and his Times*, 259.

third-party man there, soon received strong reinforcements. Leicester King, whose course in the legislature has been referred to above, was among the first, after the hurricane of 1840, to bring his legal ability and philanthropic zeal to the aid of the unpopular cause.[1] Then came Edward Wade, who in 1838 had been zealous for political action, but who in 1840 was carried off his feet by the " Tippecanoe " war-cry, and wrote a letter advising abolitionists to support Harrison. Though of gentler temperament than his better-known brother, B. F. Wade, he had all of the latter's dogged persistence and personal courage ; and from this time until his death he was an unflinching, untiring worker in the anti-slavery ranks.[2] J. Hutchins, a Democratic convert, was henceforward a persistent supporter of the Liberty party on the Reserve, and led local sentiment in Lake County. Besides these, a host of younger men joined the party in this period, including Norton Townshend, destined later to be a stumbling-block to Free Soilers. Such a group of able men as Morris, Bailey, Chase, Lewis, Wade, and the rest, could not be paralleled or approached elsewhere in the Northwest, or in any of the Eastern States, except perhaps in New York and Massachusetts. If the Liberty party, with such advocates, failed to attract public notice, the reason was evidently something else than deficient leadership.

In Indiana at this time there were in the Liberty party several men of ability and self-sacrifice, but none to equal the Ohio leaders. The most prominent leaders, perhaps, were S. S. Harding, of Ripley County, a strong radical speaker, efficient also as an organizer ; S. C. Stevens, of Madison County, an able lawyer, later a judge ; and E. Deming, a lawyer, of Tippecanoe County, the candidate for Governor in 1843. All of these men, as laborers in a field as discouraging as ever offered itself to a reformer, deserve no little credit for their devotion, courage, and persistency.

In Michigan we find the condition of things precisely opposite to that in Ohio. The Liberty sentiment was strong, the vote twice as large proportionally as that in Ohio; but for want of

---

[1] J. Hutchins, in *Magazine of Western History*, V. 680.
[2] A. G. Riddle, in *History of Ashtabula County, Ohio*, 84.

real leadership, in addition to other causes, this early promise
was not justified by later events; Michigan never produced a
Liberty man of national prominence; its leaders were as devoted as those of any other State, but they seemed to lack the
vigorous personality of the Ohio, Illinois, and Wisconsin leaders.
In the period 1840–43, the most prominent man in the State,
overtopping every one else, was J. G. Birney, who had settled
in Saginaw County after several years spent mainly in travelling over the country, agitating and organizing. His purpose
in going to Michigan seems to have been to retire from his
labors, and by farming to rest himself and repair his health
and fortunes with a view to the campaign of 1844. Hence he
seemed at first to avoid Liberty party work; but before long
he found himself in the thick of it and at the head of the movement. Dr. A. L. Porter, S. R. Treadwell, C. H. Stewart,
H. Hallock, and S. M. Holmes formed a coterie of Liberty men
in Detroit and its vicinity who well seconded Birney and on
their own account labored to promote the cause. Unlike the
leaders in other States, these Michigan men were not all lawyers, and hence did not appear very often as candidates themselves; but it is safe to say that the real management of the
party lay with the men mentioned above. Stewart, an Irish-
man, a "Repealer," and a fiery stump-speaker, was, after Birney,
the leading orator at this time.

In Illinois the cause of political abolition had passed from
such men as David Nelson into new hands. Here, as in Ohio,
there was a powerful local sentiment to build upon; and as a
result the Illinois Liberty party leaders proved from the outset
an active, enterprising group. In some respects the most
important of the Illinois abolitionists was Zebina Eastman, for
thirteen years the editor and publisher of anti-slavery newspapers. He was a hard worker, very earnest and practical in
both speeches and writings, but sometimes open to the charge of
prosiness. In contrast to him was Owen Lovejoy, who, having
knelt on the grave of his murdered brother, Elijah P. Lovejoy,
to swear eternal enmity to slavery, was a zealous, persistent
agitator, eloquent in speech, radical, and sometimes bitter to
the point of virulence, a man capable of inspiring the greatest

respect and confidence in the anti-slavery men of the north-eastern counties, and for fourteen years the leader and personification of Illinois abolitionism. F. Collins was from the first a consistent Liberty man, and from his business ability and devotion to the cause was a favorite anti-slavery candidate. Dr. R. Eells and C. V. Dyer also deserve mention as leading agitators, as well as the radical, fiery-tongued Ichabod Codding, formerly of Maine and Connecticut, who in 1843 joined the Illinois forces. In short, the Liberty men of the northern counties, although not equal perhaps to the group of Cincinnati leaders, were fully the peers of the Western Reserve men in point of ability and of enterprise.

In Wisconsin, which had just begun its work in this period, leaders had not yet shown themselves. Jacob Ly Brand, Vernon Titchener, an able lawyer, and S. Hinman were at this time prominent, but later yielded to the leadership of others. As will be seen later, the eventual Liberty leaders were Charles Durkee, of Racine, a prosperous and extremely popular farmer, a clear-headed and reliable man; E. D. Holton, of Milwaukee, a business man and a banker, a good speaker, and a fine figure-head; S. M. Booth, formerly of Connecticut, later an editor, agitator, and leader in Milwaukee, and defendant in the famous fugitive slave case of Ableman *v.* Booth, a tireless, sharp-tongued radical, of just the kind needed to give an impetus to the anti-slavery cause ; S. D. Hastings, formerly a Liberty pioneer in Pennsylvania ; and some others of less prominence. The Wisconsin leaders were not men of such strength as their Illinois or Ohio coadjutors, but their success proved them fully equal to the leaders of Indiana or of Michigan.

These, then, were the men at the head of the new movement. Their methods were much the same as those of the old anti-slavery societies ; but, owing to their more definite immediate aims, they showed a more organized activity. The first thing the third-party men in each State tried to do was to establish a paper, for they well knew that a press was indispensable to their party's success. In Ohio, the *Philanthropist* continued under Dr. Bailey to be the organ of the southwestern counties, and to exercise a great influence.[1] In 1840-41 there were several attempts to establish a paper in Cleveland, but none succeeded on the Western Reserve until the *Liberty Herald* at Warren, Trumbull County, was established in 1843.[2] In Indiana, Arnold Buffum tried for some time to start an abolitionist paper, and for a time published the *Protectionist;* but he finally abandoned the project. In 1841-43 the *Free Labor Advocate,* a Quaker paper of New Garden, Wayne County, was the organ of Indiana abolitionists. In Michigan, the *Michigan Freeman* of Detroit was finally superseded by the *Signal of Liberty,* published at Ann Arbor in 1841. In Illinois, Z. Eastman started the *Genius of Liberty* at Lowell, Lasalle County, in 1841. It ran until 1843, when the editor moved to Chicago, where, under the auspices of the State society, he started the *Western Citizen,* which soon became the organ of Illinois, Wisconsin, and Iowa anti-slavery sentiment.[3] In Wisconsin, after one attempt, in 1844, to start a paper at Racine, the *American Freeman* was in the same year begun, at Southport (later Kenosha), with the aid of the State society.[4] In Iowa no attempt was made in this period to establish anti-slavery papers.

The policy of the Liberty party during these three years was consistent and simple. It asserted the overmastering importance of the one question of the existence of slavery, and the necessity of bringing about a separation of the national government from all connection with the institution. It claimed no unusual powers, believing that its sole opportunity of attacking slavery lay in the District of Columbia and in the Territories, and that for slavery in the States it had no direct responsibility. For this reason the *Philanthropist* said that it was incorrect to style it the "Abolition Party," for its purposes were not directed toward abolition anywhere except in these two places.[5] This caused some amusing outbursts. Said one

[1] A file may be found in the Western Reserve Historical Society, Cleveland, Ohio. See Appendix B, below.

[2] *Ibid.*

[3] File in Chicago Historical Society.

[4] File in Wisconsin Historical Society, Madison.

[5] *Philanthropist,* Feb. 16, 1842.

correspondent of a new York paper: "We are amazed, astounded, dumbfounded, at the leading article from the pen of Dr. Bailey. . . . Let us understand each other. Where are we? . . . We look upon it as a direct and bold attempt to sell the abolitionists of Ohio to one of the political parties, and we cry, Beware!!"[1]

The means adopted by the political abolitionists to gain their end, was the building up of a new party whose sole purpose should be to urge the separation of the national government from slavery. This party was to remain absolutely distinct and separate from all pre-existing organizations, indifferent alike to Whig and Democrat; it was to nominate and vote for those only who accepted in detail all its tenets in regard to slavery and party action; and, for gaining political success, it was to rely simply and solely upon the presentation of its principles to the people. The adoption of such a course was inevitable after the reaction from the non-partisan questioning expedient of 1830–39, and the consequent loss of all faith in the possibility of reforming the old parties; but the alternative now chosen by the Liberty party presented several difficulties equally grave with those avoided. If the old method left the anti-slavery voters at the mercy of the nominating conventions of the old parties, which seldom resulted in the presentation of a man whom they could fully trust, it did allow them a direct influence on the results of elections. The Liberty-party methods, on the contrary, prevented anti-slavery voters from securing any representation or from directly influencing the results of elections, until they were, in any given district, more numerous than either of the opposing parties. Practically, the only hope of success for Liberty men lay in the possibility that Whigs or Democrats would unite with them in nominating a Liberty man, a contingency extremely unlikely to happen. The political self-effacement required in joining the new party was beyond the reach of many who sympathized with its doctrines, and hence its growth was slow.

Moreover, the new party had to meet a still more fatal difficulty, in that it was unable to convince people that the slavery

[1] *Philanthropist*, March 16, 1842.

5

question was at the time paramount to all others. In 1840–43 the bank struggle was in its expiring agonies, and the tariff question was hotly debated in Congress: to the eyes of most people these seemed the real issues. Slavery was just what it had been since the beginning of the Union; though not attractive to a farmer of northern Indiana or Ohio, it was certainly not a grievance with him; and attacks disturbing the *status quo* seemed unnecessary, if not dangerous. Had either of the old parties adopted an anti-slavery plank, many of their adherents would have acquiesced; so long as this was not done, the anti-slavery platform of the Liberty party, devoid of reference to tariff, bank, public lands, internal improvements, or any of the commonplaces of politics, was not likely to prove attractive. The " one idea party," as it was commonly called, was trying to force an issue, — almost to create one.

During this period the old parties and their organs at first said little about their new opponents. In 1840, as we have seen, there had been occasional outbursts of condemnation; but after the election the party papers either ceased to notice the new organization, or dismissed it with a few contemptuous words. During the whole period of 1841–43, Democratic men and newspapers, whenever they spoke of abolition, generally condemned it. Now and then they went to considerable lengths, as in the following outburst of the *Madison* (Wisconsin) *Democrat:* " It is quite apparent that these people as a political party will soon pass away. . . . Providence has doomed them to that certain fate which in an intelligent age and among an honest people must sooner or later overtake all political factions whose existence and support depend upon ignorance and hypocrisy. . . . We firmly believe Providence decreed that the white race should guard and protect, clothe and feed the negro race, and that the latter should be hewers of wood and drawers of water for those who feed and protect them. God has made the two races so distinct that on earth they can never be equal." [1] Such language could not hurt the Liberty party; in fact, it was calculated rather to help it; and the Liberty newspapers and speakers took comparatively little notice of the Democrats.

[1] Oct. 12, 1843.

Between the Whig and Liberty parties in the Northwest, however, the case was quite different. Each recognized in the other
a dangerous antagonist; the success of the Whigs was imperilled by third-party organization; the very existence of the
Liberty party was endangered by the Whig position. When
the Liberty party rose out of the decay of the old anti-slavery
society movement, the majority of those abolitionists who refused to follow Birney went into the Whig party, claiming that
in so doing they were fully as desirous to help the cause as were
the Liberty men. Some, in their revulsion of feeling after
1841–42, returned to the third-party ranks, furnishing probably
most of the increase in the Liberty vote; but the majority continued to adhere to the party of Clay, Webster, and Adams; and
the result was a bitterness between the anti-slavery Whigs and
the Liberty men which very largely occupied the interest and the
energies of the latter. Some of the Whig opinions of 1840 have
been quoted; the main purport of them was that the Whig party
was really opposed to slavery, and that the Liberty party, by
drawing from the Whig ranks, was wasting its vote and was
virtually electing pro-slavery Democrats. In the period under
discussion such expressions occurred with increasing frequency
as time went on. At every election the cry was repeated, in
the words of the *Detroit Advertiser :* " Let every Whig abolitionist remember that every vote cast for the third party is in
effect, if not in intention, cast for the locofoco ticket." [1]

The growth of the Liberty party in this period had no effect
upon the legislation of the Northwest. We find the southern
section of the three Ohio River States still dominant in the State
government; and the same expressions of disgust at abolition
and of dislike for the negro. In Ohio a Whig legislature did,
it is true, repeal the Fugitive Slave Act of 1839; but efforts
made at the same time to repeal the Black Laws met with
crushing defeat. In February, 1842, resolutions were adopted
denouncing John Quincy Adams for presenting a petition for
the dissolution of the Union.[2] In 1843 the House of the Illinois
legislature, composed mainly of natives of the slave-holding

[1] Nov. 11, 1842.
[2] *Philanthropist,* Feb. 9, 1842; *Laws of Ohio* (1841–42), 213.

States, signalized itself by adopting resolutions which from any point of view can be considered only humiliating. The preamble stated that the distributions of public land were unduly favorable to the South, which would not consent to any change unless it received some concession; that the legislature of Illinois "viewed with deepest concern the continual increase of desertion of the slaves of our brethren of the slave-holding States," and thought that measures to check the evil should be taken. Therefore, it recommended to the States of Louisiana, Mississippi, Alabama, Kentucky, Tennessee, Arkansas, Missouri, Indiana, Ohio, and Michigan to meet in convention at Jonesborough, Illinois, on July 4, to make arrangements in regard to the public lands and in regard to a new fugitive-slave law.[1]

With the year 1843 the formative period of the Liberty party was complete. Its leaders had done their best; its newspapers had cried aloud and spared not; its lecturers had traversed all the States; at three elections all the faithful had cast their votes unflinchingly for men whom they knew they could not elect; and still the party remained diminutive, almost insignificant. The experiment of forcing an issue upon an indifferent people had been tried, and, as always, it had proved futile.

[1] *National Era*, June 3, 1847.

CHAPTER VI.

THE LIBERTY MEN HOLD THE BALANCE OF POWER.

1843–1845.

In the year of the national election of 1844, the Liberty party of the United States suddenly found itself in the presence of a new and pressing issue, in the outcome of which it was vitally interested. The annexation of Texas had been since 1836 the subject of intrigue, but in this year for the first time it loomed up as a probable event. In the winter of 1843–4 it became evident that while the South almost as a unit was in favor of annexation, the two old organizations, in the Northern States at least, seemed inclined to divide upon this question. There was no need for the Liberty party to force or to create an issue; there stood one, threatening, unavoidable. How were they to meet it?

Pursuant to a resolution adopted at that New York convention of 1841 which had nominated Birney and Morris, the Liberty party, after the elections of 1843, met in national convention at Buffalo. At the Ohio Liberty Convention in January, 1843, Morris had withdrawn from the nomination, feeling that, as so many able and leading men had joined the cause since the spring of 1841, it would be only fair to allow the party to choose one of them, if it thought politic or desirable. The business before the convention, then, consisted in filling the vacancy caused by Morris's resignation and in organizing the party for the campaign of 1844 ; and for the first time was seen a really national, or at least a Northern, political anti-slavery gathering. No longer was the management, as in 1841, almost entirely in the hands of New York and Massachusetts men; for the Western delegates showed on the whole greater distinction than did the older leaders of the cause. The Ohio constellation in particular took the lead : Leicester King presided ; Samuel Lewis was a vice-president, speaking often with great effect; and Chase drew up the resolutions. Among other Northwestern men those from Illinois were prominent, C. V. Dyer being a vice-president, and Owen Lovejoy a secretary. Regular procedure was adopted, modelled on that of the Whig national conventions. Birney and Morris were unanimously renominated with great enthusiasm ; a long series of well-written resolutions embodying the party creed was adopted ; and the convention adjourned with cheerfulness, if not with all the high hopes that had been cherished in 1841. An interesting incident was the appearance in the convention òf Stephen S. Foster and Abby Kelly, of the Garrisonian or non-resistant abolitionists, who made various remarks, partly conciliatory and partly otherwise, until the patience of the members was exhausted, and the zealous Abby Kelly was with difficulty silenced.[1]

The Liberty party, then, in the opening of 1844 had its Presidential ticket in the field, but had no statement in its platform in regard to Texas ; for at the time the platform was adopted that question had not risen into prominence. In January and February the local Liberty organizations started in on the long campaign, calling conventions, passing resolutions, and, in general, continuing the processes used in the three preceding years. They condemned both the old parties, urged the necessity of separating the national government from slavery, and reiterated the usual arguments, now beginning to be familiar. Presently the Texas matter began to come into view; and, as the year wore on, the fact grew more and more evident that Democrats and slave-holders favored annexation and Whigs opposed it. This condition of things did not, however, suggest to the Liberty party any alteration in the line of conduct which they had been pursuing. Though the Whigs and Democrats were divided over the slavery issue, how did that concern the Liberty party? The Whigs, on the contrary, thought that it concerned

---

[1] For the Liberty convention of 1843, see *Emancipator*, Sept. 7, 14, 1843; *Albany Patriot*, Sept. 12, 1843; R. B. Warden, *Life of Chase*, 300.

the Liberty party very closely whether or not Texas were annexed ; and in the spring and early summer of 1844 they began
with a vehemence hitherto unknown to urge upon abolitionists
that the only way to keep Texas out was to vote the Whig
ticket for Presidential, Congressional, and State offices. After
Polk was nominated, and it became still more evident that the
Democratic party was committed to annexation, their appeals
and arguments came with increasing fervor. " Friends, Chris-
tians, honest men," said the *Indiana State Journal*, " how can
you, by throwing away your votes, hazard the election of Texas
and slavery men to the legislature from this county? Our opponents . . . are tickled to death with the prospect of thus using
you as tools. Shall it be done? Will you minister to their
success? Ponder on these things."[1]

The abolitionists were forced to ponder, particularly those
who had been Whigs in 1840. The exigency seemed pressing,
but there was no provision for anything of the sort in the
Liberty programme. All their training in the years 1841–43
bade them to ignore or to condemn the old parties, and to scorn
as a temptation of Satan the idea of voting for a Whig, even
though an anti-slavery man, unless he were also an abolitionist
in good standing and already a Liberty nominee. Yet there
stood Texas, a whole slave empire in itself, waiting only the
election of a Democratic President and Congress in order to be
annexed. So long as there was any hope of preventing this
step by direct action, to vote for a third party seemed, as the
Whigs said, simply to minister to Democratic success.

Had the Whigs at this juncture offered a candidate who by
any stretch of logic could be called anti-slavery, the existence of
the Liberty party would have been imperilled; but the Whigs,
fortunately for the Liberty men and unfortunately for themselves, had at the head of their ticket the one man least likely
to attract abolition votes. In Henry Clay, the idol of Whigs
North and South, the abolitionists could not find a redeeming
trait. He was himself a slave-holder, a fact which, according to
the Liberty creed, hopelessly disqualified him. Moreover, for
seven years he had publicly deprecated their aims, and ridiculed

[1] Aug. 3, 1844.

and condemned their methods. His only possible claim to their
support was his avowed opposition to Texas annexation; and
this in the summer of 1844 he destroyed by his famous Alabama
letter, saying that he should "be glad to see it annexed . . .
on honorable terms." In spite of these patent facts, the Whig
appeals for Liberty support continued so vigorous, and the
exigency seemed so pressing, that desertions from the Liberty
ranks began, and the third-party leaders became alarmed. And
now the least lovely traits of the political abolitionists came into
view: their insistence that a candidate completely conform to
their creed; their mastery of the art of exasperating abuse. To
prove that Clay was no abolitionist was easy; to show that
he was unsound on the question of Texas was not difficult; but
with this the Liberty men were by no means satisfied. They
attacked him on altogether irrelevant grounds, impugning his
personal character as that of a gambler and a duelist, and employing the old-time anti-slavery language in calling him a "man-
stealer" because he held slaves. The Ohio State Convention
at Akron, June 6, adopted a resolution offered by Edward Wade,
that "no law-abiding citizen can support Mr. Clay for President,
because he is a duelist."[1] When excited, the Liberty men
sometimes went beyond all bounds of prudence. M. R. Hull, of
Indianapolis, for example, having been mobbed by a Whig
crowd, published a letter in a Democratic paper saying: "This
is the party whose leader is a gambler, a man-stealer and a duelist; this is the party, with all their bitter, bloody, burning out-
rages on abolitionists, that has the impudence to call on Liberty
men to support their gambling, dueling, negro-robbing chief."[2]
Devotion to Henry Clay was almost a cardinal point in the
Whig creed; they could hear their party and their platform
abused, but attacks on Clay they could not stand. As an indignant anti-slavery man had written to the *Philanthropist* in 1842:
"I think too much of Henry Clay to longer support a paper
that abuses him as much as you do."[3] Consequently these
bitter Liberty attacks on Clay's character drove the Whigs

[1] Warren *Liberty Herald*, June 12, 1844.
[2] *Indianapolis Sentinel*, Sept. 5, 1844.
[3] *Philanthropist*, Sept. 17, 1842.

simply to madness. Argument vanished in a flood of mutual invective.

Meanwhile in the Northwest the Liberty forces had been for some months preparing for the election. In Ohio, on February 7, a State Convention in Columbus, with J. H. Paine presiding, adopted a long series of resolutions, appointed Presidential electors, and nominated Leicester King for Governor. One hundred and sixteen delegates were present, representing all parts of the State. Their temper is shown by one of the resolutions: "That Liberty men should . . . suffer no election, local or general, to go by without nominations and a struggle; our constables and justices of the peace, our trustees, clerks of townships, school directors, our judges, sheriffs, coroners, and clerks of courts, our representatives and senators in the legislature and in Congress, our Governor, President and Vice-President and all the other officers of our State and National Government should be Liberty men."[1] From this time on, not a week passed without Liberty meetings somewhere in the State; and in June a regular campaign began, with stumping tours in the southwest and on the Reserve. King was in the field with Brisbane, Sutliff, Morris, Wade, Chase, and William Birney; and by the end of the summer, as the time for the October State election approached, the Liberty party of Ohio was better organized than ever before.

In Indiana a State Convention, on May 30, nominated electors, and adopted measures to circulate a quantity of anti-slavery literature. The calm and undisturbed course which third-party men had held, when left to themselves by the old parties, was now interrupted, and the conflict of 1840 returned. In every county where Liberty men were strong, Whig candidates made direct appeals for their votes. In the words of the Democratic *State Sentinel*, "The stump orators made speeches which the abolitionists themselves declared were up and down abolition speeches in everything but voting for Henry Clay."[2] At the Liberty State Convention, the same Mr. Rariden who four years before had played a prominent part in preventing the Indiana State Convention from ratifying the nomination of Birney, now

[1] Warren *Liberty Herald*, Feb. 22, 1844.
[2] *Indianapolis Sentinel*, Aug. 15, 1844.

reappeared, and spoke twice urging Liberty men to support Clay.[1] Consequently the Liberty vote in the Indiana State election in August showed the effect of this concerted Whig attack. As the *Free Labor Advocate* said, " The new-born zeal of the Whig orators against the annexation of Texas had made a strong impression in their favor . . . and the argument in favor of voting wrong this one time . . . in order to save the country prevailed." [2] During the interval between this and the national election the abolitionists of Indiana made strong efforts to act together; but, although matters were somewhat improved by November, their organization was still very incomplete.

In Michigan the Liberty organization created by Birney and his sympathizers in the preceding year was working effectively. The usual State and local conventions met, and by the middle of the summer a full ticket for Congress and the legislature was in nomination. The State campaign became active when Birney took the stump in July and by a joint debate with Z. Platt in Detroit excited wide-spread interest.[3] The differences between Whigs and Liberty men reached an acute stage in Michigan sooner than in any other Northwestern State; and by July the newspaper controversy became acrimonious to a degree, which gave intense delight to the Democrats.

In Illinois we find much the same state of things.[4] The northern counties, hotbeds of anti-slavery feeling, were busy from early in the year; and Lovejoy, Codding, Eastman, Dyer, and the others by their activity brought about a distinct increase in the Liberty vote at the State election in August. In the Fourth District the vote was 1,408, as against 1,174 in 1843, and the other returns were said by the *Western Citizen* to be equally encouraging.[5] The Illinois leaders, Lovejoy and Codding, were fortunately of a temperament to be exhilarated rather than discouraged by the Whig abuse poured out in the summer of this year.

---

[1] *Emancipator*, July 3, 1844.   [2] Quoted *Ibid.*, Aug. 28, 1844.

[3] *Ibid.*, Aug. 14, 1844.

[4] *Western Citizen*, April 18, June 20, 1844.

[5] *Ibid.*, July 4, Aug. 8, 1844; quoted in *Emancipator*, July 23, Aug. 19, 1844.

In Iowa Territory there was as yet little anti-slavery feeling, and no attempt at Liberty organization; but in Wisconsin the methods of Illinois were being imitated. The Liberty men of that Territory could not participate in the national election, nor even in any general State election; but they ran local tickets with considerable vigor, and were extremely active in organizing. Their vote as returned by the *Western Citizen* was at least 450, and probably more, — a substantial increase over the 152 of the preceding year.[1] The Territorial Anti-Slavery Association, in its annual report, pointed with pride to the fact that " in Walworth County the Whigs ascribe their defeat in the election of county officers to the influence of the Liberty Party."[2]

By October, then, the Liberty men in all the Northwestern States were hotly engaged in the fiercest conflict which they had as yet experienced, their attitude on the Texas issue being well illustrated by a quotation from the Michigan *Signal of Liberty:* "Liberty men! Now is the time to act! Stand forth for your principles and show that you are men. . . . Polk is for immediate annexation, Clay for it as soon as it can be had upon such terms as he may think peaceable, etc. The question is not, shall Texas be annexed? but when and how shall it be annexed? What have Liberty men to do with this issue? Let the pro-slavery parties settle it between themselves."[3]

In opposition to this view, the appeals of Whigs grew more urgent, and their denunciations sharper, fairly drowning in a flood of vituperation the Liberty replies, bitter and violent as they became. Here and there in the Liberty ranks appeared signs of weakening, which were loudly trumpeted by Whig papers to all corners of the country. In Michigan and in New York manifestoes appeared signed by anti-slavery men, announcing their reluctant purpose of supporting Clay on the Texas issue;[4] but although here and in Indiana the third party sustained some losses, Ohio abolitionists held firm, and in the October election increased their vote even more than Illinois

---

[1] *Emancipator*, Nov. 20, 1844.

[2] Racine, *Wisconsin Ægis*, March 2, 1844.

[3] Quoted *Detroit Free Press*, Sept. 12, 1844.

[4] *Cincinnati Gazette*, Oct. 1, 1844.

had done in August. The official return was as follows: Democratic — Tod, 146,461; Whig — Bartley, 147,738; Liberty — King, 8,411.[1] Again, as in 1842, the Liberty men showed that they held the balance of power.

In October, however, there came to light in Michigan a most remarkable state of things, which, more than any possible Whig arguments or abuse, damaged the Liberty cause. It was learned that, on September 28, just after starting on an electioneering tour to the East, James G. Birney, one of the founders of the party and its candidate for President, had been nominated for the legislature by a Democratic convention. Nothing could have been more opportune for the Whigs. In their indignation at Liberty obstinacy, they had been crying that nothing could explain it except a bargain between Birney and Polk; and here was an incident that seemed to confirm their claim. As soon as the discovery was reported to the Michigan Whig Committee, then under the lead of Jacob M. Howard, the news was sent all over the country. "There is no earthly doubt of this," said Howard, in a letter to R. C. Winthrop, of Massachusetts. "Use it then! It will influence 20,000 votes in the North."[2] The news, accompanied by stinging comments, appeared in every Whig paper, followed often by a crop of stories regarding statements made by Birney to the effect that he preferred Polk to Clay, and admissions that he favored free trade and, most incredible of all, the annexation of Texas![3]

The effect on Liberty men was stupefying. In spite of all Birney's sacrifices, his labors, his repeated condemnations of Democrats and of slavery, it seemed to many as if he had actually played them false, or had at least committed a stupendous piece of folly. Birney himself hastened to explain, though

---

[1] *Whig Almanac*, 1845. These published figures are almost certainly incomplete, for there are no returns for Carroll, Cuyahoga, or Highland County, and but 16 for Harrison County; whereas these had given 715 votes in 1843. A later version, also official, makes a total of 8,898, giving Harrison 216 Liberty votes, and Cuyahoga 364; but even this count seems inadequate. The Liberty vote was probably over 9,000.

[2] *Emancipator*, Oct. 21, 1844.

[3] *New York Tribune*, Oct. 10, 19, 26, Nov. 2, 1844.

not to satisfy. In letters to the *New York Tribune* and to the Liberty party at large he made it evident that the nomination was simply the result of local questions in Saginaw County; that the Democrats in nominating him had done so without regard to anything but a desire to break up a local ring which had been mismanaging affairs; and that he himself, when he gave them permission to nominate him, regarded the nomination as coming from the people and not from any party.[1] The fact remained, however, that it was an extraordinary performance on his part, particularly since the Michigan State Liberty Convention, which nominated him for Governor in 1843, had resolved: " That in the opinion of this Convention great injury will be suffered by the Liberty party if the members permit their names to be placed on the tickets of other parties unless they are taken up by them distinctly as Liberty men, and this ought to be ascertained by the fact of their nomination then existing on the Liberty party ticket."[2]

Birney denied the accuracy of the stories regarding his alleged preference for Polk, but admitted the truth of their main contention, namely, that he preferred Polk to Clay. The reasons which he assigned were, that Clay, as well as Polk, had expressed himself in favor of annexation, and that Clay could and would lead his party, while Polk was incompetent to lead his. The question suggests itself at once whether Polk's party needed any leading to bring it to favor annexation. Birney's position was not perfectly logical, and his statement was a piece of very unnecessary frankness; for the Whig papers, in the heat of the campaign, brushed aside without ceremony his fine distinctions, as weak attempts to justify Democratic leanings; and they continued to repeat phrases taken from the affidavit of one Driggs, who had been sent by the Michigan Whig Committee to investigate the matter and to work up the case against Birney, and who reported that the latter " had sought the nomination, . . . expressed himself a Democrat, [and] had promised if elected not to agitate the slavery question in the legislature."[3]

---

[1] *New York Tribune*, Oct. 10, 19, 1844; *Emancipator*, Oct. 15, 1844.
[2] *Emancipator*, March 16, 1843.
[3] Driggs's affidavit, *New York Tribune*, Oct. 26, 1844.

Seasoned abolitionists knew Birney too well to heed the uproar ; but recent recruits became doubtful. In Ohio, Giddings, always a tower of strength to the Whig party, spoke with great effect, never missing an opportunity to excoriate Birney; until, in alarm at the havoc that he was making among the abolitionists of that region, the Ohio Liberty Committee issued an address written by Chase begging Liberty men to stand firm and to trust in Birney: "To say that such a man has united himself to the Democratic party, bound as it is at present by the atrocious resolutions of the Baltimore Convention, is base beyond measure. . . . Reject with scorn this gross libel. . . . We entreat you to stand! For God and Duty stand! Stand this once!"[1]

Perhaps the Liberty men would have stood, had matters rested at this stage ; but suddenly, one or two days before the national election, there appeared in most of the Northern States a copy of a letter written by Birney to J. B. Garland, of Saginaw, sworn to by Garland himself, and taken from a copy of the *Genesee County Democrat Extra* of October 21. In the letter Birney concluded to accept the Democratic county nomination, authorized Garland to say that he was a Democrat of the Jeffersonian school, and promised if elected to forego the agitation of the slavery question in the State legislature.[2] This document, apparently unimpeachable, was sprung upon the country with consummate skill. It appeared on the same day in Portland, Boston, Washington, Columbus, Cincinnati, and elsewhere, in other cities a little earlier, in Detroit, significantly enough, considerably later. It was printed as a handbill and distributed by the Indiana Whig Central Committee.[3] It was circulated all over the Western Reserve, endorsed by the Ohio Whig Central Committee,[4] and carried, as indignant Liberty men said, "by the hands of deacons and church members."[5]

[1] A. G. Riddle on J. R. Giddings, in *History of Ashtabula County, Ohio*, 81 ; *Philanthropist*, Oct. 23, 1844.

[2] Washington *National Intelligencer*, Nov. 2, 1844.

[3] W. Birney, *J. G. Birney and his Times*, 355; *Indianapolis Sentinel*, Nov. 21, 1844.

[4] *Liberty Herald*, Nov. 6, 1844.

[5] *Herald and Philanthropist*, Nov. 13, 1844. In this year a daily edition of this paper took the name *Cincinnati Herald*.

Birney was at this time travelling westward; but the letter was not published in western New York, — Rochester, Syracuse, and Buffalo, — until he had passed by,[1] and he did not see it himself until he reached Painesville, on the Western Reserve. As soon as he read it, he pronounced it an utter forgery throughout;[2] but it was too late: the document had done its work. Following after his Democratic nomination and the flood of Whig innuendo, containing the very phrases repeated by the Whigs and seeming to confirm them, signed and sworn to with all due forms, it had turned hundreds of abolitionists from Birney to Clay, had kept hundreds more away from the polls, and had in New York and Ohio seriously reduced the Liberty vote. In New York the vote was 1,000 less than in 1843; in Ohio it was probably at least 1,000 less than in the State election a month before.[3] Even in far-off Illinois, the *Western Citizen* reported that fifty voters in one county were kept from the polls.[4]

But argument, appeal, and Garland forgery together, failed to save the Whigs in the November election. In spite of all distractions, enough Liberty men supported their candidate in the State of New York alone to give the electoral vote to Polk. Had there been no Liberty party, most of those who composed its membership would probably have voted for Clay, — enough of them, the Whigs claimed, to make his election certain. Whether this last assertion is true, it is of course impossible to say; but in any case it is safe to conclude that, had not Birney been in nomination, Whig chances would have been much better.

The Liberty vote in the country at large in this year amounted to 62,000, showing a very slight increase over that of the preceding year. In the Northwest each State made a substantial increase except Ohio, whose decrease from October we may

---

[1] *Detroit Free Press*, Dec. 15, 1844.

[2] *Cincinnati Gazette*, Nov. 5, 1844. See Garland's affidavit, *Detroit Free Press*, Dec. 18, 1844.

[3] For the Garland forgery, see W. Birney, *J. G. Birney and his Times*, 354 *seq.*

[4] *Emancipator*, Dec. 7, 1844.

ascribe in no small degree to the effect of the Garland forgery on the Western Reserve.[1]

The election of 1844 was decisive for Liberty men; for by their own conduct they had succeeded in putting out of their own reach all success along the line which they were pursuing. From the Democratic party they had from the outset nothing to hope, since its strength lay in the South and in the ruder classes of the North and West, among whom anti-slavery principles would be the last to penetrate. To the Whig party alone could they look; and now after 1844 accessions from that quarter were rendered infinitely less likely than heretofore. Liberal people were repelled by the intolerance of the Liberty men for any opinions but their own; practical men were displeased by their adherence to Birney, when by voting for the other candidates they would have influenced directly the election in regard to Texas; Old-Line Whigs were disgusted at their refusal to accept the Whig view of the duty of anti-slavery men, and were enraged beyond control by their unsparing and bitterly personal condemnation of Clay. In the opinion of hundreds of thousands of Whigs, the persistence of Birney in running in 1844 could be explained only on the theory that he was a Democrat in disguise, subsidized by Polk to aid the latter's election. When the news of his nomination by the Democrats of Saginaw County, of his own honest but ill-judged acceptance of the name " Democrat" " in the true sense," and of his still more unwise preference for Polk over Clay were spread abroad, the last shadow of doubt vanished, and from 1844 to the end of the Whig party's career neither Birney nor the Liberty party was ever forgiven.

In the fall of 1844 and the winter of 1844–5 Whig execrations fell heavily on the heads of the culprits. That any other causes had co-operated to defeat Clay never entered their heads;

[1] The vote was as follows : —

	Democratic.	Whig.	Liberty.	Per cent.
Ohio . . .	149,117	155,057	8,050	.027
Indiana . .	70,181	67,567	2,106	.015
Michigan . .	27,703	24,037	3,632	.064
Illinois . .	57,920	45,528	3,570	.033

that Clay's own vacillation in any degree accounted for his failure they never admitted: for upon the Liberty party alone they laid the blame of their idol's defeat. "Refine and revise as we please," said the *Cincinnati Gazette*, "the responsibility of this whole matter rests with the third party." [1] "We believe that thousands of political abolitionists," said the *Chicago Journal*, "if they had their own votes to cast over again would cast them for Henry Clay. . . . If their mission was the unloosing of the bonds of the captive, and the giving of liberty to the slave, they have proved recreant to their holy trust. For, instead of circumscribing the area of slavery, they have added to it, . . . have given the slave-holders a power which will prove for years if not for centuries resistless. Their work has been surely done, and a fearful and awful work it is." [2] "Where's the Liberty party?" asked the *Ohio State Journal*. "The leaders have gone over to the Texas and slavery party; will the rank and file follow? The next we shall see of their leaders, with Mr. Birney at their head, will be hanging about the executive offices at Washington receiving their pay." [3] More influential in the Northwest than any local paper, the *New York Tribune* thus poured out its wrath: "You third-party wireworkers forced this man [Polk] upon us instead of the only anti-Texas candidate who could possibly be elected. On your guilty heads shall rest the curses of unborn generations! Riot in your infamy and rejoice in its triumph, but never ask us to unite with you in anything." [4]

It was upon Birney himself that the hatred of the ultra-Whigs was especially poured forth.[5] Their feeling is best shown in a letter of J. M. Howard, of Detroit, to Birney, in the spring of 1845: "Will the low arts of the demagogue,

---

[1] Aug. 22, 1844.   [2] Nov. 19, 1848.

[3] Quoted in *Milwaukee Sentinel*, Dec. 7, 1844.

[4] Nov. 28, 1844.

[5] The *Detroit Advertiser*, for example, during the campaign, said that there was no scandal too low, no perversion of truth too glaring for his use, . . . his whole speech was a tissue of rancorous personal abuse, sly and unmanly innuendo, and harsh and brutal calumny," . . . that he "added cowardice to falsehood," and was "a Polkat in the skin of a mink."—*Detroit Advertiser*, July 11, 1844; *Emancipator*, Aug. 14, 1844.

assaults upon private character, the petulant whining tone of a
charlatan who has been detected in a dirty transaction . . .
will these miserable follies break the shackles of a slave? . . .
You well knew that if left to themselves nine-tenths of your
followers would vote the Whig ticket. . . . You knew and saw
with your own eyes that the Democratic party was anxious that
you should thus act.   They encouraged you, . . . you knew it
and they knew it.   Talk of it as you may — sneer at it — explain — deny as you please, this is evidence of a conspiracy in
favor of slavery which . . . no arguments can ever remove or
shake." [1]

In the course of a year or two the Whig party began to recover from its soreness ; but the bitterness between the two
parties remained.   In the Northwest, the efforts of the Michigan
Liberty men to unearth the forgers of the Garland letter nour-
ished hard feeling.   The history of this curious matter is not,
perhaps, worth relating at length; but it should here be completed.   The Whig papers, after the election, all admitted that
the letter was a forgery, but they admitted it often in the most
irritating way possible.   The *Ohio State Journal* remarked on
the needless folly of the forgers, "when it is considered that the
evidence of a coalition between the leaders of the Loco and
Liberty parties was manifest from the evidence furnished by
Mr. Birney himself in his letters and speeches." [2]   The *New
York Tribune* said that the Garland letter was of questionable
authenticity, but that "there was much internal probability of
the verity of the letter." [3]   Several of the Whig papers, it is
true, said that they hoped the forgers would be hunted down ;
but the avowed disposition to retract promptly and to act
was [4] due probably to the recent libel trials of James Feni-
more Cooper, the outcome of which led all newspapers to act
circumspectly ; when the Michigan Liberty Committee tried
to get evidence, the Whig editors and leaders obstinately
blocked the way.   They refused to tell where they got the let

---

[1] *Milwaukee Sentinel*, March 28, 1845.
[2] Quoted in *Indiana State Journal*, Nov. 9, 1844.
[3] Nov. 2, 1844.
[4] *Indiana State Journal*, Nov. 9, 1844.

ter, refused to let the supposed original be seen, declined in any way to assist the Liberty Committee, and covered them with abuse.   The result was an envenomed newspaper controversy in Michigan and elsewhere, ending finally in the refusal by the Whigs to continue the subject.[1]   The Liberty Committee, working with what clews they could get, managed to trace the forged " Extra" to the Michigan *Pontiac Gazette* press-room, and implicated as its printers one of the editors of the *Detroit Advertiser*, and one or two leading Whigs.   Their evidence, however, was not very strong from a legal point of view, and the obstinate silence of the Whigs finally succeeded in preventing a complete exposure.   By the time the *Emancipator*, the organ of the American and Foreign Anti-Slavery Society, felt able in 1846 to print what evidence it had, the matter was already lapsing from the public memory, and after some abortive libel suits the whole affair was suffered to drop.[2]   Jacob M. Howard, who had done most to spread the forgery, was not among those named as involved in its concoction, although the Liberty Committee would have been glad to find him guilty. Thus in 1846 the last echoes of the election of 1844 died away; but in the hearts of Henry Clay Whigs its memory remained, keeping alive a consuming hatred of the Liberty party and of all political abolitionists.

When we consider what the Liberty party was, how it had been formed and built up by years of hard work, and what were its aims, it seems not quite just to condemn it for not dissolving in 1844.   Its leaders as a rule were neither statesmen nor politicians, but rather philanthropists and agitators; and with such men, and with their followers, the doctrine that means are justified by any end is not likely to flourish.   The Liberty party was formed to support anti-slavery candidates, by men whose consciences would not allow them to vote for any others.   Henry Clay was in no sense an anti-slavery man, except

---

[1] *Detroit Free Press*, Dec. 15, 1844.
[2] Final statement in *Emancipator*, March 4, 1846; quoted in *Cleveland American*, March 18, 1846; *New York Tribune*, April 6, 1846.   W. Birney *J. G. Birney and his Times*, 355) thinks that the forgery was concocted in New York.   He offers no proof.

that as an advocate of preserving the *status quo* he was inclined
to object to slavery encroachments; and when his Alabama letter appeared, even this claim was gone.   Had the Liberty men
voted for Clay in 1844, the step might have proved an act of
magnificent statesmanship, or more likely a useless sacrifice;
as it was, they simply acted consistently, although in so doing
they seemed in the eyes of the Whigs to wreck their own cause.
The fault, however, was Clay's, not theirs.   The case for the
Liberty party cannot be better stated than by Birney himself, in
a letter to the *New York Tribune*, in 1852: " It was Mr. Clay's
indecision about the admission of Texas that defeated him.
His letters, even if they were not so intended, made many of his
friends believe that he was undecided. From his supposed
wavering on the subject he lost the votes of many that were
opposed to the annexation of Texas as well as those who were
in favor of it.   That in either event Texas would have been in
the Union now appears very certain to me, as I believe it does
to most others, though a decided party man might express himself differently." [1]

[1] Quoted in *National Era*, March 11, 1852.

CHAPTER VII.

DISCOURAGEMENT OF THE LIBERTY MEN.

1845–1847.

THE Liberty party, in the three remaining years of its existence, was even more isolated than before 1844. It held conventions, nominated candidates, voted for them, and continued to agitate, but with less effect than heretofore.

The Liberty work in Ohio in 1845 was chiefly local, the activity of the State Committee being exercised in stimulating county and district conventions, and in nominating for legislative and local offices. "We earnestly recommend," it said, "the nomination of full Liberty tickets in each county where there are Liberty men enough to form a ticket. We are aware that many reasons are urged why under peculiar circumstances Liberty men should make no nominations, but we are fully satisfied that it is a bad policy to pursue such a course under any circumstances."[1] The Liberty vote in the fall seems to have been about the same as that in 1844, incomplete returns giving 7,954 as against 7,449 in the same counties the year before.[2]

One leader whose voice had long been heard was now missing. On December 7, 1844, ex-Senator Thomas Morris died suddenly, at the age of sixty-eight; and by his departure the Liberty party lost an indefatigable worker, a clear thinker, and a man of incorruptible courage and honesty. Unfortunately for his posthumous fame, Morris's modesty was so great as to

[1] *Herald and Philanthropist*, Aug. 6, 1845.
[2] Scattering returns in *Liberty Herald*, 1845, and in *American Liberty Almanac*, 1846.

lead him, in the period from 1841–44, to prefer to exercise his talents in the comparatively humble sphere of local canvassing. He shrank from, or at least made no effort to retain, the prominence warranted by his legislative record in Ohio and at Washington, and allowed men more eloquent, but of far less political ability, to overshadow him. Although his age made his chosen work very exhausting, he continued up to the day of his death, in spite of ill health and family afflictions, to labor in his self-appointed sphere. Morris's death was deplored and his memory honored in resolutions of local and State societies; but a few years sufficed to cause him to be forgotten except by Bailey, Chase, and others of his fellow-workers, who realized, as Chase said, that " Thomas Morris was far beyond the time in which he lived." [1]

In Indiana, as in Ohio, there was at first a continuation of interest into the winter and spring of 1845. A new paper was started, the *Indiana Freeman ;* local conventions nominated candidates for Congress and for township and county offices; and a State Convention at Indianapolis, on May 30, nominated S. C. Stevens and S. S. Harding for Governor and Lieutenant-Governor respectively in the campaign of 1846; but in August this impetus, surviving from 1844, began to die out, and the vote in six out of ten districts was 1,755, in counties where Birney had received 1,975 votes. [2]

In Michigan the interest in the controversy over the Garland forgery lasted into the spring of 1845. The Democratic press, delighted at the chance to defame Whig leaders, printed all Liberty documents in full, and quoted with zest every editorial of the *Signal of Liberty* which condemned Whig leaders and methods ; until the Whigs, exhausted with raging at Birney, decided to ignore his existence and that of his party so far as possible, a policy which from this time was fairly well adhered to. Partly to show their confidence in Birney, and partly because he was the natural leader, the State Liberty Convention, which met at Marshall on June 9, nominated him for Governor. In the campaign that followed — if campaign it can be

[1] B. F. Morris, *Life of Thomas Morris*, Introd., xi.
[2] Official returns in *Whig Almanac*, 1846.

called where no resistance but indifference is offered by the party attacked — Birney's Democratic principles came out clearly in a series of replies to questions about his views on State policy. He disapproved of internal improvements, wished salaries and offices reduced, and used much the same language as that of the traditional Democratic creed.[1] He was at this time gradually coming to the opinion that the "one idea" was not broad enough for successful action, but that a general reform party would stand a better chance. In the fall election the Liberty vote showed the same falling off as had appeared in Indiana, the total amounting only to 3,363, marking a decline of 269 from the vote of the preceding year.[2]

Illinois abolitionists, as they had surpassed their fellow-laborers in their success in 1844, now exceeded them in their reaction after it. In 1845 there were hardly any conventions, few nominations, and a decided falling-off in the Liberty vote. There are no general returns accessible.

In Wisconsin the growing Liberty sentiment found an outlet this year in voting for a delegate to Congress. The Territorial Convention, meeting on February 9, nominated E. D. Holton, of Milwaukee, and local conventions met in a majority of the southeastern counties. In the fall election the vote for delegate stood: Democratic — Martin, 11,803; Whig — Collins, 10,788; Liberty — Holton, 790; showing an increase of about 300 over the Liberty vote of the preceding year.[3]

In Iowa an effort was made in this year to run local Liberty tickets. In the anti-slavery cause this State was eight years behind the other Northwestern communities: at a time when the Liberty party was strongest, the Iowa movement was still in the lecturing and church-action stage. The attempt to begin a Liberty party seems to have drawn a slight vote, 60 being returned from one county; but in the condition of things in 1845 the step was premature.[4]

[1] *Emancipator*, Oct. 29, 1845.

[2] Partial returns in *Whig Almanac*, 1846; others in *Emancipator*, Jan. 27, 1847.

[3] Moses M. Strong, *History of Wisconsin Territory*, 481; *Emancipator*, Oct. 22, 1845; *Milwaukee Sentinel*, Oct. 8, 1845.

[4] *Cleveland American*, Oct. 8, 1845.

In the summer of 1845 an effort was made to unify Western sentiment by holding a "Great Southern and Western Convention" at Cincinnati, on June 11 and 12. Although the call said : "It is not designed that this convention shall be composed exclusively of members of the Liberty party, but of all who . . . are resolved to use all constitutional means to effect the extinction of slavery,"[1] neither Whigs nor Democrats would attend, and the convention amounted practically to a Liberty meeting. Two thousand delegates were in attendance from Ohio, Indiana, Kentucky, Michigan, Illinois, Virginia, and Wisconsin, and considerable enthusiasm was manifested; but there appeared certain tendencies new to the Liberty party and destined to trouble it hereafter. Those most prominent in this meeting, besides Birney and Chase, were Dr. Bailey, Samuel Lewis, Owen Lovejoy, and Rev. E. Smith, like Lovejoy a political minister of the gospel. Letters were read from Cassius M. Clay, Governor Seward, and others. Horace Greeley aroused some anger in the convention by a letter, written in bitterness of soul over the recent Whig defeat, which was due, as he firmly believed, to the Liberty party; but aside from this incident the proceedings were harmonious.

S. P. Chase, like Birney, participated in the reaction against the Whigs, and, as a natural consequence of his views on slavery, had begun to conceive of himself and of the Liberty party as "Democratic" in the same sense as the "Loco-foco" wing of the Democracy; the only difference in his eyes was that the "Loco-focos" had neglected to carry out their Democratic principles logically, to include anti-slavery.[2] When it is borne in mind that at this time Chase was the author of as many Liberty resolutions and addresses as he could be induced to write, the importance of this change of mind is evident.

In writing the resolutions of this convention, Chase introduced some phrases explaining his creed. "That party only," he said, "which adopts in good faith the principles of the Declaration of Independence and directs its most decisive action

[1] *Herald and Philanthropist*, April 23, 1845.
[2] *Cleveland American*, June 26, 1845.

against slavery . . . is the true Democratic party of the United States."[1] Birney, who presided, undoubtedly sympathized to some extent with Chase's views; but recent events in Saginaw County had taught him a severe lesson, and he now was keenly on guard against the appearance of evil. When Chase submitted the "address to the people" which he had prepared, Birney detected in it certain passages that might be interpreted as proposing a coalition with the Democratic party, and by his skill as a manager secured the reference of the address to a committee, by whom the obnoxious passages were expurgated. The address was then adopted by acclamation.[2]

In this year another movement began in the Liberty ranks which was destined to disrupt the little party a few years later. This was the appearance of the doctrine that the United States Constitution was "an anti-slavery document," a questionable theory at best, but one very welcome to the souls of impatient abolitionists. Conventions in Illinois, Michigan, and Ohio took this ground, as did also a great Eastern "Convention of the Friends of Freedom" at Boston in October, which had been called as a complement to the Southern and Western Liberty Convention just described.

In 1846 the Liberty party in the Northwestern States put all its energy into what proved to be its last great effort; but the rising enthusiasm of 1841-44 was lacking. A complaining tone, sometimes perilously near that of desperation, permeated its utterances, even when matters seemed to be going well. In fact, the Liberty party was beginning to realize its failure. A convention for the Northwest, held this year in Chicago, proved in every respect inferior to the Southwestern Convention, of the preceding year. J. G. Carter, of Massachusetts, presided, flanked by five vice-presidents and two secretaries. None of the Ohio leaders were present; and in their absence E. S. Hamlin, an anti-slavery Whig of the Western Reserve, spoke for Ohio with liberality and good sense, holding to his Whiggery, but avoiding anything that could rasp his Liberty audience. G. W.

[1] See the Proceedings of the Convention, published in pamphlet form, 1845.

[2] W. Birney, *J. G. Birney and his Times*, 364.

Clark, the famous Liberty singer from New York, was also present and aroused enthusiasm.

The real management of the convention, however, was in the hands of Codding, Lovejoy, and Eastman of Illinois, by whose influence an attempt to "broaden the platform" of the Liberty party was defeated. Birney since 1845 had begun to think that the party ought to have more than one idea, and in 1846 many of the Michigan leaders had fallen in with his plan. Two of these, Foster and Beckly, of the *Signal of Liberty*, advocated declarations in favor of making the Liberty party an agency of general reform; but after a prolonged debate this proposition was defeated, nearly all the leading men opposing it.[1] One of the most important things done by the convention was the appointment of a committee to consider the plan of starting a newspaper at Washington. The committee did their work admirably, and in 1847 succeeded in establishing the *National Era*, with Dr. Bailey, of Cincinnati, as editor, and this paper did more than any other, until 1854, to promote anti-slavery action in the North.[2]

In Ohio in this year took place the last, and in many respects the most interesting, State Liberty campaign. As its result turned on a new development in the Ohio Whig party, it may be well to notice how that organization had changed since the days when it condemned Thomas Morris for misrepresenting Ohio. It was no longer possible entirely to ignore questions relating to slavery. The Whigs of the Reserve were for all practical purposes abolitionists, and in case of an unsatisfactory Whig nomination there was nothing to prevent them from voting the Liberty ticket, except indeed the bitterness between the two organizations. This exasperation, it is true, had since 1842 been continually on the increase; but there were signs in 1846–47 that it would fail to prevent bolting in the last resort.

[1] *Cleveland American*, July 15, 1846; *New York Tribune*, July 11, 1846; *Emancipator*, July 15, 1846. For an account written by one of the other side, see *Signal of Liberty*, July 4, 1846.

[2] *Emancipator*, Nov. 4, 1846. The committee was: C. V. Dyer and Zebina Eastman, of Chicago; Charles Durkee, of Wisconsin; J. J. Deming, of Indiana, and C. Beckly, of Michigan.

On the subject of the Black Laws the Western Reserve was a unit, and by 1846 had succeeded in forcing the subject into prominence. In 1845 bills to repeal the Black Laws had been defeated by a smaller margin than before. In 1846 another repeal bill met defeat; but a majority of the Whig members favored it, and the Reserve was of course solid on that side. Although the convention of the two regular parties nominated candidates for the campaign of 1846, without taking any ground on the subject, so large a portion of the Whig press began to advocate repeal that the question was certain to enter into the election.

The Liberty State Convention had met, December 31, 1845, nominated Samuel Lewis for Governor, and adopted some resolutions written by Chase, — among others one declaring " that we professedly revere the doctrine of true Democracy." [1] Early in February Lewis began an extraordinary campaign of stump-speaking. From February 18 until September 28, with the exception of a few weeks in the summer when he was ill, this indefatigable apostle of freedom traversed Ohio, arousing interest where Liberty speakers had never been heard before, and in places like the Reserve creating great enthusiasm.

Soon interest centred in the position of the three candidates with regard to the Black Laws. Tod, the Democratic nominee, tried the virtues of silence ; Lewis, of course, favored the abolition of the laws; and, to the delight of the Western Reserve, Bebb, the Whig candidate, took the unheard-of step of coming out boldly in favor of the repeal of the law invalidating negro testimony against whites.[2] From the first, Liberty men suspected him, but could find no good cause for denying his sincerity. So consistently did he hold to his position while he traversed the Reserve that the Liberty eaders found their party's growth seriously threatened. The Democrats, who had hitherto been enjoying the spectacle, thought the tide seemed to be setting towards Bebb, and, in hope of sustaining the courage of Liberty men, printed an absurd and unreal eulogium

[1] *Herald and Philanthropist,* Jan. 7, 1845.
[2] *Ibid.,* Feb. 25, 1846; *New York Tribune,* July 6, 1846.

on Lewis in the *Ohio Statesman*.[1] In the Twentieth Congressional District an attempt was made to bring the Liberty party to support Giddings. As usual, the effort failed; for, said the *Cleveland American*, " he [Giddings] would vote for a slave-holder for President, provided he were pledged to Northern rights. Is this Liberty ground? Will Liberty men vote for a slave-holder on any considerations whatever?"[2] Edward Wade received the third-party Congressional nomination, and took the stump against Giddings.

In September, the Democrats, hitherto silent on the subject of the Black Laws, were unwillingly drawn into the fray by the discovery that Tod, in 1838, when a candidate for the legislature, had replied to anti-slavery questioners that he favored repeal. In their alarm at this appalling revelation, Democratic papers violently disclaimed any such position, attacking Bebb as a man who would make Ohio a receptacle for broken-down and runaway negroes.[3] The three-cornered fight grew hotter, with Lewis on one side, Tod's supporters on the other, and Bebb, now beginning to be alarmed at the possible effect of his speeches in the southern counties, trying to hold the balance. He wanted the anti-slavery Whig and the Liberty vote, but he wanted still more the Southern Whigs from the Ohio River region. He therefore told a quite different story in speeches in southern counties, admitting that he was in favor of equalizing blacks and whites before the courts, but asserting warmly that he was opposed to equal political or educational advantages, and suggesting that a good way to keep negroes out of the State would be to lay a special tax on their land.[4] This was, to say the least, sharp practice; but owing to the difficulties of communication between the northern and southern parts of the

1 " Mr. Lewis, the candidate of the Liberty party, is winning golden opinions. Mr. Lewis sets out to discuss a great principle and his whole bearing is marked by a candor and sincerity which induce his listeners to respect even his errors. Mr. Bebb is his antipode. His special pleading commands no more respect than his grimaces." Quoted in *Herald and Philanthropist*, July 15, 1846.

2 Sept. 2, 1846.

3 *New York Tribune*, Sept. 9, 1846.

4 *Cleveland American*, Oct. 22, 1846.

State, the fact was not known on the Reserve until after the election. In the meantime, Bebb's anti-Black-Law utterances had saved him. At the last moment, B. F. Wade, who had retired from politics, but was still dear to Western Reserve people for his anti-slavery record in 1838–39, made a vigorous appeal in his behalf; and thus Bebb, while he was advocating negro exclusion in the southern counties, carried the Western Reserve on his anti-slavery professions.[1] The vote in October stood: Democratic — Tod, 116,489; Whig — Bebb, 118,857; Liberty — Lewis, 10,799.[2] This result marked an increase for the Liberty vote over its highest previous total; but, as all agreed, the gain was not so great as it would have been but for Bebb's advocacy of Black Law repeal. It is needless to say that the Liberty men were sore and angry, and felt in regard to Bebb that " his election to the gubernatorial chair has been secured by one of the vilest frauds that ever disgraced a political contest." [3]

In Indiana, in 1846, there was an attempt on the part of Liberty men to increase their vote. Left strictly alone by the old parties, their campaign lacked the interest of that in Ohio, and it suffered furthermore from lack of organization. " There does not seem to be any common understanding among the friends scattered in different parts of the State," complained the *Herald and Philanthropist;* [4] and again, "this is a hard State, in which little has been done." The *Indiana Freeman* said: " Liberty men seem to forget that the Liberty party originated in a firm belief that slavery could never be abolished until such a party was formed. If this conviction was well founded, Liberty men ought not to absent themselves from the polls on election days." [5] In August, 1846, the vote stood: Democratic — Whitcomb, 64,104; Whig — Marshall, 60,697; Liberty — Stevens, 2,278.[6] This result showed an increase of only 172 over the vote in 1844. The cause had evidently come to a standstill.

---

[1] *Cleveland American*, Nov. 4, 1846.
[2] Complete returns, *Ibid.*, Nov. 11, 1846; also in *Whig Almanac*, 1847.
[3] *Cleveland American*, Oct. 22, 1846.
[4] *Herald and Philanthropist*, Nov. 12, 1845.
[5] Quoted in *Emancipator*, Oct. 28, 1846.
[6] Official in *Indianapolis Sentinel*, Sept. 12, 1846.

In Michigan the party had a good organization and a compact band of workers; but in the autumn of 1845 it lost its leader, and decay seemed at once to begin. James G. Birney suffered an accident which so injured his brain that, while his mental faculties remained unimpaired, his speech was almost lost, and writing became painful and at times impossible. The Liberty cause in Michigan and in the country at large thus sustained a loss that it could not repair. Mr. Birney was an able, active man, a born organizer and manager, a good judge of men and of measures. His principal fault, strangely enough, lay in his inability to realize that frankness in a candidate is sometimes almost as great a mistake as undue secretiveness, and that expediency may advantageously be regarded in connection with dealings outside as well as with those inside the party. He would undoubtedly have played a large part in later political history, had not his injury put an end to his career. From this time until his death, in 1858, he remained in retirement, writing letters occasionally, but in the main observing quietly, although with keen interest, the course of politics.

With his retirement the anti-slavery cause in Michigan seemed at once to decline. His candidacy in 1845 had brought the Liberty vote nearly to the level of that of the year before; in 1846 it fell off. On February 4 the State Anti-Slavery Society met and received a communication from Birney advocating a broader basis. After due consideration the convention voted: " It is neither consistent with our present objects, nor expedient, to add to our present political principles." [1] Shortly afterwards, at the annual Liberty convention at Ann Arbor, the same proposals were made, but after an animated debate were again postponed.[2] Having disposed of this question, the Liberty men proceeded to organize, and by October had reasonably full tickets in the field. On the eve of the election the Central Committee issued a hopeful address, saying: "This year we have endeavored to do something. We have effected a good State organization. Almost every town has its committee. Be assured, friends, that our vote for 1846 will startle friends and

[1] *Emancipator*, March 18, 1846.
[2] *Cincinnati Gazette*, March 12, 1846.

foes by its increase if we are faithful."[1]   The vote did indeed
startle the friends of the cause;[2] for it resulted in a decrease of
478 from that of the year before, and of 747 since 1844, and it was
larger than the vote in 1843 by 110 only.   The mortified Liberty men attributed their loss to lack of organization; but that
was not the real reason.   The abolitionists of Michigan were
beginning to tire of the apparently hopeless effort to build up a
new party.   Since Birney's retirement they were without any
very strong leader; the struggle over the broader platform had
diminished confidence and caused quarrels;[3] and, under the circumstances, no amount of organizing could bring them to the
polls.

In Illinois, the northeastern counties, after their relapse of
1845, returned to the charge with redoubled vigor, and in this
year reached their highest point.   Although a State ticket was
to be elected, the main anti-slavery interest lay in the Fourth
Congressional District.   On January 14 a convention at St.
Charles, attended by crowds from ten or twelve counties, unanimously and with great enthusiasm nominated Lovejoy for
Congress.   In Chicago arrangements were made early in the
year to hold bi-weekly meetings in every precinct, and to build
a permanent Liberty headquarters.[4]   On May 24 the State
Convention nominated Richard Eells for Governor and A.
Smith for Lieutenant-Governor; candidates for Congress were
nominated in all the districts except "Egypt"; Codding, St.
Clair, and Cross were constantly in the field; and a flood of
tracts were issued.[5]   So great was the enthusiasm in the Chicago

---

[1] *Emancipator*, Oct. 14, 1846.

[2] It was as follows: —

	Democratic.	Whig.	Liberty.
First District . .	7,877	6,442	777
Second District . .	9,515	8,678	1,127
Third District . .	6,492	5,780	981
Total . .	23,884	20,904	2,885

See *Whig Almanac*, 1848.

[3] *Signal of Liberty*, May 11, 18, 1846.

[4] *Emancipator*, Feb. 11, March 11, 1846; *Herald and Philanthropist*,
May 20, 1846.

[5] *Western Citizen*, June 10, 1846; *Chicago Journal*, July 24, 1846.

district, that the *Western Citizen* began to hope that Lovejoy would lead Kerr, the Whig, and thus be next to " Long John Wentworth." Although this hope proved vain, Lovejoy polled in his own district a Liberty vote equal to the Liberty vote of the whole State in 1844. One of the most serious difficulties encountered by Lovejoy in his canvass was the bad impression left by preceding abolitionist orators. At Lowell, for example, he could do little, for a " rash, violent, ranting, denunciatory preacher" had spoiled everything. "I wish," he said, " our ministers would learn to be a little more prudent, use a little more oil and not so much of the fire and hammer." [1]

The vote for Governor resulted as follows: Democratic — French, 58,576; Whig — Kilpatrick, 36,937; Liberty — Eells, 5,147. For Congressmen the total Liberty vote was a little larger, — 5,221. In the Fourth District the vote was: Democratic — Wentworth, 12,026; Whig — Kerr, 6,208; Liberty — Lovejoy, 3,531. In De Kalb, Kane, Kendall, Lake, and McHenry counties, the Liberty vote was ahead of the Whig, and in Bureau and Du Page practically equal to it. [2]

In Iowa, there is no record of any Liberty vote in 1846; but there was a gradual strengthening of anti-slavery sentiment. The State Anti-Slavery Society resolved on November 26 to establish a newspaper and to hold a convention in the winter of 1847, preparatory to organizing a State Liberty party. Wisconsin had no general territorial ticket; but there were members of a Constitutional convention to be chosen, for which the Liberty party in many places ran separate tickets. Agitation by lecturing and the establishment of a newspaper occupied anti-slavery interest in the Territory.

The year 1846 marks the flood tide for the Liberty party in the United States. In some of the New England States, indeed, it kept on growing after this, but in the Central and Northwestern States it fell off. Already in 1846 the coming decline was foreshadowed in New York, Pennsylvania, and Michigan; but

---

[1] *Western Citizen*, June 10, 1846.

[2] Returns in *Whig Almanac*, 1847; district returns in *Cincinnati Herald*, Sept. 16, 1846; some county returns in *Emancipator*, Sept. 9, 1846.

on the whole the Liberty vote in this year reached its maximum, in a total of 74,017, against 62,200 in 1844.[1]

The next year, 1847, was uneventful; for other questions had risen which drew the attention of anti-slavery men away from local politics. In Ohio there was no State Convention, nor was there any action of importance beyond some county nominating conventions and two general meetings in the Western Reserve, engineered by J. H. Paine and Edward Wade. The vote for local offices in the fall was less than at any time since 1841.[2] Three thousand votes are reported for counties which cast 4,300 in the preceding year. In Indiana there was about the same state of things; local organization was kept up and nominations were made; but the main interest was not in the election, and no record of any vote is known, beyond a few county returns. In Michigan, even a State election for Governor failed to arouse much interest, or to stop the local Liberty party on its downward course. The State Convention nominated C. Gurney for Governor and H. Hallock for Lieutenant-Governor. There was almost no campaign, no interest in the election, and a very small vote in September. In the absence of any State election, Illinois leaders devoted themselves to agitation and organization. Local conventions met and deliberated, and a Liberty convention for southern Illinois was held at Eden, in Randolph County. Delegates were present from seven counties, — for even in the vicinity of "Egypt" there were traces of anti-slavery sentiment.[3] Iowa, now a State, remained in much the same condition as Illinois: her anti-slavery men were able to agitate, but did not feel strong enough to form a Liberty organization. In Wisconsin the local Liberty party remained unaffected by the lassitude

[1] Maine	9,244	New York	12,027
New Hampshire	10,403	Pennsylvania	2,028
Vermont	6,671	Ohio	10,797
Massachusetts	10,134	Indiana	2,278
Rhode Island	155	Michigan	2,885
Connecticut	2,248	Illinois	5,147

[2] According to some papers the vote was as follows: Democratic, 105,385; Whig, 103,822; Liberty, 4,379. See *National Era*, Nov. 11, 1847.

[3] *National Era*, Sept. 30, Oct. 28, 1847. For a notice of Madison County in this region, see A. C. McLaughlin, *Lewis Cass*, 302.

which had seized upon it in the other States. In the winter a
State constitution was submitted to the people, and with it, on
a separate ballot, the question of negro suffrage. This subject
stirred up Liberty interest; but, although the party labored hard,
it produced little effect upon territorial sentiment, and negro suffrage was rejected by a vote of 14,615 to 7,664.[1] At this time
Ichabod Codding and G. W. Clark, the Liberty singer, came from
Illinois to make a lecturing tour of the Territory; and Codding
remained for a time in order to help the new *American Freeman.*
His presence was a great stimulus, and helped the Liberty men
in October to increase their vote as follows: Democratic — M.
M. Strong, 9,648; Whig — J. H. Tweedy, 10,670; Liberty —
C. Durkee, 973.[2]

In 1847, then, the Liberty party in the Northwest and in
the country at large seemed to be slackening its efforts. The
tide had begun to ebb; for, as Dr. Bailey said, "Not to advance is to recede; no new and small party can live simply by
holding its own."[3] The fact was, that many adherents were
getting tired of the bootless work of seven years and were impatient for change. Hence, about this time we find a number
of new doctrines springing up among Liberty men, and a tendency toward faction threatening to shiver into fragments the
party, already none too numerous.

One such phenomenon, already noted above, was the growth
of a theory that the United States Constitution was an anti-slavery
document, and, as a sort of corollary, that slavery must be unconstitutional in the States.[4] The latter doctrine was worked
out with ingenuity by Lysander Spooner on historical and legal
grounds; but although he and William Goodell, who had reached
the same conclusion by a different method, had a considerable following in the Eastern States, they found little support
west of New York. It was evident that their view, if accepted,
would vastly broaden the opportunities for anti-slavery action;

    [1] F. E. Baker, *The Elective Franchise in Wisconsin*, in Wisconsin His-
torical Society, *Collections*, 1894, p. 9. See below, Appendix D.

    [2] Official returns in *Whig Almanac*, 1848.

    [3] *Herald and Philanthropist*, Nov. 12, 1845.

    [4] Lysander Spooner, *The Unconstitutionality of Slavery*, Boston, 1853.

but it was so entirely contrary to the received Liberty creed that the practical Ohio and Illinois leaders looked on it with disfavor. In Ohio, in 1845, a few county conventions resolved that Congress could abolish slavery in the States; [1] but in 1846 the Black Law campaign caused theoretical questions to be laid aside. In 1847 the idea gained renewed vigor from the discussions in the East, and again Ohio abolitionists defined their position. The *Cleveland American* [2] inclined toward Spooner's views; but the *Philanthropist*, now under the name of *National Press and Herald*, and edited by Stanley Mathews, held to the received doctrine. Local conventions also seemed to have grown conservative. Logan County, which two years before had resolved that the Constitution was an anti-slavery instrument, now voted down a resolution declaring slavery unconstitutional; [3] and Hamilton County also rejected the new doctrine. [4]

In Indiana, a convention at South Bend, in 1845, had resolved that slavery was unconstitutional, [5] but the matter does not seem to have aroused much interest; nor is there any record of controversy on the subject in Michigan. In Illinois, a convention at Fulton, in 1845, had resolved that the Constitution was an anti-slavery document; [6] but in 1847, when the subject was brought up at the convention for southern Illinois, the traditional interpretation prevailed. [7] Wisconsin had shown a tendency toward radicalism by adopting at its Liberty Territorial Convention, in 1845, the position that the United States Constitution was anti-slavery; [8] but after that time its interest ceased to rest upon theoretical questions, until in 1847, with the Liberty League (hereafter mentioned), these questions arose once more.

Another tendency toward altering the Liberty programme was that shown by Chase in his use of the term "democracy" as synonymous with "anti-slavery." In 1845 he had given indications of a tendency in this direction, and by 1846 his correspond-

---

[1] *Herald and Philanthropist*, March 5, Sept. 17, 1845.
[2] March 31, 1847.   [3] *National Press and Herald*, Sept. 1, 1847.
[4] *National Era*, Sept. 23, 1847.
[5] *Emancipator*, May 14, 1845.
[6] *Ibid.*, April 2, 1845.   [7] *National Era*, Oct. 28, 1847.
[8] *Emancipator*, July 30, 1845.

ence shows a rapid growth in his mind of the conviction that the Democratic party was the natural ally for anti-slavery men. "I think that the political views of the Democrats are in the main sound," he wrote to Giddings in August, 1846, "and the chief fault I have to accuse them of is that they do not carry out their principles in reference to the subject of slavery. . . . I have sometimes thought," he added, "that if all the anti-slavery men whose opinions are Democratic should act with that party in this state they might change its character wholly." [1]   In the same vein he wrote to John P. Hale: "At the present moment there are doubtless more abolitionists in the Whig party than in the Democratic party, but I fear that the Whig party will always look upon the overthrow of slavery as a work to be taken up or laid aside as expediency may suggest, whereas if we can once get the Democratic party in motion regarding the overthrow of slavery as a necessary result of its principles, I would have no apprehension at all of the work being laid aside until accomplished." [2]   For holding such views, Chase and the whole Ohio Liberty party, which he was supposed to represent, were looked upon with suspicion by many abolitionists.   In 1846, a letter to the Northwestern Convention, in which he suggested a new non-partisan league, caused the editors of the Michigan *Signal of Liberty* to say: "This last proposal confirmed our previous impressions that the Liberty party of Ohio did not expect or wish to be a permanent National party, but are ready when an opportunity offers to merge themselves in some other body." [3]

A more important movement was one started by Birney to transform the Liberty party into a general radical reform party. The "one idea" had proved too narrow; if the platform should contain planks pledging the party to all kinds of reform, many men favoring one or more of these might come in who would otherwise be unable to do so. This movement began in Michigan, with a letter from Mr. Birney, and a circular sent by Beckly and Foster of the *Signal of Liberty* to all the leading Liberty newspapers in the country, requesting co-operation in bringing the

[1] August 15, 1846: J. W. Schuckers, *Life of Chase*, 99.
[2] May 12, 1847: R. B. Warden, *Life of Chase*, 312.
[3] *Signal of Liberty*, July 4, 1846.

party to broaden the platform.[1] In Ohio this project attracted almost as little notice as did the dogma of the unconstitutionality of slavery. Chase might possibly have favored it, had he not been at the time contemplating " Democracy "; others found it unnecessary. On December 30, 1845, the State Liberty Convention laid on the table resolutions on the Free Bank law and on sugar duties; and this action is the only suggestion of any move to broaden the platform.[2] In Indiana Mr. Birney's plan produced no disturbance ; but in Michigan, where the movement originated, it aroused much debate. In February, 1845, the State Anti-Slavery Society, as has been said, rejected the proposal to broaden the party, and at a later meeting the State Liberty Convention did the same. In Illinois, as we have seen, at the Northwestern Convention, a motion to broaden the platform was made, but was defeated. Again, in 1847, at the Convention for the Fourth District, at Elgin, a resolution looking in that direction was laid on the table, but adopted later, in a very mild form.[3] In Wisconsin alone of the Northwestern States did the new doctrine meet with much welcome. In 1845 the Territorial Liberty Association resolved that " the one idea embraces opposition to sin and tyranny in all forms ";[4] and in 1847, while it asserted the paramount importance of the slavery question, it reiterated its purpose to oppose evil of all kinds.[5]

Nevertheless, advocates of a broader platform went forward, until their movement culminated in the formation, by William Goodell and some of his sympathizers, of a new radical party called the " Liberty League." Their convention at Macedon Lock, New York, in June, 1847, nominated Gerrit Smith and Elihu Burritt for the Presidency and Vice-Presidency respectively, and adopted a long series of resolutions setting forth the views of Goodell and Spooner. Even among those who sympathized with the idea of a radical party, this movement found little support, except in New York. In the Northwest, when-

---

[1] *Emancipator*, March 18, 1846.
[2] *Herald and Philanthropist*, Jan. 7, 1846.
[3] *National Era*, March 18, 1847; *American Freeman*, March 17, 1847.
[4] *Emancipator*, July 30, 1845.
[5] *American Freeman*, Feb. 10, 1847.

ever the action of the Macedon Lock convention was noticed by newspapers or by conventions, it was generally with regret. The *Cincinnati Herald* said: " It will be as impossible for the Liberty party to support the nomination of Mr. Goodell's universal reform party, as it will to vote for the Whig or Democratic candidates, and to propose it in either of these cases is a betrayal of the party." [1]   Even Wisconsin Liberty men regretted the action.   The Milwaukee *American Freeman* called the address of the Liberty League " a truly able one," but added "to support Messrs. Smith and Burritt, Liberty men as such cannot labor. To do so would be to make the manifesto of Goodell and others the creed of the Liberty party and to exclude from . . . our support . . . any believers in even a revenue tariff. . . . Still we have no quarrel with these men." [2]   The Wisconsin Liberty Association resolved, on July 14, that "we regret the organization of a new political party, and regard it as uncalled for." [3]

During part of this period another circumstance undoubtedly tended to a certain extent to distract the Liberty party: this was the growth of a Garrisonian movement in Ohio and Michigan.   At first, after 1840, there had been no organizations other than the old State anti-slavery societies; but in a short time the followers of Garrison rallied and set up their separate State associations.   Stephen S. Foster and Abby Kelly, and later Parker Pillsbury, made frequent lecturing tours on the Western Reserve and in Michigan, and succeeded in securing a certain following for the " Disunion " movement.   Once started, this comparatively small body showed a persistency and a unity of purpose which entirely surpassed the ardor of the bulk of the Liberty party.   From 1845 onward, they supported a newspaper, the *Anti-Slavery Bugle*, at Salem, Ohio, while Liberty papers, one after another, with a nominal support ten times as large, rose and fell by the wayside on the Western Reserve.

The sentiments expressed by these persons did not, however, attract very much attention, except when, as not uncommonly happened, they were accredited to the Liberty party by Old

[1] June 2, 1847.
[2] *American Freeman*, July 14, 21, 1847.
[3] *Ibid.*, July 28, 1847.

Line Whig and Democratic presses. Almost the only formal action taken with regard to them by the political abolitionists was a resolution adopted at a convention at Elgin, Illinois, on February 16, 1847: "We regret, as evil in its tendencies, the dogma of the so-called Garrisonian or non-resistance abolitionists."[1] At about the same time, the Wisconsin Territorial Convention passed a resolution to the effect that voting was a Christian duty.[2] In general, there was not that intense bitterness between Liberty men and Garrisonians which prevailed in New England. Outside sentiment was made plain when in 1847 Garrisonian disunion petitions were presented to the Ohio legislature; a committee indignantly advised that a copy of Washington's farewell address be sent to every school district in the State, in order to prevent any similar occurrence in future.[3]

By 1847 the Liberty party was showing signs of fatigue and discontent. It had done good work, it had stood to its guns, firing them apparently into vacancy for seven years, and yet popular sentiment failed to support it. In spite of all its efforts, the densest ignorance of its aims and methods prevailed in many of the free States, as is well illustrated by a letter from Morgan County, Illinois, dated June 20, 1845: "Quite a large portion of our Western people who are anti-slavery in principle and who will subscribe to all the views of the abolitionists when presented to them in private conversation, still abhor the name abolitionist. They attach to the name everything that is false, such as amalgamation, circulating inflammatory papers among the negroes . . . and a desire to do away with slavery by physical force. They also attach to the name all the views of Garrison. Many of them are honest men . . . but they believe multitudes of false stories that are studiously circulated on purpose to prevent honest people from coming to the light."[4]

As the election of 1848 drew near, all the diverse elements in the Liberty party began to demand a nomination and a platform which would be a ratification of their own peculiar position.

[1] *National Era*, March 18, 1847.
[2] *American Freeman*, Feb. 10, 1847.
[3] 16*th Annual Report of the Mass. Anti-Slav. Soc.*, 1848.
[4] *Emancipator*, July 16, 1845.

Lysander Spooner wanted the convention to declare slavery unconstitutional; Goodell and his sympathizers wanted it to adopt
the principles of the Liberty League, and thus turn itself into a
universal reform party; conservative Liberty men desired it to
keep on in the same old rut, separate, sufficient unto itself; and
Chase, Lewis, Leavitt, and others hoped by a more liberal nomination and platform to place the party in a position to gain
from existing circumstances.

These last, with truer insight than the other leaders, realized
that since 1844 the Liberty party had deliberately chosen to
exclude itself from action with regard to a living issue, and had
thus made its task infinitely harder than it would otherwise
have been. Ever since the Texas annexation project had been
brought up, the question of the extension of slave territory had
been boiling in the ranks of the old parties, growing more noisy
and more violent as the Mexican War came on, and still further
annexation for the benefit of the South seemed inevitable. Men
were making reputations as anti-slavery leaders in both Whig
and Democratic parties; splits over slavery questions took place
in State organizations; John P. Hale, in New Hampshire, for
doing the same thing that Thomas Morris had done, received
Morris's punishment, but, instead of dropping unnoticed, he
carried with him in revolt a large section of his party. Still
the Liberty men clung to their old isolation. It was in fact
an impossible situation: either the Liberty party must use the
existing circumstances to its profit, or it must inevitably fall
to pieces.

CHAPTER VIII.

THE LIBERTY PARTY IN THE WILMOT PROVISO CONTROVERSY.

1846–1848.

In 1848 the Liberty men were confronted with a new set o conditions, which gave them unexpected allies. Before going on into the history of the memorable campaign of 1848, we must clearly understand the complications caused by the issue of territorial slavery. Although in the years before 1840 the mass of the people in the Northwest declined to follow the abolitionists, and repudiated the Liberty party, it was not because they liked slavery more, but agitation and innovation less. They wanted above all things to preserve the *status quo*, and objected to abolitionism because it sought innovation; but they were just as likely to object to any alteration of the existing state of things in favor of slavery. This fact was first clearly brought out in the Missouri Compromise struggle, when the North unmistakably showed that it was opposed to the extension of slave territory. Again, after 1836, when the project of annexing Texas was agitated, signs of a distinctly Northern attitude appeared in the form of legislative protests, such as that of one House of the Indiana legislature in 1836.[1] In 1837 there were some public meetings which resolved that it was "inexpedient and ruinous to the best interests of the United States of America to admit the province of Texas into this government."[2] In 1838 a committee of the Michigan House of Representatives reported, on January 19, a joint resolution

[1] *Anti-Slavery Examiner*, No. 8: *Correspondence between F. H. Elmore and J. G. Birney*, 1838, p. 14, note.
[2] *Philanthropist*, Oct. 24, 1837.

declaring that the annexation of Texas would "create discontent which might endanger the stability of the Union," and instructing the Senators and Representatives to oppose the project; and this resolution passed the House by a vote of 42 to 4;[1] a similar report in the Senate seems to have produced no result.[2] In Ohio, B. F. Wade reported from a select Senate committee a strong series of resolutions condemning the proposed annexation of Texas as "unjust, inexpedient and destructive of the peace, safety and well-being of the nation;" and it passed both Houses by large majorities.[3] These protests indicate that in 1837–38 the same legislatures that passed resolutions condemning abolitionists were aware of the objection to the extension of the area of slavery.

After the election of 1844 had seemed to show that the country would sanction annexation, the project advanced rapidly to its consummation, in the last days of Tyler's administration. Since the Democratic party, which carried all the Northwest except Ohio, was committed in favor of annexation, no protest was raised in Indiana and Michigan, where objections had been made seven years before; and Michigan even went so far as to instruct its Senators and Representatives "to use all proper exertions" for the annexation of Texas "at the earliest practical period."[4] Ohio, which was under Whig control, continued its opposition to slavery extension by passing resolutions, on January 13, 1845, instructing its Senators to oppose the annexation of Texas on anti-slavery grounds.[5] Both the Senators, however, Allen and Tappan, were Democrats, and felt no obligation to regard the wishes of a Whig State legislature. Their disregard of the instructions is said to have aroused no little irritation even in the Democratic press of the State; but in Ohio there was nothing like the popular and legislative protests, party upheavals, bolts, and

---

[1] *Philanthropist*, Feb. 13, 1838.

[2] *Report of a Committee of the Senate on State Affairs in relation to the Annexation of Texas*, etc., 1838.

[3] *Philanthropist*, Jan. 30, 1838; *Laws of Ohio* (1837–38), 407.

[4] *Laws of Michigan* (1844–45), 154.

[5] *Laws of Ohio* (1844–45), 437; *New York Tribune*, Jan. 22, 1845.

other interesting events that disturbed the Eastern States at this time. No Northwestern Representatives except Giddings and later Jacob Brinkerhoff made anti-slavery reputations; for in these Ohio River States the Southern-born element still controlled politics, and in Michigan the prominence of Lewis Cass kept the State from joining its natural allies in New England in opposing slavery extension.

When the Mexican War broke out, a few conservative Whig papers, like the *Cincinnati Gazette*, protested; but the martial temper of the Northwest was too strong to allow much opposition. Legislatures of several of the States adopted resolutions laying the blame of hostilities on the perfidy of Mexico, and urging a vigorous prosecution of the war; and for a time the undercurrent of Northern feeling was buried by an outburst of militarism. When, with the successful prosecution of the war, came the prospect of new annexations, this feeling rose to view once more. In every Northwestern State the Whig party, which since 1844 had been more or less avowedly anti-slavery, became strongly in favor of excluding slavery from all newly acquired territory; and in the northern counties of the four southernmost States, and in many localities in Michigan and Wisconsin, anti-slavery Democrats began to adopt the same position. It was the South which now threatened the *status quo*, and Northwestern conservatism found itself at once ranged on the other side.

In 1846 the Wilmot Proviso discussion began to be active in the Northwest; and by 1847 numbers of Whig newspapers had declared themselves in favor of it. "We are against any new territory," said the *Cincinnati Gazette*, "any new slave territory . . . and against extending the constitutional inequality in favor of slave-holders beyond the states already in the Union."[1] "We are satisfied," remarked the *Ohio State Journal*, "that the free states will never consent to the annexation to this republic of slave territory."[2] The *Chicago Journal* repeated the foregoing, and added: "We will always be found on the side of freedom against oppression whatever shape it assumes. The Whig party has a great duty to perform in this

[1] Oct. 7, 1847.   [2] Quoted in *National Era*, Aug. 12, 1847.

matter, . . . to avoid on the one hand the untempered zeal and fanaticism of the Liberty party, and on the other the opposite extreme into which warring against this is too apt to lead." [1]

In this year began a " boom " (to use the modern phrase) for General Taylor. With memories of 1840 ringing in their ears, Whigs found the idea of a military candidate very fascinating; and, as the year advanced, newspapers began with increasing fervor to advocate his nomination. But Taylor was a slaveholder, and his views on the Wilmot Proviso, as well as on all other Whig measures, were entirely unknown. Among antislavery Whigs in the Northwest much repugnance was exhibited toward his candidacy, though in most of the States it was not loudly expressed. A correspondent wrote from Indiana to the Wisconsin *American Freeman :* " A strong distrust of Taylor can be found among Hoosier Whigs, but an unholy fear of party proscription restrains multitudes from saying or doing anything." [2] The *Chicago Journal*, whose anti-slavery utterances are quoted above, became alarmed at the threatening attitude of anti-Taylor Whigs in the East, and said: " However much the Whigs of Massachusetts and the North may differ from their political brethren in other states in reference to slavery and its evils, yet in National politics they are simply Whigs." [3]

There was one place in the Northwest, however, where antislavery Whigs were thoroughly aroused on the subject of slavery in the Territories. From the beginning of the year 1847 the Western Reserve had been filled with ominous mutterings. Whig conventions in Cuyahoga and Trumbull counties resolved to "support no man unless he is openly pledged against any further annexation of territory or extension of slavery." [4] The Cleveland *True Democrat*, founded by E. S. Hamlin as a radical Whig paper, declared "that at the next Presidential election we will not support a slave-holder for President or Vice President." [5] Still more significant was an incident at a meeting in Ashtabula County: Giddings, hitherto an inde-

[1] July 1, 1846.   [2] *American Freeman*, Sept. 1, 1847.
[3] Dec. 5, 1846.
[4] *National Era*, Sept. 16, 1847; Cleveland *True Democrat*, Jan. 4, 1848.
[5] Jan. 3, 1847.

pendent Whig, "became much excited, and boldly proclaimed
. . . 'Sooner shall this right arm (lifted above his head) fall
from its socket and my tongue cleave to the roof of my mouth
than I will vote for Zach. Taylor for President . . . and I think
I can say the same for every true Whig of Ashtabula.'" The
meeting then resolved with enthusiasm that "we will support no
man . . . who is not fully and publicly pledged against the
extension of slavery."[1]

While anti-slavery Whigs were growing alarmed at the progress of Taylor's candidacy, anti-slavery Democrats in the
Northwest had been showing equal solicitude in regard to
the question of slavery in the Territories. As early as June,
1846, the *Cleveland Plain Dealer*, the leading Democratic paper
on the Reserve, said boldly: "The West has but to say that no
more slave territory shall be annexed to this Union, and the dark
tide of slavery will be stayed. . . . It is time that the lovers of
freedom should unite in opposing the common enemy by fixing
bounds to their aggression."[2] In the same year the Hamilton
County Democratic Convention demanded that the Ordinance
of 1787 should be extended "over our Pacific empire present
and future."[3] In 1847 Democratic papers in Ohio continued
with increasing emphasis. "We shall not discuss the question
whether the exclusion of slavery [from the Territories] is a
needful rule," said the *Ohio Press;* "public opinion has long
since decided it. Such is the almost unanimous opinion of
the people of every Northern state."[4] The *Sandusky Mirror*
defied Southern dictation: "So far from the conduct of the
South being any reason for yielding in the matter, we see in it
only additional reasons for standing by the Proviso and carrying
out its principles regardless of all opposition."[5] Democratic
conventions for Paulding, Richland, Jefferson, Columbiana, and
several other counties passed resolutions against the extension

---

[1] *Cleveland American*, May 26, 1847 ; *National Era*, June 10, 1847.

[2] Quoted in *New York Tribune*, June 29, 1846.

[3] *National Era*, June 29, 1848.   [4] Quoted *ibid.*, Sept. 16, 1847.

[5] Quoted *ibid.*, Dec. 9, 1847. Similar sentiments were uttered by the
Springfield Democrat, Cincinnati Morning Signal, Ohio Patriot, and
Wayne County Democrat. Ibid., Sept. 16, 1847.

of slavery.[1]   In Michigan some Democratic papers spoke out boldly.   Said the Ann Arbor *True Democrat,* in October: "The North is strong enough to submit no longer like Southern slaves to the dictation of the South, especially when it is asked to extend slavery beyond its natural boundaries."[2]   In Illinois the Democrats of the northeastern counties, much in sympathy with the Barnburner faction of the New York Democracy, were uttering vigorous sentiments.   Said the *Chicago Democrat,* owned by John Wentworth: "The acquisition of territory is unavoidable, . . . the question then must arise, shall the wide domain which will be added to our country be given up to slavery?"[3]   The Jacksonville *Prairie Argus* said: "We acknowledge and will ever defend the vested rights of the South.   But here our acknowledgement and defence conclude.   We will never consent to an extension of slavery over countries which we may acquire and in which it does not exist."[4]

The growing feeling in the Northwest in favor of the Wilmot Proviso led to the passage of strong resolutions in two State legislatures.   On February 15, 1847, the Ohio legislature adopted a joint resolution instructing the Senators and requesting the Representatives to vote so as to secure the exclusion of slavery "from Oregon Territory, and any other territory which may hereafter be annexed to the United States."[5]   At the same time Michigan spoke more directly by resolving "That in the acquisition of any more territory . . . we deem it the duty of the general government to extend over the same the Ordinance of 1787 with all its rights, privileges, conditions and immunities."[6]   J. H. Cravens, a Whig, introduced similar resolutions into the Indiana legislature; but they failed to pass.[7]

Had this not been an "off" year in politics, the question would undoubtedly have played a part in elections; but Ohio and Illinois were without any important contests, and in Michi-

---

[1] *National Era,* June 29, Sept. 30, Dec. 9, 1847.
[2] Quoted *ibid.,* Dec. 9, 1847.   [3] Quoted *ibid.,* Sept. 16, 1847.
[4] Quoted *ibid.,* June 10, 1847.   [5] *Laws of Ohio* (1846–47), 214.
[6] *Laws of Michigan* (1846–47), 194.
[7] *National Era,* Feb. 4, 1847.

gan and Wisconsin interest was very slight. In Indiana only, where there was an election of Congressmen in the summer of 1847, did the Wilmot Proviso enter largely into the result. The effect on the Northwest will be shown later.

It was evident, then, by the summer of 1847, that anti-slavery questions bade fair to play in the coming Presidential campaign an even larger part than in 1844, and that in all probability they would be accompanied by great party changes. What was the Liberty party to do in this contingency? It was an undoubted fact that since 1844 anti-slavery sentiment had increased a hundredfold in each of the old parties; and yet the Liberty party had come to a standstill. Chase stated the case very clearly in a letter to John P. Hale: "I see no prospect of greater future progress, but rather of less. As fast as we can bring public sentiment right the other parties will approach our ground and keep sufficiently close to it to prevent any great accession to our numbers. If this be so, the Liberty party can never hope to accomplish anything as such, but only through its indirect action upon the other parties." [1]

In such circumstances, it is not surprising that Chase, Leavitt, Stanton, and others came to the conclusion that it was time to adopt a new policy, and by some appropriate nomination and platform to place the Liberty party in a position to absorb discontented Whigs and Democrats without insisting on the full Liberty creed. Such a proposition ran directly counter to Liberty precedent. Thus far it had been the rule to vote for no man who would not separate from the old parties; coalition had been decried as treason to liberty, as practical perjury, as a sin against God's law. In the Northwest and in the country at large scarcely any cases of Liberty fusion occurred in the first five years of the party's existence. In Lorain County, on the Western Reserve, E. S. Hamlin, an anti-slavery Whig, had received Liberty votes in 1843; [2] and in Wayne County, Indiana, there was one case of Democratic and Liberty fusion in 1844; [3] Indiana furnished another case in 1845. J. H. Cravens,

---

[1] May 12, 1847: R. B. Warden, *Life of Chase*, 312.

[2] *Philanthropist*, Nov. 8, 1843.

[3] *Emancipator*, Aug. 28, 1844.

a Virginian born, who " hated human slavery with an intensity akin to madness," had lost a renomination to Congress because of his anti-slavery opinions. On becoming a candidate for the legislature, he issued an address giving under thirteen heads his views on slavery, which agreed substantially with the opinions of Giddings. " I do not believe the Whigs," he concluded, " will incorporate a pro-slavery article in their political creed. Should they do so they will drive many good and true men from their ranks in grief and sorrow." This address won the hearts of the Liberty men of his district; they resolved, under the lead of S. S. Harding, to support him; and, in spite of disaffection in his own party, he was elected.[1] Except in these cases, nearly every attempt to induce Liberty men to support candidates of the old parties had been defeated, the nearest approach to success being in Indiana in 1845, when the Liberty convention for the Tenth Congressional District refused by a majority of one to support the Whig candidate, who had made a direct appeal for their support.[2]

Perhaps the place where the Liberty leaders found it hardest to keep their followers true to the party creed was in the Twentieth Ohio Congressional district on the Western Reserve, where Giddings enjoyed unmeasured popularity. His relations to the Liberty party up to 1844 have been already referred to as peculiar. In 1842, when he was censured, and resigned from Congress, Liberty men voted heartily to secure his re-election; and Chase and some other Liberty leaders tried hard to get him to join the new party.[3] He did not think, however, that the time had come for an organization separate from the Whigs, and explained his reasons, over the name " Pacificus," in a series of letters published in the *Ashtabula Sentinel*. The result was that strict Liberty men found themselves unable to support him in 1843, and nominated Edward Wade. True, as the *Liberty Herald* of Trumbull County admitted, Giddings had done all that a man

[1] W. W. Woollen, *Biographical and Historical Sketches of Early Indiana*, 276.

[2] *Emancipator*, May 28, July 30, 1845.

[3] See letters of Chase to Giddings, in G. W. Julian, *Life of J. R. Giddings*, 130.

could do in Congress, but he was still a member of the Whig party. "No Liberty man therefore could vote for Mr. Giddings without voting with and for the Whig party." The *Liberty Herald* concluded this exhibition of rigid partisanship by crying, with whimsical inconsistency: "Liberty men, abolitionists, Whigs, Democrats, and all, come out and vote for Edward Wade!"[1]

Giddings at once took up the challenge thus offered. So great was the effect of his criticisms of the Liberty party that in this election, wherever he spoke, its vote fell off.[2] In 1844 the breach widened; for the Liberty men found in Giddings a formidable obstacle to their progress, and Giddings recognized in them a possible source of danger to the Whig party. J. Hutchins and L. King each had joint debates with him; but, in spite of all Liberty efforts, his popularity was so great as to hold the Whigs firm, and even to draw from the Liberty ranks. The result was that, in the Presidential election, Ashtabula County, where he had been working, cast a heavier majority for Henry Clay than any other county in the country.[3] The animosity of the Liberty men toward Giddings now became bitter in the last degree. He had believed implicitly in the Garland forgery, and had used it with deadly effect; and when its spurious character was proved, he couched his apology in terms that added vigor to the Liberty hatred. He had believed in it, he said, because "no man of the intelligence which Mr. Birney was supposed to possess could close his eyes to the consequences which were likely to result from a division of those who were opposed to the annexation of Texas," and because collusion with Democrats was the only rational explanation. He still believed that Birney was in league with Polk, and that the letter "was a fabrication based almost entirely upon truths existing previously to the writing of the letter and wholly independent of it."[4] The anger of Liberty men was so great that when, in 1845, Abby Kelly and Stephen S. Foster made a lecturing tour on the Western Reserve, the *Liberty*

[1] *Liberty Herald*, Sept. 28, 1843.   [2] *Ibid.*, Oct. 12, 1843.
[3] G. W. Julian, *Life of J. R. Giddings*, 167.
[4] *Ohio American*, April 24, 1845.

Herald, in terms that can scarcely be regarded as less than scurrilous, accused Giddings of having imported them for the purpose of breaking up the party.[1]

Yet his popularity with the masses was still so great that, in 1846, a Liberty convention at Painesville resolved that the District Congressional Convention ought not to nominate, but that it should leave the field open in his favor. The District Convention promptly repudiated the suggestion, saying: "We stand ready to unite with Whigs or Democrats in a political organization for the overthrow of slavery, but we spurn all overtures of union for the attainment of any mere party triumphs."[2] Nevertheless, Liberty men on the Reserve could not help understanding that Giddings really represented their principles in Congress, nor could seven years of separatism prevent them from desiring to support him. The *Cleveland American* found it necessary to devote pages to a definition of its position. In January, 1847, it said: "We had supposed that no one could misunderstand by this time our views in relation to Mr. Giddings. . . . And yet a friend assures us that when we publish a speech of his without comment, our views and motives are liable to misconstruction. . . . As a faithful anti-slavery Representative we give and have always given him full credit, but it is his deportment to the Liberty Party . . . his utter refusal to say after all that he would not continue to vote for slave-holders . . . these and other inconsistencies we have condemned and shall continue to condemn. . . . It has been fear of the Liberty Party that has driven the wire-pullers of his party to keep him in Congress . . . and yet he will condemn and abuse and misrepresent the Liberty Party without stint, and after election taunt it with having been unable to elect its candidates or with having decreased its vote because Liberty men had been deceived and wheedled by his blandishments."[3] The idea of rugged Joshua Giddings offering blandishments to any body of men may seem ludicrous; but to the Western Reserve Liberty men it was a very real danger. So great was their suspicion

[1] *Liberty Herald*, April 17, 1845.
[2] *Cleveland American*, Sept. 2, 1846.
[3] *Ibid.*, Jan. 20, 1847.

that, in 1847, when Giddings in his wrath swore publicly never to vote for Zachary Taylor, his action was looked upon as a Whig trick. " That a deep plot," said the *Cleveland American,* " is laid by the universal Whig party to absorb or use up the Liberty movement in the canvass of 1848, is evident." [1]

When such a man as Giddings was looked upon as unfit for Liberty support, it was evident that Chase, Bailey, and the others who favored a nomination for the sake of expediency, had a hard task before them. In 1847, however, the strictness of Liberty action seemed in several places to be breaking down. In Ohio, in places where there were no Liberty nominations, it was stated that "there was considerable fusion or rather voting of Liberty men for old party candidates;" [2] and in Indiana, in the election of congressmen there was a general return to fusion and to the old system of interrogation. This election has peculiar interest as the only one in the Northwest in which the Liberty party turned its back on the usual programme and gave itself up to coalition. One reason for this course was probably that its adherents were few and were tired of third-party action; but another reason, without doubt, lay in the interest displayed by Indiana Whigs and Democrats in the question of slavery extension. Perhaps, also, they took to heart the case of New Hampshire, where in 1845–46 a fusion of Whigs, Liberty men, and independent Democrats had overthrown for the moment the " Loco-foco " rule of the State, and had sent to Congress John P. Hale and Amos Tuck as the first independent anti-slavery men. If this departure from the Liberty programme had proved so successful, why might not another have a like success?

Early in April, signs of an intention to coalesce led the *Anti-Slavery Chronicle* to insist on straight-out independent action; [3] but such advice was of no avail. In the summer Liberty nominations for Congress were made in three districts; but all of the nominees eventually withdrew in favor of the Whig candidates.

[1] *Cleveland American,* May 26, 1847.
[2] *National Era,* Oct. 28, 1847; *National Press and Herald,* Oct. 20, 1847.
[3] Quoted *National Era,* April 29, 1847.

In the Fourth District, the centre of anti-slavery sentiment, the Wayne County Convention resolved " That to vote for any man, on account of his antislavery profession, to fill any office, who would under any circumstances support the candidate of [the Whig or Democratic] party would be an act of consummate folly." [1]   A district convention also resolved that " there is no safety or propriety for us as Liberty men in adopting or pursuing any other course than that of nominating good and true men who will not bow the knee to the dark spirit of slavery " ; [2] but, in spite of these resolutions, T. R. Stanford, the Liberty candidate, withdrew in favor of C. B. Smith, the Whig nominee.   In the Fifth District the Liberty party propounded a series of questions to the Whig and Democratic candidates regarding the admission of new slave States, the Mexican War, and other matters not usually deemed of vital importance by abolitionists ; and it nominated D. W. De Puy, the editor of the *Indiana Freeman*, with instructions to withdraw should either of the other candidates answer properly.   This he did, in favor of McCarthy, the Whig, although McCarthy's answers were not very strong. [3]

Even in districts also where abolitionism had little strength, the slavery question disturbed the course of politics.   In the Third District, on the nomination of a " War " man by the Whigs, there was a bolt centring around J. H. Cravens ; but the latter eventually withdrew.   In the Second District H. J. Henly, the Democratic candidate for renomination, who had voted against the Wilmot Proviso, became so alarmed at the consequences that " he declared most emphatically and unequivocally . . . that he was in favor of the Wilmot Proviso and had always been in favor of it . . . and that he intended to vote for it and support it with all his power, and farther that he had always supported it when introduced, *and had never voted against it.*" [4]   When the election occurred, the Whigs gained two members on this issue : Owen, Democratic, lost in a strong Democratic district ; Henly's majority of 843 in 1845 was reduced to 40 ; Wick's majority was reduced from 1,400 to

[1] *National Era*, July 8, 1847.   [2] *Ibid.*, July 29, 1847.
[3] *Ibid.*, July 1, 29, 1847.   [4] *Ibid.*, Jan. 6, 1848.

8, — the loss resulting in each case from the candidate's record ;ainst the Wilmot Proviso.[1]

Time for maturing any well-defined plans was not, however, rmitted to the advocates of a new policy; for in the spring of 47 began a movement to call the National Nominating Conntion in the ensuing fall. This was exactly what the expedicy men did not want; for by an early nomination the party ight put out of its power an opportunity to profit by the rising ilmot Proviso excitement. The coming session of Congress omised to be of immense importance, and a nomination and a atform adopted a year before the election might prove hopesly unsuited to the conditions.

A brisk newspaper controversy sprang up over the date of e convention. The Eastern press, and those who favored rrit Smith, William Goodell, and the new " Liberty League," shed an early day; but most of the Western papers, except se in frontier Wisconsin, preferred some time in the spring 1848. In Ohio the *National Press and Herald* strenuously posed. "We have observed with regret," it said, "an effort on the part of some influential Liberty papers to precipitate party into a nomination of its candidate for the next Presincy. Would it not be better to wait the developments of xt winter in Congress and of the other political parties?"[2] ter it argued: "There are thousands of good men and true the Whig and Democratic parties. . . . It would be a great ect to secure their co-operation with us, which can only be ne by a charitable and conciliatory course. . . . We are will to accomplish it by the sacrifice of anything short of our n anti-slavery principles."[3] It said that the sentiment of Ohio s strongly in favor of postponement: "We do not know one ividual who has been specially active and self-sacrificing in Liberty movement who favors a nomination this fall."[4] The veland American* agreed with these sentiments, as did also *Liberty Advocate*, the Indiana *Free Labor Advocate*, and the

National Era, Aug. 19, 1847.
National Press and Herald, April 21, 1847.
Ibid., June 2, 1847.   [4] *Ibid.*, June 30, 1847.

Michigan *Signal of Liberty*.[1]   The *Western Citizen*, of Chicag
said: "Our opinion is that the Convention should not be he
till the middle of the month of May, 1848.   It is folly for us
shut our eyes to the future and act regardless of consequence
As there is no special haste for a nomination, let us wait and s
what Providence and the course of events may develop for t
next twelve months before we are committed to our candidates.
The Michigan State Liberty Convention in June, by a thre
fourths majority, passed a resolution in favor of postponemen
On the other hand, the *New Lisbon Aurora* in Ohio, and t
American Freeman in Wisconsin, desired an early conventio
"We have been from the beginning for an early nomination
said the *Freeman;* "it is difficult for mankind at large to be he
together without a representative. . . . Real anti-slavery acti
by either the Whig or Democratic party is out of the que
tion . . . then why wait?"[4]   The small band of third-par
men in Wisconsin was decidedly more radical than Bailey, Chas
and other founders of the party; for the Wisconsin Liber
Association resolved to "approbate the decision of the Nation
Committee of the Liberty Party to call a convention to nom
nate in the ensuing autumn."[5]

The question was settled by the Liberty National Committ
appointed in 1843, who, against the protests of Chase of Oh
and Stewart of Michigan, issued a call for a convention
October 20, 1847.   On that date, accordingly, met at Buffa
the third and last National Convention of the Liberty par
There were present one hundred and forty regular delega
quite fairly proportioned among the Northern States, includi
twenty-three from Ohio, eight from Illinois, five from Michiga
four from Indiana, and three from Wisconsin. Besides the
many Liberty League men were present and a considera
number of voluntary delegates, all of whom, according to t
somewhat irregular habits of anti-slavery conventions, parti
pated on an equal footing with those regularly appointed.   T
Liberty Leaguers had adopted Spooner's doctrines; and at

---

[1] *National Era*, June 24, July 8, 1847.
[2] Quoted *ibid.*, May 20, 1847.   [3] *Ibid.*, July 8, 1847.
[4] *American Freeman*, June 2, 1847.   [5] *Ibid.*, July 28, 1847.

ery outset, before the Convention was organized, Bradburn of
Cleveland moved not to nominate any one who did not believe
that slavery was unconstitutional. This motion was laid on the
table; and the convention organized, with Western men as
usual in prominent positions. Sam Lewis[1] was president, and
six of the sixteen vice-presidents and secretaries were Northwestern men.

The proceedings of the convention are too much involved
with parliamentary questions and with discussions over methods
of voting to be discussed in detail; for the purposes of this study,
will be enough to summarize their results. The struggle began when Joshua Leavitt reported a series of resolutions from
the Business Committee. The first of these resolutions, asserting
the object of the Liberty party to be the abolition of slavery in a
constitutional manner, was adopted unanimously. The second,
declaring that the Constitution gave the government no power
to institute slavery, was also adopted unanimously. The third
resolution, however, which stated that slavery was unconstitutional in the Territories, proved a crucial point; for here Gerrit
Smith offered an amendment that slavery was unconstitutional
in the States also. A long discussion followed between Smith,
Goodell, and others on one side, and the conservatives on the
other. In the evening session the amendment came to a vote
and was rejected, 137 to 195. The fourth resolution stated that
the duty of anti-slavery members of Congress was to vote for
the repeal of slavery in the District of Columbia, for the repeal
of the Fugitive Slave Act of 1793, and against the introduction
of slavery into the Territories. More debate followed; but the
amendments of Gerrit Smith were all voted down, and the
remaining resolutions were adopted without a struggle.

When the resolution to nominate was offered, Chase moved
to postpone action until May, 1848; but after a long debate the
convention rejected his amendment, 37 to 128, and proceeded to
nominate. Here the expediency party made a great effort,
determined that if they must nominate they would present the
right kind of man. Ever since the spring they had been advo-

[1] Lewis's name was Samuel; but he was always called Sam by the press,
infallible sign of popularity.

cating the selection of John P. Hale, now the national anti-
slavery champion in the United States Senate, whose election
had been brought about by Whig, Democratic, and Liberty votes.
He was not technically a member of the Liberty party, a fact
which, in the eyes of dyed-in-the-wool abolitionists, was enough
to condemn him; but when Lewis Tappan, one of the originators
of anti-slavery action, read before the convention a letter from
Hale expressing his willingness to run on a Liberty ticket,
scruples were so quickly quieted that on the first ballot Hale
had 103 votes to Gerrit Smith's 44, and was thereby nominated.

To designate a Vice-President two ballots were necessary,
Leicester King being successful over Owen Lovejoy on the
second. The convention then appointed a National Liberty
Committee, and after an address by Sam Lewis adjourned.
had been in some respects a drawn battle: Chase and the
Western men who favored postponement had been defeated,
but had secured the nomination of Hale; the conservatives had
maintained the Liberty platform practically unchanged, but
they would have preferred some other candidate. The Liberty
League people alone had been routed at every point.[1]

Hale's nomination aroused much discontent among the narrower Liberty men of the East; but in the West it proved very
popular. Only in Wisconsin Territory did it meet with disapproval, and there it seemed to be a bitter pill. " As for John
P. Hale," said the *American Freeman*, " we are slow to believe
it necessary to leave the circle of noble men who have been the
life of the cause. . . . We will put his name at the head of our
column, but do not wish to be considered pledged." [2] The
Wisconsin Liberty Association showed a similar regret when it
resolved " That, although the course taken by the Buffalo Convention last fall was of doubtful propriety, . . . yet if John P.
Hale shall be found to espouse the great principle which is the
basis of our organization . . . we will support him." [3] Even as
late as the spring of 1848, Wisconsin leaders continued to protest
against Hale's candidacy, and to show strong signs of a desire
to join the Liberty League.

[1] Proceedings of the Convention, in *National Era*, Nov. 11, 1847.
[2] Nov. 10, 1847.   [3] *American Freeman*, Feb. 2, 1848.

CHAPTER IX.

COMBINATION OF THIRD-PARTY MEN ON THE FREE SOIL ISSUE.

1848.

AFTER the Liberty nomination, the prediction of Bailey, Chase, Stewart, the *Cincinnati Herald*, and the *Western Citizen* proved true; for so great was the change in public sentiment, and so high the excitement over the question of slavery in the Territories, that by the summer of 1848 national politics were in a state hardly dreamed of by Liberty men in October, 1847. The anti-slavery sentiment of which the growth in both Whig and Democratic parties had for two or three years been gradual, now increased with unparalleled rapidity, until it was powerful enough to do in one year what the Liberty party had been unable to do in seven, namely, to split the old parties in nearly every Northern State.

When the year 1848 opened, it became almost certain that Cass would receive the Democratic nomination; but, although he was a representative Northwestern pioneer statesman, there were very many Democrats in each of the Northwestern States to whom the prospect was anything but pleasing. Anti-slavery sentiment had much increased in the ranks of the Democratic party. In Ohio the year opened with a resolution in favor of free territory by the Hamilton County Convention;[1] and on January 8 the Ohio State Democratic Convention, breaking with all precedents, resolved " That the people of Ohio look upon slavery as an evil in any part of the Union, and feel it their duty to prevent its increase, to mitigate, and finally to eradicate the evil."[2] This resolution was by no means clear as

[1] *National Era*, June 29, 1848.   [2] *True Democrat*, Jan. 14, 1848.

to the particular question at issue; but, considering the fact that
it came from a Democratic convention, it was an immense forward stride. No other State Convention took so strong ground.
Michigan, Wisconsin, Indiana, and Iowa Democrats ignored the
subject of slavery; and the Illinois Convention, dominated by
members from "Egypt," condemned the Wilmot Proviso
movement "as an intemperate discussion and an unnecessary
agitation of the subject." [1]

Several of these conventions, including that of Ohio, went
so far as explicitly to recommend Cass for the Presidency; but
in many localities distrust of him could be neither placated
by anti-slavery resolutions nor frowned down by State Conventions anxious above all things for harmony. Even in Michigan protests were heard. "How General Cass reconciles his
views with those expressed by the Democrats of the State
which he has the honor to represent we do not know," said the
Pontiac Jacksonian. "Michigan is fully committed to the Wilmot Proviso. Our last legislature, almost wholly Democratic,
passed a resolution in favor." [2] When in February, sixty-six
Democratic members of the legislature signed a paper recommending Cass as their choice for the Presidency, five refused to
sign, including F. J. Littlejohn, a favorite Democratic stump
speaker. This was the first token of a Democratic discontent
which was destined to trouble Cass thereafter. [3]

The region where Democratic anti-slavery views were strongest
was the northeastern counties of Illinois and the contiguous
southeastern counties of Wisconsin. Here, in addition to
anti-slavery objections, Cass's probable nomination met with
hostility on the ground of his suspected disapproval of internal
improvements. This last feature deserves more attention than
can here be given, for the question of river and harbor im-
provement was one peculiarly interesting to the Northwest. In
the years preceding 1848 nearly every Northwestern State
legislature had demanded national aid to interstate commerce,
and nothing had so disgusted Western business men as Polk's

---

[1] *Chicago Journal,* May 1, 1848.
[2] Quoted in *Detroit Advertiser,* Jan. 19, 1848.
[3] *Ibid.,* Feb. 9, 1848.

to. A great Northwestern River and Harbor Convention had
en held in Chicago on July 5, 1847, to which Cass, as a repre-
ntative Northwestern politician, was invited. Faced by the
lemma of either failing to support Polk or displeasing a
ong popular sentiment, he took the futile course of writing a
te, saying, without a word of comment favorable or other-
se, that circumstances would prevent his attendance. This
empt at dodging was of course a lamentable failure, and pro-
ced unmeasured ridicule. Northwestern Democrats lost con-
ence in him at once; for their pockets were so vitally affected
bars in harbors and snags in rivers that with them Polk's
erpretation of the party creed had little weight.

The dozen or more anti-slavery counties in Illinois and Wis-
nsin were equally urgent for internal improvements, and they
w protested vigorously against Cass. When it was reported
t the Wisconsin delegates to the Democratic convention
re pledged to Cass, the *Southport Telegraph* remarked: "If
h be the case, Wisconsin will be most outrageously misrepre-
ted, for we firmly believe that of the Democratic voters five
t of six would prefer some other man to Cass. . . . If his
uthern subservience were not in itself sufficient to condemn
n in their eyes, his standing in relation to national works of
provement . . . would most effectually do it." [1] In northern
nois four or more Democratic county conventions passed
olutions demanding the Wilmot Proviso; [2] and the Chicago
arnburners," — as they called themselves, in imitation of
New York Free Soil Democrats, — not satisfied with ex-
ssing their own opinions, proceeded to suppress utterances
opposing views. At a meeting called "to sustain the
ninistration and blink the Wilmot Proviso," a number of
partisans of "Long John Wentworth" moved anti-slavery
olutions. The chairman, amid a violent clamor, declared
meeting adjourned; but the anti-slavery men, led by
mas Hoyne and I. N. Arnold, called a new meeting on
spot, and after a bitter struggle carried the resolution:
hat while the Democracy of Chicago . . . will adhere to

[1] Quoted in *Milwaukee Sentinel*, May 1, 1848.
[2] *National Era*, May 4, 1848.

the compromises of the Constitution . . . they declare their u
compromising determination to prevent the extension of slave
into territory now free which may be acquired by any action
the Federal Government."[1]

On May 22 the Democratic National Convention nominat
Lewis Cass upon a platform framed to suit the South; and fro
all over the free States broke out at once cries of rage and d
appointment. In New York the revolt of the Barnburners
once shattered the Democratic party from top to bottom; a
though this bolt was due as much to factional hatred of Ca
as to anti-slavery feeling, the action found a response in eve
Northwestern State. Only in Illinois and Wisconsin, howev
did revolt break forth at once; in the other States Democr
sulked and nursed their wrath, waiting for events. In Wisc
sin the *Racine Advocate* said: "We do not put the names
Lewis Cass and W. O. Butler at the head of our columns, b
cause we can in no event cordially support the nomination
the Baltimore Convention, and very probably may not be a
to support it at all. . . . The course of General Cass on t
Wilmot Proviso was one that ought to have the reprobation
men of all parties. . . . We honestly hope another nominati
may be made by Democrats."[2] The *Southport Telegraph* sai
"We do not place at the head of our columns the name
Lewis Cass or W. O. Butler. . . . We do not consider the
or at least the Presidential nominee, as a fit representati
of Democratic principles. . . . There is not a Democr
editor in the state, however he may try to deceive hims
and his readers, but thinks a more unfortunate and objecti
able nomination than that of Lewis Cass could not be made
Shortly after this a call appeared for a meeting of the "Den
crats of Racine and vicinity opposed to the election of Le
Cass";[4] and the first straight bolt in the Northwest h
begun.

In Illinois, John Wentworth's paper, the *Chicago Democrat*,
fused, in spite of the taunts of the Whig *Chicago Journal*,

[1] *National Era*, April 6, 1848.
[2] Quoted in *Milwaukee Sentinel*, June 1, 1848.
[3] Quoted *ibid.*, June 5, 1848.   [4] *Ibid.*, June 15, 1848.

place Cass's name at the head of its columns.[1] In June the
Fourth District Congressional Convention met, and after a
stormy time refused to ratify Cass's nomination, and renomi-
nated Wentworth for Congress without a platform. The Cass
delegates, forty in number, then bolted, and nominated J. B.
Thomas. An Illinois Presidential elector of 1844 wrote:
" There are thousands of voters . . . who will never vote for
Cass. . . . You can scarcely conceive the enthusiasm for the
Wilmot Proviso." [2]

By the end of June the Democratic opposition to Cass, led by
the New York Barnburners, had taken definite form in a convention at Utica, which with tremendous enthusiasm nominated
Martin Van Buren for the Presidency. This meeting had a
semi-national character; for delegates were present from Massachusetts and Connecticut, Ohio, Illinois, and Wisconsin, those
from the last-named State having been regularly chosen by an
anti-Cass Democratic meeting at Racine. J. W. Taylor, of Ohio,
made a speech promising aid to the Barnburners, and two interesting telegrams were read. One from Lafayette, Indiana,
declared: " We have our eyes upon you. Desire prompt
action. Will throw heavy vote. An enthusiastic mass meeting.
Whigs and Democrats in Tippecanoe have spoken in unmistake-
able terms." The other, signed by Woodworth, the mayor of
Chicago, T. Hoyne, I. N. Arnold, " and one hundred others,"
said: " Please to make known to the Convention that Northern
Illinois is ready to fraternize with New York. The undersigned
Democrats, with thousands of others, are ready to second any
national movement in favor of Free Territory and would suggest
a National Mass Convention." [3]

When the news of the nomination went over the country,
coupled with a call for a national convention at Buffalo, Northwestern Democrats fairly broke loose, and ratification meetings
were held in every State. Wisconsin and Illinois, as usual, felt
the greatest excitement. In Wisconsin, the *Southport Telegraph*

[1] *Chicago Journal*, June 3, 1848.
[2] *National Era*, June 22, 1848.
[3] *The Great Issue*, New York, 1848, 107, *seq.*, describes the Utica
Convention.

and *Racine Advocate* ran up the Van Buren flag; the *Rock County Democrat* remarked: "In this vicinity truth compels us to say that the Utica nomination is well received by a large portion of the Democracy. . . . If there were any prospect of a general uprising, if the question of free territory could be brought to a direct issue, . . . we would cheerfully take hold and help."[1]

In Illinois, the protesting Chicago Democrats rivalled their New York friends in noisy excitement. "Had a bombshell fallen into our quiet city yesterday," said the Whig *Chicago Journal*, "it could not have created more consternation. . . . Our Barnburning friends fairly swarmed and were in ecstasies. . . . Knots of men on every corner were busy canvassing the merits of the nominees. . . . They evidently gloated over the prospect of the defeat of Cass."[2] A call very soon appeared, signed by several hundred of the most influential Democrats, for a meeting in favor of Free Soil and Van Buren. On July 4 the meeting convened, "numerous and enthusiastic," and after making fiery speeches for Van Buren, and scoring Cass, resolved "That General Cass having . . . avowed the opinion that Congress has no Constitutional power to prohibit slavery, . . . no man can support him without an utter abandonment of the great principle of Free Soil."[3]

Meanwhile, Whig bolters had been keeping pace, step by step, with the Free Soil Democrats in the Northwest. Whig State Conventions in Ohio and Michigan passed resolutions in favor of restricting slavery; but in Indiana, Illinois, Wisconsin, and Iowa the subject was not mentioned. By the beginning of 1848 the Taylor "boom" was so powerful that nothing seemed able to stand before it, and anxious Whigs could only protest unavailingly or watch in gloomy silence. What made their situation the more trying was the fact that the papers which supported Taylor were the loudest in asserting anti-slavery principles. "The Whig party, North, is the true anti-slavery party of the Republic!" cried the *Detroit Advertiser*.[4] In Illinois,

---

[1] Quoted in *Milwaukee Sentinel*, July 4, 1848.
[2] June 24, 1848.   [3] *National Era*, July 20, 1848.
[4] Feb. 17, 1848.

the Cook County Whig Convention resolved that the Wilmot Proviso " is now and ever has been the doctrine of the Whigs of the free States," and that " the Whig party has ever been the firm, steady, and unchanging friend of harbor and river appropriations." [1] The *Milwaukee Sentinel* claimed: " It is known to the whole Union that the Whigs of all the free States are . . . uncompromisingly opposed to any further extension of slavery "; [2] and it invoked the people of Wisconsin to vote the Whig ticket in the spring election in order to " bear testimony, in favor of Free Soil and against the further extension of slave territory." [3]

With their party papers making such vigorous assertions, Whigs in most of the Northwestern States refrained from open complaint; but on the Western Reserve such circumstances had no weight. By the beginning of 1848 the anti-slavery Whigs of that region were preparing for the worst. The State Whig Committee made some efforts to keep them quiet by advocating McLean or Corwin as a candidate; but nobody was deceived. Every one knew that Taylor's nomination was inevitable; yet, with their eyes open, Whig conventions in Trumbull, Lorain, Warren, Stark, Cuyahoga, Belmont, Lake, Geauga, Green, Clinton, Ashtabula, and other counties resolved " That we will support no man for the office of President in 1848 who is not a true friend and an earnest advocate of the Ordinance of 1787." [4] The *True Democrat* began to consider the possible necessity of bolting. " Can party allegiance," it asked, " relieve a man from the discharge of moral obligations? Suppose the Whigs nominate General Taylor for President, must we as Whigs vote for him? Can party obligations bind us to become accessory to the extension of slavery? " [5]

As the spring approached, the excitement of Ohio anti-slavery Whigs increased. A " Clay " meeting in Cincinnati, taken possession of by anti-slavery men, passed a resolution not to support any man " not avowedly and heartily in favor of the exclusion of slavery from all the Territories." [6] Evidently times

[1] *Chicago Journal*, April 3, 1848. [2] April 28, 1848.

[3] May 2, 1848. [4] *True Democrat*, Jan. 4, 1848.

[5] *Ibid.*, Jan. 10, 1848. [6] *Ibid.*, April 11, 1848.

had changed since 1844, if such sentiments were deemed appropriate at a "Clay" meeting. In Cincinnati, early in March, there was circulated among Whigs a paper receiving a large number of signatures, declaring: "We, the undersigned, having acted with the great Whig party of the United States, . . . while we would not meddle with slavery where it now exists, yet deem it our duty to use all lawful and peaceable means to stop its progress, . . . and we do most solemnly pledge ourselves to vote for no man . . . who is not known to be, or who will not most positively declare himself, opposed to the introduction of slavery into any of the territory now owned by these United States or into any territory that may be acquired by purchase or otherwise." [1]

When, on the 10th of June, the Whig National Convention nominated Zachary Taylor without any platform and howled down the Wilmot Proviso, the Western Reserve Whigs rose as one man to repudiate him. "As we anticipated," said the *True Democrat*, "the Whigs have nominated Zach Taylor for president! And this is the cup offered by slave-holders for us to drink. We loathe the sight. We will neither touch, taste nor handle the unclean thing. We ask the Whigs of Cuyahoga County to live up to the pledge they have made." [2] They did so. Within a week after Taylor's nomination, in every county of the Western Reserve a people's meeting, without regard to party, had repudiated Taylor and demanded a national Free Soil candidate. Eight Whig newspapers bolted without hesitation. [3] Outside of Ohio, open bolting was not common; although the *Lafayette Journal* of Indiana said: "The nomination of Gen. Taylor is a disgrace to the Convention and an insult to the intelligence and virtue of the American people. The Whig party is basely betrayed — aye, sold to the Southern slave-holder. For ourselves we are against the nomination might and main, heart and soul." [4]

---

[1] *Cincinnati Gazette*, May 1, 1848.   [2] June 10, 1848.

[3] *True Democrat*, June 30, 1848; A. G. Riddle, *Rise of the Anti-Slavery Sentiment on the Western Reserve*, in *Magazine of Western History*, VI., 145–156.

[4] Quoted in *American Freeman*, July 18, 1848.

When so many Whigs and Democrats were filled with anti-slavery sentiment and with disgust at their respective party nominations, common action was inevitable. As early as the summer of 1847, non-partisan Wilmot Proviso meetings were held in Ohio on the Reserve and in Cincinnati;[1] these became more common in 1848; and as the spring advanced and every day made the nomination of Taylor and Cass more certain, they grew larger and more emphatic. Finally, May 20, a call appeared in the *Cincinnati Gazette*, signed by three thousand voters of thirty counties, for a great State Mass Free Territory Convention to express the sentiment of the people on the extension of slavery. "We ask no man to leave his party," it said, "or surrender his party views. . . . Let all come who prefer free territory to slave territory and are resolved to act and vote accordingly. If candidates have been already nominated who represent our principles, let us approve them; if not, let us ourselves form a ticket we can support."[2] This call was written by Chase, whose position in this matter will be explained below.

After Taylor was nominated at Philadelphia, a meeting of dissatisfied Whigs was held in a committee room, among whom were Vaughn, Campbell, Galloway, and two others, besides Stanley Mathews, the Liberty party editor of the *Cincinnati Herald*. After much discussion, it was resolved to hold a Free Soil convention at Buffalo; and in order to get an impressive non-partisan call, it was deemed advisable to ask the Ohio Free Territory Convention to issue it.[3] On June 21 the People's Convention met at Columbus, with one thousand delegates, including prominent Whigs, Democrats, and Liberty men. J. C. Vaughn made an address urging the calling of a national convention; and the meeting so resolved, expressing the opinion that it should be held in August at Buffalo. The presiding officer was N. Sawyer, of Cincinnati, a leading Democrat, and the other officers were nearly all Whigs and Democrats. A letter from Giddings was read by E. S. Hamlin,

---

[1] *National Era*, July 29, 1847; *National Press and Herald*, Oct. 6, 1847.
[2] *National Era*, May 25, 1848; R. B. Warden, *Life of Chase*, 316.
[3] Henry Wilson, *Slave Power*, II., 142.

9

committing the old warrior fully to the movement for a new party. Liberty men also were very much in evidence; Chase Lewis, and Birney addressed the convention, and Harding, of Indiana, made a speech claiming that his State would poll a large vote for an independent candidate. It would be profitable to repeat the admirable series of resolutions, written of course by Chase; but it must suffice to say that they were practically the same as those which the later Free Soil platform adopted at Buffalo. One noteworthy feature was the wide recognition which they gave to anti-slavery action by mentioning with honor men of all parties, — the New York Barnburners, McLean, Giddings, Palfrey, Wilmot, Henry Wilson, L. D. Campbell, and John P. Hale.[1]

With the call for a national convention issued simultaneously by this meeting and the one held at Utica, the movement for independent action grew with intense rapidity. In Ohio, anti-slavery men rushed into non-partisan conventions in nearly every county of the State, until in July the *National Era* said: "We could not find room for even brief notices of all the Free Soil meetings in Ohio. The people there seem to be cutting loose *en masse* from the old party organizations."[2] Most of these conventions passed strong, even violent, resolutions, going far beyond the mere question of slavery extension, and into abolition ground; and many of them chose delegates to Buffalo.

The other States did not lag behind. In Indiana, Free Soil conventions held in several localities passed resolutions and elected delegates to Buffalo. On July 26 a State Convention was held at Indianapolis, over which the mayor, J. B. Seamans presided. Disregarding the objections of some Taylor men, the convention went on with great enthusiasm to pass uncompromising resolutions, elected delegates to the Buffalo Convention and appointed a State Central Committee.[3] Michigan kept pace with Indiana. In June and July meetings without distinction of party were held, which resolved to "bury all political

---

[1] *National Era*, June 29–July 6, 1848; *True Democrat*, June 27, 1848; J. W. Schuckers, *Life of Chase*, 84.

[2] July 20, 1848.

[3] *National Era*, Aug. 10, 1848; *Free Territory Sentinel*, Aug. 16, 1848.

imosities and strike hands for the one great cause of Free
oil and Free Labor." [1]   On July 3 the State Convention
ppointed a Central Committee, made arrangements to start a
ree Soil newspaper, and elected delegates to Buffalo.   The
nn Arbor *True Democrat* and the *Monroe Advocate*, which had
first followed the Baltimore nomination, pulled down the Cass
ag and turned to Van Buren; and leading Democrats followed
eir example.   At one Free Soil convention, two former presi-
ents of Cass ratification meetings took part.[2]

In Illinois, the excitement, already prodigious, increased ten-
ld with the call for a national convention.   The Democrats of
e Fourth District, who had begun their bolt on a party basis,
w cordially joined the " People's " movement.   Early in July
ass meetings in Cook and Lake counties, without respect to
rty, nominated independent Free Soil candidates, the first
parently in the Northwest.[3]   Kendall, Dupage, and other
unties followed, electing delegates to Buffalo and passing
sounding resolutions, until by the end of July the whole
rthern section of the State seemed to be throwing itself heart
d soul into the third party.   Wisconsin Democrats were fully
reast of their neighbors.   Non-partisan meetings flourished
the central and the southeastern counties, and on July 26 a
ate Free Soil Convention met at Janesville, attended by men
all shades of political opinion, although most of the officers
re Democrats.   The meeting adopted resolutions, and after
rring speeches appointed twenty-five delegates to the Buffalo
nvention.[4]   Lastly, signs of life appeared in Iowa, hitherto
rren territory.   Free Soil non-partisan meetings were held in
e southeastern counties, where New England men had settled,
d measures were begun for a State organization.[5]   Thus the
onths of June and July passed with constantly swelling excite-
ent, until, on August 9, the movement reached a climax in the
mous Buffalo Convention, one of the landmarks of anti-slavery
tion in the United States.

---

[1] *Detroit Advertiser*, July 15, 1848.   [2] *Ibid.*, Aug. 10, 1848.
[3] *Chicago Journal*, July 17-31, 1848.
[4] *American Freeman*, Aug. 9, 1848; *Milwaukee Sentinel*, Aug. 1, 1848.
[5] *National Era*, Aug. 10, 1848.

But what had the Liberty party been doing all this time, whi
Vermont, Massachusetts, New York, Ohio, Illinois, and Wisco
sin seemed rushing bodily into anti-slavery action?   By Jul
1848, events had gone far beyond the wildest dreams of th
Liberty convention of 1847; but they had gone also withor
any regard to the Liberty party.   True, the nomination of Ha
was very suitable for the support of anti-slavery Whigs an
Democrats, but in 1848 most of the bolting members of the ol
parties seemed entirely to ignore it.   Some Whigs, perhaps,
Indiana and Ohio looked upon the Liberty platform with favo
but no Democratic bolting conventions ever considered it for
moment.   By July, 1848, Van Buren had been nominated at Utic
and seemed to be the popular choice to lead the new movement

What were Liberty men to do?   Were they to continue th
old policy of separation, or should they join the new movemen
The latter alternative was rendered difficult by the fact th
they had a party ticket already in nomination.   It was a tryin
situation, and there was great vacillation throughout the cou
try.   What orthodox Liberty men feared most was some devia
tion from the line of strict abolitionist consistency.   On Ju
6, the executive committee of the American and Foreign An
Slavery Society issued a warning address, urging at great leng
that " non-extension is not abolitionism although included in
and it will be time to consider overtures of coalition from fello
citizens who have recently awakened to see the disastrous p
icy of slavery extension when they shall have embraced the gre
anti-slavery principles we avow. . . . Neither can we believe
it added, making an indirect but evident allusion to Van Bure
" that any Liberty party man will cast his vote for a politici
who has, when in power, proffered his aid to the slaveocracy.
This address was signed by the Tappans of New York and
nine others, making a bare majority of the executive comm
tee.   The names of William Jay, A. Stewart, Arnold Buffu
and others were conspicuously absent.   On the other hand, t
National Era threw its powerful influence in the direction
conciliatory measures ; and between these two positions Liber
men throughout the country wavered.

[1] *National Era*, July 6, 1848.

In Ohio, matters tended from the first in the direction of co-operation with the new movement. The *Cincinnati Herald*, which, through the prestige of Birney and Bailey, was still the leading Liberty paper in Ohio, warmly advocated a union of all anti-slavery men, and condemned the American and Foreign Anti-Slavery Society manifesto as "too transcendental for our common sense."[1] Swayed by these counsels, the party abstained from its usual midwinter and spring activity. Such conventions as were held discussed and resolved, but did not nominate. Chase, Lewis, King, and Wade were waiting. In the spring Liberty leaders began actively to co-operate with the Free Soil movement; and several of them, as we have seen, were prominent at the Free Territory Convention. Chase in particular welcomed the Barnburner movement; for a large part of the Democratic party, whose redemption had occupied his thoughts since 1845, seemed actually on the point of becoming anti-slavery. He threw himself with great vigor into the cause, wrote letters right and left, and after the autumn of 1847 participated in non-partisan meetings. He wrote the call for the People's Convention and also furnished the resolutions, although, through fear of seeming too prominent, he caused them to be introduced by some one else,[2] and he induced a number of Cincinnati men of all parties to unite in inviting Hale to pay them a visit.

After the call for the People's Convention had been issued, another call appeared, signed by Chase, Lewis, Mathews, and others, summoning a Liberty State Convention to meet at Columbus on June 21, with an avowed purpose of influencing the action of the Free Territory Convention. "Let us attend," ran the call, "and share the deliberation of the Independent People's Convention. If possible, let us agree with them; if not, let us nominate, and go into the approaching contest with resolution and energy."[3] This convention adopted resolutions approving the Buffalo Convention, but declaring that the party would support no man who would not adopt Liberty principles.

---

[1] *Cincinnati Herald*, July 19, 1848.

[2] R. B. Warden, *Life of Chase*, 316.

[3] *National Era*. May 4, 1848.

A State Committee was appointed, and the convention adjourned. This was the last official meeting of the Liberty party in Ohio.[1] Among the most significant illustrations of the recent change of mind among Ohio Liberty men was a resolution passed at a convention for Lake and Ashtabula counties. A favorite taunt of the Western Reserve Liberty men against Giddings had been that the local Whig party kept renominating him only through fear of losing abolition votes; now that he was repudiating Taylor, the same men who had fought him bitterly for six years resolved that " his re-election does not now depend on our opposition, but may consist with our co-operation."[2]

Indiana followed more slowly in the same course. On June 12, a State Liberty Convention passed resolutions in favor of Hale and King, demanding the Wilmot Proviso and condemning the old parties; and it nominated an electoral ticket; but in July, with the call for a national convention, abolitionists altered their course and began to join the Free Soil movement. When the State Free Territory Convention met on July 26, S. S. Harding and S. C. Stevens, the two leaders of the Indiana Liberty party, both wrote approving letters.

The Michigan Liberty party met in convention on February 4, 1848, and nominated an electoral ticket. A last echo of the struggle in the Liberty National Convention of 1847 occurred, when this body found itself obliged to reject a proposition to endorse the platform of the Liberty League.[3] Resolutions were introduced at this meeting inviting Whigs and Democrats to join the Liberty party in supporting Hale, and proposing an alliance with the Whigs in order to carry the State against Cass. After some debate they were withdrawn; but a little later a Liberty man, in a letter to the *Detroit Advertiser*, renewed the discussion, and suggested a Whig and Liberty " deal," the Liberty party having the electors, the Whigs taking Congressmen and the State ticket.[4] These suggestions came to nothing; but, as will be seen, there was something in them

---

[1] *National Era*, July 6, 1848.
[2] *True Democrat*, May 31, 1848.
[3] *National Era*, Feb. 24, 1848.
[4] *Detroit Advertiser*, Feb. 17, 1848.

almost prophetic of later Michigan politics. By July, Michigan Liberty men were joining heartily with the Free Soil organizations.

The Illinois Liberty party in this year stood in a somewhat peculiar position. On February 9 and 10, at a State Convention, the party, recovering with its usual elasticity from the inaction of 1847, prepared for a vigorous canvass. Later in the year a convention for the Fourth Congressional District renominated Lovejoy, who took the stump at once, trying, amid the turmoil and excitement of the spring and summer months, to hold the local third party together. On July 4, at a time when Liberty men in Ohio and Indiana were in the thick of the Free Soil movement, Illinois abolitionists held a State Convention at Hennepin, and nominated Dr. Dyer and H. H. Snow for Governor and Lieutenant-Governor respectively. When the election took place, it was found that the Liberty vote had fallen off; but, considering the distraction of the time, its showing was creditable: Democratic — French, 67,453; Liberty — Dyer, 4,748. In the Fourth District, Lovejoy made a fair showing, but did not urge his cause with the vehemence which he had shown two years before. His sympathies were always with practical measures, and he saw that the time had come to abandon separate action.[1]

In Wisconsin a State election occurred to retard the union of Liberty and Free Soil men. The adoption of a State constitution having necessitated an election in the spring, the Wisconsin Liberty party met in convention on April 19 and nominated a full ticket. It was in this frontier State, it will be remembered, that John P. Hale's nomination had met with the greatest condemnation, and that the tendency of the local party had been toward Gerrit Smith and the Liberty League. This convention elected delegates to a convention called by the Liberty League

---

[1] *Chicago Journal*, Aug. 4, 1848. The Liberty vote in this Congressional election was as follows: —

	Democratic.	Whig.	Liberty.
Fourth District . .	11,857	8,312	3,130
Sixth District . . .	9,302	10,325	666
Seventh District . .	7,201	7,095	166

to meet at Buffalo in June; but it refused to adopt Goodell's favorite doctrine, that the Liberty party ought to be a national reform organization. It did declare, however, that the United States Constitution was an anti-slavery document, and it laid on the table resolutions to support Hale. When a resolution was introduced offering to unite with any or all parties who would pledge themselves to support the Wilmot Proviso, it was unanimously rejected.[1] On this rigid and narrow basis the Wisconsin Liberty party made an active campaign, and succeeded, in May, 1848, in increasing its vote as follows: Democratic — Dewey, 17,238; Whig — Tweedy, 14,049; Liberty — Durkee, 1,134.

After the local election of 1848, the question of the relation of the Liberty party of Wisconsin to the Free Soil movement absorbed all the interest of the party. When, in June, the purpose of the Ohio Liberty men to join the People's Convention became apparent, the *American Freeman* in great disgust said: " In doing this they have left the platform of the Liberty party. . . . That was established not to enact the Wilmot Proviso, but to abolish slavery throughout the Union. . . . We regard this movement as an abandonment of the Liberty party. And so Wilmot Provisoism and not abolitionism is henceforth to be the creed of the Liberty party! We wash our hands of all participation in this business ! " [2] But by the end of June, the direction of the current had become so obvious that the more practical Wisconsin abolitionists realized that they must do as their brethren were doing, or be stranded. Therefore Charles Durkee and others called a State Convention, which met at Southport, and after prolonged debate adopted resolutions favoring the Buffalo Convention, with the proviso that "the Liberty party of Wisconsin can sustain no candidates except those who are not only pledged against the extension of slavery, but are also committed to the policy of abolishing it." [3] It then appointed thirteen delegates to Buffalo; and thus the Liberty party of Wisconsin finally placed itself in line with that of the other States.

[1] *American Freeman*, April 26, 1848.
[2] *Ibid.*, June 7, 1848.   [3] *Ibid.*, July 26, 1848.

In Iowa the State Liberty party was organized in December, 1847, and in 1848, at Fort Madison, A. St. Clair began the publication of an anti-slavery paper, the *Iowa Freeman.* In the August election the party ran separate candidates for the legislature in Des Moines and Van Buren counties, and succeeded in defeating the Whigs.[1] Before the organization could do much, however, it was swallowed up by the Free Soil revolt.[2]

All over the Northwest, then, Liberty men, as well as anti-Taylor Whigs and Wilmot Proviso Democrats, were anxiously awaiting the action of the great Buffalo Free Soil Convention.

[1] *Iowa Free Democrat*, Jan. 15, 1850.
[2] *National Era*, April 12, 1849.

CHAPTER X.

CAMPAIGN OF THE FREE SOIL PARTY.

1848.

DETAILED study of the Buffalo Convention as a national movement belongs to the general history of the country; for our purposes, it will be enough here briefly to summarize its action and to give some account of the part played in it by leading Northwestern men. In this spirited assemblage were mingled at least four diverse and not always harmonious elements: the Liberty men; "Conscience" Whigs; Free Soil Democrats; and, distinct from the preceding, the New York Barnburners. To find a common platform and candidate for these incongruous groups bade fair to be a difficult task. In the first place, would the Democrats be willing to adopt any platform more radical than the Wilmot Proviso, pure and simple? It did not seem likely. On the other hand, would Liberty men accept anything less than their full party creed? And, thirdly, would a merely anti-slavery platform of any kind satisfy the Western men, who thought a demand for internal improvements indispensable? In the matter of candidates there was certain to be friction, since there were already two anti-slavery nominations in the field, Hale and Van Buren; while the "Conscience" Whigs had their own favorites in Giddings, McLean, and C. F. Adams. Of all the men named, Hale was personally the most popular: Liberty men were zealous for him; Whigs had profited once by an alliance with him in New Hampshire and felt kindly disposed; and the great mass of Democrats outside of New York would undoubtedly have been well satisfied with his candidacy. Van Buren, however, had the prestige attaching to an ex-President, and, still more important, was the candidate of the strongest single element of the convention. The New York Barnburners, in contrast to Hale's supporters, were a united body, led by trained politicians, and were masters in the art of wire-pulling and convention management, whereas Liberty men and Whigs were philanthropists rather than politicians.

Had the tumultuous mass of delegates which, on August 9, invaded Buffalo voted at once on a candidate, Hale would have had as good a chance as Van Buren; but such a proceeding would have been far too irregular to satisfy the leaders. A Committee of Conferrees was arranged, in which each State had a number of delegates equal to three times its Congressional representation; and by this body of some five hundred men was transacted the business of the convention, instead of by the thousands in the public square. While fiery orators declaimed and the crowd shouted itself hoarse, the leading members of the Liberty and Barnburner factions were privately arranging a " deal," which practically decided the outcome of the convention. Three Liberty men, Chase, Leavitt, and Stanton, had become convinced that the Barnburners would have Van Buren or nobody, but that they were not very particular about the platform. On their part, they cared more for a plank regarding the duty of separating the national government from slavery than they did for the nomination of Hale; and on this basis they determined to approach the Barnburners, offering them the candidate in exchange for the platform. The Democratic sympathies of Chase inclined him powerfully in favor of Van Buren as against McLean, Giddings, Adams, or any former Whig; and at this crisis his belief that the real hope of the country for anti-slavery action lay in the Democratic party seemed to be justified; hence he worked from the outset in complete harmony with Preston King and B. F. Butler, of New York. At some informal caucuses a provisional platform was adopted, and a plan of operations agreed upon, which, on August 10, was carried out in the Grand Committee. A Committee on Resolutions, after full discussion, reported a platform drawn up by Chase, containing planks enough to equip any party. The following is a condensed summary: — [1]

Whereas the nominations of the old parties are unfit ones, and circumstances demand a "union of the people under the banner of free Democracy," therefore be it resolved that: — 1. We plant ourselves on the national platform of freedom in opposition to the sectional platform of slavery. —— 2. Slavery depends on State law alone, and Congress has no power over slavery in the States. —— 3. The early policy of the Union was to discourage slavery. —— 4. The Federal Government has no power to deprive of life, liberty, or property without due process of law. —— 5. Therefore Congress cannot institute slavery; —— 6. And it is the duty of the Federal Government to abolish slavery where it possesses power; —— 7. And to prohibit slavery extension. —— 8. "No more slave states, no slave territory." —— 9. We condemn the recent attempted compromise in Congress. —— 10. We demand freedom for Oregon. —— 11. We favor cheap postage, retrenchment, abolition of unnecessary offices, and election of officers, where suitable, by the people. —— 12. We favor internal improvements. —— 13. We demand a homestead law. —— 14. We favor the early payment of the public debt and a tariff for revenue. —— 15. We inscribe on our banner Free Soil, Free Speech, Free Labor, and Free Men, "and . . . under it we will fight on and ever until a triumphant victory shall reward our exertions."

The sixth resolution satisfied Liberty claims; the twelfth and thirteenth attracted Western approval; and the demands for cheap postage, economy, and tariff for revenue, together with the phraseology flowing naturally from Chase's pen, served to give the platform a Democratic air. This admirably constructed document served to give all a common ground at the outset, and it was adopted with enthusiasm by the convention. By satisfying Liberty men it also promoted Van Buren's success, for, with a platform to suit them, the Liberty party cared, as usual, much less about having their own candidate.

The question of nomination now came up; and B. F. Butler

---

[1] The full text of the platform is in Stanwood, *Presidential Elections*, and in many other compendiums.

a long speech presented the name of Van Buren, explaining
s candidate's position on public issues, and asserting, in
iswer to questions, that the same President who in 1836 was
.edged to veto a bill for abolition in the District of Columbia
)w stood ready to sign one. Joshua Leavitt, on his part, with
.e sanction of Chase, Lewis, and Stanton, read a letter from
ale submitting his name to the will of the Convention.
iddings was also nominated, and some others; but the choice
ridently lay between the Barnburner and Liberty candidates.

Another name which might have roused the Convention was
ithheld. McLean was a favorite among antislavery Whigs;
id during 1847–48 Sumner, as a representative of the "Con-
ience" Whigs of Massachusetts, had corresponded at length
ith Giddings and other Western men, and also with Chase,
ho was McLean's son-in-law, in the endeavor to make out
cLean's position. The latter, however, was cautious in his
:terances as to principles, and fairly sphinx-like whenever the
ibject of a nomination was broached, and Chase exhausted his
igenuity without coming to any definite conclusion. At the
uffalo Convention, Chase was obliged to take the responsi-
ility of managing McLean's case, and, under the impression
iat he was not desirous of a nomination, and believing that
an Buren was the man for the hour, he prevented the name
om coming before the Committee of Conferrees.[1]

On the first ballot, Chase, Leavitt, and numerous Liberty men
)ted for Van Buren instead of Hale, the vote resulting as fol-
)ws: Martin Van Buren, 244; John P. Hale, 183; Joshua
. Giddings, 23; Charles Francis Adams, 13; scattering, 4.[2]
his gave Van Buren a clear majority of 21 over all; but since
)me Hale men voted for him in order to make a nomination
n the first ballot, and since the Giddings and Adams men

[1] Cleveland *True Democrat*, Aug. 4, 1852.

[2] The figures as above given are impugned in an indignant letter to the
ational Era, September 14, 1848, from that centre of radicalism, Salem,
olumbiana County, Ohio. The writer says that there were only sixty-nine
hio delegates in the Grand Committee, and that the vote of that State was
)t 37, but 27, for Van Buren. If this be the case, the totals were: Van
uren, 234; Hale, 183; all others, 40; giving Van Buren a majority of
ily 11.

would undoubtedly have preferred Hale to Van Buren, it seen
clear that but for the bargain Hale would have had a goo
fighting chance. When the vote was announced and the wi
applause of the Barnburners silenced, Joshua Leavitt, an origin
abolitionist since 1832, rose, and with deep emotion moved th
the nomination be made unanimous. Samuel Lewis second
the motion, and it was carried amid rapturous exciteme
Charles Francis Adams was then quickly nominated for Vic
President, and the convention adjourned *sine die*. Most of
leaders, except possibly the far-sighted Barnburners, suppos
that they had founded a new and a powerful party, the "Fr
Democracy" of the United States.

During the proceedings, Western men had been very prom
nent. Of the Democratic contingent, Brinckerhoff and Gill
of Ohio, and Wilson and Miller of Michigan, made addresse
and Chandler and Sawyer of Ohio, Wright of Indian
Christiancy and Wilson of Michigan, Arnold of Illino
Crocker and Wilson of Wisconsin, and Miller of Iowa, serv
on committees. Among the smaller contingent of Wilm
Proviso Whigs, Giddings was exceedingly prominent. H
name was greeted with enthusiastic applause by the mass mee
ing, and he was repeatedly called on to speak. Other an
slavery Whigs who spoke or served on committees were Brigg
Vaughn, and Hamlin of Ohio, and Julian and Cravens
Indiana. More important than any of the foregoing bolte
from the two great parties were the Western Liberty me
Judge Stevens of Indiana called the meeting to order, a
with Harding of the same State, Treadwell of Michigan, Lov
joy of Illinois, and Codding, Booth, and Holton of Wisconsi
served on committees. The Ohio galaxy, however, sho
brighter in the convention than any other body of men, excep
perhaps, the New York Barnburners and the Massachusetts Li
erty delegates. Lewis, Smith, and Paine addressed the conve
tion ; and Guthrie, Townshend, and others served on committe
or held offices. Chase was the most influential person in th
convention, with the exception of Leavitt and Butler. H
· agreement with Butler, which his position on the Committee o
Resolutions enabled him to carry out, his own literary an

olitical skill, which placed the convention on a strong plat-
orm, and his support of Van Buren, carrying with it the
otes of numerous other anxious Liberty men, — all these cir-
umstances contributed essentially to the outcome of the
onvention.[1]

As the news of the nomination and the platform travelled
ver the country, it aroused various feelings among anti-slavery
en. Free Soil Democrats were of course delighted at the
noice of an undeniably Democratic candidate on a platform
rgely Democratic; Liberty men, satisfied with the platform and
npressed by the large part taken by Leavitt, Chase, Stanton,
nd Lewis, in the proceedings at Buffalo, put aside, for the time,
npleasant memories of Van Buren, and applauded the new
arty; Hale and King shortly withdrew from the Liberty nom-
ation of October, 1847; and no reason remained why enthusi-
stic abolitionists should hesitate to support the ticket. As
dward Smith said in the Buffalo Convention, "The Liberty
arty had secured its principles, and it was no more than fair to
ive others the men."

The Free Soil ferment, which during the Convention had
almed down, now broke out again with redoubled vigor.
atification meetings were held, from district school assemblies
p to State Conventions. Especially noteworthy for enthusiasm
ere the great meetings in Cincinnati on August 25, in Chicago
n August 22, and in Milwaukee on August 26; in all of which
emocrats and Liberty men took the leading part. Almost
multaneously organization and campaign work began. Chase
nd Vaughn stumped the Reserve, and Giddings traversed the
outhern counties of Ohio. It is almost impossible to keep
ount of all Free Soil meetings on the Reserve. Those reported
verage two a day from August 10 to the eve of the election.
y the first of September, Brinckerhoff, Lewis, and Root were
n the stump, pushing organization; and the Free Soil Central

---

[1] For details of the Buffalo Convention, see Oliver Dyer, *Phonographic
'eport*, etc., published in pamphlet form in 1848, and *Great Senators*, 93
q.; also *National Era*, Aug. 17, 24, 31, 1848. The inside history espe-
ally of the dealings between the Liberty men and Barnburners has yet to
e written.

Committee, to stimulate local activity, issued an address writte
by E. S. Hamlin. "We are stronger than the most fearful o
our adversaries admit," it said; "we are stronger than our ow
most sanguine estimate. In every township, in every county
let some trusty Free Soil man be present at the polls wit
tickets for all. Your committee call upon each of you to len
your whole aid and influence to carry this state." [1]

In Indiana a State Convention met on August 30 at Indian
apolis, and after lively debate, in which Liberty men took
leading part, nominated an electoral ticket with alternates, th
list containing the leading Liberty men and the prominen
Whig and Democratic Free Soilers of the State. Local mee
ings then began to be held, but not with such vociferou
enthusiasm as in Ohio.

The Michigan Free Soilers opened a lively campaign led b
Littlejohn, Christiancy, Clark, and other former Democrat
many of whom found a motive for bolting in their dislike o
Cass, rather than in their antislavery sympathies. County con
ventions began organization in August, and on September 20
State Convention at Ann Arbor nominated a full set of electors
In this list, as in those of Ohio and Indiana, former members o
the old parties were given the lion's share of positions, Libert
men being willing to stay in the background. [2]

More ardent and more numerous than Indiana or Michiga
Free Soilers, the Barnburners of Chicago and northern Illino
rushed with enthusiasm into the new movement. A State Con
vention at Ottawa, on August 30, in which sixty-six countie
were represented, nominated with great harmony an elector
ticket composed mainly of former Democrats, and claimed f
Illinois a Free Soil vote of 40,000. Following this beginnin,
local meetings kept the northern counties in a constant up
heaval until the election.

In Wisconsin it seemed for a time as if the whole State wer
rushing into the Free Soil ranks. A mass State Convention
on August 24, at Janesville, chose a central committee an
ratified the nomination of Van Buren, and another State Con

[1] *Cincinnati Globe* (*Herald*), Sept. 1, 1848.
[2] Ann Arbor *True Democrat*, Sept. 28, 1848.

vention at Madison on September 27, attended by delegates from twelve counties, nominated a ticket of electors, mostly Democrats. Meanwhile county conventions were held to nominate independent tickets; and Codding, Durkee, and dozens of others were on the stump. An enumeration of the various meetings in Wisconsin would require almost as much space as would a list of those in Ohio.

In Iowa the news of Van Buren's nomination gave strength to the incipient Free Soil feeling, which in August led to local conventions, and in the latter part of September to a People's State Convention at Iowa City. This meeting passed the usual resolutions, and nominated a set of electors comprising two Democrats, one Whig, and one Liberty man.

By September, then, it seemed to be shown conclusively that the radical anti-slavery men of the Northwest were prepared to follow the Buffalo movement; but, beneath all this noisy activity, there lay in the minds of the more sagacious observers the consciousness that the Buffalo Convention had not united all the anti-slavery sentiment of the North. Orthodox Liberty men felt Van Buren's nomination as a slap in the face: the man who in 1836 had announced his purpose to veto any bill abolishing slavery in the District of Columbia, who in his long career had never by word or deed shown the slightest sympathy with abolitionists, was little better suited for their support than Henry Clay, whom, four years before, they had repudiated because they could never vote for any but an abolitionist. Notwithstanding this feeling, when the nomination of Van Buren was made upon a thoroughly anti-slavery platform, most of them joined the new party. Here and there a few zealous abolitionists declined to follow Chase and Leavitt; and to such Gerrit Smith's nomination and the Liberty League offered an easy asylum. The wonder is, that, trained in a school of narrowness for seven years, so few of the faithful refused to follow the Buffalo movement; and even they preferred to sit in dejected silence, while their less sensitive brethren stifled scruples by joining the Democratic Free Soilers in vigorous work for the new party.

In most of the States the Liberty organization vanished with the news of the Buffalo Convention; but here and there the name survived for a short time. In Ohio a Liberty convention in Medina County made a local nomination and stuck to its own ticket throughout the campaign, although a subsequent Free Soil convention ratified the Whig candidate. In Michigan the State Liberty party formally dissolved. In the latter part of August, a State Convention at Jackson unanimously resolved to support the Buffalo ticket, thus " putting an end to all the hopes of the Cass and Taylor factions that Liberty men would distract the Free Soil party by adhering to their separate organization."[1] The Liberty leaders, with very few exceptions, were the first to join the new party, although many of them did it with wry faces. In Indiana, for example, at the State Free Soil Convention, S. S. Harding said publicly that " it was with some difficulty that he got his own consent to go for Van Buren."[2] In Wisconsin, on the contrary, where for some months the local party had seemed on the point of joining the Liberty League, a sudden revulsion of feeling carried the leaders heart and soul into the new party; even the radical Booth, of the *Milwaukee Freeman*, returned from Buffalo a strong supporter of Van Buren, though a week earlier he had been threatening to vote for " the *Man* of this nation, Gerrit Smith."[3]

If the Liberty men, with a platform drawn by one of their own number, found it hard to join the new party, the anti-slavery Whigs of the country found it still harder. Great as was the abolitionists' dislike of Van Buren, it was nothing compared to the traditional Whig hatred, dating from the very foundation of their party. He was the same Van Buren in 1848 that he had always been; not one of the distinctly " Locofoco" doctrines had he abjured, except, perhaps, that of the unconstitutionality of internal improvements. He had not made a single concession. The ex-Whig editors of the Indiana *Free Territory Sentinel* could find no heartier praise than to say: "For our part, although we have hitherto acted with the Whigs and have opposed Mr. Van Buren (as we probably

[1] *Detroit Advertiser*, Aug. 31, 1848.
[2] *Indiana State Journal*, Sept. 1, 1848.
[3] *American Freeman*, Aug. 2, 1848.

should do again under the circumstances), yet . . . we cannot agree with Taylor men in charging him with being an absolute Demon. . . . That he has faults we readily admit, . . . but looking at the crisis in which our country is now placed, . . . we feel bound by the most solemn considerations, moral and political, to do what may be in our power in advocating the claims of Mr. Van Buren."[1]

Moreover, aside from the nomination, there were many things at the Buffalo Convention which failed to satisfy "Conscience" Whigs. Their delegates returned to their homes in New England, New York, and Ohio with long faces, and not infrequently gave vent to assertions of trickery and underhanded bargaining on the part of Chase and the Barnburners; in this opinion many Liberty men joined, feeling that Chase, Leavitt, and Stanton had played them false and had sacrificed Hale. Besides, things had too Democratic an air; Barnburners were too much in evidence, insisting on their own "regularity"; and the name "Free Democracy" applied to the new party had an unpleasant sound. Antislavery Whigs, outraged as they were at the conduct of their own party, felt their opposition to Taylor die away when the only opportunity offered them by the Buffalo Convention was that of supporting an unmitigated Democrat on a Democratic platform against their own party. Giddings, in close touch with the people, saw this clearly, and wrote to Sumner: "Our letters from Ohio assure us that it can be carried for any other man than Van Buren, and probably with him. There is a large class of Whigs, however, that would come to the support of almost any man who will not support him."[2] It was evident to the dullest observer that, should the Taylor advocates in the North have the shrewdness to take Free Soil ground, the chances were strong that Whig Free Soilers would return to their old ranks.

Political animosities developed new and strange forms in this campaign. Throughout the Northwest, Old Line Democrats — that is, either men of Southern birth or those on whom

[1] *Free Territory Sentinel*, Aug. 30, 1848.
[2] July 23, 1848: Sumner MSS.

anti-slavery principles had made no impression — acted in one way. At first deprecating the action of the New York Barnburners, they soon came to condemn it; and when the Utica and Buffalo nominations were made, they broke out into bitter maledictions. No term was too harsh, or sometimes too vile, to apply to Van Buren, the "traitor," the "hypocrite," the "Judas Iscariot of the nineteenth century." Everything that had ever been said against "abolitionists" was raked up and used again, to blacken the character and the motives of the ex-President. Far more dangerous to the success of the Free Soilers, however, was the attitude of those Democrats who, while supporting Cass, claimed to be fully as antislavery as Van Buren's followers. At the present day it seems incredible that these Free Soil Democrats could have believed, in view of the Nicholson letter, that Cass was a suitable anti-slavery candidate; yet such is the force of persistent assertion that it seems highly probable that its power was successful in hundreds of cases. Democratic papers, without a shadow of evidence to sustain them, claimed "Cass and Free Soil" as their party cry. "The Democratic party of Wisconsin is the true Free Soil party," said the Milwaukee *Wisconsin*[1] again and again. "Will you believe," cried W. P. Lynde, a Democratic Congressman from Wisconsin, "that Lewis Cass, whose interests and associations are all identified with the West, is not a Free Soil man? No! Gentlemen!"[2] "Gen. Cass," said the *Waukesha Democrat*, "is the friend of Free Territory, and his course on this subject is and has been consistent!"[3] The Democrats of the northern counties of Illinois went farther than this, and had the effrontery — no milder term is adequate — to issue an address to the Free Soilers, saying: "Gen. Cass is a Northern man and Western man, — born among the free hills of New England, reared and educated in the free West. At no one period of his life did he ever bend to the slave power. No one act of his long public career ever went to favor slave institutions."[4]

[1] Oct. 24, 1848.　　　　　　　　[2] *Wisconsin Freeman*, Aug. 30, 1848.
[3] Quoted *ibid.*, Sept. 20, 1848.
[4] *Chicago Journal*, Oct. 27, 1848.

With the Whigs matters took a somewhat different course. At first they were inclined to applaud the Free Soil movement, with the expectation that it would be confined to the Democratic party. " We rejoice that a portion of the Democrats of our State," said the *Detroit Advertiser*, " have given in their adhesion to the *Whig principles* of the Wilmot Proviso."[1] " Cheering indeed it is to Whigs," said the *Chicago Journal*, " to see this movement on the part of those against whom they have so earnestly battled. Whatever be the course of the [Buffalo] Convention, Whigs can look on without anything to fear from its action. . . . We are therefore pleased to see this Free Soil movement."[2] When the Buffalo Convention met, however, and the action of Massachusetts and Ohio Whigs, together with the spectacle of a son of John Quincy Adams on the ticket, showed that members of the party might, and probably would, vote the new ticket, a rapid change took place in the Whig attitude. Complacency vanished, and a vigorous denunciation of the new party took its place. From this time onward the Whigs aimed to prove two things : that Van Buren was unfit for any Whig to support; that the Whig party, with Taylor, was for free soil. " We claim to be as much opposed to the extension of slavery as any other person," said the *Indiana State Journal*. " If Gen. Taylor stood pledged, as Cass does, to veto [the Wilmot Proviso], we could not vote for him. Gen. Taylor stands upon the only true ground, — that of submission to the will of the People."[3] " What possible benefit," asked the *Detroit Advertiser*, " is to accrue from the deliberations of the Buffalo Convention? They can say nothing in favor of free soil, free men, or free speech that is not said daily by the Whig party. The members of that Convention know full well that the Whig party is the true anti-slavery party of the country. To ask a Whig to vote for Martin Van Buren is an insult."[4]

When the Liberty men participated in the new movement, all the smouldering rancor of 1844 flamed up to aggravate Whig objections. " The readiness with which the political abo-

[1] Jan. 15, 1848.
[2] July 24, 1848.
[3] July 31, 1848.
[4] Aug. 4, 1848.

litionists fraternize with the new faction calling itself the Free Soil party," said the *Indiana State Journal*, " is conclusive proof that it is but another name for abolitionism. The past acts of the abolitionists will best test the sincerity of their convictions." [1]   After rehearsing the " crime " of Birney in 1844, the *Milwaukee Sentinel* said: " And now the same leaders who helped to fasten these wrongs upon us are engaged in a like hopeful task. . . . Now can it be that any Whigs, with a keen remembrance of the campaign of 1844 still in their minds, will lend themselves to a repetition of the same third-party swindle? " [2]   The Whig State Central Committee of Michigan summed up the argument by saying: " Every Whig vote given to a third candidate helps to elect Cass.   The Whig party of the North has always gone to the utmost verge of the Constitution in its opposition to the slave power.   It is, it ever has been, a true free soil party. . . . Beware of the impracticable course which in 1844 made the loudest professed friends of freedom the means of annexing Texas." [3]

With all three parties claiming to be in favor of free soil, and each assailing the candidates of the other two as liars and hypocrites, the campaign had by September grown acrimonious to the last degree.   In two places, particularly, the bitterness reached its greatest strength, — in the Fourth Congressional District of Illinois, and on the Western Reserve of Ohio.   In Illinois everything hinged upon Wentworth's course.   He had been a staunch Wilmot Proviso man, and in his paper, the *Chicago Democrat*, had constantly advocated Free Soil principles; and although he placed the name of Cass at the head of his columns, not a word of comment appeared.   Day after day passed and still no sign was made, in spite of the taunt of the Whig *Journal*, " Keep it before the people that Wentworth dares not say a word in favor of Gen. Cass." [4]   While Wentworth was " on the fence," the district Democratic Convention met, and, under his influence, tabled a resolution supporting Cass, thus causing a bolt and a separate nomination

[1] July 31, 1848.   [2] Sept. 18, 1848.
[3] *Detroit Advertiser*, Oct. 10, 1848.
[4] *Chicago Journal*, June 3, 1848.

of J. B. Thomas as an "Administration Democrat." Had Wentworth at this juncture possessed the courage to throw in his lot with the new party, the history of Free Soil in the Northwest might have been different; for his personal popularity, joined to the intense anti-slavery feeling of that region, would have insured his election to stand beside Giddings and Durkee, and might have made the counties of northern Illinois as famous as the Western Reserve. After Taylor's nomination, however, the *Democrat* began to support Cass; and, to the disappointment of thousands in Illinois and Wisconsin, it was apparent that "Long John" had chosen to stay with his party. The bolting candidate then withdrew, and Wentworth was again triumphantly elected over Scammon and Lovejoy.

In Ohio, as usual, we expect to find the most interesting events during the time that elapsed between the Buffalo Convention and the national election. Since the Free Soil revolt was greatest among Whigs, the fight between Taylor men and Free Soilers was a repetition, on a larger scale, of the struggle of 1844. At the head of the Ohio Free Soil Whigs stood Giddings, whose popular hold on the Reserve was very strong; his power is only realized when we consider that he was able in one year to split in two the Whig party of that region, and to turn the strongest Whig district of 1844 into one of the strongest for Van Buren in 1848, and this in the teeth of a Free Soil Presidential nomination as distasteful to the Reserve as could possibly have been devised.

It would be interesting and profitable to consider the causes of Giddings's hold, and the ways in which it was manifested in 1848; the biographer of Cass sums it up in a sentence: "John Q. Adams led his district and showed it the way. But Giddings was the child of his surroundings, the voice and expression of the will of his constituents."[1] Upon his head fell the curses of all those Whigs who clung to the old party. When, in January, 1848, he refused to vote for Robert C. Winthrop for Speaker, and justified his course in a public letter, the *Chicago Journal* said: "It will take more than one such letter to convince the Whigs of his district and the country that he acted a

[1] A. C. McLaughlin, *Lewis Cass*, 253.

manly or patriotic part;"[1] and the *Cleveland Herald* said warn-
ingly: "We tell Mr. Giddings that for all he is, he is directly
indebted to the Whig party. Their caucuses have nominated
him. Whig votes have elected him. For twelve years he has
been fed and clothed upon Whig bounty."[2] From this time
the dislike of regular Whigs for Giddings increased daily, until,
when he renounced the Whig party, the *Indiana State Journal* called his action "the most cheering news we have heard
lately,"[3] and the *Chicago Journal* observed: "It is usually the
case when individuals part with their honor they abandon themselves to the worst passions of human nature."[4] On the Reserve itself, in spite of his "apostasy," enough Whigs stood by
him, at the regular convention of the party, to bring about his
nomination by 71 out of 95 votes. This was more than the
Taylor men could endure, and they supported an independent Whig candidate, in whose favor the regular Democratic
nominee presently resigned. In the intense bitterness of the
struggle, a former law instructor of Mr. Giddings, Mr. Elisha
Whittlesey, issued a printed leaflet charging Giddings with
having drawn unnecessary mileage as Congressman; and this
sheet was distributed all over his district.[5]

While this three-cornered fight was raging, the State election
took place in October. As the Free Soilers had no ticket,
and seemed to hold the balance of power, they counted on
deciding the election, and eagerly expected the result to show
their strength. Between Seabury Ford, the Whig nominee,
and J. B. Weller, the Democratic, no true anti-slavery man could
hesitate for a moment. Ford was not especially strong in his
opposition to slavery, but he was at least inclined that way,
whereas Weller was unqualifiedly pro-slavery; indeed, it was he
who had moved the censure of Giddings in 1842. Though not
supporting Ford with any enthusiasm, Free Soil papers in general
advised their readers to vote for him in order to rebuke Weller;[6]

[1] Jan. 15, 1848.   [2] Quoted in *True Democrat*, Jan. 8, 1848.
[3] July 12, 1848.   [4] July 18, 1848.
[5] See G. W. Julian, *Life of J. R. Giddings*, 253–255; and A. G. Riddle,
in *Magazine of Western History*, VI., 154–156.
[6] *True Democrat*, Oct. 9, 1848.

and it was confidently expected that the Whig ticket would receive a handsome majority. Ford, in order to avoid the fate of Henry Clay in 1844, absolutely refused to commit himself on political questions farther than to say that he should vote in November "by ballot." When the vote was counted, however, to the amazement of all, the expected Whig gains did not appear; and after some days, during which Weller was credited with the victory, Ford's election by a bare majority was finally conceded, as follows: Whig — Ford, 148,666; Democratic — Weller, 148,321.[1]

The effect of this vote on the Whig managers in Ohio was terrifying. In their alarm they at first tried to make it appear that more Free Soilers had voted for Weller than for Ford ; but this supposition was manifestly absurd. They were soon left face to face with the fact that their State candidate, aided presumably by the major part of the Free Soilers, was just able to win. It therefore seemed likely that, in November, Ohio, though a Whig State in national elections since 1836, would now go for Cass through the defection of former Whigs, now Free Soilers, to Van Buren. Such cries of rage went up, and such urgent appeals for help, that from every side Whig leaders rushed to the rescue. Said the *National Era :* "The most powerful efforts are being made to break down the Free Soil movement in Ohio. Messrs. Granger and Seward, we perceive, are to make a descent on the Western Reserve, and a large importation of Kentucky orators is announced. Horace Greeley, too, over his own name issued a few days since a manifesto as long as a Presidential Inaugural, appealing with weeping and wailing and lamentation to the Buckeyes to come to the help of ' Old Zach.' "[2] To these influences Tom Corwin, Ohio's favorite son, and B. F. Wade added their eloquence ; they stumped the Western Reserve; while, as the Cleveland *True Democrat* said, "the country was flooded with New York *Tribunes.*"

The closing weeks of October were stirring times. After the Whigs and Democrats of the Northwest had exhausted the capabilities of the English language in condemning, abusing, and vilifying the Free Soil party and its leaders, and in claiming for

---

[1] *True Democrat*, December, 1848.　　　[2] Oct. 26, 1848.

themselves the true Free Territory position, they now seemed to unite in an effort to cry down the new movement. It was asserted and reiterated *ad infinitum*, from Maine to Iowa, that the movement was dying away, that former Whigs and Democrats were returning to their parties, that the people had seen through the Buffalo swindle, and that on election day the discredited and exposed leaders of a hopeless cause would be left with only those behind them who four years before had followed the fanatic Birney. The Free Soilers, on their part, kept on hitting right and left, and with each succeeding week grew more and more determined. In spite of its newness, the party had no lack of mouthpieces, for there were at this time probably sixty-five or seventy newspapers in the Northwest that supported Van Buren.[1] In Ohio and Wisconsin, up to the eve of the election, the Free Soilers talked as if they really expected to carry the State. There was no flagging, except among a few Whigs, and no loss of courage. As the storm of abuse grew fiercer, the Free Soilers responded in kind, and from stump and newspaper hurled back their defiance and hatred of Cass and Taylor in terms fully as opprobrious as those with which Van Buren was assailed.

The campaign came to an end on November 9, after a contest of unparalleled bitterness and blackguardism. In the country at large the vote stood as follows: Taylor, 1,360,099; Cass, 1,220,544; Van Buren, 291,263. Cass carried every Northwestern State.[2] Distasteful as was his attitude on slavery and on internal improvements to many people, particularly to

[1] Of these the names of fifty-three are known, of which eight were Liberty, eight Whig, thirteen Democratic, and twenty-four campaign papers. Ohio had twenty-one, Illinois eleven, Indiana eight, Michigan eight, Wisconsin six, Iowa two. On the Reserve alone there were nine papers.

[2]

	Cass.	Taylor.	Van Buren.
Ohio	154,775	138,360	35,354
Indiana	74,745	69,907	8,100
Michigan	30,687	23,940	10,389
Illinois	56,300	53,047	15,774
Wisconsin	15,001	13,747	10,418
Iowa	12,093	11,144	1,126

See official returns in *Whig Almanac*, 1849.

business men, there were thousands of farmers and backwoods-
men to whom these matters were of small account beside the
fact that the Democratic candidate was a representative Northwestern man and a pioneer. Nevertheless, in Illinois and Wisconsin the Free Soil revolt came very near giving these States
to Taylor. In Ohio, on the contrary, Cass profited directly
from the third-party movement, for there the Whig revolt was
much greater than the Democratic, so that, though Cass received the highest Democratic vote on record, the Whig vote
was less than that of 1844.

In the States taken separately the Free Soilers had varying
fortunes, but in none of them, except perhaps in Wisconsin, did
they begin to approach the success which they had anticipated.
In Ohio the total Free Soil vote of 35,000 was less than it
might have been because of Van Buren's candidacy, especially
on the Western Reserve ; for, as the *True Democrat* said, " In
no portion of the Union were prejudices so strong against
Martin Van Buren. . . . There were many Free Soil men who
could not vote for Mr. Van Buren, they had not confidence in
the man. . . . John P. Hale, Judge McLean, or any other man
would have received at least 10,000 more votes on the Reserve
than were cast for Martin Van Buren." [1] The net diminution in
the total vote was 8,474, nearly all of which was due to disappointed Whigs and Liberty men, who in the event of another
nomination would have voted the third ticket. The low vote in
the State at large, as well as on the Reserve, was charged by
Chase to the efforts of the Whig orators who had stumped the
State in October. Of Corwin's work he said: " He traversed
the whole State speaking to large assemblies and to small, at
the principal points and in obscure villages, saying, '*I know*
Gen. Taylor will not veto the Proviso.' Though we did all
we could to counteract it, yet, being scattered over a large

---

[1] Nov. 14–18, 1848. This claim is probably not excessive, for the votes
of 1844 and 1848 compare as follows: —

	Democratic.	Whig.	Liberty.	Total.
1844 . . .	20,460	28,017	3,254	51,731
1848 . . .	12,876	14,511	15,870	43,257
	− 7,584	− 13,506	+ 12,616	−8,474

territory with hardly any pecuniary resources and a very imperfect organization and little or no mutual concert or co-operation among our committees or speakers, all our efforts did not avail much."[1] The result merely goes to show how difficult it is, when party feeling is high, to get men to abandon old associates for new. Chase, Lewis, Giddings, Root, Brinckerhoff, had done all that men could do; yet the Free Soilers outside the Reserve were but slightly more successful than the Liberty party had been.

In Indiana, the vote of 8,100, although large as compared with the previous Liberty maximum of 2,278, was too slight to have much significance in the result. It seems to have been composed of Whigs and Democrats in equal proportions. In Michigan, Cass's personal popularity raised the Democratic vote considerably above any previous mark. The Free Soil vote of 10,389 was almost three times as large as the Liberty maximum, and singularly like it in details of composition and distribution; it was drawn largely from Whigs and was very evenly scattered over the State. The leaders of the party were mainly Democrats.

In Illinois, the total of 15,774, almost exactly three times the Liberty vote of 1846, came from the northwestern counties, and was drawn almost entirely from Democratic ranks.[2] Had Wentworth thrown his influence on the side of Van Buren, it seems not unlikely that the Free Soil vote, increased to still greater extent in this region, might have drawn enough Democratic votes to give the State to Taylor. Wisconsin made the best proportional showing in the Northwest, its 10,418 Free Soil votes marking an increase of 9,284 over the vote of the Liberty party, and making twenty-six per cent. of the total. The intimate connection of the vote with local conditions of settlement without regard to State lines is indicated by the fact that it was concentrated in the southeastern counties, closely contiguous to the Free Soil regions of Illinois. Of the new members of the party

[1] Chase to Sumner, Nov. 27, 1848: Sumner MSS.

[2]		Democratic.	Whig.	Antislavery.
	1846	58,576	36.939	5,147
	1848	56,300	53,047	15,774

rather more were Democrats than Whigs. Iowa made its first appearance in a national election with an anti-slavery vote of 1,126, concentrated in the southeastern counties bordering on Illinois. Many, probably half, of the Iowa Free Soilers were Liberty men ; the remainder were largely Whig.[1]

In Congressional and State elections the Free Soilers of the Northwest exhibited toward the old parties all possible relations, from complete identity to absolute separation. The phrase " Free Soil " had no significance in local matters during the summer, for it was as freely claimed by candidates of the regular parties as by the followers of Van Buren. Since the Buffalo Convention was not held until August 9, the Free Soil party had no time to organize in those States which held elections in summer or in early autumn. Men who had intended to support Van Buren voted as they saw fit, usually for men of their previous political faith, in whose behalf, from August to October, the cry of " Free Soil " was raised in deafening chorus by eager partisans of both parties, in every district where the anti-slavery sympathies of voters might affect the result. In Ohio, Giddings and several other Congressmen who were classed as Free Soilers were put in regular nomination by Whig conventions, and were elected. Fusion, properly so called, was absent ; but confusion reigned. In the State legislative elections the same conditions existed, " Free Soil " Whigs and Democrats being chosen, as well as unclassified members of the old parties, together with two or three independents.

The Indiana State election occurred in August, while as yet the Free Soil movement was inchoate. No Free Soilers as such were chosen, although there were some coalitions of Liberty men and Democrats. Illinois and Iowa, having summer elections also, usually lacked distinct Free Soil candidates; although in Illinois the Liberty party still existed and in Iowa some third-party tickets were run. Wisconsin and Michigan alone in the Northwest, held State and national elections on the same day and hence had time to disentangle the new party from the old ones. In both States separate Free Soil candidates were nominated for each Congressional district, and many separate

[1] Letters of I. H. Julian to the author, May, 1896.

legislative and local nominations were made. By November, Wisconsin Free Soilers were more thoroughly organized than those of any other Northwestern State ; and in the election they had the extreme satisfaction of electing to Congress, from the southeastern district, a stanch Liberty man, Charles Durkee ; they also chose nearly twenty members of the legislature, some of them by coalition.

In Michigan the course of events took a different turn. In October, after Free Soil organization had progressed far toward completeness, a movement began toward Whig coalition. In Oakland, Wayne, Monroe, and probably in other counties, conventions of these two parties fraternized, and united on common tickets. " We do not differ upon any question of State or local policy now before us," said the Wayne County Free Soilers ; " let us arouse from our slumbers, throw to the winds our dissensions, and present a common front to our common foe." The fact that the name of S. M. Holmes, hitherto a leading Liberty man, was attached to the foregoing appeal indicates a radical change in anti-slavery policy. Still farther to signalize this feeling for union, D. C. Lawrence, the Free Soil nominee for Congress in the Second District, in a public letter resigned in favor of W. Sprague, the Whig candidate. This action was greeted with a salvo of Whig applause, the same newspapers which the day before had been vituperating the Free Democracy now beginning to find the new party not wholly bad. " The Hon. D. C. Lawrence," said the *Detroit Advertiser*, " shows a devotion and attachment to Free Soil principles alike honorable to himself and the cause of freedom. . . . Is it policy under these circumstances to contend about men while the enemy secure the victory? We think not. Let those among the Free Soil [*i. e.*, Wilmot Proviso] candidates who have done most in the cause during the campaign be united upon and supported." The self-abnegation of the Michigan Free Soilers might be excellent policy ; but some element other than mere devotion to principle is suggested by the fact that coalitions were all between Free Soilers and Whigs. The real reason lay in the strong per

1 *Detroit Advertiser*, Oct. 31, 1848.
2 *Ibid.*, Nov. 1, 1848.

sonal antagonism felt toward Cass by very many of the Free Soilers, who, in their desire to destroy his hold on the State, were willing to go to the length of union with Taylor Whigs.[1]

Michigan's action was the first unmistakable sign that the Free Soil party, in spite of the large admixture of Liberty men, was to adopt a fundamentally different policy from that adhered to by political abolitionists since 1840 ; but in every Northwestern State there was in this election a confusion between parties, a vagueness in the sense of the term "Free Soil," and a willingness to coalesce, all pointing the same way. If the new party was ready for coalition, this election of 1848 opened a wide field ; for in each Northwestern State the Free Soilers held the balance of power. This advantage was not unprecedented in Liberty party annals ; but, owing to the separatist policy of the abolitionists, hitherto it had not been pushed to its result ; thenceforth it was destined to become of the utmost importance.

[1] Ann Arbor *True Democrat*, Sept. 21, Oct. 12, 1848.

CHAPTER XI.

THE OHIO SENATORIAL CONTEST.

1849.

WHEN the election of 1848 was over, the exhausted Free Soil leaders of the country sat down to consider the state of their cause. It was evident even to the most enthusiastic among them that the political revolt, dramatic as it had been, had failed to create at a blow the hoped-for Northern anti-slavery party. No State had been carried for Van Buren; nor was the Free Soil ticket higher than third in number of votes, except in New York, Vermont, and Massachusetts. Possibly this result was due to the fact that Van Buren's candidacy had hurt the cause by repelling anti-slavery Whigs; for it is certain that thousands who, after the Philadelphia Convention, had vowed never to support Taylor, preferred to eat their words rather than to vote for the hated "little Van." "The recent vote," said an Iowan, "was no test of opinion in the Northwest. Many strong Free Soilers would not support the Van Buren ticket for various reasons, — dislike of the man and of the managers and of some points in the policy of the party, and because they believed that to vote for it was virtually to defeat the object in view."[1] The *Western Citizen*, of Chicago, said: "By the nomination of J. P. Hale as candidate, the Free Soilers would have secured a much firmer hold upon the moral sentiment of the country. . . . Mr. Hale would have polled a much larger vote than Van Buren. He probably would not have secured as many from the old Democratic party, but we mistake if the de-

[1] Quoted by H. Von Holst, *Constitutional History of the United States*, III., 403, note.

ficiency would not have been more than made up by adherents from the Whig ranks." [1]   In any case, regrets were of no use, and the Free Soil leaders recognized their failure.

Had the new party, then, any reason for continuing?   Had not the Barnburners done all that could be expected by their effective protest against Cass?   Would it not be proper in State matters to allow other considerations than the Wilmot Proviso to shape the course of the party?   The Buffalo platform had resolved " to fight on, fight ever, till victory shall reward our efforts " ; and now in 1848 the Free Soil press in the Northwest almost unanimously avowed itself in favor of keeping up the party until its objects should be attained.   " The campaign of 1848 is now ended," said the Cleveland *True Democrat*, " but not so the mission of our party.   Yesterday's sun went down upon a field of political strife where truth and principle were worsted.   To-day it rises in glory upon our invincible host; . . . this day begins the campaign of 1852." [2]   " Rapid as has been our progress," cried the Ravenna *Star*, " from this hour we date the commencement of a more rapid progress.   *Fight on !*" [2]   The Sandusky *Daily Mirror* asserted : " There is nothing in the present aspect of affairs to dishearten the friends of Freedom. . . . The great Northwest will stand shoulder to shoulder with New York in the contest." [3]   The *Western Reserve Chronicle*, after a regretful farewell to the Whig party, said, " By the conduct of the Hunkers our organization is made a distinct one, and it becomes our duty to use every laudable exertion to extend Free Soil influence by electing Free Soil champions to office." [4]   " The present Free Soil movement is not restricted to a single election," said the *Western Citizen*.   " Even if we should be successful and elect our candidates we should not disband.   Much less will we do so before we have elected any to carry into execution the will of the Free Soil people.   We feel more encouraged to work on and fight on.   The right will triumph, though the reformer may be despised and a radical party overborne by numbers for the time being.   Work on and keep working." [4]

[1] Quoted in the Milwaukee *Wisconsin*, Nov. 17, 1848.
[2] Quoted in *National Era*, Nov. 23, 1848.
[3] Quoted *ibid.*, Nov. 30, 1848.   [1] Quoted *ibid.*

If the new party were to be permanent, it was confronted by the same problem which had vexed the Liberty men for seven years, — the task of building up a new political organization until it should be strong enough to supplant one of the older ones. This end the Liberty party had tried to attain by absolute separation; but such a course the Free Democracy, in 1849, almost without exception, declined to adopt. They preferred instead to bring their influence to bear directly upon State and Congressional candidates of other parties, whenever it was possible to do so, — a decision that plunged the new party into a career of intrigues, bargaining, and "practical politics," strikingly unlike the open, independent action of its predecessor.

The policy of opportunism was more thoroughly carried out in the Northwest than elsewhere, owing to the peculiar nature of the Western parties. In New England, although coalition played a small part, the Free Democracy showed much of that fixity which since 1841 had characterized the Liberty party. In the Middle States the Free Soil party simply vanished, more completely even than had the Liberty party after 1844 ; but in the Northwest the third party, having some of the toughness of the New England wing, exhibited a greater daring in coalitions and political manœuvres, which led to prodigious fluctuations. In each State the local organization so followed its own course that in no two do we find a closely similar, or even parallel, party history; until in 1852 a Presidential campaign brought local managers once more into line. To treat the States together chronologically is, then, impossible, and the method adopted will be to take each separately for the years 1849–50.

The new party suffered in Ohio as in all the other Western States except Wisconsin, from the fact that it had not had time to disentangle itself entirely from the old parties till after the State election in October. Hardly was the national election over, when the evil results of this confusion became apparent. In the Senate of the legislature which met in December, 1848, there were seventeen Democrats, fourteen Whigs, and three Free Soilers; there were thirty-two Democratic Representatives, thirty Whigs, and eight Free Soilers; besides some contested seats.[1] A serious difficulty, which confronted the legislature at the outset, was a dispute over a law passed by the Whigs the year before, dividing Hamilton County into Representative districts. The Whigs expected thus to gain two members; but the Democrats held the law unconstitutional both in its substance and in the manner of its enactment. To mark their convictions, the Democrats of Hamilton County had voted without regard to the new law; and to their candidates, Pugh and Pierce, a Democratic election clerk had given certificates. Party feeling ran high, overriding for the time even national issues. When the day for convening the Legislature arrived, in December, the Democrats, breaking into the Capitol at an early hour, swore in all their claimants, and, when the astonished Whigs appeared, were in session as the regular legislature. Without any hesitation the Whigs formed a House of their own in another part of the room, and a dead-lock was the result, neither side willing to yield an inch. This was the great opportunity of the eight so-called Free Soil members, who held the balance of power; but they lost their heads and went with their former parties. Five had been elected by Whig votes, one by Democratic, and two only, Townshend of Lorain, and Morse of Lake, as independent third-party men.

In the Senate, meanwhile, the Free Soilers, holding the balance of power, had controlled organization by an arrangement with the Whigs; and their example inspired the House Free Soilers to recover themselves and take the lead in overtures for some plan of organization. For this purpose A. G. Riddle was sworn into both the rival lower Houses, serving as an official mouthpiece. Townshend, a former Liberty man, was first in the field, with a proposal to begin by excluding all the contestants till the House should have appointed certain designated persons as temporary officers; and then to make it the first business to decide the contested cases, no man being allowed to

---

[1] For general accounts of the Ohio session of 1848-49, see A. G. Riddle, in *Magazine of Western History*, VI., 341 *seq.*, and in *Republic*, IV., 179 (1875); N. S. Townshend, in *Magazine of Western History*, VI., 623; D. J. Ryan, *History of Ohio*, 144 *seq.*; *Ohio Standard*, Dec. 7, 1848-Feb. 28, 1849.

vote on his own case. To this proposition the Democrats agreed; but the Whigs were unwilling by any such arrangement to admit even temporarily the Democratic Representatives from Hamilton County to whom the clerk had illegally given certificates, and hence refused to adopt it. Some days passed in bitter wrangling, until Riddle brought forward a second plan much like Townshend's; and after nearly three weeks of unseemly division the Houses finally came together on the basis thus suggested.

So far the Free Soilers had acted successfully and skilfully; but meanwhile trouble was brewing. In anticipation of the success of their scheme for organization, they had held a caucus to determine their action in regard to offices. "There was present," says a survivor, "a gentleman of large political experience, although not a member of either House, who counselled perfect unity of action."[1] This may have been E. S. Hamlin, formerly a Whig Congressman, J. A. Briggs of Cleveland, or, less likely, S. P. Chase, all of whom were in Columbus at the time; but, whoever it was, his advice was not conclusive. Two of the Free Soilers, Morse and Townshend, both elected independently, and the latter a Liberty man since 1841, were not willing to pledge themselves to follow the caucus, because they felt strong suspicions of the other Western Reserve members, on the ground that they had too recently become members of the Whig party to act impartially. The results were hard words and a split, Morse and Townshend ceasing to consult with the others. Nevertheless, with the hope of conciliating the two recusants, the Free Soil caucus planned to nominate Townshend for Speaker and Mathews for clerk; but on the day of the election Townshend declined, and Johnson, a Free Soil Whig, was nominated in his place, and the Whig caucus also designated him.

In fact, two distinct intrigues had begun between the separate factions of the Free Soilers and the old parties. Riddle, Lee, and the other ex-Whigs had entered into a "deal" with the Taylor men in regard to the offices, hoping to get their support later in the one overshadowing event of the session, the election of a

[1] N. S. Townshend, in *Magazine of Western History*, VI., 626.

United States Senator to succeed William Allen.   On the other hand, Morse and Townshend, with the active assistance of S. P. Chase, and of E. S. Hamlin, the editor of the *Ohio Standard*, had, with the same purpose in view, begun negotiations with the Democrats.[1]   Chase's Democratic leanings, continually growing in strength since 1845, had now reached such a point that he felt himself in all essentials a member of the national Democratic party, and held firmly the conviction that in that party lay the hope for anti-slavery action.   In his eyes the Free Soil party was as "Democratic" as the Old Hunkers themselves.   There was in his mind no room for doubt that the Democratic view in the Hamilton County case, as in all other matters, was correct; and to this opinion he soon brought Hamlin, Morse, and Townshend, although, by the testimony of many persons, Townshend had declared in 1848 that the Whig statute was constitutional.[2]

The first inkling of the truth in regard to the position of Townshend and Morse came to the other six Free Soilers when, immediately after temporary organization, the House, according to programme, voted upon the Hamilton County contest. Townshend voted for the admission of the Democrats, and had Morse done likewise they would have been admitted.   To the surprise of both parties, the result was a tie, 35–35.   The Democrats, who had been led by Chase to think that the two independent Free Soilers would vote with them, were furiously angry; but Chase's efforts soothed them.[3]   The other six Free Soilers, on their part, and the Whigs also, scented mischief. "It is a question upon which men may and do honestly differ," wrote J. A. Briggs to the Cleveland *True Democrat*, " but there are strange rumors." [4]

The next day came a second surprise.   Townshend and Morse, in the election of Speaker, voted for Breslin, the Democratic nominee, electing him over Johnson, the " regular " Free

---

[1] R. B. Warden, *Life of Chase*, 329.   See entries in Chase's diary, Jan. 1 and 2, 1849.

[2] *True Democrat*, April 4, 1849.

[3] R. B. Warden, *Life of Chase*, 330 ; Chase's diary, Jan. 2, 1849.

[4] *True Democrat*, Jan. 6, 1848.

Soil and Whig candidate, by a vote of 36 to 34.   Stanley
Mathews, like Townshend a former Liberty man and a personal
friend of Chase, was then by Democratic votes elected clerk
over Swift, the Free Soil and Whig nominee.   It was evident
that Townshend and Morse held the power in their own hands,
and were using it without regard to the wishes of the other six
Free Soilers.   When this fact became generally known, anti-
slavery men in all parts of the State began to take sides.   In
Cincinnati, the home of Chase and Mathews, they congratulated
themselves on the successful course of matters in the legislature,
and applauded Townshend and Morse ; but on the Western
Reserve, where a majority of Free Soilers had been Whigs, and
where Democratic success was utterly hateful, there was an outbreak of dismay and distrust.   " We don't see how they can justify their conduct," said the *True Democrat;* " we shall not
undertake to do it for them."   " There is a good deal of unpleasant feeling here," wrote J. A. Briggs from Columbus. "We
are afraid that the ambition of some *individual* for a seat in the
Senate will lead Free Soilers to pander to Loco-focoism." [1]
This shaft pointed directly at Chase, whose activity in arranging
matters could not pass unnoticed.   Townshend, on his part,
wrote a defiant letter.   It seems that some Free Soiler had approached him with the proposal that, if he were elected Speaker,
he should resign to let in a Whig.   This he construed as an
insult, and so voted for Breslin to " save the Free Soil party
from being dissolved in Whiggery."   " The whole charge of
bargain and sale amounts to this," he concluded, " that Messrs.
Chase, Hamlin, Morse, and myself were not willing to be sponged
up and identified with Whiggery." [2]   Naturally, such a letter as
this failed to help matters, and by the second week of January the
split between the two and the six was hopeless.   In the Senate,
meanwhile, to keep up the excitement, an outbreak occurred
when Randall, the Free Soil Speaker, announced the election of
Governor Ford.   At this news the Democrats, who had hoped
to get in Weller, raved and cursed and threatened violence.[3]

[1] *True Democrat*, Jan. 10, 1849.

[2] *Ibid.*, Jan. 19, 1849 ; *Ohio Standard*, Jan. 23, 1849.

[3] *Ibid.*, Jan. 13, 1849.

During these days of intrigue and distrust, the first delegated State Free Soil convention met at Columbus. D. R. Tilden, an ex-Whig, presided; and after a prolonged debate, in which considerable diversity of opinion was manifested, a platform was adopted to define the new party's position in State affairs. The main points emphasized were, a repeal of the Black laws, a proportional property tax, homestead exemption, a ten-hour law, opposition to the chartering of corporations and to the banking law, and a demand for a new constitution, — matters hitherto foreign to anti-slavery platforms. Many ex-Whigs from the Western Reserve, according to a correspondent of Dr. Bailey, " dissented from all in the platform of a Democratic character and tendency, and especially from the last resolution which contemplated a permanent organization. Only one, however, declared openly that he could not act with us as a distinct and permanent party." [1] The convention adjourned without having made much impression on public feeling; for, in view of the state of things in the legislature, declarations of harmony counted for little.

Meanwhile the course of politics pursued its tortuous way. An election committee of five was appointed by the chairman, with Townshend, the Free Soil Representative, in possession of the casting vote ; it reported in favor of the Democratic contestants from Hamilton County, and, by the usual majority of two, Pugh and Pierce were given the contested seats. Townshend and Morse, however, still held the balance of power. The Whig party all over the State was by this time fairly maddened by these continual Democratic successes, and raised a chorus of vituperation against Townshend, Morse, and especially Chase, who by common consent was accused of having come to Columbus during the session with the sole purpose of lobbying for his own election as Senator. The Democratic press said little; and Chase's only defence was found in the *Cincinnati Globe*, formerly edited by Stanley Mathews, who, it will be remembered had been elected clerk by the " deal"; in the Washington *National Era*, whose editor, Dr. Bailey, was one of Chase's warmest admirers, and who gained his knowledge of the pro-

[1] *True Democrat*, Jan. 4, 1849; *National Era*, Jan. 18, 1849.

ceedings at Columbus mostly from Chase himself; and in one or two other papers. These journals claimed that Townshend and Morse were the only independent men in the legislature ; that the Whig Free Soilers pressed their views in caucus "with an earnestness bordering on dictation"; that they were " mere nominal Free Soil men whose object appeared to be to make the Free Soil organization subservient to the success of mere Whig measures and ideas"; and that, if Townshend and Morse were not sustained, " they must not be surprised to see the Free Soil organization resolve itself into its original elements." As to Chase, they said that the insinuation of a bargain for the Senatorship was " purely gratuitous and utterly false," that "the political position of Mr. Chase could have been suggested by no other considerations than the most disinterested convictions of duty."[1] "It is true," said the *Ohio Standard*, edited by E. S. Hamlin, " that Mr. Chase, by the solicitations of many Free Soilers, is a candidate for the United States Senate. He has a right to be a candidate for that or any other office, and the fact that he is such is no evidence that he is for selling out the party."[2] Having arranged the organization of the House and the settlement of the Hamilton County case, Chase's " duty" no longer kept him at Columbus. He returned to Cincinnati, but continued in daily communication with his friends.

Morse now brought forward a bill to repeal the Black Laws, which on January 30 passed the legislature as follows: Senate, 24–11; House, 56–10. Thus the " blot on the statute book," the object of anti-slavery attack for fourteen years, was finally removed by a bargain with the Democrats. In view of the large majorities, it was claimed by the Whig Free Soilers that no bargain was needed, and that Townshend and Morse could derive no credit from the repeal; but this claim seems not very plausible.[3] The prevailing sentiment among Democrats was so strongly against repeal, that without a bargain it seems doubtful whether enough of them would have voted with the anti-slavery Whigs and Free Soilers to carry the measure. As it was, they voted

---

[1] *Cincinnati Globe*, Jan. 24, 1849.   [2] Feb. 2, 1849.

[2] A. G. Riddle, in *Republic*, IV., 183 (1875).

only under severe party pressure. One of them, together with a Whig, tried by hiding to dodge the vote, and had to be dragged in by the sergeant-at-arms amidst the ironical applause of the Assembly Chamber.[1]

The legislature was next obliged to face the questions of a choice of a Senator and two State judges. The Whig Free Soilers had been from an early date hoping to elect their idol Giddings to the Senate, while the *Cincinnati Globe* and the *National Era* had been urging Chase. As early as October 26, 1848, Dr. Bailey in the *National Era* suggested Chase as " a man uniting in an eminent degree fitness for Senatorial office, trustworthiness and availability." The *Cincinnati Globe* preferred him to Giddings, saying: " Mr. Giddings' peculiar sphere of usefulness and distinction is on the floor of the American Commons. The omission to select him for the present vacancy should be regarded as the best tribute to his character and position. . . . We respectfully present the name of S. P. Chase as a worthy and capable candidate." [2] The *True Democrat*, on the other hand, said: " The Free Soil men will present J. R. Giddings as their candidate. . . . S. P. Chase has been named. . . . Mr. Chase is a young man and high honors yet await him. Work and wait is a good motto." [3]

By January, 1849, it was perfectly well understood that the choice lay between these two, and feeling ran constantly higher. Chase, anxiously watching affairs from Cincinnati, wrote numerous letters to Dr. Bailey, who in Chase's interest urged upon Giddings to use his influence to calm the excitement of his followers. Bailey wrote to Chase: " He is modestly ambitious, would like to be U. S. Senator . . . if the Free Soil men will unite on him. If they cannot or will not . . . he says that you and you alone, by all means, are the man. I told him he ought to write to one of his Free Soil friends in the legislature." [4] Giddings at once wrote to Randall, Townshend, and others, urging them to combine on Chase if he himself were out of the question. A little later, finding the breach still unhealed, Chase

[1] *Cincinnati Globe*, Feb. 7, 1849.   [2] *Ibid.*
[3] Jan. 24, 1849.
[4] Chase to E. S. Hamlin, Jan. 20, 1849.   Chase MSS.

wrote directly to Giddings, practically asking him to withdraw. No sooner was the letter gone than he repented, and wrote to his friend Hamlin at Columbus: "I said to him that he being in Congress, and I out, the interests of the cause required my election or that of some other reliable man rather than his. I may be wrong in this, misled perhaps by the ' ambition ' so freely ascribed to me. If so, let Giddings be chosen, I shall not complain. I cannot help thinking, however, that the election of one who has been longer convinced of the necessity and is more thoroughly identified with the policy, of a distinct and permanent free Democratic organization, will do the *cause* and the *friends of the cause* more good." [1]   Naturally, Chase's "ambition" did not prevent his friends from continuing to work hard in his interest, so long as such excellent reasons were furnished. Moreover, Giddings's modesty led him to agree with Chase as to the advisability of remaining in the House.   He wrote in his journal, January 24: "By the mail of this evening I received letters from Columbus which speak cheerfully of my prospects for the Senate.   One from Dr. Townshend gives me some little hope of election, for which however I do not feel anxious, as I think I can do more good in the House, where I have established an influence, than I can in the Senate, where I should meet with intellects of a higher order, — men of nerve, experience, and of far greater intelligence.   But the moral effect of my election would be great, and on that account I feel a desire to succeed to that office." [2]

No combination could be formed for Giddings.   During the month of January the ex-Whig Free Soil men made persistent but vain efforts to get all the Taylor men to support him.   Though a majority of the Whig caucus were willing, the members from Cuyahoga County could not be induced to condone his " apostasy," [3] and the attempt finally had to be given up.   "For some time past," said the *Standard*, "the Whigs have been urged to consent to vote for Giddings . . . but they have steadily refused. Why?   They were afraid that by so doing they would render

---

[1] Chase to E. S. Hamlin, Jan. 28, 1849.

[2] G. W. Julian, *Life of J. R. Giddings*, 267.

[3] *Ibid.*

themselves offensive to the incoming administration. On all questions of National policy they knew him to be a Whig. But if elected he would not sustain the administration in its pro-slavery course. This they knew, and because of this he was defeated." [1]

The way, then, seemed clear for the ex-Whig Free Soil members to follow Giddings's advice by uniting on Chase; but even with Giddings out of the race they would try some other man rather than unite with Townshend and Morse. The Whig caucus offered to support Judge McLean, but he telegraphed his refusal.[2] At the last minute an effort was made to unite on J. C. Vaughn, but it failed, and the Whigs and Free Soilers went into the senatorial convention with their original candidates, Ewing and Giddings.

Townshend, Morse, and Hamlin as Chase's agent, had taken an impartial course: they had offered to support Giddings for Senator and to vote for Whig nominees for judges, or to support Chase and vote for Democratic caucus candidates for the judge-ships. Townshend's belief that the Whigs, anxious to save what they could from the wreck of the session, would all accept the offer, proved ill founded. Eventually the Democrats proved more complaisant, as they had every reason to be, and an arrange-ment on the basis of Townshend's offer was perfected. When the fateful day came, the result of the balloting showed Chase to be elected by the fifty-three Democrats with Townshend and Morse, the other Free Soilers voting to the last for Giddings, and the Whigs, except three, adhering grimly to Ewing.[3] One

---

[1] *Ohio Standard*, Feb. 23, 1849.

[2] Notes of an interview with E. S. Hamlin, taken by Albert Bushnell Hart; see also *National Era*, Feb. 22, 1849.

[3] The four ballots ran as follows: —

	I.	II.	III.	IV.
Chase	14	52	55	55
Ewing	41	41	39	39
Giddings	9	8	9	11
Vaughn	—	—	2	1
Allen	27	1	—	—
Scattering	4	—	—	—
Blank	11	4	2	—

The third ballot was void, since there was one vote too many.

of the Whig Free Soilers, A. G. Riddle, who throughout the
session had shown greater independence than his colleagues,
stood ready to vote for Chase if his support should be necessary
to secure his election; but the others would sooner have seen
even a pro-slavery man go in. The "deal" was then consum-
mated by the election, as judges, of R. P. Spaulding and W. B.
Caldwell, Democrats, over Edward Wade and B. S. Cowen, the
Free Soil caucus nominees; and the legislature soon adjourned,
after one of the most important sessions in the history of the
State.

The repeal of the Black Laws and the election of an anti-slavery
Senator met with approbation on every side, even from Free
Soil Whigs, who loathed from the bottom of their souls the
means by which these results had been accomplished. "No
event has given us more satisfaction than the election of Mr.
Chase," said the *Western Citizen*, although it admitted that
Chase's "conservatism" had caused "many of his friends
to suspect his unwavering constancy to the anti-slavery movement."[1] The *True Democrat*, swallowing its wrath, said: "The
election of Mr. Chase will be gratifying to the Free Soil men of
the country. . . The slave propagandists will find him a match
for the strongest."[2] "Hurrah for Ohio!" cried the *Western Reserve Chronicle*. "Our first choice has been Mr. Giddings. We
preferred his election not because we thought him *the* best man,
. . . but out of personal preference. . . . Our next choice was
Mr. Chase. We certainly have no regrets."[3] The *Ashtabula
Sentinel* called the election of Chase "a triumph of principle,"
and the *National Era* and the *Cincinnati Globe*, which had all
along supported him, were of course delighted.

On Townshend and Morse, however, and in a less degree on
Mathews and Hamlin, fell condemnation more violent than had
been heard since the days of Birney and the Garland forgery.
They were accused of bargaining away their principles for office,
and of changing front on the Hamilton County question for the
sake of obtaining Democratic votes. An extract from the
Cleveland Herald illustrates the amenities of the Whig papers.[4]

[1] Feb. 27, 1849.   [2] Feb. 24, 1849.   [3] Feb. 28, 1849.
[4] "Of all wretches known in the records of infamy none can compare

What cut the Western Reserve Free Soilers to the heart was the vote of Townshend and Morse for Spaulding and against Edward Wade, on the ground, as E. S. Hamlin said, that " after obtaining the Senator the Free Soilers could not well obtain the Supreme judges." " Out upon such ethics, away with such hypocrisy ! " cried the *True Democrat ;* " it smells of corruption." [1] Even the mild *Western Reserve Chronicle*, while approving the election of Chase, added: " We do not hesitate to condemn in strong terms the election of Mr. Spaulding." [2] It would be easy to fill pages with the laments and bitter maledictions of the ex-Whig Free Soilers; but perhaps the recent statement of one of the leading participants in the election shows how deep an impression this incident made upon the minds of Ohio Whigs: " Whatever may be said of the morality or the expediency of the course pursued, no doubt can exist of its effect upon Mr. Chase and his career. It lost to him at once and forever the confidence of every Whig of middle age in Ohio. Its shadow, never wholly dispelled, always fell upon him and hovered near and darkened his pathway at the critical places in his political after life." [3]

Just what verdict to pronounce on this memorable contest is a question hard to decide. Judged by the results, it was a great success and an equally great failure, for, though it elected an anti-slavery Senator to stand beside John P. Hale, it nearly ruined the Ohio Free Soil Party. A bargain of some sort, however, was inevitable; and to condemn Townshend and Morse, as the other Free Soilers did, because they co-operated with the Democrats, was really absurd, though it seems that the same end might have been attained with less friction, and consequently

with this black-hearted miscreant from Lorain County. Of Morse I say little. He is so far below the heathen in everything that goes to make a man that time spent over him would be poorly appropriated. He is more fool than knave, and a good deal of both. It would require an act of omnipotence to bring Townshend up to the level of a Judas Iscariot, or a Benedict Arnold . . . or Morse to the level of a fool. The Free Soil party is as badly treated by the traitors as Jesus Christ by Judas Iscariot or the American army by Benedict Arnold." Quoted in *True Democrat*, Feb. 1, 1849.

[1] *Ibid.*, March 1, 1849.　　　　　　　[2] Feb. 28, 1849.

[3] A. G. Riddle, in *Republic*, IV., 183 (1875).

with less heart-burning. The real burden of the complaint was not that a bargain was in itself blameworthy. Most of the Whigs would have supported Giddings in return for the judgeships. The real crime was coalition with the " Loco-focos." Chase, Hamlin, Townshend, and Morse, when the immediate results of their operations are considered, accomplished all that could have been done in the repeal of the Black Laws and the election of an anti-slavery Senator. For Free Soilers to vote against Edward Wade was not agreeable ; but, from the nature of things, such a bargain must have a seamy side, and a Whig arrangement would undoubtedly have presented some similar requirement. We may, then, at the outset dismiss all talk of " bargain and corruption," as entirely beside the mark. The mistake made by Townshend and Morse lay in their defiant attitude, taken up at the very beginning of the struggle. The ex-Whig Free Soilers were no more prejudiced in favor of their old companions than Chase was in favor of the Democrats. In bolting from the Free Soil caucus, Townshend and Morse made a tactical mistake ; for it threw on them, as the minority of a party, the burden of proving that they were right, and it needlessly enraged both their fellow Free Soilers and the regular Whigs.[1]

Precisely what part Chase played in the matter is not easy to make out. He seems not to have thrust himself into affairs, but when once involved he took a leading part in arranging the early stages of the bargain. That his planning, as the Whigs asserted, went so far as to include his own nomination for Senator, is almost certainly untrue. There is no trace of this aim in his private letters to Hamlin, his confidential friend at Columbus ; and the men connected with him at the time, especially Mathews, Hamlin, and Townshend, have all repeatedly said that he did nothing in his own favor. Nevertheless, his nomination was only the logical working out of the bargain ; for Chase and Hamlin well knew that if the Democrats were to unite with the Free Soilers in voting for a Senator, Chase and nobody else would be the man. The *Cincinnati Globe,* in answer

[1] See a speech of Townshend in the Ohio Legislature, reprinted in the *National Era,* March 22, 1849.

to Chase's critics, said: " His intercourse with members of the General Assembly and others was characterized by a frankness which no one should misconstrue and a delicacy which a fair opponent cannot fail to appreciate." [1] Chase was frank in one sense, in that he told no lies; but between his guardedly correct statements and the open frankness of a man like Giddings lay a world of difference. At this juncture Chase minded his own business strictly, made no public appearances, gave the soundest advice to Townshend and Morse, wrote the most unimpeachable letters to the *National Era* about " conscientious action," " regard for the cause of liberty," etc., and, while so doing, with the utmost skill he paved the way for his own advancement. His whole connection with the affair, his dealings with Townshend and Morse, his intense anxiety to settle the Hamilton County case in favor of the Democrats, and especially his action toward Giddings, leave an unpleasant impression. One cannot point to a single questionable act on his part ; but the feeling remains that, in this emergency, a man like Lewis or Giddings would have paid less attention to the settlement of the Hamilton County snarl and the rights of the Democrats, and more to the unification of the Free Soil party.

[1] Jan. 24, 1849.

CHAPTER XII.

COLLAPSE OF THE FREE SOIL PARTY IN THE THREE OHIO RIVER STATES.

1849–1850.

So great was the bitterness stirred up among Free Soilers by the circumstances of Chase's election, that the prospect for harmonious action in the campaign of 1849 seemed gloomy. The whole Western Reserve was fuming over the Democratic successes, Whigs were cursing, and Democratic legislators were trying to explain to irate constituents how and why they came to vote against the Black Laws and for Chase. In the midst of the turmoil, Giddings exerted himself to bring about peace. He would undoubtedly have been very glad to get the senatorship, and he had fairly earned promotion by ten arduous years of single-handed fighting; but he showed no signs of irritation. "From the bitter attacks made on Messrs. Morse and Townshend for their support of Mr. Chase, you may suppose," he generously wrote to Sumner, "that I am dissatisfied with them. Such is not the case. They both acted by my advice in that election. . . . I felt neither mortification nor disappointment at his success over me. On the contrary, I regarded his election as a great victory." [1] "Mr. Chase," he wrote in a later letter, "is an able man, and will prove an able Senator"; but, putting his finger on the weak spot, he added, "he lacks a knowledge of popular sentiment and is not qualified to lead a party." [2]

With this feeling, Giddings, through his organ, the *Ashtabula Sentinel*, worked for harmony, and urged that the matter might drop, that recriminations might cease, and bygones be by-

---

[1] G. W. Julian, *Life of J. R. Giddings*, 267.

[2] Giddings to Sumner, Oct. 19, 1849: Sumner MSS.

gones.[1] Such magnanimity was beyond the attainment of most Ohio Free Soil men; and consequently the quarrel went on until a vigorous effort to allay enmities was made at a convention for the Western Reserve, which met on May 2, 1848, at Cleveland. To symbolize reconciliation, Edward Wade, Morse, Townshend, and others were assigned dignities and were placed together on committees. A series of resolutions, reported by Giddings with the design of setting affairs to rights, urged an "early, efficient, and thorough party organization;" and said that "the existing controversy relative to the law dividing Hamilton County and all other questions of a mere partisan or temporary nature are of minor importance and ought not to be the subjects of strife or tests of fidelity with men pledged to the great principle of Human Freedom."[2] Conciliatory speeches were made by Giddings, Riddle, Vaughn, and Townshend; and for the time being it seemed as if, in the words of the *True Democrat*, "the spirit of discord was allayed, and mutual confidence was restored."[3]

This meeting, at the suggestion of Indiana Free Soilers, appointed a committee to call a convention at Cleveland to celebrate the Ordinance of 1787, in other words, the Wilmot Proviso. This step was presently taken, and on July 12, 1849, the convention met, with a large attendance. The time of the opening exercises was announced to the assembled crowd by the firing of cannon. Could Thomas Morris have returned to earth, he would undoubtedly have felt that time brings its revenges; for in the president's chair sat the very man who ten years before had supplanted him in the senatorship, the Honorable ex-Senator, Benjamin Tappan. With him were five vice-presidents, one from each of the States preserved for freedom by the Ordinance of 1787. Addresses were made by Ellsworth of Indiana, Austin Willey of Maine, Giddings, Taylor of the *Cincinnati Globe*, and, most eloquent of all, John Van Buren. In addition, Bibb, the fugitive slave, who for several years had been prominent in Michigan anti-slavery work, made a speech, as did also Judge Spaulding, whose election by Townshend and

[1] *Cincinnati Globe*, March 28, 1849.
[2] *National Era*, May 17, 1849.   [3] Quoted *ibid.*

Morse had caused ex-Whig Free Soilers to wince. Letters were received from a dozen eminent men, including Martin Van Buren, Henry Clay, J. A. Dix, J. G. Palfrey, Horace Mann, C. F. Adams, Charles Sumner, Lewis Tappan, and C. M. Clay; and a series of strong resolutions was adopted reiterating the Buffalo platform.[1]

These two peace-making conventions seemed, for the moment, to have done something to reunite anti-slavery men, and to put the Ohio third party on its feet; but, as the summer advanced and organization began, appeared a tendency — new, and, for Ohio, abnormal — toward Free Soil and Democratic coalition. Why should the Free Soilers coalesce at all? And, above all, why should they seek allies among Cass Democrats, among those whose leaders at Washington were slave-holders and advocates of slavery extension? This paradox demands explanation.

In the first place, the fundamental reason why the Free Soilers coalesced and the Liberty men did not, was that the new party was led to a considerable extent by politicians, with whom immediate gains were of much more relative consequence than had been the case with the philanthropists of the Liberty party. The New York Barnburners, the Western Reserve Whigs, the Michigan, Illinois, and Wisconsin Free Democrats wanted, if possible, to make their influence felt in every election; and if any party or body of men were willing to unite with them on a common platform, or on common candidates, so much the better. Another reason why Free Soilers in Ohio and in some other places coalesced with Democrats is found in the overshadowing influence of the New York Barnburners, who formed undeniably the strongest single numerical element of the new party, and were to a great extent its founders. Now, it was the boast of the Barnburners that they were " regular " Democrats, and that in voting for Van Buren they were more " regular," and more " Democratic," than the followers of Cass. The party name adopted at Buffalo, although seldom used in 1848, was the " Free Democracy "; and from this fact an impression prevailed, similar to the belief held by Chase since

[1] *National Era*, July 26–Aug. 2, 1849.

1845, that the Free Soil party was essentially an offshoot of the Democratic. If, then, there were to be any union, what more natural than that it should come about between the two kinds of Democrats?[1]

In Ohio, by far the larger part of the third-party vote of 1848 was Whig in origin; yet we find this idea of the Democratic character of the Free Soilers very prevalent. Its currency was undoubtedly increased by the sudden development of an anti-slavery spirit in the ranks of the Old Line Democracy. Early in 1848 the party convention had adopted a Free Territory clause in its platform, and its mouthpieces after the election used language that would have seemed extreme in a Birney organ of 1844. "Rather than see slavery extended one inch beyond its present limits," cried the *Cleveland Plain Dealer*, "we would see this Union rent asunder!"[2] Similar expressions, hardly less violent, may be found in the *Mahoning Index*, *Norwalk Experiment*, and in other Democratic papers in the northern counties. It is not, then, surprising that, with the Democratic press of the North incessantly calling for a "re-union," and the Barnburners of New York and the Free Soilers of Vermont negotiating terms of coalition, local conventions in Ohio began to yield to the current. In April a "union Demo-cratic" ticket was nominated in the Sandusky city election, and the same thing occurred in Cleveland and Toledo, to the great disgust of many ex-Whig Free Soilers. Later, Portage, Summit, Carroll, and Tuscarawas, Lucas, and Henry, Erie, Morgan, and Washington, Montgomery, Warren, and Medina counties, all saw Free Soil and Democratic conventions unite on a common ticket. In a few places, such as Summit and Ashtabula coun-ties, where the Whigs made an effort to gain Free Soil aid by adopting its full platform, their offers were laughed to scorn. Democratic fusion swept nearly every county, even on the Reserve.

In many places the Hamilton County question, for a time suppressed, boiled up again. In Lorain County, where the Free Democratic convention renominated Townshend, a minor-ity seceded and coalesced with the Whigs. In Summit County

---

[1] See *Cincinnati Globe*, Jan. 3, 1849.   [2] Nov. 17, 1848.

the Whigs made an effort to gain Free Soil votes by nominating McClure, an anti-Taylor man. The Free Soilers, however, nominated Spelman, who took the Democratic view of the Hamilton County affair; whereupon the Democrats indorsed him, " and thus," said the *True Democrat*, " the principles of Free Soil are merged in a little dirty squabble about an apportionment law." [1] In Cuyahoga County, Johnson, the Free Soil candidate for Speaker in the preceding legislature, found Edward Wade's views on the Hamilton County case unsatisfactory, and, in a public letter, went back to the Whig party. All the bitterness which the Western Reserve and Northwest Ordinance conventions had begun to allay, blazed up again with redoubled vigor.

All this time Chase was working hard to secure complete Democratic and Free Soil fusion. From the outset he felt that his reputation was at stake on the Hamilton County case, and he spared no efforts to secure vindication in the next election. Giddings tried to induce him to let the matter drop; but he replied at great length that it was impossible, that the question was one of principle and must be decided at the polls, and that the Free Soilers could not ignore it. [2] Accordingly he wrote scores of letters in all directions, urging fusion. " To me it seems clear that the true interest and duty of the Democracy in the free States," he wrote on August 6, " points to union with the Free Democrats instead of alliance with the slaveholders. . . . I am rejoiced to hear that in Portage and Summit the two wings of the Democracy will be united on principle. I wish it could be done throughout our State." [3] The *National Era* and the *Cincinnati Globe* also applauded " reunion." Said the former: " The union so far as it has taken place has been honorable to both parties, the work of reformation has begun in the right place." [4] The *Globe* went farther: " Aside from the slavery question," [as if that were a minor matter,] " there

<hr/>

[1] Sept. 27, 1849.

[2] Chase to Giddings, April 4, 1849: Chase MSS.

[3] Chase to L. W. Hall and to A. Dimmock, Aug. 6, 1849: R. B. Warden, *Life of Chase*, 332.

[4] *National Era*, Sept. 20, 1849.

are numerous things common to the old Democracy and the Free Democrats," such as strict construction, " superior reverence for human nature and human rights, hostility to special privileges, progress, *et cetera*. . . . It has now become the interest of the Democratic party . . . to seek the alliance of Free Soil men . . . to promote the cause of Freedom and Right." [1] To many ex-Whigs, of course, the whole series of fusions in New York, Vermont, and Ohio seemed woful mistakes. The *True Democrat* cried : " We can have no coalitions ! It would be treachery to the cause of the people to enter into them "; it called them "adulterous connections," "nefarious schemes," [2] and considered them all to be part of a plot to ruin the Free Soil party.

When the election day came, the Democrats profited to some extent by these coalitions, electing six more members of the House than before, and one more Senator. How the Free Soil party fared it is difficult to make out. As before, they had eleven members of the legislature, four of whom had been Whigs, one a Democrat, and six Liberty men. Since most of these were elected by Democratic fusion, the Free Soil vote cannot well be estimated. It seems, for the most part, to have held its own proportionately wherever there were separate tickets.[8] Giddings thought that the vote had fallen off, and laid the blame to Chase. " His policy last winter," he wrote to Sumner, " came near ruining us in this State. Had we on the Reserve adopted his plan of making the division of Hamilton County a test we should have been blown sky high. It was a most singular coincidence that the Old Hunker Whigs and Democrats and Mr. Chase were at the same time all laboring to make that *the question*. On the Reserve we took a bold determined position to have no reference to it but leave our Representatives to act as they pleased in regard to it. *It was that subject alone that diminished our vote*." [4] The stormy year

---

[1] *Cincinnati Globe*, May 16, 1849.

[2] April 12, Sept. 20, 1849.

[8] The Free Soil vote in eleven counties in 1848 was 14,457; in 1849, 12,811.

[4] Oct. 29, 1849: Sumner MSS.

1849 thus came to a close, and for the time being no man could say just where the Free Soil party of Ohio stood. The only thing certain was, that it would take a prolonged, strenuous effort to place it again where it had been in August, 1848, united, self-reliant, enthusiastic, and ready to " fight on, fight ever."

The next year carried the Ohio Free Soil party still farther on the downward path. In the legislature nothing of import-ance took place except squabbles over organization. In the House mutual distrust, arising from the Hamilton County case, caused the Free Soilers again to divide. After some futile bal-loting, in which A. G. Riddle, supported by Whigs, came within one vote of being elected Speaker, Leiter, a Democrat, secured the office by an obscure intrigue, much as Breslin had done the year before. Beyond some squabbling over this inci-dent, nothing of further interest took place in the House. In the Senate the irrepressible Hamilton County case made trouble; for a Whig claimant appeared, whom the Whig clerk of the preceding Senate insisted upon swearing in. This made one Senator too many, a fact which blocked all organization. For some weeks the Senate wrangled, taking three hundred and one ballots, all illegal, since each party teller insisted on receiv-ing the votes of all the Senators of his own party. At length, through a union of Free Soilers and Whigs, organization was effected and the extra Senator disposed of.

In the spring, elections were held for a Constitutional Con-vention, and again fusion was the order of the day. Only in the two election districts of Trumbull and Geauga, and Ashtabula and Lake counties, where the two old parties united, did the Free Soilers stand alone; of eight men classed as Free Soilers who sat in the convention, three were elected independently, one by Whig votes, and four, including Dr. Townshend, by Democratic coali-tion. The main interest of the country in this year centred upon the Congressional struggle over Clay's compromise. With Southern threats of disunion filling the air, and with President Taylor, on the other hand, ready to use force to prevent the execution of those threats, local elections became more or less perfunctory, particularly as they could not in any way influence the state of affairs at Washington. The Free Soil State Convention met at Columbus on May 2, 1850, and adopted some resolutions which indicated that the unlimited coalition which for over a year had bewildered anti-slavery men had begun to lose its charm. "While we deprecate affiliation with any other political organization," said the convention, "we will hail with pleasure accessions."[1] The meeting was thinly attended, and many of the southern counties were unrepresented. A strong desire was shown to nominate Sam Lewis for Governor. On his refusal, D. R. Tilden, of Summit County, formerly a Whig Congressman, was designated; but he, in turn, felt obliged to decline, although adhering strongly to the Buffalo platform, and "highly gratified by the honor" of the nomination.

To fill this vacancy, a "mass convention" met at Cleveland on August 22. The few persons present are said to have represented the extreme radical element of the Western Reserve, and they signalized themselves by passing the most remarkable resolution ever entertained by a Northwestern Free Soil convention. After nominating for governor Rev. E. Smith, an old-time Liberty man, and adopting the customary platform, the convention resolved: "That notwithstanding slavery is necessarily the creature of local State law, yet in the language of Madison, 'if it becomes a source of expense or endangers the stability of the nation, it ceases to be local and becomes a fit subject for the legislation of the General Government.' That time has now come. . . . We therefore hold that it is not only the duty of the General Government to forbid its extension, but that humanity, justice, mercy, and self-preservation demand, and the constitution permits, its immediate extermination in all the States and Territories."[2] No body of men claiming to be Democrats ever unanimously adopted a more remarkable resolution, in which a dictum of one of the "fathers" served as the sole basis for a proposed line of conduct which had hitherto been held to be absolutely unconstitutional by everybody in the United States, except the extremest abolitionists. Through the

[1] *National Era*, May 30, 1850.
[2] *Western Reserve Chronicle*, Aug. 28, 1850; Author's correspondence with G. Hoadly, May 10, 1894.

vigorous opposition of George Hoadly and others the resolution was reconsidered and finally laid on the table; yet its previous adoption was well known outside, only the small size of the convention and the general lack of interest in the Ohio campaign prevented the fact from being used with annoying effect against the party.

In the Congressional elections the third party made little exertion. Fusion still continued, although the "union" conventions showed a sinister desire to nominate nothing but Old Line Democrats.[1] In the Nineteenth Congressional District, on the Reserve, the Free Soilers nominated Newton, and the Whigs ratified the ticket. In the Twenty-first District a convention of the United Democracy nominated Norton Townshend for Congress, and "Old Line Hunkers" for local offices. Therefore a bolt took place, and a separate Free Soil nomination of J. M. Root was made, more with the hope of defeating Townshend than for any other reason.[2] Here and there became visible a similar tendency to withdraw from Democratic coalition, the Fairfield County Convention resolving that "we cannot as consistent Free Soil men longer act with said party."[3] Although there were separate Free Soil Congressional tickets in seven districts, the campaign was dull. Except on the Reserve, scarcely any effort was made to bring out the vote; and a feeling spread among anti-slavery men that the party's usefulness had ended and that they might as well return to the old organizations.

Both the old parties in this year made a distinct effort to draw back into the fold wavering bolters of 1848. The Whigs, on their part, were unreservedly anti-slavery, from Governor Ford's message of January, which adopted the entire Free Soil platform, to their State Convention of May 6, which nominated Johnson, a former "Whig Abolitionist," and made the Wilmot Proviso one of its planks. "The indications are," said the *National Era*, "that the Whigs of Ohio have determined to carry that State at the next election by adopting the faith of the Free Soilers."[4] The Democrats, on their part, on January 8,

---

[1] *True Democrat*, Sept. 4, 1850.
[2] *Ibid.*, Sept. 28, 1850.
[3] *Ibid.*, Sept. 6, 1850.
[4] Feb. 21, 1850.

1850, re-adopted verbatim their anti-slavery resolution of 1848, and nominated for Governor Judge Wood of the Supreme Bench, a Western Reserve anti-slavery Democrat. "A better nomination," said the *National Era*, "aside from political considerations, could hardly have been made."[1] In spite of the reluctance shown by many Democrats in adopting the Free Soil resolution, their attitude and the nomination proved so attractive to many still under the sway of Chase's logic that, from early in the year, Free Soilers of 1848 began to show signs of an intention to vote for Judge Wood. Chase, delighted at the prospect, found time at Washington to write frequent letters to Ohio urging with incessant reiteration the necessity of Free Soil and Democratic union. "I still strongly hold the faith," he said, "that it is to a regenerated Democracy that the country must look for final deliverance from the thralldom of the Slave Power"; and again, "I am anxious, as you know, for union with and in the Democracy. I believe that Democratic principles supply the only safe ground on which the battle with the slave power can be fought."[2] There were, of course, vigorous protests on the other side. "Is the Whig or Democratic party," asked the *True Democrat*, "now any more sound on the human rights question than in 1848?"[3] "Let every one feel," wrote Sam Lewis, "that a vote for Wood or Johnson is a vote for sustaining and extending slavery, not that they as individuals would do it, but their parties cannot exist on any other principle."[4]

The tide, however, was setting against the third party: individuals and groups rejoined the old parties; newspapers like the *Toledo Republican* turned to Wood; and when the election day came the vote stood as follows: Democratic — Wood, 133,092; Whig — Johnson, 121,095; Free Soil — Smith, 13,802.[5] In the Congressional election Giddings was the only successful third-party man, Townshend being elected by Democrats in

[1] Jan. 17, 1850.
[2] Chase to E. S. Hamlin, Jan. 12, Feb. 2, 1850: Chase MSS. Also in letters of March 16 and May 21.
[3] Aug. 29, 1850.   [4] *True Democrat*, Sept. 18, 1850.
[5] Vote in *Whig Almanac*, 1851.

spite of a Free Soil bolt, and Newton by Whig coalition. The Whigs, in most places outside the Reserve, even where there were three tickets, received Free Soil votes and made some gains in the Congressional delegation. They also gained some seats in the legislature and, as compared with the Presidential vote of 1848, increased the vote for Governor. In this result we trace to a slight extent the effect of a popular reaction against the Democracy on account of the behavior of its Southern leaders in Congress.

More striking, however, than anything else was the drop in the Free Soil vote. Since 1848 it had lost 21,526, or nearly two-thirds, of which about 15,000 vanished from the counties outside the Reserve. In other words, the Western Reserve, which in 1848 cast less than half of the total third-party vote in the State, now, in spite of a decline, cast about three-fourths. The fact that it was an " off " year does not explain this decrease; for the Whig and Democratic losses were both numerically and proportionately less. Where had the absent Free Soil voters gone? Several thousand did not vote at all; these, doubtless, were the same persons who had voted the Liberty ticket in 1844 and the Free Soil in 1848, but did not trouble themselves about State elections; in other words, they were part of the regular stay-at-home vote. There were more, however, who returned to their old parties, feeling that the Free Democracy had shot its bolt; or that, since the local parties had nominated anti-slavery candidates on anti-slavery platforms, principle no longer required them to act independently. In this connection, Chase's notion of the " Democracy " of the Free Soil party proved a double-edged tool: if it made the return of Democratic Free Soilers to the Old Line easy by minimizing their difference; it also made Whigs feel out of place in the " Free Democracy," and anxious to get into more congenial company. There were, moreover, since the repeal of the Black Laws, no State issues for the third party. The sole remaining difference in principle between them and the old organizations was anti-slavery action; and that distinction both the old parties, by their platforms and nominations, had taken away.

When any persistent abolitionist tried to act independently, the effect of the coalitions of 1849 became manifest in the absence, in most of the central and southern counties, in 1850, of any Free Soil organization separate from the Democratic. So marked was this inanition that it paralyzed all Free Soil action, and reduced the third-party vote in these regions to a figure smaller than any Liberty vote in a State election since 1842. Outside the Reserve the Free Soil voters of 1850 were probably nearly all Liberty men, and on the Reserve itself there were only some five thousand faithful Whig or Democratic Free Soilers of 1848. For all practical purposes, the Free Soil party of Ohio ceased to exist in 1849; and in 1850 there emerged to view once more the original, unreconciled Liberty party of 1840–47. Liberty leaders once more assumed the management of the cause, and, with the exception of Giddings, Root, Brinckerhoff, Riddle, and a few others, the enthusiastic bolters of 1848 sank into the background. The Free Soil revolt had plainly failed in Ohio, and, in spite of the results obtained by coalition, succeeding years had only emphasized its failure. In the autumn of 1850 the third-party men realized that they stood once more at the foot of the ladder, with all the weary work of agitation and organization to do over again.

The Free Soil party of Indiana had at no time in its career any such stirring episodes as those which enlivened the winter of 1848–49 in Ohio; but with even swifter pace it ran the same course as did its eastern neighbor. For some months after the Presidential election, newspapers and politicians of both the old parties continued with unabated fervor to advocate the Wilmot Proviso. The Democrats, though they had a clear majority in the legislature, refused to re-elect Hannegan because of his equivocal position in regard to slavery in the Territories, and chose in his place Ex-Governor Whitcomb, whose answers to Free Soil questions had been eminently satisfactory. On January 3, 1849, the Whig State Convention "calmly but firmly expressed the conviction that the extension of slavery over the newly acquired territories ought to be prohibited by law," and urged that "all constitutional and proper means should be adopted to free our National Capitol from the last vestige of human bondage ";[1] and local Whig conventions echoed these sentiments.   At about the same time the Democratic State Convention resolved that, since "New Mexico and California are in fact and in law free Territories, it is the duty of Congress to prevent the introduction of slavery within their limits."[2]   It seemed as if an anti-slavery millennium were at hand.[3]

In spite of such inducements for the abandonment of separate action, the Free Soil party had for some months after the election of 1848 showed much activity in organizing; and the press spoke at first very courageously.   "Who says the Free Soilers ought to disband?" asked the *Tippecanoe Journal*.   "Bless your soul, neighbor, you don't seem to understand anything about the Free Soil movement.   No, Sir, the Free Soil party — or Free Democracy as some prefer calling it — WILL NOT DIS-BAND! . . . Ours is the campaign of Freedom, and it cannot be closed until Freedom and Right, Liberty and Equality, have finally triumphed."[4]   "Shall we," asked the *Free Territory Sentinel*, "having espoused a cause which all admit to be right, and having already accomplished great good, shall we now abandon it? Organize! Organize! We must relax none of our energies.   Self-respect forbids that we should go back to our old party allegiance after having been denounced and stigmatized without stint for doing what we firmly believed to be our duty.   We are therefore distinctly in favor of organization as an independent and permanent party."[5]

In January, 1849, the State Free Soil Convention met at Indianapolis, and, still thrilling with the excitement of the recent campaign, seemed at that time to be in favor of independent action.   When J. H. Bradley, a Free Soil elector, moved that the convention, instead of making nominations, pass resolutions in favor of the Whig ticket and adjourn, his proposal was voted down; and J. H. Cravens and J. W. Wright were

---

[1] *Free Territory Sentinel*, Feb. 17, 1849; *Indiana State Journal*, Aug. 24 1853. See App. C.

[2] *National Era*, Jan. 25, 1849.

[3] *Ibid.*, Dec. 21–28, 1848; *Indiana State Journal*, July 29, 1854.

[4] Quoted in *Free Territory Sentinel*, Dec. 6, 1848.

[5] *Ibid.*, Nov. 18, 1848.

selected for the State ticket on the Buffalo platform.[1] In its enthusiasm, the convention issued a call for the mass meeting described in the preceding chapter, to be held at Cleveland, July 13, 1849, to commemorate the Ordinance of 1787. H. L. Ellsworth duly appeared as a delegate appointed by the Indianapolis Convention.

During the spring, however, the unanimous chorus of Whig and Democratic anti-slavery professions began to have its effect. In most of the Congressional districts where there were any Free Soilers, the policy of questioning was resorted to by the especial advice of the Free Soil Central Committee, who issued an address containing a suitable list of questions.[2] When the August elections drew near, the campaign presented the spectacle, hitherto unprecedented in Indiana, of all the candidates claiming to be on the same anti-slavery ground. The term "Free Soil," as describing a party, ceased to have any meaning when it was assumed by every Whig candidate and by nearly, if not quite, all of the Democrats. "We believe there are few Whigs or Democrats," said the Democratic *Indiana Register*, "that do not believe in the principle of non-extension."[3] "There exists no possibility of the election of the Free Soil candidates," said the Whig *State Journal* to the new party; "then what is to be gained by voting for them? By doing so you may prevent the election of men who agree with you on every single political question, including the question you place above all others. Is it the part of wisdom thus to act?"[4]

Some Democratic candidates for Congress outbid even the Whigs. Dr. Fitch in the Ninth District, when questioned in regard to the principal points in the anti-slavery creed, asserted: "If no older or abler member whose influence for them would be greater than mine introduces them to Congress, I shall do so myself, if I have the honor of holding a seat there."[5] It was little wonder that, with such appeals re-echoing on every side, the Free Democrats of Tippecanoe County, which had been a

---

[1] *Free Territory Sentinel*, Jan. 24, 1849; *National Era*, Feb. 8, 1849.

[2] *Ibid.*, June 13, 1849; *National Era*, July 12, 1849.

[3] Quoted in *National Era*, Aug. 23, 1849.

[4] Quoted *ibid.*, July 5, 1849.   [5] *Ibid.*, Sept. 20, 1849.

hot-bed of revolt in 1848, now concluded to make no nominations, "inasmuch as both the Democratic and Whig candidates
in answer to letters of inquiry declared themselves in favor of
the Wilmot Proviso, prohibition of the slave trade in the District
of Columbia, and the removal of the seat of the Federal Government to a Free State."[1]

The only place where the Free Soilers cut any figure in this
Congressional election was in the Fourth District, where there
were special conditions. This region contained a large Quaker
population, and had been a centre of abolitionism ever since the
movement began. The Whigs had hitherto shown a large majority; but in the summer of 1848 a great number had followed
the lead of G. W. Julian in support of Van Buren; and it was
seen that unless these bolters could be induced to return, the
Whig party was fatally weakened in this stronghold. On a reduced scale, the situation resembled that on the Western Reserve
in Ohio; and here as there the Democrats, who hitherto had
had no hope of success, tended strongly to favor coalition with
the Free Soilers. Consequently, when the Free Soilers of the
District nominated Julian for Congress in 1849, and began a
vigorous campaign, most of the Democratic local conventions
adopted anti-slavery platforms and joined in his support.

The Whigs had been angling for Free Soil votes ever since
the preceding year; and the call for the Henry County Whig
Convention had proclaimed that "Free Soilers generally, and
especially Free Soil Whigs who voted for Van Buren, or did not
vote at all, are invited to attend."[2] S. W. Parker, the regular
Whig candidate for Congress, claimed to have been an abolitionist for twenty years, that is, since 1829, and made direct
appeals for Quaker support. Upon Julian, the "renegade," a
flood of contempt was poured; and as Julian when aroused
was a hard fighter, the contest became extremely bitter and
personal. "This district," he wrote later, "in the matter of
liberality and progress was in advance of all other portions of
the state; and yet the immeasurable wrath and scorn which
were lavished upon the men who deserted the Whig party on

[1] *Cincinnati Globe*, July 25, 1849.
[2] *Free Territory Sentinel*, Nov. 29, 1848.

account of the nomination of Gen. Taylor can scarcely be conceived. The friends of a lifetime were suddenly turned into foes and their words were often dipped in venom. The contest was bitter beyond all precedent."[1] Every effort was made by Whig papers to spread the impression that Julian was a nonentity, feeble physically and mentally, hardly more than half-witted; and the Free Democrats, on their part, exhausted their energies in proclaiming Parker a lying hypocrite, a blasphemer, and a sanctimonious bully.[2] So much were the Free Soilers engrossed in this contest that the fact that there was an anti-slavery State ticket was entirely overlooked. On the day before the election, the *Free Territory Sentinel* suddenly recollected it in time to remark apologetically: " We have said little in regard to these two offices, but we wish Free Soilers will not forget that our candidates are in the field . . . good and true men. They should receive the vote of every Free Soiler."[3] In August, 1849, Julian was elected over Parker by a narrow majority; and elsewhere in the State the Democrats, profiting by their Free Soil professions, carried every district but one, and elected their State ticket.

In this way it happened that Indiana, from an anti-slavery standpoint the most backward of the Northwestern States, came to have a Free Soil Representative in Congress to stand beside Giddings, Root, and Durkee. This result was due to coalition, and seemed completely to justify the system; but the vote for Governor presented a different aspect of the matter. It stood as follows: Democratic — Wright, 76,996; Whig — Embree, 67,218; Free Soil — Cravens, 3,018.[4] As compared with the vote of the year before, the total vote was smaller by 5,000; but this loss was confined to the Whigs and Free Soilers, who had lost 2,000 and 5,000 respectively, whereas the Democrats had gained about 2,000 over the preceding year. Possibly some of this Democratic gain was due to the return of a few Taylor Democrats to their old party; but in the main, no

[1] G. W. Julian, *Political Recollections*, 72.
[2] For both sides, see *Free Territory Sentinel*, Aug. 1, 1849.
[3] *Ibid.*
[4] Official figures in *Indianapolis Sentinel*, September, 1849.

doubt, it was composed of Free Soilers. The logic of the Free Soil Central Committee had been destructive to the party's success; for if it was proper to vote directly for local candidates of the old parties, why not for Governor also, particularly since both candidates were Wilmot Proviso men? In Julian's district so cordial was the feeling between Democrats and Free Soilers that a correspondent wrote to the *National Era* that they were permanently united.[1]

The result of this year's operations was, that after the fall of 1849 the State Free Soil party of Indiana simply ceased to exist. There was no life left; there were no leaders except Julian, and he was in Washington. A call for a State Convention at Indianapolis to establish a central newspaper fell absolutely flat;[2] nor in the winter of 1849–50 did even the hitherto reliable Henry, Wayne, and Randolph County anti-slavery men take any action. Now and then, as the spring approached and elections were coming on for a Constitutional Convention as well as for local offices, individuals called for action in the columns of the *Indiana True Democrat;*[3] but still nothing was done. "What has become of the friends of the slave?" asked Daniel Worth, a lifelong abolitionist. "Where is the zeal, devotion, and sacrifice of former years? I have watched with deepest sorrow the declension of the anti-slavery spirit. It is so long since we have had a meeting, let us look each other in the face ";[4] but he appealed in vain.

When nominations were finally made, whatever Free Soil activity existed found its outlet in renewed coalition. In Wayne County a Free Soil convention, on June 8, 1850, did nothing more than nominate to fill certain gaps which a previous Democratic convention had left invitingly in its list.[5] In Henry County a similar union took place. In Union County a mass union convention met; and in Cass County a Free Democratic convention at Logansport, on July 27, selected a ticket out of

---

[1] *National Era*, Sept. 20, 1849.
[2] *Free Territory Sentinel*, Nov. 7, Dec. 5, 1849.
[3] Known until 1850 as the *Free Territory Sentinel*.
[4] *Indiana True Democrat*, May 22, 1850.
[5] *Ibid.*, June 12, 1850.

those already in nomination by the old parties.[1] All these fusions aroused again the bitter wrath of Whigs, and called out protests from some Free Soilers. Why is it, asked one, that Free Soil Whigs never receive any nominations? Is it because they are Whigs? or is it through intrigue and management on the part of the leading old abolitionists and old Democrats?[2]

The summer elections of 1850 showed that coalition had begun to lose its effectiveness; for in Wayne County the fusionists were beaten, and to the State Constitutional Convention but one Free Soiler was elected, I. Kinley, from Henry County. The Free Soil party of Indiana had ceased to be a power of any sort in the State. Without any of the bitter internal struggles that convulsed the party in Ohio, it had sunk into a state of almost complete decay. The only men who still adhered to its principles and preferred a separate organization were some of the old-time Liberty men and a few Whigs, in all a mere corporal's guard. All this had been accomplished without any reference to the Compromise of 1850, but solely through the full acceptance by the Indiana Free Soilers of the anti-slavery promises made so profusely by both Whigs and Democrats in 1849 and 1850.

In the autumn of 1848 the Free Soilers of northern Illinois seemed on the threshold of a brilliant career. They were concentrated in several contiguous counties in two Congressional districts, one of which for five years had been the " banner " liberty district of the country. Their leaders were experienced politicians, their enthusiasm had been tremendous, they had an active newspaper press, and they stood a good chance of carrying a dozen counties for the legislature and of electing one congressman, perhaps two. Yet in spite of all this promise, no third party experienced a more ignominious drop than did the Illinois Free Soilers in the two years, 1849–50. For this fall may be assigned several reasons, an important one, without doubt, being the change brought about in the political situation by the new constitution adopted in the spring of 1848. This

[1] *National Era*, Aug. 8, Sept. 5, 1850.
[2] *Indiana True Democrat*, June 19, 1850.

13

instrument gave the Governor a four years' term, and made legislative elections biennial. The first election held under these requirements had been in August, 1848, before a separate Free Soil party had been organized; consequently there were no third-party Congressmen or members of the legislature. This circumstance at the outset left the new organization with no accredited mouthpieces, with nothing more tangible than principles to support, and with no immediate prospect of anything else. In the next place, there would be no State or national election of any importance until 1850; and thus the new party was left for two years with nothing to do. The situation was calculated to make the revolt of 1848 seem merely a temporary outburst; and since the Barnburners of " Long John Wentworth's " district found no necessity for committing themselves at once on the point of a separate organization, they had plenty of time to cool their Wilmot Proviso enthusiasm of 1847–48.

Yet at first in Illinois, as in Indiana, it seemed as if Free Soil sentiments ruled the State. All the papers of the northern counties talked boldly; on January 24, 1849, the legislature, in which the Democrats had a large majority, by a strict sectional vote of the northern counties against " Egypt," instructed its Senators and Representatives to vote for the Wilmot Proviso. Party lines could scarcely be said to be drawn; but when the *Western Citizen* claimed this action of the legislature as a triumph of the Free Soil Party principles, the *Chicago Journal* in its anti-slavery enthusiasm retorted that it was good Whig doctrine. " Every Whig in both houses," it said, " voted for these resolutions, as they have done on similar ones before the humbug of the Free Soil party had a beginning." [1] The instructions were so repellent to Senator Douglas that an effort was made to sweeten them to his taste by the introduction of a resolution covering him with flattery, and begging him, in case he disagreed with the instructions, not to resign. Even the members from " Egypt " declined to stoop so low, and the resolution was rejected with scant courtesy. [2] In the election of a Senator the Whigs were powerless, and there

[1] Jan. 13, 1849.   [2] *National Era*, Feb. 1, 1849.

was no distinct struggle on the slavery question; but the Wilmot Proviso received recognition by sending to the Senate General Shields, who was reported to be in favor of its principle.

The next year (1850) came a Congressional election, and the Free Soil party of Illinois had an opportunity to assert itself. By this time, however, matters were much changed since 1848: coalition had run its course in the Northwest, and — most impressive of all to Illinois ex-Democrats — the New York Barnburners had rejoined the Hunkers. The excitement of 1848 had died away, and the " Union-saving " cry of 1850 had begun to be strong. Nevertheless, in spite of inaction among Illinois Barnburners during 1849, and of their apathy in 1850, local Free Soil conventions continued, as if independent action were the course to be followed; and, as usual, interest centred in the Fourth District, where in 1848 the Free Soil vote for President had been larger than that of either of the old parties. The party was now, however, in a rather disorganized condition. Its three elements were more irreconcilable here than in any other Northwestern State, and each thoroughly distrusted the others: the Liberty men of the Lovejoy type felt ill at ease beside the Barnburner politicians, Hoyne and Arnold; and both of these groups were to the Whigs equally repugnant.

In the summer of 1850, while all eyes were turned toward Washington, Free Soil county conventions passed vigorous resolutions, and on August 28 the district convention nominated for Congress W. B. Ogden, a former Democrat. Apparently the coalition examples of their brethren in other States were to produce no result. The Lake County Convention, having been approached by the regular Democrats, resolved " That we regard all overtures made by either of the old parties to unite with us as unworthy of serious consideration,"[1] — a show of independence which proved delusive. Shortly after this the Democratic district convention nominated Dr. Molony, but from the conflicting accounts it is not clear whether it adopted a Wilmot Proviso platform. At any rate, Molony, extremely

[1] *Chicago Journal*, Aug. 29, 1850.

anxious to get the Free Soil vote, hastened to declare himself a strong anti-slavery man. Apparently the Barnburners were waiting for some such sign, for within a few days Ogden, their nominee, resigned in Molony's favor, "thinking two Democratic nominations needless"; and without further hesitation the majority of those who in 1848 had shouted the loudest for Van Buren marched back into the old ranks.[1] Some local meetings declared outright that the Free Soil party was at an end. If the *Chicago Journal* is to be believed, a Bureau County Union Convention resolved "That the Democratic and Free Soil parties be united and that so far as the action of this meeting can effect this end they are hereby united one and inseparable now and forever."[2] To Lovejoy, Codding, and others of the old Liberty guard, this action was simply intolerable, and on October 23, in a convention at Aurora, they signalized their devotion to a third party by nominating in Ogden's place an old-time Liberty candidate, J. H. Collins.[3]

Meanwhile the Illinois Whigs were talking pure Free Soil doctrine. Local conventions in Kane and McHenry counties, for example, resolved "That we are ceaselessly and eternally opposed to human bondage, and we believe it to be the duty of Congress to prohibit by positive enactment its increase."[4] Finally the Fourth Congressional District Convention nominated C. Coffing, a strong anti-slavery man, on an outright Free Soil platform. If Free Soilers wished an unexceptionable candidate and platform, there stood the Whigs ready to receive them; and it is probable that many of them, in their disgust at what they called the Barnburners' "betrayal," voted for Coffing. In any case, the Congressional vote in November showed the astonishing fact that the Illinois Free Soil party, without much formal coalition, had simply ceased to be. Only in the Fourth District was there any third-party vote, and there it was smaller than any Liberty vote since 1843. On the contrary, the Whigs gained so largely in this district and all over the northern par

1 *National Era*, Oct. 24, 1850.
2 *Chicago Journal*, Oct. 7, 1850.
3 *Ibid.*, Oct. 17–25, 1850.
4 *Chicago Journal*, Oct. 17, 1850; *Milwaukee Sentinel*, Aug. 22, 1850.

of the State, that one can believe what was asserted at the time, — that most of the Free Soilers voted the Whig ticket.[1] Even in the Fourth District, Coffing "ran" Molony so closely as to indicate that, had Collins been nominated a little earlier, Coffing might possibly have won. But the leaders of the Barnburners were once more safe at home in their old party, and the brilliant Free Soil promise of 1848 had faded into darkness.

What distinguishes the fate of the Illinois Free Soil party is the quiet way in which it died out, with none of the bitter struggles of Ohio, Michigan, and Wisconsin. Its end shows, as does the similar fate of the party in Indiana, how shallow in its anti-slavery basis was the Democratic bolt of 1850 in these two Ohio River States. The hard contest that Cass waged in his own State with members of his own party, the sharp dealings of 1849 in Wisconsin and Ohio, were unknown alike in Indiana and in Illinois, where the Free Soil party of 1848 disintegrated almost without a struggle.

---

[1] The vote in 1850 stood as follows : —

		Democratic.		Whig.		Free Soil.
Fourth District	Molony	11,231	Coffing	10,587	Collins	804

Collins's vote is elsewhere stated as 1,213; in any case, it was about equal to the liberty vote of 1843, which was 1,174. See figures in *Whig Almanac,* 1851, and in *Chicago Journal,* 1850.

CHAPTER XIII.

COLLAPSE OF THE FREE SOIL PARTY IN MICHIGAN, WISCONSIN, AND IOWA.

1849–1850.

IN the three northernmost States of the Old Northwest, coalition assumed more ambitious forms than in Ohio, Indiana, or Illinois; but the result on the Free Soil organization was quite as disastrous. In Michigan the one great difference at the outset was that the State, unlike its neighbors, was in the hands of a "boss." Lewis Cass, though an honest, able man, was a thorough politician and partisan, and kept a controlling hand over every movement of his party in the State. On accepting the Baltimore nomination of 1848 he had resigned his seat in the Senate; and when, after his defeat for the Presidency, he returned to offer himself as a candidate for re-election, he met with violent opposition on every side. Whigs and Free Soilers were eager to complete his discomfiture in every possible way, and (still more ominous) there were signs of a strong anti-slavery revolt in his own party.

When the legislature had convened, Governor Ransom directly challenged Cass's position by a message arguing strongly in favor of the power of Congress to prohibit slavery in the Territories, and crying, "Should it be suffered to extend a single line into territory now free? No, never!"[1] Following this, members of both parties introduced resolutions instructing Senators to vote for the Wilmot Proviso, and on January 9 and 13 such a series was passed by votes of 14 to 7 in the Senate, 35 to 26 in the House: nothing could have been more clearly defiant of Cass, or more ominous for the success of a candidate

[1] *Detroit Advertiser*, Jan. 3, 1849.

who thought the Wilmot Proviso unconstitutional. When the matter of choosing a Senator came up, it looked as if Cass were doomed; for seven Democratic Senators and ten Representatives signed a declaration that they could not vote for Cass, because he had been improperly nominated for President by the Baltimore Convention, because they disliked his opinions on slavery, and because it was the turn of the western half of the State to have a Senator.[1] The seven Senators holding the balance of power prevented a joint session for several days. It was generally believed that there would be no election, but at last one of the seven gave way, finding party pressure too severe to endure; the bolters thus lost control of the Senate, and on January 23 General Cass was re-elected by a vote of 44 to 38. It was the narrowest escape from defeat that the "boss" of Michigan experienced until the rise of the Republican party in 1857.

Encouraged by the presence of so much Free Soil sentiment in Cass's own party, the various elements of opposition began to think of combining against him and his followers in the coming State election. In the early months of 1849 the Whigs especially showed a strong desire to make common cause with the Free Soilers, a course for which a precedent was furnished by several instances of coalition in 1848. Negotiations were soon under way, and by June matters had progressed to such a point that Whig and Free Soil State conventions were called for the same day, the Whigs taking the initiative to secure the coincidence. Their action, however, met with strong opposition in both parties; for the "regular" Whigs were, of course, alarmed at any appearance of coalition, while many of the Free Soilers, particularly the leaders, looked for allies rather to the anti-Cass branch of the Democratic party than to the Whigs.[2] The *Detroit Advertiser*, which, it will be remembered, had been Birney's severest critic in 1844, now took the lead in advocating a coalition of Whigs and anti-slavery men; it asserted that the non-extension of slavery was "part and parcel of the Whig creed," whereas the Democrats had adopted it purely for par-

[1] *Detroit Advertiser*, Jan. 23, 1849.
[2] *National Era*, May 17, 1849.

tisan purposes; and it called for co-operation. " We ask you, Free Soil men of Michigan," it said, " is it not better that we should work together and teach these hypocrites that the principle of Free Soil with us is something which cannot be put on and off at pleasure?" [1] The two conventions met on the appointed day, but no coalition resulted, in spite of the *Advertiser's* hints, and of the evident desire for union on the part of very many of the delegates in both. The Whig convention had been preceded by a mass meeting, which, under the lead of J. M. Howard, adopted resolutions supporting Taylor and declaring slavery extension not a party question. [2] Although the State Convention adopted six resolutions comprising the Buffalo platform, and offered them through a conference committee to the Free Soilers, the latter could not overlook the resolution of the preceding day, and declined to co-operate. Accordingly, separate candidates were nominated, the Whigs selecting John Owen for Governor, G. A. Coe for Lieutenant-Governor, and H. H. Duncklee, of the *Detroit Advertiser*, for State printer; the Free Soilers presenting F. J. Littlejohn, A. Blair, and E. Hussey, a Democrat, a Whig, and a Liberty man respectively.

During July and August, politicians of all three parties continued actively at work. The Free Soilers undoubtedly hoped that the anti-Cass Democrats would swing their party convention in favor of Littlejohn, who, until the preceding year, had been a very prominent Democrat; or that they would bolt from an unacceptable Democratic nomination. During the summer, however, Cass himself entered the field, determined to save his own credit by making the State Convention nominate one of his followers and indorse his policy. By September his exertions had begun to tell, and little by little the Democratic press, hitherto nearly unanimous for the Wilmot Proviso, changed front. It was evident that General Cass and his machine were too strong for the opposition; but when the Democratic Convention met on September 19, it was equally evident that without Cass's personal exertions the Democratic party of Michigan would never have indorsed him. The opposition maintained a

1 *Detroit Advertiser*, June 4, 1849.   2 *Ibid.*, June 22, 1849.

steady vote of 57 to Cass's 65; consequently, the change of but five votes would have been enough to alter the outcome. On a test vote of 65 to 59, McClelland, a Free Soil Democrat, was defeated for Governor by Barry, Cass's choice; and when one of the western delegates moved the Wilmot Proviso as an amendment to the regular platform, it was met with hisses and cries of " no niggerism." The convention then adopted some vague anti-slavery-extension resolutions, and adjourned. Cass had a second time saved his credit by the narrowest of margins, and through his own extreme exertions.[1] Immediately after this, he made a tour of the State, " under the guise," said the *National Era*, of " attending county agricultural fairs," but really for the purpose of whipping local Democratic organizations into line.[2] In this aim he was eminently successful, the *National Era* enumerating eight Democratic county conventions, previously Free Soil in doctrine, which now swung over to Cass's position of non-interference with slavery in the Territories.

The Free Soil party had, then, nothing to hope from the Michigan Democracy so long as Cass was at its head. All that it could expect was some accession from the defeated minority. At this juncture the Whigs reopened the coalition question. Early in the summer their candidate for Governor, Owen, had resigned, and the Whig managers began the task of getting the party into a frame of mind to support Littlejohn. In this action the *Detroit Advertiser* took the lead. Finally a Whig convention was called to meet directly after the Democratic convention on September 21. The *Advertiser* said : " It is not to be disguised that upon the subject of state nominations there exists at the present time a wide and marked difference of opinion in the Whig party. It is the duty of all good Whigs to take care that this subject be there harmonized and set at rest."[3]

The convention, after four ballots, nominated F. J. Littlejohn, the Free Soil candidate, thereby consummating the union for which the Whig leaders had been so anxious; but the opposi-

[1] *Detroit Advertiser*, Sept. 22, 26, 1849.
[2] *National Era*, Oct. 25, 1829.
[3] *Detroit Advertiser*, Sept. 17, 1849.

tion which this action aroused was alarming. After the nomination two members of the Central Committee resigned, and
others broke out into violent language. "Who is Littlejohn?"
cried Kellogg, of Allegan County. "He is an arrant radical
Loco-foco — I say he is a Loco-foco! Is this a Whig Convention? I beg of you, I entreat, nay, I pray, do not nominate
this man." Another called the nomination "a miserable farce,
too barefaced to merit contempt," "a bitter and nauseating
draught," and "many delegates declared openly that if they
voted at all it would be for Barry. It was a choice between
Loco-focos." [1] Littlejohn accepted the nomination in a letter
full of Free Soil doctrine, but without anything which could
by any remote interpretation be called Whiggism; and Austin
Blair, the Free Soil nominee for Lieutenant-Governor, then resigned in favor of Mr. Coe. From the outset, however, the
chances for the success of the ticket seemed poor. True, the
Democratic party was torn in two by feuds; but the prospect
that the anti-Cass men would vote for Littlejohn was lessened
by the Whig indorsement. The Whigs also showed unmistakably that the coalition had failed to attract them. The Detroit
Advertiser worked heroically. On September 24 it said: "By
accepting the nomination of the Whig Convention, Mr. Littlejohn becomes *one of us*, so far at least as our state interests are
implicated"; and again: "It is useless to disguise the fact that
a difference of opinion and feeling has existed upon this question, but it is now full time . . . to come up as one man to the
rescue of the ticket . . . to drag down into the grave forever
the prospects and aspirations of Lewis Cass, the traitor to the
rights and feelings of those whom he misrepresents." Again
it said, and reiterated the statement: "Recollect, Whigs, the
only source to which our opponents look for success in the approaching canvass is to your disaffection." It would be interesting to quote more from the *Detroit Advertiser* and from other
papers, such as the *Adrian Expositor* and the *Grand River Eagle*,
which, though "frank to admit that there were some Whigs upon
whose ears the name of F. J. Littlejohn would grate harshly, yet
upon full and careful consideration . . . became thoroughly con-

[1] *Detroit Free Press*, Sept. 29, 1849.

vinced that the policy pursued was the wisest and best."[1] It is enough to say that, by the end of October, party discipline and hatred of Cass and Barry had brought every Whig newspaper in the State to give its support to the ticket.

In local matters, fusion between Whigs and Free Soilers went on at a rapid pace. In at least eleven counties the two parties united completely; indeed, the Whigs and Free Soilers were so inextricably confused that, before the election, the *Detroit Advertiser* printed the list of candidates without any attempt to distinguish one from the other. In the Munroe County district the regular Democratic convention, — by advice of Cass, it is said, — made an attempt to get Free Soil votes by nominating I. P. Christiancy; but as both Whigs and Free Soilers joined in the nomination, the move proved fruitless. One of the humorous aspects of the campaign appears in the way in which Democratic and Whig papers regarded coalition in other States. The *Detroit Free Press*, while loudly applauding " Democratic reunion " in New York and elsewhere, thought that nothing could explain Free Soil and Whig fusion except " an unhallowed thirst for spoils "; and the *Detroit Advertiser*, in the intervals of its hard work to get Whigs to support Littlejohn, found time to condemn the " venal truckling and dicker coalition between the Cass Hunkers and Abolitionists in Vermont."

The election came off in November, and the legislature showed some Whig and Free Soil gains; but in the vote for Governor the coalition was decisively beaten. The vote was as follows : Democratic — Barry, 27,837 ; Fusion — Littlejohn, 23,541.[2] The decrease in the total vote as compared with that of 1848 was 13,638. The explanation is probably to be found in the fact that great numbers on both sides refused to vote at all, including, besides the usual "off year" indifferents, Democrats who hated Cass yet would not aid the Whigs, and Whigs who found it "a choice between Locofocos." Plainly Whig discontent was the greater, since the coalition vote was less than the combined Free Soil and Whig vote of 1848 by fully 10,788, while the Democratic vote had fallen off but 2,850. In

---

[1] *Detroit Advertiser*, Oct. 6, 1849.

[2] Partial returns in *Whig Almanac*, 1850, and in *Detroit Advertiser*.

commenting on the election, the *Advertiser* undoubtedly told the truth when it said: "Many of our friends looked upon a union of Whigs with the Free Soil party upon any terms as pregnant with mischief, and as having a direct tendency to *denationalize* the Whig party. Many Whigs who were in favor of a union disliked the terms upon which the union was effected, thinking that in the present numerical ratio of the two parties too much was conceded to the Free Soil party on the ticket; while still another portion was actuated by a strong distaste toward the gubernatorial candidate. These causes combined produced a general apathy through the state in the Whig ranks and gave rise to open opposition . . . in other portions of our state, giving to our opponents an easy victory and a large majority."[1]

Irritation was inevitable between the two wings of the defeated coalition, and lively recriminations were exchanged. The Old Line Democrats gleefully contributed to increase the discontent and mortification of the Whigs by constantly asserting that "the Democratic Free Soilers would not coalesce with the Whigs, but went for Barry and Fenton; this is true both of the rank and file and of the leaders";[2] until the *Detroit Advertiser*, apparently convinced, said bitterly of the Free Soilers: "If the non-extension of slavery is the only great, ultimate object for which that party was organized, it becomes more and more difficult to reconcile with the prosecution of that object the results which have just taken place."[3] The *Peninsular Freeman*, on the other hand, said: "The Free Soil men generally turned out and voted the union ticket, while large numbers of Whigs absented themselves from the polls and hundreds of others voted the Barry ticket entire or the union ticket with the names of the Free Soil candidates erased."[4]

The next year carried on the struggle between Cass and his opponents to a further stage, and again the Free Soilers, in

---

[1] *Detroit Advertiser*, Nov. 9, 1849.
[2] *Detroit Free Press*, Nov. 13, 1849. [3] Nov. 13, 1849.
[4] Quoted in *National Era*, Nov. 22, 1849. The election returns in some degree substantiate this latter claim; for of the twenty-one counties where full returns are found, Coe led Littlejohn in seventeen by from 20 to 140 votes, having a net lead of 845 votes.

their eagerness to oppose him, threw away their consistency as a party. In the legislature of 1850, in spite of the efforts of Cass's friends, Free Soil sentiment was still strong enough to secure in February the passage of resolutions instructing Senators and Representatives to favor the admission of California as a free State. By March the efforts of Webster, Clay, and Cass together began to have some effect on public sentiment in Michigan, long before they were felt in Ohio or in the other Northwestern States; and although a resolution formally eulogizing Clay and Cass for their efforts in behalf of the Union was defeated, yet Cass's desires were finally satisfied by the passage of resolutions rescinding the Wilmot Proviso instructions of a year before. Cass affected to consider this action an expression of the will of the State; but in view of the way in which the resolution was passed his claim seems hardly admissible.[1] In the House the vote was 24 to 20, with twenty-two absentees, and in the Senate the resolution was carried only by the casting vote of the Lieutenant-Governor, who during the previous election had posed as a Wilmot Proviso man. " The vaunted expression of Michigan," said a correspondent of the *National Era*, " is an expression of a minority of the Legislature obtained by treachery and deception." [2] In the spring, elections were held for a Constitutional Convention; and in a few places, where Democrats were rash enough to resolve in favor of the rescinding resolution, Whig successes were the result. In general, however, as in Ohio and Indiana, the Democrats were in a great majority, the delegation standing as follows: Democratic, 75; Whig, 18; Free Soil, 3. This convention and those of Indiana and Ohio will be considered together later.

The Free Soil party of Michigan did not in this year drop into the inanition of that of Indiana. It still retained spirit enough to hold two conventions, one in May, 1850, which resolved against Clay's Compromise and urged a thorough organization; and another in September, which nominated a full ticket for Secretary of State, auditors, and for other minor offices. Still, the main interest of the Free Soilers

---

[1] See A. C. McLaughlin, *Lewis Cass*, 273.
[2] *National Era*, Sept. 5, 1850.

was not in the general State election, but in the choice of Congressmen.

The year 1850 was to set the Democratic party free from that anti-slavery opposition which had been annoying Cass ever since 1848; for the intimate connection of Cass with the Compromise measures brought his followers in Michigan into line before those in any other Northwestern State. As the Congressional campaign came on in the summer, the Democratic press called for conservative nominations, objecting particularly to K. S. Bingham, who, elected in 1848 as a " Free Soil Cass man," had voted in Congress entirely without regard to his distinguished superior; and to Sprague, chosen by Whig and Free Soil fusion in 1848, and now a strong Wilmot Proviso man. " We want a delegation in Congress," said the *Jackson Patriot*, " who will labor for the nomination of our great statesman. We want no more Binghams in Congress." " The delegation," said the *Kalamazoo Gazette*, " must reflect the wishes of the people and coincide in sentiment with General Cass; must be both his warm personal and political friends. We want no more Spragues or Binghams." [1] The result was the nomination in all three districts of men whom the Whigs and Free Soilers considered unmitigated doughfaces. In the Second District, Stuart was renominated; in the First, A. W. Buel, one of Cass's intimate friends; and in the Third, General Hascall, in place of Bingham. The Whigs were quick to seize their opportunity, and to these candidates opposed Williams, Penniman, and Conger, all sound Whigs and anti-slavery men. In the Third District, K. S. Bingham at first appeared as an independent candidate; but after J. S. Conger, the Whig nominee, had written, in reply to questions asked by a Free Soiler, his full acceptance of the Free Soil creed and his condemnation of the Fugitive Slave Law, Bingham withdrew in his favor.[2] The Free Soilers made no nominations, but joined the Whigs in all three districts. The *Peninsular Freeman* said in regard to Penniman: " Their support of him will be given freely, cordially and without solicitation, bargains or pledges on the part of Mr. Penniman.

[1] Quoted in *Detroit Advertiser*, Aug. 31, 1850.
[2] *Ibid.*, Oct. 23, 1850.

. . . Decency requires the election of Mr. Penniman and the defeat of Mr. Buel." [1]

The campaign that followed was very brisk; for General Cass, bound to secure " vindication," took the stump himself in Buel's district. For once, however, popular sentiment found a chance to express itself directly, with the result that Buel and Hascall were decisively beaten and Stuart barely succeeded.[2] Had the whole Democratic ticket, State and Congressional, been defeated, the Whigs and Free Soilers could not have been more exultant than they were over their partial victory. Buel was Cass's right-hand man; he had voted for the Fugitive Slave Law; and Cass's labors on the stump had not saved him! In this election the Whigs profited more by the sins of their opponents than by their own virtues; for their State Convention had adopted resolutions in favor of the Compromise, and during all the campaign the party organs, so zealous in appealing to the Free Soilers a year before, had ignored the existence of the latter party, and had avoided discussion of the slavery question whenever they could. After the election the Whig papers expressly denied any coalition, and it is true that there was no formal union; nevertheless, the Whigs owed their success to Free Soil votes; but the Free Soil party of Michigan had by this time practically disappeared, having been absorbed in the Whig ranks.

The Free Soil vote for Secretary of State was about the same as the Liberty vote of 1842, — Democratic, 32,372; Whig, 26,331; Free Soil, 2,228. Probably none but a few former Liberty men voted the ticket, for in a majority of the counties the Free Soil organizations had disappeared.

In Michigan, Whig coalition had proved quite as deadly to the growth of the Free Soil party as had Democratic coalition

---

[1] Quoted in *National Era*, Nov. 14, 1850.
[2] The vote this year was as follows : —

	Democratic.		Opposition.	
First District	Buel	8,909	Penniman	10,741
Second District	Stuart	11,923	Williams	11,508
Third District	Hascall	8,427	Conger	8,623

See returns in *Whig Almanac*, 1851.

in Ohio and Indiana; but unlike the Free Soilers in the latter States, who had Chase, Giddings, and Julian to represent them in Congress, the Michigan anti-slavery men had no party gains in the national government to recompense them for the sacrifice of party consistency.

Wisconsin was a State from which Free Soilers had apparently very much to hope. In the fall of 1848 they had one-fourth of the total vote, a good organization, and a Representative at Washington, Charles Durkee, elected from the southeastern district. In this State, however, the local Democratic and Whig parties were both as anti-slavery in 1848 as the Free Soilers themselves, and now after the election they began to insist with increasing emphasis that a third party was unnecessary. The Wisconsin Democrats in particular began to clamor for "reunion," with a vigor surpassing that of the New York Hunkers themselves.

In the legislature of 1848–49 Wisconsin had to choose a Senator, and before the Free Soilers could form any settled policy they found themselves in the midst of the struggle. The Democrats had a nominal majority over both Whigs and Free Soilers; but many of their number were Wilmot Proviso men, and by a coalition of some sort it would have been possible to defeat the party candidate. Although some negotiations were begun, none were seriously prosecuted; and, after a little reluctance on the part of the House of Representatives, the two bodies of the legislature met in joint convention and by a vote of 45 against Whig 18, Free Soil 18, scattering 4, re-elected I. P. Walker, chosen in the preceding June as a strong Wilmot Proviso man. Had any coalition been attempted between Whigs and Free Soilers, it would have met the same fate as did that in Ohio; for from the outset two men elected to the legislature as Free Democrats acted with the "Old Line," attending their caucus and voting for Walker.

When the State Free Soil Convention met at Madison on January 11, the feeling in favor of Democratic reunion carried everything before it. After adopting the Buffalo platform, with sundry additional planks in favor of land reform, free trade, direct taxation, and election of all federal officers by popular vote, it resolved " That we are ready to unite and co-operate with any party or the members of any party that cordially approve the principles embodied in the foregoing Resolutions."[1] Moses M. Strong, a "regular" Democrat, then appeared and spoke in favor of union. Nothing could have presented a more striking contrast to the Liberty convention which, engineered by Booth, Codding, and some of the very men most prominent in this Free Soil meeting, had less than nine months before refused to co-operate on the basis of the Wilmot Proviso. The Whig elements of the party were thoroughly alarmed at this tendency to unite, and no less at the free trade resolutions; but their occasional protests passed unheeded, and every day seemed to bring the Wisconsin Free Soilers and Democrats together, to the joy of such papers as the Oshkosh *True Democrat.* "We have a strong love for the Democratic party," it said, "and after having left it we look with yearning anxiety to see it assume a position that will warrant our return to its support."[2]

The legislature adopted by large majorities a set of instructions, introduced by S. D. Hastings, directing their Senators and Representatives to vote for the Wilmot Proviso; but Senator Walker, although elected as an anti-slavery man, failed to obey them. On February 21 he introduced a scheme organizing the new Territories without providing for the exclusion of slavery, and at once he became the mark for unsparing condemnation throughout his State. So great offence at his treachery was felt by all parties in the legislature that resolutions of censure, requesting him to resign, were passed in both Houses, in the Senate 10 to 6, in the House 42 to 9. Shortly after this the final steps were taken toward Free Soil and Democratic "reunion," to which such incidents as union conventions in Waukesha and Winnebago Counties had been pointing. A conference of Free Soil and Democratic members of the Legislature was held on March 30, 1849, at which, after some discussion, the Buffalo platform was unanimously adopted as a basis

[1] *Madison Express*, Jan. 16, 1849.
[2] Feb. 23, 1849.

of action, and the following resolutions in substance were agreed
on : —

"Whereas it appears that the principles held by the great
majority of the Democratic and Free Soil parties in this state
are the same;

"*Resolved* that we recommend that the State Central Committees unite in calling a State Convention to be held at Madison September 5th.

"*Resolved* that we recommend to our friends in all parts of
the state to abandon their separate organizations." [1]

The Free Soil party of Wisconsin was running its career at a
pace calculated to startle its members. Born in August, 1848,
it had cast 10,000 votes in November, and now in April of 1849,
in the seventh month of its existence, it was joined to the "Old
Line in one grand party of progress." By June, however, a flaw
appeared in the new union. The Free Soil Central Committee
had invited the Democratic Central Committee to co-operate
with them as suggested by the resolutions of March 30; but
for nearly a month the latter body had refused to make any
reply. The Democratic members of the legislature had gone
rather too fast for their constituents, and Old Line Democrats
wished to pause. At the end of June a reply came in the shape
of a call for a Democratic State Convention, with an explanation
appended to the following effect: Union, it said, was desirable,
but for the Democratic Committee to act outside its own party
was to exceed its powers; moreover, no practical method had
been suggested; two simultaneous conventions were clumsy
and would quarrel over officers; one convention composed
equally of the two parties would be unfair to the Democrats, who outnumbered the Free Soilers one-half; and, finally,
since the point on which the Free Democrats had separated
had no reference to State issues, they might as well express
their preferences in the regular Democratic primaries, for "a
return would be attended with no degradation of feeling." [2] This
proposal was a dash of cold water which left the bewildered
Free Soilers gasping. The dream of power in which most of

[1] Milwaukee *Wisconsin*, April 11, 1849.
[2] *Ibid.*, July 5, 1849.

them had been indulging since April was rudely shattered by the information that they could, if they chose, "rejoin" the Democratic party as individuals, but not as an organization. Unless they proposed to lose their identity, there was nothing to do but to call a convention of their own. This they did, appointing it for September 7, two days after the Democratic meeting. "We are coolly told that we went off without reason," said the *Kenosha Telegraph*, "and the most we can ask is the privilege of coming back unquestioned. We see but one course for the Free Democrats to pursue. Hold their Convention, make their nominations, and elect their ticket if they can." [1]

During the summer of 1849 the Free Soil party of Wisconsin was in a chaotic state, with the Liberty element eager to act alone, the Whig members disgusted at the coalition negotiations and the free-trade platform, and the Democratic members torn between irritation at the trickery of the Democratic Central Committee and a strong desire to rejoin their old associates if they consistently could. In many of the counties local fusion took place, the union Democratic meeting choosing delegates sometimes to one State convention, sometimes to both, instructing them in nearly every case to work for harmony. On September 5 the Democratic convention met, and although composed, as the Free Soil organs claimed, of office-seekers and their particular friends, it showed much political sagacity. It nominated a full set of irreproachable Old Line Democrats, and then, to emphasize the absorption of the Free Soilers, it adopted the platform recommended in the union resolutions of March 30. Except by a few delegates, no notice was taken of the Free Soilers; consequently the feelings of the convention of that party, which met two days later, were those of almost unmixed bitterness. They saw the trap into which they had run by their offer to coalesce with any party adopting their principles; and the Democratic acceptance of their offer left them no way of escape.

Although the Free Soilers had called a "union" convention, there were present only a few more than forty delegates, of whom eighteen had already attended the Democratic meeting.

[1] July 6, 1849.

These latter, under the leadership of A. W. Randall and A. E. Elmore, moved that, since the Democrats had adopted the platform of the Free Soilers, the latter should appoint a committee to question the Democratic nominees, and then adjourn; but this course involved greater self-effacement than the majority of those present could endure. It was resolved, 25 to 18, that this was a union convention; and, 28 to 13, that it proceed to nominate; whereat the minority withdrew.[1] The remaining handful of Free Soilers nominated a ticket largely of Barnburners, headed by N. Dewey, the Democratic nominee, and attacked the Democrats' hypocrisy in nominating Old Hunkers upon a Free Democratic platform; but this ground was almost immediately cut from under their feet by the action of the seceding delegates. That faction, continuing to act together, had addressed each of the Democratic candidates, and each, in answer to a specific question, had declared that he was in favor of the platform upon which he was nominated, and that he saw no difference between it and the Free Soil platform.[2] Thus completely outwitted, the Free Soil party approached election day without a leg to stand on, presenting to the public merely the spectacle of a band of men who, denied the spoils for which they had hoped, refused to live up to their promises. In all the history of political manœuvring in the Northwest, there is nothing to surpass the consummate ease and skill with which Wisconsin Democrats in this year took the Free Soilers at their word, deprived them of logical consistency, and put them in the wrong.

During these intrigues the Wisconsin Whig party had been keeping on its own way, filled, of course, with holy horror at the corrupt coalition, but in the main enjoying heartily the Democratic quarrels. "Go it," said the *Wisconsin Express*, when there was a prospect of a Democratic Union Convention; "we shall like to see these elements of corruption come together; the effervescence would be beautiful."[3] On September 11 the Whig State Convention nominated a set of regular party

---

[1] *Kenosha Telegraph*, Sept. 21, 1849.

[2] Milwaukee *Wisconsin*, Oct. 20, 1849.

[3] Madison *Wisconsin Express*, July 17, 1849.

men, passed resolutions indorsing Taylor, and also demanded "the invariable application of the Anti-Slavery clause of the Ordinance of 1787 to every law organizing a new Territory or creating a new State."[1] Such a platform offered an attractive refuge to Whig Free Soilers, who were disgusted at the coalition fiasco; and there is little doubt that, parallel with desertions to the Democratic party, a slight exodus of returning Whigs took place from the Free Soil ranks. Before the election day, to complete the Free Soil discredit, one member of their Central Committee resigned, "seeing no necessity for a separate organization;" and Dewey and one other candidate refused to run on the Free Soil ticket. Their places were filled by W. Chase and E. D. Holton respectively, through a mass convention on October 11.

The vote in November was as follows: Democratic — Dewey, 16,649; Whig — Collins, 11,317; Free Soil — Chase, 3,761.[2] As compared with the preceding year, the Democrats had gained 1,648, the Whigs had lost 2,430, and the Free Soilers 6,657. If the parties had maintained their proportional strength, the Democrats and Whigs would have lost about 2,700 apiece, and the Free Soilers 2,000; as it was, the Democratic gains indicate that about 4,000 Free Soilers voted the Democratic ticket, about 200 the Whig, and that some did not vote at all.

By these interesting operations the Free Soil party of Wisconsin had at the end of 1849 reduced itself to a condition of almost complete helplessness. Its press, broken-spirited and dejected, knew not how to meet the exultant assertions of Whigs and Democrats that the Free Soil party was dead and would never run another independent ticket. "What shall the Free Soilers do?" asked the *Kenosha Telegraph*. "At present it strikes us the Free Soilers have nothing to do except simply to keep an eye upon the dominant party. It is not at all important to us who has our thunder, so it is used, and used effectively. Let us quietly observe the dominant party."[3] In the next year (1850) the party made no sign of life except through three newspapers which still remained faithful, and through the

[1] *Milwaukee Sentinel*, Sept. 17, 1849.
[2] Vote in *Whig Almanac*, 1850.   [3] Nov. 30, 1849.

few local conventions which coalition had not swallowed up. In the Legislature nothing of note occurred except the fusion of Free Soil and Democratic Senators "under a call for all those in favor of the Resolutions of the Democratic State Convention," [1] and later the unanimous passage of resolutions instructing Senators Dodge and Walker to vote for the Wilmot Proviso.

As in Michigan and Ohio, the political interest of the State centred, in 1850, in the election of Congressmen. In the Second District, where Orsamus Cole, the Whig incumbent, had an excellent anti-slavery record, and where Eastman, the Democratic candidate, pledged himself in favor of the Wilmot Proviso, no Free Soil nomination was made, nor was any party action taken. In the Third District, J. D. Doty, like Bingham in Michigan, was thrown over by the Democrats on account of his Free Soil action in Congress. After a short time Doty came out as an independent anti-slavery candidate, and as such received the enthusiastic support of both Whigs and Free Soilers. The campaign in his district became extremely embittered; for Doty carried with him five bolting Democratic journals, and the personalities and abuse which passed between these papers and their old associates were of full frontier flavor. It was in the First District, however, that the Free Soil sentiment of the State centred. As the Western Reserve in Ohio was now standing faithful and alone, so the southeastern counties of Wisconsin — Walworth, Racine, and Kenosha — alone kept up Free Soil organizations, and it was their absorbing purpose to re-elect Charles Durkee. In the hope that his good record in Congress might procure him an unopposed return, no formal nomination was made; but a petition of a thousand names was sent, urging him to stand. To this request he acceded in September. Some Free Soilers undoubtedly hoped that the Democratic machine would indorse him; but when the Democratic district convention met and nominated A. E. Elmore, one of the seceders from the union convention of a year before, the last flickering hope of Democratic and Free Soil coalition died out. The Walworth County Free Soilers resolved, "That the course of the leaders

---

[1] *Kenosha Telegraph,* Jan. 18, 1850; *National Era,* Jan. 31, 1850.

of the old Democratic party of this State subsequent to the last State Convention . . . in their marked hostility to the re-election of Messrs. Doty and Durkee," shows that " the adoption of the Free Soil party platform in the Convention of September 5th last was faithless and hypocritical . . . and it will be the fault of the Free Democrats themselves if they shall hereafter be deceived by any reiterations of the same professions." [1]

Now happened an unexpected piece of good fortune. The Whig papers began to shower praise on Durkee; and when the local Whig conventions nominated J. H. Tweedy for Congress, that gentleman instantly resigned in Durkee's favor. As in Michigan, this line of action met with strenuous opposition; and when a second Whig convention adjourned without nominating, a public meeting was held in Milwaukee to censure this conduct as an abandonment of Whig principles. The Whig leaders, however, with the *Milwaukee Sentinel, Madison Express,* and *State Journal,* fell upon the protestors with such energy that the revolt was nipped in the bud. Tweedy " did not hesitate to avow a decided preference for Mr. Durkee as an upright, honest, reliable man. He characterized the resolutions [of censure] as insidious, dastardly, and uncalled for." [2] Through the vigorous support of the Whig papers, the preference of many Free Soil Democrats for Elmore over Durkee was counteracted, and in the election the latter gained a well-earned victory.[3]

Thus, by the end of 1850, the Free Soil party in Wisconsin was indistinguishable as a separate organization, except in the southeastern counties. There anti-slavery sentiment insured the return of a real Free Soiler to Congress; but even this success was due to Whig help. In 1849 coalition had dragged the Free Soil party into the dust, where it lay during 1850; but so long

---

[1] *Milwaukee Sentinel,* Oct. 8, 1850.   [2] *Ibid.,* Oct. 28, 1850.

[3] The vote in the three districts was as follows: —

	Democratic.		Opposition.	
First District	Elmore	5,574	Durkee	7,512
Second District	Eastman	7,262	Cole	5,852
Third District	Hobart	5,374	Doty	11,159

See *Whig Almanac,* 1851.

as coalition could secure the return of a man like Durkee, Free Soil prospects in Wisconsin were by no means in total eclipse.

The Free Soil party of Iowa, diminutive as it was, in comparison with those of Michigan and Wisconsin, held a similar balance of power, and consequently in 1849 found itself involved in coalition. Little was to be hoped from the local Democratic party. Its members were of the same stamp as those of " Egypt " and of Missouri, and its record in the legislature and in Congress had been uniformly such as would seem to put coalition out of the question. Nevertheless, in some localities efforts were made to bring the two " Democratic " parties together,[1] and there is reason to think that local fusion did take place, — a circumstance merely indicating how much stronger was the feeling for " Democracy " than for anti-slavery.

In Henry County, the centre of anti-slavery sentiment, a union ticket was formed to overthrow Whig control, which the Mt. Pleasant Free Soil paper called " the intolerable domination of truckling doughfaces." [2] In Washington County the Old Line Democrats placed three active Free Soilers upon the county ticket; but the Free Soil convention, though it ratified these nominations, declined to complete the union by accepting the other Democratic nominees. Some hopes were occasionally expressed that the State Democratic party might " reunite " with the Free Soilers; and it was asserted by the *Capitol Reporter* that Kelsey, the editor of the *Iowa Free Democrat*, attended the State Convention on June 28 with hopes of making some " deal." However that may have been, the action of the Democrats, who deprecated sectional parties and deemed it " inexpedient to add to the further distraction of the public mind by demanding in the name of the Wilmot Proviso what is already amply secured by the laws of the land," [3] settled definitively that no honorable coalition could take place between the two Democracies.

The local Whigs were on a different footing; for in Iowa their party contained whatever anti-slavery sentiment was to be found

[1] *National Era*, July 26, 1849.   [2] *Iowa Free Democrat*, July 31, 1849.
[3] *National Era*, Aug. 16, 1849.

outside of the little band of Liberty men. Its members in the legislature frequently spoke and voted in favor of anti-slavery petitions and measures ; and although it had supported Taylor and the Mexican War, and disclaimed, as did the Whig party in most of the Northwestern States, any sympathy with abolitionists, it seemed to furnish the most promising ally to the Free Soil body. The Free Soil State Convention, early in 1849, nominated for State offices two Free Soilers, and W. H. Allison, a Whig, whose record in the legislature was very creditable from an antislavery point of view. On June 29 the Whig State Convention adopted a solid Free Soil plank, and concurred in the nomination of Allison,[1] to the intense scandal of every Loco-foco in Iowa, and of very many " Silver-gray " Whigs. An avalanche of billingsgate descended upon the "disgusting coalition," the "amalgamation," the "marriage of Whiggery to abolitionism," the "sale of the abolitionists to the Whigs " ; while the *Free Democrat*, on the other side, justified the partial fusion as "manly and independent," and the *Whig and Reporter* held up to scorn the " ribald abuse and vulgar blackguardism " of the Democrats.[2] On the face of things, the coalition seemed to have a fair chance of success, for according to the vote of 1848 the Free Soilers held the balance of power; but the election of August showed as complete a fiasco as did the Whig and Free Soil coalition in Michigan two months later.[3]

Just what caused the failure of the arrangement is not obvious. Very probably Free Soilers of Democratic antecedents were so repelled by the nomination of a Whig that they preferred to act with their old party, in spite of its recent action; it is also likely that some " Silver-gray " Whigs bolted their own ticket out of dislike to Allison's anti-slavery record; so that (as some dissatisfied Free Soilers claimed openly) the

---

[1] *National Era*, July 26, 1849.

[2] *Iowa Free Democrat*, July 31, 1849.

[3] The vote stood as follows : —

	Democratic.	Whig.	Free Soil.
Secretary	Williams 12,154	Allison 10,978	
Public Works	Patterson 11,672	McKean 10,960	Dayton 564

See *Whig Almanac*, 1851.

defeat of the ticket was due to Whig treachery.[1]   Probably both causes operated.   In the part of the ticket where there was no coalition we see the usual results; for the Free Soil vote of 1,126 in 1848 was reduced exactly one half.   After such a defeat, with numbers shrunk to a mere handful, it is surprising to find that the Free Soilers of Iowa continued their activity into the next year.

In the early months of 1850 there was some talk of renewing the coalition.   W. P. Clarke, a leading Free Soiler of Whig antecedents, wrote a letter urging that the two parties were practically agreed on anti-slavery matters, and ought to co-operate against their common enemy, the Democrats; but the reception given to the letter showed that the time for fusion had gone by.   The *Iowa Republican* admitted that the two parties occupied the same ground, and spoke favorably, although in general terms, of the union of all true men; but the *Muscatine Journal,* representing the conservative Whigs, said sharply: "We are decidedly opposed to having anything to do with the Free Soilers and will not support any amalgamated ticket.   Let us have a *Whig* ticket or none at all."[2]   The Democrats looked on with jeering indifference, the *Iowa State Gazette* remarking that " to the Democrats these movements are important only as passing events of the day . . . Experience proves that such coalitions frequently detract from the efficient strength of a party instead of serving to augment it.   A striking illustration of this truth was furnished by the result of the last election and . . . an equally emphatic condemnation awaits any attempt that may be made in August next to unite the Whig and abolition forces."[3]

Thus the Free Soilers went on by themselves.   Local conventions in Linn, Henry, Lee, and other counties, passed courageous resolutions; on May 8, 1850, a State Convention, led by W. P. Clarke and S. L. Howe, nominated a full ticket,[4] and by August there were two Congressional tickets in the field.   The manner in which these nominations were received led the *True*

---

[1] Letter in *Indiana True Democrat,* March 13, 1850.

[2] Quoted in *Iowa Free Democrat,* Jan. 15, 1850.

[3] Quoted *Ibid.,* Jan. 22, 1850.

[4] *Iowa True Democrat,* May 28, 1850, same paper as the *Free Democrat.*

Democrat to comment on the transparent hypocrisy of the old parties: " The Cassite glories in our spunk in nominating a Congressional candidate, but emphatically condemns the county nomination ; whilst the Taylorite rejoices in our county nomination, but utterly abhors the Congressional. We hope," it concluded, " we hereafter shall be able to maintain moral stamina enough to resist all machinations of all the political demagogues of all the political parties who approach us with their fraudulent and delusive temptations." [1] Great efforts at organization were made ; the party held three successive State Conventions ; but in spite of an active campaign, the result of the election was disheartening.[2] The Free Soil party was evidently reduced to its lowest terms, and under existing circumstances could hope for no more than 600 votes at the outside. Nevertheless, the Iowa abolitionists refused to admit their failure ; and immediately after the election the party showed its persistence by holding a State Convention at Yellow Springs, on October 30, which condemned the Fugitive Slave Law and planned for further organization.[3]

The Iowa Free Soil party, it is evident, lost the greater part of the Barnburner, or Democratic, elements in 1849, just as happened in the other States ; but the remainder showed an elasticity under defeat, and a persistence in organization, quite different from the complete depression into which the party fell in every other State except Ohio. The reason for this elasticity lay in the fact that the Iowa Free Soilers were practically all abolitionists ; consequently their activity in 1850 should not be compared with the almost total collapse of their Illinois and Wisconsin neighbors in that year. It finds its parallel in the Liberty Party action of 1841–44 in the latter States, and exhibits the same courage, persistency, and zeal which that party had shown before it was weakened by years of disappointment.

---

[1] *Iowa True Democrat,* June 25, 1850.

[2] The figures are : —

	Democratic.	Whig.	Free Soil.
For Governor	13,192	11,082	574
For Congress	13,182	11,710	479

See *Whig Almanac,* 1851.

[3] *National Era,* Jan. 23, 1851.

CHAPTER XIV.

CAUSES OF THE FREE SOIL COLLAPSE.

1849–1850.

WE are now in a position to take a general view of the years 1849–50 in the Northwest. It is obvious that beneath the various forms of political surface movements in the six States ran a common undercurrent which, by the end of 1850, had either engulfed the Free Soilers into the mass of the old parties, or had left a small remnant stranded high and dry, in much the same situation as that of the Liberty men of four years before.

The causes of this phenomenon have been suggested incidentally in connection with the various States, but they may here be summed up. The first reason why the Free Soilers desired coalition lay in the character of the leaders of the movement. In 1848, in every Northwestern State, the men in the forefront of the new party had been prominent, ardent partisans and practical politicians, who aimed at electing their candidates, — Giddings, Hamlin, Riddle, Randall, and others, in the Western Reserve; Christiancy, Littlejohn, Blair, in Michigan; Ellsworth, Cravens, Wright, in Indiana; Hoyne, Arnold, Ogden, in Illinois; Marshall M. Strong, Chase, Randall, Elmore, in Wisconsin. These men and many others were active Whigs and Democrats up to the time of the revolt, and most of them had been or were office-holders. With such men the attainment of office as an immediate end is of vastly greater importance than the building up of a party by separation, agitation, and appeal to popular sentiment. The best way to affect the popular mind, in their opinion, was to get some public representative. If such a result could be gained by separate action, well and good; but if only by coalition, what did it matter, provided that principles were not violated?

Secondly, it should not be forgotten that the years 1848–50 were a period of crisis. All eyes were on Congress, from its meeting in December, 1848, until the final consummation of the Compromise in the autumn of 1850. So long as the question of slavery in the Territories was undecided, while California clamored for admission, while the South threatened secession, and Clay, Webster, and Cass pleaded for compromise, it was obviously of the first importance to get the best antislavery men possible elected to places where they could vote on the main question; and it was no time to split hairs over the propriety of coalition, if that means would serve to secure this result. With such ideas the Liberty men were not familiar; but when brought to the point few of them flinched. In Ohio, in fact, Chase outstripped his ex-Whig associates in his interpretation of the new doctrine.

Wherever the Free Soilers were willing to coalesce, the old parties as a general rule met them more than half-way. From the election of 1848 down to the very passage of the Compromise of 1850, Democratic and Whig leaders, papers, and conventions avowed the Wilmot Proviso as an integral part of their creed. At no time in any State could the Free Soilers claim to be the only anti-slavery party. In Ohio, Indiana, and Wisconsin both parties asserted Free Soil principles; and in Illinois the local Whig and Democratic organizations in the northern part of the State proclaimed anti-slavery doctrines. In Michigan only did the Democratic party in 1850 drop its Free Soil attitude, and even then two of its Congressional candidates, Hascall and Stuart, wrote letters advocating the non-extension of slavery.[1]

What determined the direction of coalition? To some extent, the prepossessions of the politicians who led the new party. A majority in the Northwest, outside of Ohio, were former Democrats, and when their old party offered them the same principles as the new one, the desire to return was inevitable. A still

[1] *Detroit Advertiser*, Nov. 7, 1850.

more powerful motive lay in the general tendency existing toward Democratic coalition. The Buffalo nomination and platform had been a combination, in which Liberty men had the platform, Democrats the candidate; and now, after 1848, the influence of the New York Barnburners continued. They were and continued to be Democrats, regarding themselves as the only legitimate New York State organization; and when, in 1849, negotiations began between them and the Old Line Democrats, the example powerfully affected other sections. Throughout the Northwest, local ex-Democratic Free Soilers found themselves adopting the Barnburners' vocabulary, and freely speaking of "Democratic reunion," though a few months before they had been urging each other to "fight on, fight ever, till victory shall crown our cause."

To this tendency was added a strong feeling that the Democrats, as the party beaten in 1848, were on the point of taking anti-slavery ground. "Our opinion is," said the Oshkosh *True Democrat*, "that there are to be only two parties in the state, the Free Democratic and the Taylor; that the latter will be composed of conservatives from the Cass Democratic and Whig parties, while the former will embody the radicals of all parties and be largely in the majority." [1] "The Democracy of the Free States," said the Ann Arbor *True Democrat*, "are released from all further responsibility of protecting the supposed rights of the slaveholders against the growing encroachments of Freedom. The Taylor party have taken their place. The Democratic masses will now join the standard of Freedom and Progress. . . . The Buffalo platform is the only firm standing ground amid the general wreck of old worn-out questions; . . . the mass of the party will adopt these principles and become one with us. . . . All our institutions must be made thoroughly Democratic." [2]

Moreover, the influence of names, pure and simple, should not be ignored. The name, "Free Democracy," was in itself a strong plea for Democratic union; for if the Old Line Democracy should become "Free" by adopting proper principles, where was the difference between the two parties? The as-

---

[1] March 23, 1849.   [2] Nov. 16, 1848.

sumption of the democratic character of anti-slavery principles fascinated even the ex-Liberty men into believing themselves Democrats; and hence such men as Chase were inclined to expect the reformation of the pro-slavery, annexation, filibustering, secession-threatening party of 1845–50, simply because it called itself "Democratic." So effective did this fallacy prove that, astonishing as it seems at the present day, the anti-slavery men of 1849 almost uniformly looked for allies to the Democratic party rather than to the Whig, even in places where, before 1848, such action was unthinkable. In Ohio, where, outside of the Liberty party, nine-tenths of the Free Soil voters of 1848 were Whigs, Democratic coalition swept everything; also in Illinois, where one-third of the party were Liberty men; in Indiana, where numbers of them were Whigs, and throughout Wisconsin.

Whig coalition took place in those regions only where Whig principles were most widely spread, or where the nature of the local Democratic party forbade Free Soil and Loco-foco union. In Ohio, in 1849, the coalition of Whigs and Free Soilers in the legislature, and in 1850 the union in the Twenty-first Congressional District, were due to the fact that on the Reserve the Free Soilers were largely ex-Whigs; but it is noteworthy that even here in 1849 coalition was chiefly with the Democrats. In Wisconsin in 1850, in Iowa in 1849, and in Michigan in 1849, Whig coalition did not take place until Democratic fusion had become clearly out of the question. In these States the Free Soil leaders themselves, though desirous of Democratic union, were usually passive when Whig aid was proffered. Had it not been for Cass's personal influence in Michigan in 1848–49, it seems possible that Democratic rather than Whig fusion would have occurred; but when once the tide had turned in the latter direction, the Free Soilers without hesitation continued to coalesce with Whigs in local and Congressional matters, until nothing was left of their old separate party.

It is sometimes said that the Compromise of 1850 killed the Free Soil party. In the Northwest this was certainly not the case; for although, when it did come, it put an end to the widespread Wilmot Proviso feeling, the Compromise was not completed until after coalition had run its course and the Free Soil party was already reduced to its lowest point. In the only elections that occurred after its passage — those in Michigan and Wisconsin — the Compromise seems to have had little effect, for in these States the Whig party continued anti-slavery up to the time of the election.

Nevertheless, the fact should not be overlooked that the circumstances of the year 1850 tended powerfully to obliterate party lines, and thereby to render exit from the Free Soil ranks easy. In every Northwestern State the threatening attitude of the Southern Democrats, coupled with the position taken by Cass and Douglas, brought about a reaction against the Democrats, which led many Free Soil men, especially in Michigan, Wisconsin, and Illinois, to join the Whigs, not merely coalescing, but entirely abandoning all third-party action. In 1850, then, the Free Soil party was hardly distinguishable as a separate organization in the Northwest; in only three of the States did it run third tickets, and in those it polled only a small fraction of its former strength. Most of those who, in 1848, had been the loudest in their devotion to the Wilmot Proviso had gone back either to the Democratic or to the Whig party, their return in every case being made easy by the strong anti-slavery platforms of the old organizations.

Coalition for immediate results had played its part, and in the various States had achieved some success. Ohio had a Free Soil Senator, three Free Soil Congressmen, and several Free Soil members of the legislature; through their balance of power in the legislature, the Free Soilers twice secured Wilmot Proviso resolutions and the repeal of the Black Laws. Indiana had one Free Soil Representative, and a Senator, and several Congressmen who avowed Free Soil doctrines. Michigan had several Free Soil members of the legislature and two Congressmen. Illinois had one Democratic Congressman, who, to secure his election, had been obliged to advocate Free Soil views. Wisconsin had one Free Soil Congressman, and two Senators who asserted Free Soil doctrine; and it also had several third-party Representatives in the legislature. Iowa alone had nothing to show. For a party polling in the six Northwestern States only eleven per cent. of the total vote, this record was cred-itable. As compared with that of the Liberty party, it showed a vast difference in results; but also another difference: in 1841 the Liberty men made a better showing for a separate party than did the Free Soilers in 1850. Coalition was a two-edged tool, every time it was used it hurt the user almost as much as the object attacked. So effective in both respects had it proved to the Free Soilers that, by 1850, when it practically ceased for a time, it ceased because the Free Soil party was virtually dead, and its former members had thus lost the power of compelling concessions.

15

CHAPTER XV.

THE FREE DEMOCRACY STANDS AGAINST FINALITY.

1850–1851.

IN the opening months of 1851 it seemed as if the last remnants of the Free Soil party might as well disband. A course of almost uninterrupted coalition had well-nigh destroyed among them both the wish and the power for independent action, had deprived them of faith in their own resources and in each other, and had reduced their State and local organizations to impotence.

To this disintegration the Compromise of 1850 — passed in September, 1850 — came as the finishing blow. People were tired, thoroughly tired, of the slavery struggle; they desired never to hear the words "Free Soil" or "Wilmot Proviso" again; all they wanted was peace, and this the Compromise offered.

In reality, the Compromise settled nothing; it left the territorial question much as it had been before; but this fact people agreed to ignore, and with one accord statesmen, politicians, and newspapers, hitherto strong for the Wilmot Proviso, joined in the cry that slavery agitation must now cease, that a settlement which was a "finality" had been reached. In the face of this clamor the Free Democratic party for the time being vanished from sight: its principles, just claimed by both parties, were now repudiated with the oft-repeated assertion that, since the question of slavery was settled, no one but a rank disunion abolitionist would still maintain them. The Barnburners in particular, who had already rejoined their old associates, now reviled their temporary allies of 1848 as constitution-breakers, fanatics, and fools, because they too did not cease struggling.

Nevertheless, this year, when things were at their lowest ebb, really marks the beginning of a new phase in the anti-slavery history of the Northwest. There was a feeling that in the hurly-burly of the last two years anti-slavery sentiment had become perverted, that a return to first principles was demanded; and consequently there was a reappearance of religious, moral, and non-partisan anti-slavery agitation, reminding one of the days previous to 1840. The Compromise measures included a statute against which anti-slavery people the country over could band themselves; it was the new Fugitive Slave Law, which indeed, upon its passage, had produced a sort of explosion in the Northwest. In Ohio, the Western Reserve rose as one man to condemn the obnoxious bill. Free Soil, Whig, and Democratic papers lamented its passage, and public meetings without respect to party uttered fiery denunciations coupled with threats of disobedience. Clergymen took an active part, and anti-slavery men who had hardly met since the days of 1838 found themselves for the moment side by side.

A few examples will illustrate the uproar. "We deem it the duty of every good citizen," said a meeting in Cleveland, "to oppose and resist by all proper means the execution of said law."[1] In Highland County a meeting, managed by Mr. Chase and the old time abolitionists, John Rankin and Samuel Crothers, resolved that "Disobedience to the enactment is obedience to God."[2] Said Belmont County: "If the Federal Government has any slaves to catch it may catch them, — we will not aid or assist, nor do we believe any respectable or high-minded citizen of the Union will."[3] Washington County resolved "That any man who in any way aids in the execution of this law should be regarded as false to God and totally unfit for civilized society."[4] Similar sentiments were expressed in Indiana, where one of the meetings, rising on the wings of eloquence, resolved "That we will not assist, if called upon,

[1] *True Democrat*, Oct. 14, 1850.
[2] *National Era*, Dec. 5, 1850.
[3] *Ibid.*, Nov. 14, 1850.   [4] *Ibid.*, Dec. 5, 1850.

in capturing or securing a fugitive slave under this act, although the penalty for refusing should deprive us of all our possessions and incarcerate us between dungeon walls."[1] A Michigan meeting resolved that "Any commissioner or marshal who will not rather resign his office than consent to aid in carrying this law into effect, has too little soul to appreciate the blessings of freedom, and is unworthy of our confidence or respect."[2] The northern counties of Illinois echoed these protests. The anti-slavery sentiment of Wisconsin revolted at the new law, expressing itself in dozens of protests; and Iowa felt a ripple of the excitement and held indignation meetings.[3]

Even legislative bodies felt the heat of this fierce indignation. The Chicago Common Council passed a resolution that the city police should not be required to aid in the recovery of slaves.[4] While the feeling was at its height, an effort was made in the Ohio legislature to pass resolutions instructing Senators and Representatives to vote for the repeal of the law; but it was defeated in the House, 38 to 33. Toward the end of the session, in March, some milder resolutions were passed, asking merely for an amendment of the law so as to secure jury trial; and, in default of that, for its repeal. This request was so unsatisfactory to the Free Soil members that some of them on the final passage voted against it.[5] In Wisconsin similar resolutions passed the Senate by a close vote, but were tabled in the House.[6] By the spring of 1851 the excitement among those who were not abolitionists had burnt itself out, and people were beginning to accept the law as a disagreeable but necessary part of the Compromise.

To all thorough-going anti-slavery men, however, the Fugitive Slave Law remained an object of execration; and its repeal formed the immediate aim of their agitation, now that

---

[1] *Indiana True Democrat*, Nov. 15, 1850.
[2] *National Era*, Nov. 14, 1850.
[3] *Iowa True Democrat*, Feb. 5, 1851.
[4] A. T. Andreas, *History of Chicago*, I., 608.
[5] *National Era*, April 3, 1851.
[6] *Kenosha Telegraph*, Feb. 14, 1851.

the Wilmot Proviso had been compromised away.[1]   Anti-slavery organization began once more at first principles, — on the ground that slavery was unrighteous.   In April, 1850, during the Compromise debate, a Christian Anti-Slavery Convention, in which veteran abolitionists of 1838 took part, had been held at Cincinnati with great success ;[2] following this model a Northwestern Christian Convention was held at Chicago, in July, 1851, at which eleven States were represented by clergymen and laymen, including many of the stamp of Samuel Lewis and Owen Lovejoy.   Both of these conventions revived the half-forgotten language of 1836, insisting on the pre-eminently religious character of anti-slavery action.[3]   In the following years local Christian conventions, held in all of the Northwestern States, revived the old agitation ; and, little by little, movements began toward resuming anti-slavery political action.   Ohio and Wisconsin, it is true, did not feel this impulse so much as did the other communities ; for in these two States the Free Soil party still lived on.   Michigan anti-slavery sentiment still remained prostrate, giving little or no sign of life.

In the rest of the Northwest the work of 1841 began anew. In Indiana the old Quaker leaven began to work again, and a call appeared in Wayne County, saying: "Years have elapsed since we have had an anti-slavery meeting in the county and all this time the foes of freedom have been triumphing. We have surely lost strength by inaction. Come, let us have a genuine, good, old-fashioned anti-slavery convention."[4]   Then came a Christian Anti-Slavery Convention at Indianapolis, on May 28, 1851, followed by a "Political Anti-Slavery Convention," in which, under the presidency of Judge Stevens, some old-time Liberty men, with a few Free Soilers, adopted a long series of resolutions of the old stamp, besides denouncing the Fugitive Slave Law, advocating prohibition of the liquor traffic, on the principle of the "Maine Law," and calling for a National

---

[1] A meeting to organize a party against the law was held in Randolph County, Indiana, Jan. 1, 1851: *Indiana True Democrat*, Feb. 27, 1851.

[2] *Report of the American and Foreign Anti-Slavery Society*, 1850.

[3] *National Era*, July 10, 31, 1851.

[4] *Indiana True Democrat*, April 10, 1851.

Political Anti-Slavery Convention at Cleveland. A State Central Committee was appointed, and measures were taken to sustain the *True Democrat*.[1]

Illinois followed the example of Indiana by holding, on January 9, a State Anti-Slavery Convention at Granville. A new State Anti-Slavery Society was formed on "religious, moral, and political grounds," with J. H. Collins as president, Z. Eastman as secretary, and with a full list of officers, nearly all of whom were old Liberty men. A set of resolutions was adopted, which, like those of Indiana, rang with radicalism; so that even the *National Era* felt called upon to condemn their tenor as "illegal and proscriptive." "Our efforts," it said, "are not limited to the restriction of slavery, but we labor for its abolition. An oath to support the Constitution never implies an obligation to support any immorality it may contain. . . . Slavery like piracy has no legal existence in the United States," and, in the language of the Liberty League, "it is unconstitutional."[2] There was also a convention for southern Illinois in Randolph County, which paid its respects to the "Union-saving" cry of the Compromisers in the following prophetic language: "We do not believe the union of these States is in the slightest manner endangered by the agitation of this question. The sagacious statesmen of the slave states know that a majority of their citizens are in favor of the Union. A war destructive of slavery, perhaps of the slaveholders, must be the results of secession."[3]

Such language fell unheeded by the leaders of the old parties. To them the non-extension of slavery was a dead issue; and, therefore, in most of the Northwestern States they proceeded to rid themselves in all haste of the Free Soil doctrines which they had been upholding so vigorously, and to plant themselves squarely on the Compromise. In Indiana the legislature opened the year by choosing, for Senator, J. D. Bright, who, in contrast to Whitcomb, elected in 1849, was "avowedly the friend and ally of the South." The *Indianapolis Sentinel*, which in 1849 had claimed that the Democratic party in its opposition to

---

[1] *National Era*, June 26, 1851; *Indiana True Democrat*, June 12, 1851.
[2] *Ibid.*, Feb. 6, 1851, March 20, 1851.   [3] *Ibid.*, July 3, 1851.

slavery "occupied a position of moral strength otherwise un-rivalled,"[1] now came under the control of W. J. Brown, who, though a Free Soil Democrat in 1848, now placed his paper among the unswerving advocates of the "finality" of the Compromise. Among the requisites for Democracy he placed "adherence to the recent Compromise measures of Congress on the subject of domestic slavery, and opposition to the repeal of the Fugitive Slave Law and further agitation of the slavery question. We are for the Compromise as a whole. On this rock we have taken our stand. It is the rock of safety to the Democratic party, and the rock of safety to the Union."[2] In Illinois the Democratic party in the legislature, through the influence of Douglas, passed resolutions indorsing the Compromise measures and rescinding the Wilmot Proviso instructions of two years before.

In Michigan the Democratic party, which already, under Cass's dictation, had abandoned Free Soil ground, now signalized the disappearance of old feuds by unanimously renominating Cass to the Senate, and later by nominating for governor R. McClelland, a former Wilmot Proviso man, whose nomination in 1849 had been prevented by Cass's personal effort. McClelland had been so consistently anti-slavery that the leaders of the defunct Free Soil party, after consultation, expressly declined to put a candidate in the field against him.[3]

The Democratic majority in the Wisconsin legislature passed resolutions rescinding the censure of Senator Walker in 1849; and the State Convention, in spite of opposition from some returned Barnburners, resolved "That the Democracy of Wisconsin now stand, where all true Democrats have stood since 1836, on the platform of principles drawn by that pure and lamented statesmen, Silas Wright; and we would in their name repudiate all extraneous issues and sectional tests of party faith as disorganizing in their tendency."[4]

The Iowa Democracy had been throughout so pro-slavery

---

[1] *National Era*, July 12, 1849.
[2] *Indiana True Democrat*, March 20, April 3, 1851.
[3] H. K. Clarke, *Detroit Post and Tribune*, July 6, 1879.
[4] *National Era*, Oct. 2, 1851; *Racine Advocate*, Sept. 17, 1851.

that no recantation was necessary to bring it into line with the
national party. In 1849, its majority in the legislature had
flouted and shelved some Wilmot Proviso resolutions, after
having made sport of them by proposing ludicrous and inde-
cent amendments. Now in 1851 the Iowa legislature proceeded
to pass joint resolutions favoring the Compromise; and enacted
a law forbidding free negroes or mulattoes to settle in the State
on penalty of fine and imprisonment, adding with cutting irony:
"This act is to take effect and be in force by publication in
the *Iowa True Democrat*, a weekly newspaper published in Mt.
Pleasant."[1] The *True Democrat* naturally refused to publish
the law, saying in its disgust: "When we take into consideration this new law, making Iowa a slaveholding state for slave-
holding monopolists, we think our legislature serves the Devil
with more alacrity than even their slave-holding lords could
desire."[2]

With the Whigs matters were somewhat different. To be
sure party organs directly accessible to "influence" from
Washington said, in the language of the *Detroit Advertiser* :
"No threats of disunion will ever serve to drive a single true-
hearted Whig from the support of an administration which he
knows to be *pure* and *true*."[3] Yet the party conventions were
less eager than were their Democratic opponents to ratify the
Compromise. The Ohio State Convention resolved that, as
the Compromise and the Fugitive Slave Law were not administration measures, every Whig was at liberty to hold his own
opinion concerning them; and many local conventions passed
anti-slavery resolutions. In Indiana, although the leading Whig
newspapers assumed a non-committal attitude, party conventions in two districts condemned the Fugitive Slave Law as
"impolitic, unjust, abhorrent to our feelings and repugnant to
our habits."[4] The Michigan Whig State Convention, "while
holding it to be the duty of every citizen to abide by and support all laws constitutionally passed on the subject of slavery,

---

[1] *Laws of Iowa* (1850–51), 172–73.

[2] Quoted in *Indiana True Democrat*, March 27, 1851.

[3] *Detroit Advertiser*, Feb. 3, 1851.

[4] *National Era*, Aug. 7, 1851.

nevertheless was now as always opposed to the extension of slavery over territory now free." [1] In Wisconsin the Whigs, still bolder, declared themselves opposed to the extension of slavery, and defied the " finality" cry by saying: " We deem it the unquestionable right of every citizen to canvass the merits of every enactment, and if found to be unjust, oppressive, or of doubtful expediency, to advocate their modification or repeal." [2]

In 1851 the only elections in which organized anti-slavery action was involved were in Indiana, Ohio, Wisconsin, and in Iowa, where, although the third-party men took no State action, enough vigor remained to run Free Democratic tickets in several counties. [3] In the Fourth Congressional District of Indiana, G. W. Julian, who had been elected in 1849 by Free Soil and Democratic coalition, was now, under very discouraging auspices, nominated for re-election. The only supporters upon whom he could certainly count were the Free Democrats and Liberty men, for the Whigs of the district stood on the Compromise, and the Democrats were wavering. In spite of the efforts of W. J. Brown, of the *Indianapolis Sentinel*, seconded by those of Oliver P. Morton, the Democratic district convention stood by him, since it knew that it had no chance of success without Free Soil help; it therefore passed some resolutions in favor of the Compromise, and adjourned without nominating anybody. [4] Julian was thus left the only opponent of the Whig candidate, and he made a gallant fight. He took the stump and traversed the whole district thoroughly, combating the virulent opposition of the Whigs and the underhand disaffection of the Democrats. Some negotiations were opened for a joint canvass; but the scheme fell to the ground, and the air was filled with charges and counter-charges of cowardice. When on several occasions the two candidates did encounter each other, their speeches were envenomed with personalities, Parker losing his temper and Julian giving back with interest all that he

[1] *Detroit Advertiser*, Sept. 12, 1851.
[2] *Milwaukee Sentinel*, Sept. 25, 1851.
[3] *Iowa True Democrat*, July 23, 1851.
[4] *National Era*, July 17, 1851.

received. By his personal popularity and by his aggressive
bearing in the fight, Julian succeeded in holding the greater
part of the Democrats who had supported him two years before,
as well as a few Whigs; but the efforts of the *Sentinel* cut away
the ground from under him, and Parker was elected through
Democratic votes.[1]   The result of this contest was the end of
coalition between the anti-slavery and Democratic organizations
in Indiana.

In Wisconsin the third party raised its head in 1851 for the
first time since October, 1849, and issued a call for a State
Mass Convention of all opposed to the Fugitive Slave Law, to
be held September 9.   The convention thus called, evidently
remembered Durkee's success through Whig votes in 1850; for
it took an unusual step in nominating for Governor L. J. Farwell,
an anti-slavery Whig, expecting that the Whigs would unite on
him.   The proceedings were almost entirely in the hands of old
Liberty men, Durkee, Holton, Booth, Ray, and J. H. Paine
formerly of Ohio; but the ticket nominated had, as usual, a
large admixture of Barnburners.   Though the platform had the
ordinary Free Soil flavor, the name "Free Democrat" was
avoided by this State Convention;[2] but the affiliated local
organizations continued under their old names during the
campaign without any such qualms.

This nomination proved fortunate; for the Whigs, on their
side, ascertained that Farwell, in spite of his choice by the
"Mass Convention," was no Free Soiler, but a true Whig;
at their State Convention he was nominated on a strong anti-
slavery platform, largely through the personal efforts of S. M.
Booth, of the Milwaukee *Free Democrat*, who had gained
Farwell's assent to the plan and had managed the Free Soil

---

[1] The comparison between the votes of the two years is shown as
follows: —

	Whig.	Coalition.
1849	4,583	4,737
1851	5,102	4,540

For the details of this campaign, see G. W. Julian, *Political Recollections*,
116-18, and *Indiana True Democrat*, Mar. 13-Aug. 7, 1851, and especially
Aug. 28.

[2] *Kenosha Telegraph*, Sept. 26, 1851.

convention.[1] The Free Soilers at first did not think it prudent
to notify Farwell of their nomination, lest he should decline it.
Such fears were unnecessary; the Whigs were too much in need
of Free Soil votes to reject their unaccustomed allies; they did
not revolt even when Durkee, to quiet the uneasy consciences of
the more radical anti-slavery men, wrote to Farwell asking him
his views. The reply was so thoroughly anti-slavery that the
Free Soilers rallied to Farwell's support, and secured his election.
The Whigs thus got not only a Governor, but — for the first time
in the history of the State — a plurality over the Democrats in
the lower branch of the legislature. Although Farwell could
not have been elected without the Free Soil vote, the Whigs
considered their victory was due to advocacy of State banks; a
policy which, the Democrats said: "the enemies of the Democracy stalked forth as a kind of war-horse to operate on the
nerves of voters."[2] In the vote for Lieutenant-Governor may
be seen the usual damaging effect of partial coalition. The
Free Democratic vote had fallen now to even less than in 1849,
and, outside a few counties, comprised few except old-time
Liberty men.[3]

In Ohio in 1851 several incidents occurred which, like the
revival of anti-slavery agitation in Indiana and Illinois and the
renewal of party action in Wisconsin, marked the beginning of
a new growth. The first problem to confront the diminished
number of Free Soilers in the legislature of 1850–51 was the
question of the election of a United States Senator. For a
time it seemed as if the days of 1849 had come again; for the
third party still held the balance of power in each House, and a
Whig and Free Soil "deal" arranged the organization of the
Senate; while Morse, as though bound to repeat his achievements of two years previous, was chosen Speaker of the House
by Democratic agreement. When the time came for the sena-

---

[1] Author's correspondence with S. M. Booth, July, 1896.
[2] Letter in *Racine Advocate*, Jan. 14, 1892.
[3] The vote was as follows : —

	Democratic.	Whig.	Free Soil.
Governor	Upham 21,812	Farwell 22,319	
Lieut.-Governor	Burrs 24,519	Hughes 16,721	Spaulding 2,904

torial election, however, no coalition of any sort had been engineered: the Free Soilers held together in most exemplary fashion in support of Giddings; the Whigs voted steadily for Griswold; and the Democrats, relinquishing all hope of Free Soil aid, stood grimly by H. B. Payne. This condition of things was very exasperating to Chase. "Of course I want a man of decided Democratic sympathies and affinities," he wrote to his agent, E. S. Hamlin; and he suggested that "it would not be amiss for the Free Democrats to elect some Democrat of the Old Line in sympathy with them — say Spaulding." [1]

After thirteen fruitless ballots, it became evident that a hard struggle was inevitable; therefore the senatorial election was postponed until the end of the session. Balloting was then resumed, with the same candidates as before; until on March 13 the Free Soilers suddenly abandoned Giddings for Vaughn, gaining by this manœuvre a few Whig votes. By this time it was common rumor that coalition, if any there were, must be between Whigs and Free Democrats, a state of things which caused Chase the utmost alarm. "Any arrangement with the Whigs," he wrote, "would put a club in the hands of the enemies of our cause with which they would infallibly break our heads. If there is no hope for the triumph of our cause through the progress and co-operation of the Democrats, there is no hope for it, I see." Then, thinking of his own election, he remarked: "Thank God I have never compromised principle for political place and, with his blessing, I never will." [2]   In spite of Chase's warnings, a series of rapid changes now took place on the part of Whigs and Free Soilers, each party testing the other by some new candidate. The Free Soilers put forward Giddings, Vaughn, Sutliff, and Hildreth; the Whigs tried Corwin, B. F. Wade, Lane, Williamson, and finally Wade again, who on the twenty-ninth ballot, on March 17, received all the Whig and Free Soil votes and was elected.[3] This victory, almost the last Whig success of any moment in Ohio, caused great Whig rejoicing; for Wade, though a stalwart anti-slavery

[1] Chase to E. S. Hamlin, Dec. 9, 1850, and Jan. 15, 1851: Chase MSS.
[2] *Ibid.*, Jan. 17, 1851.
[3] *True Democrat*, Jan. 3–March 17, 1851; *National Era*, March 27, 1851.

man since 1838, had not flinched from his party in 1844, or even in 1848. All Free Soilers, also, except Chase and his followers, were well satisfied; for in the previous autumn Wade had made a fiery speech denouncing the Fugitive Slave Law, and they felt sure that he would be no compromiser. " He is a true Northern man," said the Cleveland *True Democrat*, " one who will not yield the hundredth part of an inch where freedom is at stake."[1] Giddings, however, though recognizing Wade's anti-slavery position, could not forget that he had always followed his party, and wrote to Sumner in words that sound oddly in view of later events: " I have no distrust of his present feelings. My objection to him is solely on account of his want of straightforward determination of purpose. That leads me to fear he may leave us at some future day."[2]

In the State election of 1851 it became apparent that anti-slavery principles were still a power in the land; for while Democratic and Whig parties in other States were hastening to abandon Free Soil ground, those in Ohio stood unmoved where they had been since 1848. The Whigs, meeting on June 3, resolved that, since the Compromise and the Fugitive Slave Law were not party measures, every Whig was at liberty to hold his own opinions concerning them; but this refusal to indorse the "finality" was weakened by the nomination for Governor of G. F. Vinton, who while in Congress had changed front on the slavery question.[3] The Democrats went into the campaign with high spirits; for the new State constitution, a thoroughly popular instrument, was their work, a fact by which they were sure to profit. To make success certain, in their State Convention they reaffirmed their anti-slavery plank of 1848, omitted to notice the Compromise, and renominated Governor Wood. It might be true, that the delegates greeted the news of the success of negro exclusion in Indiana with yells of applause;[4] but as that fact did not appear on the surface,

[1] March 18, 1851.
[2] March 17, 1851: Sumner MSS. See also G. W. Julian, *Life of J. R. Giddings*, 287.
[3] *National Era*, July 10–31, 1851.
[4] *True Democrat*, Aug. 8, 1851; *National Era*, Aug. 14–21, 1851.

the Democrats of Ohio went into the State election of 1851 with a platform almost as anti-slavery as that of the Free Democrats themselves.

The Free Soilers, meanwhile, plucked up courage, asserted the permanency of their party, and called for a State Convention. As usual, the Western Reserve led the way; and on May 6 a convention at Painesville fired a signal gun by passing a set of courageous resolutions under the lead of Giddings, Vaughn, Bissell, Morse, and others, recommending a Western Reserve convention on June 25, a national Convention later, and thorough local organization. The Western Reserve Convention at Ravenna, on June 25, presided over by J. F. Morse, was an able body. The attendance was 2,000; Tilden, Chase, Lewis, and Giddings made addresses; and great enthusiasm showed that, whatever might happen elsewhere, the Western Reserve was still true to independent action. The resolutions reiterated the Buffalo platform; condemned the old parties, the Compromise, and the Fugitive Slave Law; recommended a national Convention at Cleveland to organize for 1852, and appointed a committee to call a State Convention. On August 21 the State Convention assembled, and for the first time since 1848 the anti-slavery forces of the State got into good working order. All the old leaders were present; Giddings presided, J. Birney was secretary, Spaulding, Vaughn, Lewis, Root, and Hamlin spoke; and the utmost harmony reigned, except for a slight brush between the ex-Whigs and the ex-Democrats over a clause in the resolutions favoring a low tariff. A full State ticket was nominated, headed by the name of the candidate for Governor, Lewis. When the chairman of the nominating committee read Lewis's name, the veteran came forward and tried to withdraw; but suddenly Root, from the audience, broke in: " Hold, hold, sir, I beseech you! The boys who listened to you when travelling over the State and speaking in behalf of education are *men* now, and they want a chance to vote for you." Everybody rose and cheered, and amid the thunders of applause, Lewis, much moved, bowed his speechless acquiescence.[1] The convention adjourned with high hopes.

---

[1] *True Democrat*, Aug. 23–25, 1851; *National Era*, Aug. 28, 1851.

Before the campaign had fairly opened, the party received a blow between the eyes that fairly dazed it. In a long letter, dated August 25, 1851, S. P. Chase avowed his intention to act with the Ohio Democrats in this election, and to support Judge Wood against Sam Lewis. To prove that the Ohio Democrats were an anti-slavery body, Chase adduced a long list of Free Soil opinions and resolutions from local conventions and papers of the years 1849-50, and pointed out, as finally conclusive, the action of the recent convention in not approving the Compromise and in renominating Wood. " I regret," he said in conclusion, " that I cannot expect the concurrence of all the devoted friends of freedom and progress, with whom I have been accustomed to act. . . . I must abide also the censures of those Free Soilers who allow themselves to see in Democracy only a malign spirit servile to all wrongs and hostile to all good, and look to a dissolved and reconstructed Whig party for the realization of their ideas of reform. Hereafter, as before, I shall be faithful to my cause." [1] Such action on Chase's part was the logical outcome of his state of mind since 1845, as shown in his fondness for the term " Democracy; " in his refusal to recognize the Western Reserve Whigs as true Free Soilers, coupled with his unhesitating acceptance of the Barnburners as his yoke-fellows; in his efforts in 1849 to bring about local fusion; and in his letter in 1851 to Donaldson, of the Democratic National Committee, in which he said that he " greatly desired the union and harmony of the Democracy." [2] All these indications pointed one way; but he had never during the years 1849-50 separated from the Free Soil organization; and he had played an active part in organizing and attending the great convention on the Western Reserve at Ravenna. Now, in 1851, when the Democratic party everywhere except in Ohio stood on the Compromise, his adherence to the local Free Soil body seemed a matter of necessity.

Chase's letter was therefore an entire surprise to his former Free Soil associates, and tried to the uttermost the patience of the Western Reserve, as well as that of the Free Soil party at

[1] *National Era*, Sept. 11, 1851.
[2] Aug. 2, 1851: R. B. Warden, *Life of Chase*, 334.

large. Lewis wrote in disgust to Arthur Tappan: "Men lose their confidence in our political movement because so many flaming Liberty men and Free Soilers are worshipping false gods and seeking to draw us away. . . . I am a Democrat, but do not recognize the party recognizing Cass, Dickinson, and Douglas as democratic, nor can I knowingly do aught that can help such a party into power."[1]

At first the *True Democrat*, struggling hard to keep its temper, remarked that it would not condemn him: "Mr. Chase has bared his bosom to whoever will strike. We give no blow";[2] but as public discussion of the matter increased, and letters came from old-time Liberty men describing their "inexpressible surprise," it became more and more open in its condemnation, as did the *Western Reserve Chronicle*, the *Ashtabula Sentinel*, the *Painesville Telegraph*, and in fact nearly every Free Democratic paper, except the Washington *National Era.* "Mr. Chase," said the *True Democrat*, "is now opposing in Ohio Sam Lewis and supporting Reuben Wood. There is no logic which can reconcile in our minds this inconsistency or its moral clash. . . . It is all ajar."[3] It spoke of him as the "late Mr. Chase, our lamented friend," and finally said: "We believe it would have been incomparably better for the party, if it had never raised a finger to put Mr. Chase into the National Senate."[4] From Cincinnati, Chase's home, came letters, saying: "This short corner that he has turned has filled us with shame and mortification. Henceforth we must rank him with mere partisan politicians."[5] And finally the Hamilton County Free Soil Convention, revived for the first time since 1848, resolved "that as the Hon. S. P. Chase, Senator in Congress from this State, has formally withdrawn from our party, while we regret this course and hope that it may not be injurious to the cause of freedom, we feel it to be our duty to declare to the public that we do not hold ourselves responsible for his acts or recognize him as our representative."[6] On the other side, Dr.

---

[1] W. G. W. Lewis, *Biography of Samuel Lewis*, 388.
[2] *True Democrat*, Sept. 11, 1851.   [3] *Ibid.*, Sept. 27, 1851.
[4] *Ibid.*, Nov. 25, 1851.   [5] *Ibid.*, Sept. 8, 1851.
[6] *National Era*, Sept. 18, 1851.

Bailey, in the *National Era*, deprecated all this criticism, saying
very justly: "The conduct of Mr. Chase is clearly in accordance with his principles, and taking into consideration his circumstances, we are not prepared to say that he has not acted
wisely. His profound sympathy with the Democracy, the high
estimation in which he is held by a large portion of it, make his
case exceptional. The time in our judgment has not yet come
for dispensing with an independent Free Soil organization in
Ohio."[1]

The campaign of 1851 was a short one, and resulted in the
following vote in October: Democratic — Wood, 145,606;
Whig — Vinton, 119,538; Free Democratic — Lewis, 16,911.[2]
The great Democratic plurality was due probably to the popularity of the new constitution and of their candidate, Judge
Wood. The Free Soil vote had increased a little over that of
the year before, but was still less than half of the vote of 1848.
Still more discouraging was the fact that neither in the popular
vote nor in the legislature did the party hold the balance of
power: and the days of bargaining were evidently over. "It is
quite safe to affirm," said the *True Democrat*, "that the vote for
Mr. Lewis would have been larger by some thousands had
Senator Chase stood by his party. Many who had placed
great confidence in him as a leader were confounded by his
sudden abandonment of us. Many Whigs supposed the Free
Soil strength was about to be transferred to Locofocoism, and
therefore abstained. Thousands of such did not vote at all.
Upon downright earnest Free Soilers, however, we willingly
grant that Senator Chase's secession produced no practical
effect, immeasurably as it surprised them. Not one of these, so
far as we know, followed in the retrogressive footsteps of that
gentleman."[3] In this year, most of Chase's special followers
of 1849 joined the Democrats; Dr. Townshend attended the
Democratic State Convention and served on the Committee
on Resolutions;[4] and Stanley Mathews was the Democratic
nominee for judge; but upon the mass of original Liberty men

[1] *National Era*, Sept. 11, 1851. See also Oct. 2, 30, 1851.
[2] Vote in *Whig Almanac*, 1852.
[3] *True Democrat*, Nov. 25, 1851.   [4] *Ibid.*, Aug. 8, 1851.

Mr. Chase's course had little influence. Dr. Bailey, in the *National Era*, said that no disappointment ought to be felt over the vote: "Those we can rely upon at all times are mainly after all the old-fashioned Liberty men and the natural accessions to their numbers springing from the adoption of their principles;" and to support this view he pointed out the steady increase in the anti-slavery vote for Governor since 1842.[1]

In the fall of 1851 there was held at Cleveland a national convention, first proposed by Indiana and seconded by the Western Reserve. There had been a growing feeling that the time had come for a national organization of the "Friends of Freedom," a sentiment which had already found expression in Ohio, Illinois, and Michigan in proposals for the revival of the Liberty party. For example, M. C. Williams, of Hamilton County, Ohio, had written to the *National Era :* "The object of this short communication is to suggest the propriety of holding a convention in Cleveland or Buffalo some time in May next, to reorganize the old Liberty party. All anti-slavery men could unite in carrying out the principles of that party. The cause has lost much by being merged with the Free Soil movement. Many are disgusted with the bargain and sale going on in some legislatures at this time."[2]

This convention accordingly proved to be made up to a great extent of old Liberty men. Dr. F. J. Lemoyne, of Pennsylvania, presided, and of the four vice-presidents three were Liberty men. Delegates were present from some of the New England States, and from New York, Pennsylvania, and elsewhere. Among the number were Lewis, Tappan, and Cassius M. Clay; from Ohio came Giddings, Spaulding, Lewis, Brisbane, Hoffman, Bradburn, and crowds of others; from Indiana, Julian and Harding; from Illinois, Eastman; from Wisconsin, Booth; and from Iowa, Catell and Clarke. After speeches by Clay, Lewis, Stansbery of Vermont, Julian, and Giddings, the convention adopted somewhat radical resolutions, demanding, besides the essentials

[1] 1842, King, 5,405; 1844, King, 8,411; 1846, Lewis, 10,797; 1850, Smith, 13,747; 1851, Lewis, 16,911. See *National Era*, Nov. 20, 1851.

[2] *National Era*, Feb. 20, 1851. See also letters from Michigan, *Ibid.*, Aug. 7, 1851.

of the Buffalo platform, the election of all officers by the people; they roundly denounced the Fugitive Slave Law, and declared that "law is without rightful authority unless based on Justice." Some resolutions asserting that slavery was made unconstitutional "by the preamble of the Constitution," were referred to the next national convention; and a committee from eighteen States and the District of Columbia was appointed to fix the time and the place for the National Nominating Convention.[1] An interesting incident of the meeting was a slight passage-at-arms between Lewis and Chase. The former in his address "discussed with marked plainness the wisdom and the grounds of Senator Chase's recent change of position. He proved the one to be not very far-seeing and the other wellnigh baseless." Loud calls for "Chase! Chase!" brought the Senator to his feet with one of his characteristic speeches. "Though he differed — temporarily he trusted — from those with whom he had so long acted . . . he begged none would for any light reason believe him capable of faltering in his support of a cause to which the best years of his life had been devoted."[2]

The year 1851 ended with slight encouragement for anti-slavery men. The "finality" cry was lulling all but the most independent into quiet, and seemed in most of the States to have completed the ruin of the Free Soil party. The third-party press, the condition of which was a sure index of the condition of the Free Soil cause, had dwindled to a mere fraction of its numbers of three years before. In Ohio, out of about forty Free Soil sheets in 1848, only seven remained.[3] In Indiana, the Centreville *True Democrat* was the only paper remaining out of eight, and that was on the verge of suspension. In Michigan the last Free Soil paper, the *Peninsular Freeman*, died in this year. In Illinois, of some eight or ten in 1848, the *Western Citizen* alone remained; but Wisconsin kept

---

[1] On the Cleveland Convention, see *Ibid.*, Sept. 11, Oct. 2-9, 1851; G. W. Julian, *Political Recollections*, 119; *Magazine of Western History*, IX., 273.

[2] *National Era*, Oct. 2, 1851.

[3] The Cleveland *True Democrat, Painesville Telegraph, Western Reserve Chronicle, Ashtabula Sentinel, Chardon Free Democrat*, Mount Vernon *Times*, and *Ohio Star*.

three of its original eight, the Milwaukee *Free Democrat, Kenosha Telegraph*, and *Racine Advocate*. In Iowa the solitary *True Democrat*, always on the point of collapse, was maintained by the devotion of its editor, S. L. Howe, and by that of the little band of third-party men in the State.

The only encouraging signs were, that at the ebb tide of their cause anti-slavery men had drawn together for mutual support; that State and national organization had begun once more; and that, with the return to first principles, the old Liberty party was again emerging into view. The fact that the revival of 1851 was felt by the participants to be something different from the movement begun at Buffalo is shown by the abandonment of the term "Free Soil" as a party name. From the action of Illinois, Indiana, and Wisconsin, it seemed for a time as if the word "Anti-slavery" would take its place; but, through the influence of the Eastern States and of Ohio, the official title of the third party from 1851 to 1854 was the "Free Democracy," a name suggested at Buffalo in 1848, but, curiously enough, not in general use in the Northwest until the Democratic elements of the party had in large measure left it. The term "Free Soil" was for some purposes more attractive; but the single idea which it expressed was not broad enough to become the foundation of a party. Moreover, it had been intimately connected with the Wilmot Proviso, now a dead issue; and it had been used as a mere political adjective, without party signification, by Whigs, Democrats, and people of all shades of opinion. To these objections the name "Free Democracy" was not liable.

CHAPTER XVI.

THE FREE DEMOCRACY IN THE CAMPAIGN OF 1852.

1851–1852.

IN 1852 the independent anti-slavery sentiment of the country by one strong effort pulled itself together and stood again on its feet in every State. The initiative came, not as in 1848 from New York, for there the Free Soil party since 1849 had been non-existent; nor from New England, although there the third party had maintained itself for the most part intact through the troubled years 1849–51; but it came from the Northwest.

The Cleveland Convention of 1851 had appointed a committee to call a National Nominating Convention, and had sounded a trumpet call for the campaign of 1852. Its last resolution had been, "that we recommend to our friends in the several States to organize as soon as possible"; and accordingly in the autumn of 1851 and the winter of 1852 work began. No detailed account of this preparation is necessary; it is enough to say that in each State conventions were called, campaign committees appointed, and in some cases nominations made for State offices. The southern counties of Ohio, destitute of anti-slavery organizations since 1849–50, were invaded by Lewis, James Birney, Brisbane, and others. Everything had a Liberty air; old-time methods were used, especially that of employing paid lecturers; and of the nominees for eléctors, State officers, and delegates to the National Convention, all but one were former Liberty men.

A like zeal stirred Indiana: conventions of "Friends of Freedom" were held; and a State "Political Anti-Slavery Convention" met and made nominations; it adopted the old Liberty and abolitionist language, although led largely by Julian, A. L. Robinson, and other ex-Whigs; and it chose a majority of its Presidential electors from Liberty men.[1]   Michigan had to begin its organization anew, and it did so in the spirit of 1841.   A " State Delegated Convention of Friends of Freedom " met, and formed a new State Anti-Slavery Society, after resolving "that the present crisis demands a reorganization of the friends of Liberty in this state, for the purpose of co-operating with those of other states in separate political action." [2]   In Illinois we find the same old Liberty phraseology cropping out, when a State Anti-Slavery Society, led largely by old-time Liberty men, resolved "that we organize a party of Freedom to rescue the Constitution from the abuse of slaveholders and their allies." [3] Everywhere the methods, aims, and language of ten years before reappeared, until it seemed as if the formal adoption of the name was all that was needed to bring the old Liberty party into existence again.

In the spring of 1852 the Whig and Democratic national conventions were held at Baltimore.   Their action — from which few but the most optimistic among anti-slavery men expected anything — showed conclusively that in this year the Free Democratic or Liberty party, or whatever it chose to call itself, must stand alone; for both of these conventions, with entire unanimity, resolved that the Compromise of 1850 had finally settled the slavery question, and that agitation must now cease.

The Central Committee, appointed in 1851 by the Cleveland Convention, now issued, through Samuel Lewis, a call for a national convention of the Free Democracy at Pittsburg on August 11, requesting friends of the Buffalo platform to meet and choose delegates; each State to be entitled to three times the number of its Congressional delegation.   The real lack of any connection between this movement and the Free Soil outbreak of 1848 was clearly seen by Lewis; and since the intention was to form a practically new party, he felt that much depended on the wording of the call.   " We may mend or mar

[1] *Indiana True Democrat*, May 27, 1852.
[2] *National Era*, July, 1–8, 1852.   [3] *Ibid.*, Feb. 19, 1852.

this great cause," he wrote to Arthur Tappan on May 28 ; and again, " I think I have seen even from the active members of the Cleveland Convention a disposition to go for Scott. I see that our position is extremely critical and am trying not to increase the repulsive influence." [1] As finally adopted, the language of this call, in using the term " Free Democracy " instead of " Anti-slavery," gave offence to some people like Lewis, Tappan, and Lemoyne ; [2] but throughout the country it was the signal for vigorous action. There was an outburst of local meetings to elect delegates; the Western Reserve counties, surpassing all other regions in their enthusiasm, resolved to be represented each by one hundred delegates.[3]

On August 11, met the last national gathering of the Free Democratic party. This convention was a large assemblage, and, in spite of the recent destruction of the Free Soil vote in nearly all of the States, it was enthusiastic.[4] After the call had been read and explained by Lewis to the satisfaction of Tappan, and a temporary organization had been effected, with Spaulding of Ohio as chairman and Booth of Wisconsin as secretary, the Western Reserve delegation, several hundred strong, amid tremendous cheering came marching in under a banner inscribed, " No compromise with slaveholders or doughfaces." [5] After one day spent in securing organization, and part of a second day in deciding how to vote, a platform containing twenty resolutions was reported by Giddings. It was based upon the Buffalo platform, but there were additional clauses condemning the Compromise and the Fugitive Slave Law, demanding the recognition of Hayti, and favoring international arbitration ; it included also declarations of the unconstitutionality of the South Carolina seamen laws, and of the duty of the United States government to protest against European monarchical intervention, together with other matters that showed the hand of Gid-

---

[1] W. G. W. Lewis, *Biography of Samuel Lewis*, 395, 397.

[2] *National Era*, July 8, 1852.

[3] *True Democrat*, July 28, Aug. 4, 1852.

[4] *National Era*, Aug. 19-26, 1852; G. W. Julian, *Political Recollections*, 122.

[5] H. M. Addison, in *Magazine of Western History*, IX., 273.

dings.[1] A minority report offered by Gerrit Smith received little support, and Giddings's resolutions were adopted by a vote of 197 to 14.

The Presidential nomination was a foregone conclusion; for John P. Hale was the unanimous choice of the people represented by the convention. True, he had written a letter deprecating the use of his name; but this circumstance the convention refused to consider, and he was nominated on the first ballot, by 192 votes to 15 scattering for Chase, Smith, and others. At this result the enthusiasm of the assembly found vent in nine cheers. The choice of a Vice-President necessitated two ballots. There had been a strong movement in favor of nominating Sam Lewis; but to the surprise of every one the first ballot gave him only 83 votes to G. W. Julian's 104, and 23 scattering. Lewis then withdrew his name; and on the second trial, Julian was chosen, to his own astonishment. Lewis was much hurt by this rebuff, not because he coveted honors, but because he thought that Chase, Spaulding, and others had worked secretly to defeat him on the ground that he was too radical.[2] Indeed, Julian's name had scarcely been mentioned up to the time of the ballot.

At this convention nearly all the real thorough-going political anti-slavery men of the country came together; with the exception of Chase and the Barnburners, hardly any one who had been prominent as a Liberty man or as a Free Soiler was absent. Delegates attended from all the free States, and from Delaware, Kentucky, Maryland, and Virginia; but, as usual, the Northwestern men took the lead. Lewis and Giddings were the men most prominent in the convention. Also important were Spaulding, Brisbane, and Vaughn, of Ohio; Harding, of Indiana; Lovejoy, of Illinois; Paine and Booth, of Wisconsin, and Howe, of Iowa. The only Eastern men who were equally conspicuous were the Massachusetts contingent, headed by Henry Wilson, the president of the convention, and Charles Francis Adams. Throughout the convention,

---

[1] The platform was drafted by Chase: R. B. Warden, *Life of Chase*, 338.

[2] G. W. Julian, *Political Recollections*, 124; W. G. W. Lewis, *Biography of Samuel Lewis*, 401.

crowds were present, and great mass meetings on the even-
ings of both days made the air ring with applause. Never
had a small third party, with apparently nothing to hope
for in the coming election, shown a higher spirit or a steadier
determination.

Some unfriendly papers, notably the *New York Tribune*, asserted that this convention had been "worked" in the Democratic interest; and that Giddings and Vaughn, in their spite
against the Whigs, had prevented the nomination of Chase,
who would have drawn votes from Pierce — had forced Hale's
nomination in spite of his refusal by letter, and had taken care
not to notify him of his choice lest he should decline.[1] It is
true that some of the leaders of the party at Washington, including Bailey and Hale, would have liked to support Chase;
but the latter from the outset would not hear of any such
scheme.[2] Moreover, the assertion that it took any especial
effort to defeat his nomination is manifestly absurd, when the
facts of Chase's position in 1852 are borne in mind. He had
abandoned the Free Democratic party, and had not attended
its meetings since the summer of 1851; even in this year,
when the Baltimore platform of the Old Line Democrats proved
too pro-slavery for him, he insisted that he was still Democratic.
" I cannot support the nominees of the Baltimore convention,"
he wrote; " but with an independent Democracy — with a democratic Democracy I am prepared to stand ";[3] and again, " If
we could have an Independent Democratic rally, thoroughly
Democratic in name and fact, without wild extravagances and
without any shrinking from a bold avowal of sound principles,
I should support it cheerfully."[4] So long as Chase maintained
this attitude, there was no necessity to steer the convention
away from him; for by no thinkable means could his nomination
have been forced upon it. Giddings himself, far from having
worked for Hale to the disparagement of Chase or of anybody
else, thought Hale an unsuitable candidate because of the

[1] *True Democrat*, Aug. 28, Sept. 1, 1852.
[2] Chase to E. S. Hamlin, June 28, 1852: Chase MSS.
[3] *National Era*, July 15, 1852.
[4] Chase to E. S. Hamlin, June 28, 1852: Chase MSS.

letter of declination, but he yielded to the irresistible popular demand.[1]

The statement has also been made that Chase had desired the convention to ratify the nomination of Scott, and had sent his follower Townshend with instructions to work for that end. True, a number of ex-Whig Free Soilers, led in Ohio by D. R. Tilden, were anxious to unite the Free Democrats with the Whigs against Pierce; but, although they made a stir in the spring of 1852, they stood no real chance of carrying their point. In spite of Lewis's fears, mentioned above, the likelihood that the Free Democracy would indorse Scott is not worth consideration. Not only did Scott stand on the Compromise Whig platform, but Chase's Democratic prepossessions make it impossible that he could have supported a Whig; and his private letters of the time show that his interest in the Pittsburg Convention centred solely in its Democratic character. Both these stories seem to be simply the idle tales of disappointed Whigs.

Indeed, Julian's words are justified: " An assemblage of purer men never convened for any political purpose."[2] There was in the convention no plotting, wire-pulling, bargaining, or underhand dealing of any kind; nothing but the most earnest desire for harmony and for the choice of the best men for leaders. If the redundant excitement of the Buffalo Convention was lacking, so were also its trading and bargaining. In all essentials, the Free Democratic meeting of 1852 bears a far closer resemblance to the Liberty convention which nominated Hale and King in 1847 than to the Free Soil convention of 1848.

After the news of the nomination and the platform had been spread abroad, organization in the Northwestern States progressed rapidly. To describe the movement in detail would be merely to give a list of conventions and resolutions. It is enough to say that in the months of August and September the old Liberty days of 1843 came again. In every Northwestern State. Liberty men, ex-Whigs, anti-slavery Democrats, and all not under the influence of the " finality" narcotic, ratified

---

[1] *True Democrat*, Aug. 28, Sept. 1, 1852.
[2] G. W. Julian, *Political Recollections*, 122.

with real enthusiasm the nominations of Hale and Julian, and worked as they had not done since 1848.

In Ohio, the number of Free Democratic meetings on the Reserve and in the State at large again becomes too great to enumerate. The list of speakers on the stump contained nearly everybody of importance, and included an amount of talent and zeal that would seem able to convert any State to anti-slavery principles. Giddings, Edward Wade, Root, Brinckerhoff, Lewis, Spaulding, Brisbane, Bissell, and O. P. Brown were all at work. On the Reserve, to symbolize the healing of all differences, Townshend was renominated for Congress by a Free Democratic meeting; and then, with Morse and Hamlin, took the stump side by side with Riddle and Vaughn. Finally, in September, Chase himself, finding Hale Democratic enough to satisfy his scruples, took the stump, thus partially appeasing the Western Reserve, although his act did not by any means wipe out all old scores. Throughout the summer the *True Democrat* had continued to cast slurs upon him. When asked, in July, what Senator Chase would do in the coming campaign, it remarked: " That's a tough question to answer at all times, but especially now. . . . He is a Democrat, and he does not mean to forget it or allow anybody else to forget it. He will allow no conflict between his party position as a Democrat and his conduct as a public man." [1] Even after Chase had returned to the Free Democratic ranks, the *True Democrat* said: " It is not to be denied that our people regard the late past and present position of Mr. Chase with the most decided disapprobation. . . . It is a position the very purest of Earth's beings could not occupy and escape suspicion." [2]

No man ever lived more certain of his own rectitude than was Chase; but the open abuse of the Western Reserve papers stung him to the quick, and he was even more bitterly galled by the steady undercurrent of suspicion which attached to all his words and deeds. On December 9, 1850, he wrote to Hamlin: " The malice with which all of us who thought that true policy as well as clear duty required co-operation with the Old Line Democracy in 1849 have been pursued is extreme. . . . This is outrageous. The disseminators of these calumnies must

---

[1] *True Democrat*, July 14, 1852.　　[2] *Ibid*, Aug. 4, 1852.

be met and put down." [1]   Never were they met or put down
until Chase was in his grave.   The real difficulty was, that Chase
so lacked sympathy and imagination that he was entirely unable
either to understand that others doubted him or to avoid doubt-
ing others; he could not conceive of any Whig as really standing
for anti-slavery ; and it seems never to have entered his head that
his Democratic course, which seemed to him perfectly consistent, should to others appear questionable.   At any rate, he
never hesitated on that account.   In short, he fell into the same
mistake as Birney's in 1844 : he did not scrupulously avoid the
appearance of evil.   Chase was undoubtedly sincere and upright in purpose, but almost every position which he took from
1849 to 1852 had an unpleasant aspect and required elaborate
explanation.   There was especial reason for caution, inasmuch
as Chase and his especial friends were lifted into office, while
Lewis, Brinckerhoff, Root, and Giddings were devoting heart
and soul to the thankless task of third-party work.   Every Free
Soiler connected with the "deal " of 1849 got his reward : Chase
was Senator; Townshend, Congressman and member of the Constitutional Convention; Morse was re-elected to the legislature;
Mathews got a judgeship; Hamlin was a member of the Board
of Public Works.   A man of even ordinary insight should have
realized that such things do not come about by coincidence.
Neither in his public utterances, which were so correct and color-
less that most ex-Whig Free Soilers thought them hypocritical
nor in his private correspondence does Chase for an instant
notice the doubt thus naturally suggested.   He thanked God
that he had never bargained his principles for place, " conscious
as I am," he said, " of my fidelity to the cause in every thought,
word, and act, and knowing as I do what temptations to turn aside
I have resisted." [2]

The bitter editorials of the *True Democrat* led Giddings, on
August 18, to write a public letter regretting any appearance of
unkind feeling toward Chase.   As for Chase's return to the
Democratic party, he said: " I did not believe his confidence
well placed, and so expressed myself freely at the time, but I

---

[1] Chase MSS.

[2] Chase to E. S. Hamlin, Sept. 20, 1853: Chase MSS.

had full confidence in his integrity of purpose. . . . I am aware that suspicion and jealousy were awakened from reports that he was to be our nominee for President. That story was put forth without his consent. He constantly urged that Mr. Hale was the man of all others to whom circumstances pointed. . . . It is due to our cause that these facts be known." [1] Appeased by this letter, the *True Democrat* let the subject drop, saying: "We neither cherish nor feel any unkindness toward Mr. Chase. We were only afraid that he would, in 1852, as he did in sustaining Governor Wood and opposing Sam Lewis in 1851, turn his power and position against our organization with fatal effect. . . . But let all this pass. . . . Only let him be fully and heartily with us and we will stand by his side as cordially as if we had never differed in opinion." [2]

On September 14, a State Free Democratic Mass Convention met at Cleveland, presided over by Giddings. After Milton Sutliff had been nominated for Judge of the Supreme Court, to fill the place on the ticket made vacant by the resignation of Edward Wade, John P. Hale was introduced, and spoke with great effect for two hours. [3] One of the most interesting incidents of the Ohio campaign was a dinner given to Giddings by his constituents of the "Old Twentieth" Congressional District, at Painesville, on September 18. Morse presided; speeches were made by Hamlin, Chase, Hale, Wade, and Smith, and letters read from C. M. Clay, Lewis, Julian, Judge Jay, Spaulding, and others. It was a well-earned compliment to the veteran anti-slavery champion. [4]

In Indiana, Julian, Harding, Cravens, and Robinson were on the stump; but local organization was very imperfect, and anti-slavery men complained bitterly of their neglect by the party at large. "We seem to have been slighted by all men," wrote one; "the friends abroad seem to have given us over to our own defence, whilst we had the most powerful odds to contend

[1] *True Democrat*, Aug. 25, 1852.
[2] *Ibid.*
[3] *Ibid.*, Sept. 22, 1852; *National Era*, Sept. 30, 1852.
[4] See Giddings's address to his former constituents, in the *National Era*, April 7, 1853.

against of any of the Free States."[1]   In the Quaker regions, however, the old Liberty spirit flamed up and real enthusiasm appeared.   The ratification meeting in Henry County was " a glorious one, the largest political meeting ever held in the county; . . . the Free Soil ratification meeting of four years before in the same place in comparison to this was a cold and lifeless affair not one fourth as large." [2]

In Michigan, where the whole work of organization had to be begun anew, there was a vigorous campaign.   A mass convention at Ann Arbor, September 1, was addressed by Lewis and Giddings with great effect ; and a second State Convention at Kalamazoo, September 29, appointed three salaried lecturers, nominated a full State and electoral ticket, and arranged to start a Free Democratic newspaper.   Though their numbers were few, Michigan anti-slavery men returned to the task of party-building with an energy unknown since 1841.   " So far as my observation extends," wrote a correspondent of the *National Era,* " I think there has never been a period since the first foundation of the Liberty party when more zeal and spirit have been manifested than there is at the present time." [3]   In Illinois the old-time activity of the northern counties reappeared after a three years' eclipse, and in Kane, Kendall, Cook, Lake, and other counties local agitation began.   " Hale Clubs " sprang up, and organization was zealously urged.

The Wisconsin Free Democrats, better off than any of their neighbors, still had their organization of 1848 ; hence there was no such renewed uprising as took place in Illinois and Michigan, but rather a strengthening all along the line.   A State Mass Convention at Milwaukee, on September 8, nominated an electoral ticket, heard an address by Sam Lewis, and ratified the nominations of Hale and Julian with great enthusiasm. Even in Iowa the little band of anti-slavery men in the southeastern counties gained renewed life, improved their organization, nominated an electoral ticket, and assailed the old parties with fresh vigor.   " What are the Free Soilers of Iowa doing? "

[1] *National Era,* Jan. 6, 1853.
[2] *Indiana True Democrat,* Sept. 2, 1852.
[3] *National Era,* Oct. 7, 1852.

cried the *True Democrat ;* "whilst the friends of human freedom are vigilant in Ohio, New York, Massachusetts, etc., are they alone standing still in this state? With proper exertion they ought to poll in November next three or four thousand votes. . . . Let us be up and doing. Let the electoral tickets for Hale and Julian be distributed in every neighborhood. Many do not vote the Free Soil ticket because they are not at hand on the day of election. Let the electors see to this." [1]

In this year there was for the first time a beginning of national management of the campaign. The Free Soil movement had been so strong in the Northwest that the third-party leaders determined to throw their weight into that quarter; and accordingly Lewis, Giddings, Hale, and Julian stumped Ohio and Michigan. They paid especial attention to Wisconsin: that state had made an especially good showing in 1848, and anti-slavery sentiments were widespread; hence they felt encouraged to hope that they might get its electoral vote.[2] In spite of all the efforts of Free Democrats, however, this year's campaign was intensely dull. It takes two to make a fight; and the Free Democrats could provoke the active opposition of neither of the old parties. The Democrats, reverting to their old practice of 1844, ceased to notice them; and the Whigs either followed the same course, or, driven to express themselves, accused the third party of merely running as stalking-horses for Pierce. Between the two old parties the slavery question was avoided by common consent; and the same men who for years had been claiming the Wilmot Proviso as straight Democratic or Whig doctrine, now found food for debate in the tariff, or very often in less respectable topics. "The coarsest abuse of the candidates of the opposing party," wrote a correspondent of the *National Era,* "little tales of what General Pierce once did and what General Scott once said, appeals to sectarian prejudice, — any claptrap forms the staple of party appeals. The discussion of the great question, the only vital one, is carefully avoided." [3]

So recent had been the revival of the Free Democratic party

[1] *Iowa True Democrat,* Oct. 27, 1852.
[2] Cleveland *True Democrat,* Aug. 25, 1852.
[3] *National Era,* Oct. 21, 1852.

that in the summer elections it did not make a large figure. In the Ohio October election the vote for judge stood as follows: Democratic — Caldwell, 146,795 ; Whig — Haynes, 128,560; Free Democratic — Sutliff, 22,167. In Indiana no returns for the state vote are accessible ; it was probably greater than that in 1849, but how much greater cannot be accurately stated. The complaints of lack of organization were bitter. " We have already since the state election received more than a dozen letters," said the *True Democrat,* " stating that no tickets were had in the respective townships of the writers for State officers." [1] In Julian's old district the vote for Congress stood: Democratic — Groce, 6,153 ; Whig — Parker, 7,181 ; Free Democratic — Hubbard, 1,451.

In Congressional nominations the party did not feel strong enough for much independent action, although it was decidedly more active than in 1848 or 1850. In Ohio, nominations were made in sixteen districts, as against seven in 1850, and six in 1848 ; but the Liberty party had frequently surpassed this mark, nominating in eighteen districts as far back as 1843. In Michigan, inveterate habit proved too strong for the Free Democrats, and in the Second District they indorsed Williams, the Whig nominee. This action was not, however, the complete self-surrender of 1850 ; for Williams had been a Free Soiler in 1848, and was still so strong an anti-slavery man that he pronounced openly in favor of the Pittsburg platform.[2] In Indiana a single third-party nomination was made, and in Illinois there were four Free Democratic candidates in the northern districts, as compared with one in 1850 and with six Liberty candidates in 1846. In Wisconsin a complete ticket appeared in all three districts, but the interest centred as usual in the First District, where Durkee had been elected in 1850 by coalition with Whigs, and where, it was hoped, that party would now again help him ; but however much some of the Whigs would have liked to support Durkee, the managers dared not take such action in a national campaign. Consequently, a Whig candidate was nominated ; whereat the Free Democrats, in their irritation,

---

[1] *Indiana True Democrat,* Oct. 28, 1852.

[2] Cleveland *True Democrat,* Sept. 29, 1852.

turned the Whigs' cry back upon them by asserting that Durand, the Whig, was run only in order to defeat Durkee and let in Wells, the Democrat.[1]

In November Pierce received a great majority of the electors, and he carried every Northwestern State.[2] Everywhere the most striking fact was the complete overthrow of the Whig party. The falsity of its position with regard to the Compromise, together with its complete failure to meet the pressing question of the hour, made its efforts useless ; and the country had discarded it for the triumphant Democracy.

What was the lesson of the election for the new Free Democratic party? It had found itself unable in this single campaign to make up for the losses caused by the return of the Barnburners and the "Conscience" Whigs in 1849–50 ; but it had shown vitality. As Dr. Bailey said: "It was not until the year preceding the late election that the political antislavery men or the Free Democrats began the work of a separate national organization. The fact that in so short a time they were able to disentangle themselves and after a short canvass cast upwards of 150,000 votes for Freedom is evidence of power."[3] The most important fact brought out by the election of 1852 is that the centre of gravity of political anti-slavery action had swung into the West. The canvass of 1852 showed little relative change in New England, where the three parties continued with the same rigidity which had characterized them since 1844. In the Middle States the Barnburners of 1848 were now the strongest supporters of Franklin Pierce, and the rejuvenated Free Democracy polled little more than the old Liberty vote. In the Northwest, however, where immigration had been active,

---

[1] *Racine Advocate*, Sept. 29–Oct. 20, 1852.

[2] In the Northwest the vote stood as follows : —

	Pierce.	Scott.	Hale.
Ohio	169,220	152,526	31,682
Indiana	95,340	80,900	6,929
Michigan . . .	41,842	33,853	7,237
Illinois	80,597	64,934	9,966
Wisconsin . . .	31,658	22,240	8,814
Iowa	17,762	15,855	1,606

[3] *National Era*, Dec. 9, 1852.

where since 1848 the fluctuation in anti-slavery votes had been extreme, the greatest revival took place; the new party cast only 15,000 votes less than the Free Soilers of 1848, and it also cast a larger third-party vote than even New England.[1]

Who furnished these Free Democratic votes? In New England the Liberty men, and most of the same Whigs and Democrats who had revolted in 1848; in New York and Pennsylvania, few besides old-time Liberty men. In the Northwest, it seems certain that the Free Soil party had by 1850 lost nearly all of its original Whig and Democratic converts of 1848; but unlike the party in New York it mounted again, in 1852, nearly to the voting strength which it had reached in 1848. Apparently it regained few or none of its former Democratic members; for there is no assertion that any Barnburners returned to the third-party ranks in 1852, and the great increase of the Democratic vote in every Northwestern State raises a strong presumption against any such supposition. The Whig vote also increased largely, but in a smaller ratio than the Democratic; and it seems reasonable to suppose that some Whigs may have voted the Hale ticket. This conclusion is strengthened by the comparison between the votes for State and Presidential tickets in Illinois and Michigan. The main increase since 1850, however, must have come in part from some young men voting for the first time, but chiefly from the stay-at-homes, who were very numerous during the years of 1849–51. This class of persons, usually not participating in politics, — clergymen, professional men, and hard workers who scarcely knew to what party they belonged, — were interested to turn out in a Presidential contest; and they swelled the vote of the Free Democrats.

In the Congressional elections, Giddings and Edward Wade were returned from Ohio; but Townshend in his gerrymandered district was defeated; and in Wisconsin Durkee lost his seat. The Western Reserve was still the only place in the Northwest

[1] The comparison is shown by the following table : —

	New England.	Middle.	Northwest.
1844	25,754	19,071	17,358
1848	77,286	132,592	81,161
1852	57,143	34,203	66,234

where anti-slavery men, unassisted, could hope to elect their candidates ; and all Ohio was jubilant over the eighth success of Giddings. " I never knew," said a correspondent, "so much personal or political opposition concentrated in one Congressional campaign. The Whig press was weekly gorged with defamation that had in vileness no depths, in bitterness no bounds. No lie was too big for utterance. My heart sickens at the recital of the immoralities that blackened Whig electioneering."[1] " Our friends abroad," said the *True Democrat*, " cannot well measure the extent of the Free Democratic triumph in electing Giddings and Wade. These two districts, the nineteenth and twentieth, were formed expressly to defeat the Free Democracy. Against Giddings the contest was waged with merciless ferocity." Even B. F. Wade, unmindful of his old partnership with Giddings in law and in anti-slavery, and of Giddings's refusal to attack him in 1851, took the stump against the anti-slavery champion.[2]

The Presidential vote of the third party showed so great a growth since 1850 that few were disappointed ; and throughout the Northwest, except where Wisconsin Free Democrats sorrowed over Durkee,[3] the general feeling was joyful. They had released themselves from connection with the old parties ; they had given their testimony against slavery; and their ranks seemed to have all the real living enthusiasm that existed in the country. Moreover, the idea became prevalent that the Whig party was dead, and that now was the time to strike for a share of the heritage. A great cry went up for organization, especially from regions like Indiana and Iowa. " I would just suggest to our friends in the East," said a writer from the latter State, " whether in view of our infancy and weakness in Iowa and the peculiar state of the public mind among us — which is now very unsettled, just in the condition to be favorably impressed — it would not be right and expedient for them to lend us some assistance."[4] " All that is needed," said the Cleveland *True Democrat*, " is for the Free Democracy to be firm and active, to

---

[1] *True Democrat*, Oct. 20, 1852.

[2] *Ibid.*, Sept. 22, 1851.

[3] *Milwaukee Sentinel*, Nov. 4-17, 1852.

[4] *National Era*, Jan. 20, 1853.

organize, and through that organization to assault the public mind."[1] "All that is needed," came the cry from Michigan, "is a fair circulation of documents."[2] Everywhere the determination to keep on working was manifest. Said the *Indiana True Democrat* : "The Free Democrats of Indiana have no intention of grounding their arms";[3] and the *Racine Advocate* fairly expressed the general feeling when it said: "We want it perfectly understood that we cannot be conquered; that agitation of our principles cannot be prevented ; and that we mean to grow more and more earnest with every assumption of the slave power."[4]

[1] Jan. 5, 1853.

[2] *National Era*, Jan.13, 1853.

[3] Quoted *ibid.*, Nov. 25, 1852.

[4] Nov. 10, 1852.

CHAPTER XVII.

EXPANSION OF THE FREE DEMOCRATIC PARTY.

1853.

So great was the impetus given to the anti-slavery cause by the election of 1852 that, without any slackening of pace, its activity was carried over into 1853, and in this last year of its life the Free Democratic party made the best record in its history. Circumstances were propitious: the national Whig party was overthrown, and its members were dismayed and bewildered; the Democratic party, inflated beyond its real strength, was beginning to be torn by feuds. Already signs of the coming chaos in politics had begun to appear in the sudden importance assumed all over the country by the agitation for prohibition, or, as it was called from its origin, "the Maine Law." In such circumstances, men of all parties, in the autumn of 1852 and in the beginning of 1853, began to look with a certain admiration at the clear-cut, aggressive principles of the Free Democracy; at an enthusiasm different from the quarrels and bitterness in the old parties; and at a confidence and hope which had risen with renewed life from the defeats of the years 1849 to 1851.

From all sides reports of encouraging signs among members of the old parties poured in from correspondents to the *National Era* and to other Free Democratic papers. " Since the Presidential election, it is not an uncommon occurrence to hear Whigs and Democrats say that they have cast their last vote for slavery; there is a general demand for information." [1] " The Free Democrats were never in higher spirits than at the

[1] From Bridgeport, Ohio. *National Era*, Jan. 13, 1853.

present time. The Whig party have all been taken aback; . . . they now begin to manifest a willingness to pause and inquire what are the principles of Free Democracy."[1] "I have heard many Whigs and Democrats say, 'I would have voted with all my heart for Hale if there were any hope of his election.'"[2] "Since the Presidential election is over there seems to be quite an interest felt by Whigs and Democrats to obtain information in regard to our principles, as it is pretty generally conceded on all sides that the next contest will be between the Free Democrats and the Old Line Democrats."[3] " A prominent Democrat who has served several terms in the State Senate stated to me that he believed the Free Democratic party would eventually become the ruling party and that whichever party should be defeated at the coming election would mostly fall in with us."[4]

The Whig *Lafayette Courier* said : "We have heard it estimated that in the event of the defeat of General Scott the Whig party will be disbanded, and of the fragments will be formed a grand National anti-slavery party, which, by including the Liberty party, the Free Soil party, the abolitionists, and that portion of the Democrats who sustain the nominees but not the finality resolutions of the platform, may be able to control the National elections of the future. That such a party will be organized we have good reason to believe."[5] The Democratic Valparaiso *Practical Observer* remarked in similar vein : "We heard numbers say that if their votes would elect J. P. Hale he should have them. The Free Democracy are really the most thoroughly Democratic party in existence. If they are not the organized party that is to regenerate our National policy, purging it of slavery, aristocracy, and corruption, they are at least the forerunner of that party, as John the Baptist was of the Christian Church."[6] From Batavia, Illinois, came the words : " As the noble, honest Hale said at Aurora in this county there

---

[1] From Unionville, Union County. *Ibid.*, Jan. 6, 1853.
[2] From Erie County. *Ibid.*, Dec. 9, 1852.
[3] From Preble County. *Ibid.*, Dec. 23, 1852.
[4] From Jacksonville, Indiana. *Ibid.*, Oct. 28, 1852.
[5] Quoted in *Indiana True Democrat*, Oct. 14, 1852.
[6] Quoted in *National Era*, Nov. 25, 1852, March 31, 1853.

would be plenty of Free Soilers after election, so it has turned out. Many Whigs are now turning where they can carry out their principles. Some Democrats — and perhaps as many of the other party — have voted their last Old Line ticket." [1]

With such signs to cheer them, the Free Democrats of the Northwest were encouraged to strain every nerve. In four of the States, where there were only minor elections in 1853, the activity of the party was directed to organization; but in Ohio and Wisconsin, which elected State tickets this year, events of the highest significance took place; they will be considered in full after a brief review of the year in the other States.

In the autumn of 1852, Indiana rang with a cry for organization. Indignant Free Democrats in back counties wrote protests to the *National Era* and the *Indiana True Democrat.* "There has never to my knowledge been an anti-slavery lecture delivered in the county," said a correspondent from Fort Wayne; "Free Soil speakers seem to be afraid of us." [2] "We shall lose thousands of votes in this campaign simply for the want of organization," said the *True Democrat;* and it proposed a permanent society of some sort, "call it what you please — anti-slavery or anything else — with local auxiliaries." [3] A State Convention at Indianapolis, on October 21, 1852, presided over by Nathaniel Field, one of Indiana's earliest abolitionists, appointed a Committee on Permanent Organization and called a convention for January 13, 1853, to form a State League. [4] This second convention met accordingly, and under the presidency of S. C. Stevens reiterated the Pittsburg platform of 1852, and adopted the constitution of a State Free Democratic Association, which was "to continue in existence for four years from January 13, 1853," and the object of which should be "to disseminate the principles of the Free Democracy." [5] Provisions were made for local associations, and by the end of the year such bodies were formed in at least seven counties. To the value of this work the spring elections in March, 1853, bore testimony; for, according to the *Indiana Free Democrat*, the vote of the third party showed an

[1] *National Era*, Jan. 27, 1853.   [2] *Ibid.*, Dec. 23, 1852.
[3] *Indiana True Democrat*, Oct. 14, 1852.   [4] *Ibid.*, Nov. 4, 1852.
[5] *National Era*, Feb. 10, 1853.

increase of some 1,500 over that thrown in November, "the spontaneous tribute of 8,000 persons to our principles and our cause."[1]

To keep up interest, another well attended State Convention was held on May 25, at which G. W. Julian and S. C. Stevens spoke and S. P. Chase delivered the address of the day. This, said the *Free Democrat,* "was by far the best State Convention they have ever had in Indiana."[2] In the summer, Lewis, of Ohio, amid his arduous duties in his own State, found time to lend aid; and by the end of the year local organization was in a better condition than at any time since the days of the Liberty party. Julian was the life of the cause. From January to December he was hard at work lecturing and organizing, and was cheered everywhere by the most encouraging signs. The journal of the tireless campaigner is full of interest. "Labor till the campaign of 1856 closes seems to be the general demand," he wrote, January 5. "The anti-slavery cause is more decidedly onward than ever before. . . . The Democracy is awfully swollen, whilst all of Whiggery capable of salvation is preparing to come into our embrace. There is a good time coming." He repeatedly said: "I have never seen the Free Democrats in this state so much encouraged."[3]

In Michigan there was much the same state of affairs. A State Convention on January 12, at Jackson, devoted its attention to organization and to the establishment of a newspaper at Detroit. Moreover, it adopted a series of racy resolutions, to the effect that "in the present swollen condition of the Democratic party and the shrivelled condition of the Whig party we see evidences of disease"; and that "the first and most important measure of the Free Democrats of Michigan is an organization in every town in the state."[4] Thereupon county conventions began to meet and to push the matter of local organization:

---

[1] Quoted *ibid.,* March 24, 1853. The Indiana *Free Democrat* was the same paper as the Indiana *True Democrat.* Name changed January, 1853.

[2] Quoted *ibid.,* June 16, 1853. See G. W. Julian, *Speeches on Political Questions,* 83–101.

[3] MS. diary of G. W. Julian.

[4] *National Era,* Feb. 10, 1853.

as in Indiana, the result appeared in the town elections, in which, in many places, the Free Democratic vote gained prodigiously. No general campaign was attempted, however, nor did the Free Democrats throw their energies into politics so much as into organization. While the State struggled over the question of a "Maine Law," the third party worked actively in its own field.

In Illinois the Free Democrats began, even before the result of the Presidential campaign was known, to prepare for the work of 1856; and here, as in Indiana, bitter complaints of lack of organization spurred them on. "I wish I could rap the knuckles of our leading Free Soilers," wrote a correspondent of the *National Era* from Cumberland County; "would you believe it that we in this part of the state never obtained the Hale and Julian ticket nor do we know yet whether there was one formed in this state or not. Such neglect is insufferable!"[1]

The Illinois State Free Democratic Convention met at Ottawa on May 18, and took steps for an efficient organization. A plan was adopted for invading "Egypt" with a series of conventions, and arrangements were made for a permanent campaign headquarters, with salaried agents. The convention devoted much attention to the recently enacted Negro Exclusion Law, condemning it as "a foul blot on the statute book, a reproach to our people, an attempt to nullify the Ordinance of 1787, and a destruction of the equality of citizenship as guaranteed by the Constitution of the United States." Any one who attempted to enforce the act was to be considered as "a traitor to humanity."[2] As in Michigan, the principal care of the third-party men was the hard task of maintaining their paper, the *Western Citizen.*

Later in the year the "Association" system of Indiana was introduced and adopted largely in the northern counties. In the fall elections there was little attempt to nominate independent tickets, the leaders preferring to wait until their organization was completed. In Will County the effect of the

[1] *National Era*, Dec. 23, 1852.
[2] Chicago *Congregational Herald*, June 4, 1853.

changed state of national politics was visible in a Free Democratic and Whig combination, which elected two of its candidates. In Kane County the Whig convention adjourned without nominating, in order to leave the field open in favor of the Free Democrats; whereupon a bolt of "Silver Gray" Whigs set up a straight party ticket.[1] These straws showed the direction of the wind as much as did the brisk breezes in Ohio and Wisconsin, for Whig and Free Democratic coalitions were an entire innovation in Illinois.

Iowa, the only State in the Union in 1852 to increase its third-party vote over that of 1848, kept pace with Illinois in the "off year" of 1853. On the very day of the Presidential election, the *Iowa True Democrat* had urged: "We do hope the friends of freedom in Iowa will go right to work to organize for a future effective action. In this we have always failed; let us fail no longer."[2] With steady courage the little band of abolitionists kept at work. On February 22, 1853, a State Free Democratic Convention met, and, like that of Indiana, formed the constitution of a State Association. Dr. Shedd, S. L. Howe, J. W. Catell, and other veterans were present, committees were appointed, an effort was made to secure organization in every county and a State ticket was nominated. Then officers for the State Association were chosen, and a set of courageous resolutions embodying the Pittsburg platform and the Maine Law was adopted.[3] Following this action, local associations were formed in several counties.

The comparatively quiet organization in the States just described, important as it was as an index of Free Democratic purpose and feeling in 1853, sinks into insignificance when compared with the extremely interesting elections in Ohio and Wisconsin, the only States in which the Free Soil party had maintained an unbroken existence since 1848.

After the election of 1852 all Ohio was vociferous for organization. "If we had only a few enterprising speakers to take the field," said a writer from Putnam County, "we might have more than trebled our present vote. There has not been a

---

[1] *Chicago Journal*, Oct. 17–28, 1853.   [2] Nov. 3, 1852.
[3] *Ibid.*

regular Free Soil speech delivered in the County to my knowledge, except one." [1] " Let temporary Free Democratic organizations be continued for the next four years," urged the *Western Reserve Chronicle;* " let occasional meetings be held, have speeches, hold discussions." [2] In accordance with this suggestion, local Free Democrats at Ravenna, Akron, and elsewhere on the Reserve began to form associations, "to continue in force until the close of the Presidential campaign of 1856." [3] The State Central Committee, on November 17, issued a call for a State Convention in January, and urged organization. " We stand on the eve of important events," it said, " and must be prepared to meet them. . . . The old parties are undeniably in a difficult position, their old issues are obsolete. Free men of Ohio, it is in you and for you to help work out the great result. . . . Let the truth be known, circulate documents, hold meetings, agitate." [4]

The convention of January 12, 1853, proved important. Brinckerhoff presided, and nearly all of the leading Free Democrats were present, except those who were in Congress. At the beginning arose a serious difference of opinion as to the platform. R. P. Spaulding, a somewhat recent Democratic convert, reported from the Committee on Resolutions that the Pittsburg platform should be modified by introducing clauses in favor of strict construction, free trade, and direct taxation. When Root and some other ex-Whigs raised objection, Spaulding, a hot-headed man, lost his temper and indulged in personalities, until cries of " Question " cut off debate and the platform as reported was adopted. The remainder of the session went on in a different spirit; when it was moved to nominate Sam Lewis again, the enthusiasm of the convention broke out in uncontrollable cheers and cries. The veteran rose, and with deep feeling tried to withdraw, urging his age, his labors, and frequent previous campaigns, but in vain: the Convention refused to hear him. " We'll make you Governor yet! " shouted Edward Wade; and Lewis again gave way, with

---

[1] *National Era*, Dec. 2, 1852.
[2] Quoted *ibid.*, Nov. 11, 1852.
[3] *True Democrat*, Nov. 17, 1852.   [4] *Ibid.*

tears in his eyes, deeply touched by the affection and enthusiasm of the meeting.[1] "God bless you, Father Lewis," said Judge Lee, as the tears flowed down his cheeks; when he grasped the hand of his old standard-bearer in both his own; "God bless you, I believe we shall not fight this evil much longer; let us fight the harder." [2]

The rest was all harmony. Resolutions were passed indorsing Giddings and Townshend; then Lewis made an eloquent plea in behalf of Chase, which Spaulding, Brown, and Brinckerhoff seconded, and Chase also was included in the approving resolution. Hamlin, Parrish, and Wade also spoke, urging oblivion for past differences and confidence for the future; and after adopting a resolution in favor of prohibition, and establishing a central Free Democratic organ at Columbus, the convention adjourned. The close, as described by the *True Democrat*, was a reminder of the early days of the Liberty party. "It had been a hard day's work, but at the end one spirit animated all. Every rude feeling was hushed, all unkindness forgotten. Harmony reigned. As speaker after speaker dwelt upon the necessity of organization, as Samuel Lewis near midnight in his loftiest eloquence bade free men live to work and do their whole duty to God and man, the Convention in a body and amid the deepest enthusiasm adjourned, resolving to act out the heroic sentiments of this heroic man." [3]

The initiative of this convention was the signal for a steady and vigorous campaign. The free trade resolution caused a little grumbling, but even the *True Democrat* said that it was not worth the time spent on it, and the harmony of the party remained unimpaired. Campaign work began in April on a scale hitherto unapproached. Lewis, as always, threw heart and soul into the work, and repeated his brilliant canvass of the State in 1846. In May, Giddings joined him on the stump, and later Chase and Edward Smith; and these four visited every county in Southern Ohio. By June the campaign on the part of the Free Democrats had reached a height surpassing that of the

---

[1] *True Democrat*, Jan. 19, 1853; *National Era*, Jan. 27, 1853.

[2] W. G. W. Lewis, *Biography of Samuel Lewis*, 406.

[3] *True Democrat*, Jan. 19, 1853.

year before. Conventions were organizing, local speakers agitating, a campaign song-book published in Cleveland was being
distributed, and the Central Committee, to supplement the
spontaneous local meetings, arranged for Lewis a grand tour of
the state, which was to begin July 20 in Clermont County, to
take in succession all the counties in the south, east, north, and
centre, and to close on October 4, just before the election.[1]

Meanwhile the other parties, with a lassitude in great contrast
to the intense activity of the Free Democrats, had held their
conventions and made their nominations. The Democrats on
January 30 nominated Medill, and for the fourth time repudiated the national platform by re-adopting the anti-slavery resolution of 1848, 1850, and 1851. Had Chase and Townshend
desired again to seek Democratic associations, the Ohio party
was ready to receive them; but Chase had apparently had
enough of changing partners, and he stayed with the Free
Democrats. The Whigs, on February 22, by a vote of 179 to
43, nominated N. Barrere, one of the Fillmore school, over L.
D. Campbell, a Free Soiler of 1848; and they showed their
futility as a party by passing perfunctory resolutions in favor of
protection and against the Democratic State government, avoiding any reference to slavery.

In spite of the fact that the Democrats had an excellent
platform from an anti-slavery point of view, the Free Soilers
paid them very little attention; coalition with the Old Line
Democracy, no matter what their platform might be, was no
longer considered a possibility. The case of the Whigs, however, was different. So great had been the discouragement
of the latter party after the election, and so frequent were
Whig expressions of approval of Free Soil principles, that the
interest of this election of 1853 all centred in the effort by the
Free Democrats to attract Whig votes. " Calculate as you
may, Whigs," said the *True Democrat*, " count up your figures,
shout out your party cry, it will all be in vain; for your thinking voters, every anti-slavery Whig, will mock at you and spurn
an organization which has so brutally defied the claims of jus-

[1] *True Democrat*, June 22, 1853; *National Era*, Aug. 11-18, 1853; W.
G. W. Lewis, *Biography of Samuel Lewis*, 415.

tice." [1] "The very fact that the Whig press is disputing the point whether the Whig organization be dead or alive proves that it is dead. . . . The question arises whether at this juncture it is possible to bring together the true men of all parties . . . to make a party which shall be, — in the nation and State, — for freedom. That question we answer affirmatively. We know full well the partisan Democrat will deny, and the partisan Whig scout, our assertion. But among the people we hear in a hundred ways the hope expressed that a new organization will spring up, the belief boldly uttered that there should and must be one. It needs only time, and in the coming election the success of that bold, good man Sam Lewis, as Governor of Ohio." [2] Said the *Ashtabula Sentinel:* "We are informed that many leading men, and probably nine-tenths of the voters of the Whig party, are desirous of disbanding and casting their votes and influence for Justice and Liberty. Circumstances induce us to believe that the candidates of the Whig party, at least a portion of them, are anxious to withdraw." [3] These claims, of course, met with derision at the hands of the regular Whig party organs. Said the *Sandusky Commercial Register:* "The *True Democrat* betrays the weakness of its cause by the anxious eagerness with which it would seize recruits by the collar and drag them nolens volens into the meagre ranks of the Free Democracy"; [4] and the *Cleveland Herald* scouted the idea that the great Whig party "would yield to a faction of some 30,000 and do its bidding." [5] The *State Journal* felt solemn horror at the proposal of an alliance with the Free Democrats on the basis of anti-slavery opinions, for "these are sentiments that the Whig party never did and never will proclaim." [6]

Some Whig papers, however, as well as some individual Whigs, used different language. The Cleveland *Forest City* queried: "Can antislavery Whigs longer affiliate with doughface material? . . . Is it not better to dissolve partnership with

---

[1] *True Democrat*, June 1, 1853.   [2] *Ibid.*

[3] Quoted in *National Era*, June 16, 1853.

[4] Quoted in *True Democrat*, June 29, 1853.

[5] Quoted *ibid.*, June 8, 1853.

[6] Quoted *ibid.*, June 29, 1853.

these men rather than continue a connection the fruits of which
are treachery, pro-slavery, and defeat?"[1] The *Cincinnati Gazette*
admitted that the Whig party had "abandoned its principles so
far that it differed little from the Democratic, and had no real
principle in the State election"; [2] and the *Medina Whig* spoke
out boldly: "What shall the Whig party do? We love the old
Whig name, but a mere name is nothing. . . . There is no reason why the liberal Whigs of Ohio and the Free Democrats
should not unite."[3] The *New York Tribune*, always a power
with the Northwestern anti-slavery Whigs, threw its great influence in favor of one of Greeley's favorite ideas, — a union of
Free Democrats and Whigs on the Maine Law. By the end of
July it became evident that this advice would be followed.
From Portage County came a "tremendous call" signed by four
hundred names of men of all parties, demanding a "People's"
convention, to unite the issues of temperance and anti-slavery.
This was the signal for similar calls in Cuyahoga, Columbiana,
and Ashtabula counties, and in the senatorial district of
Huron, Erie, Sandusky, and Ottawa. Chase was doubtful; but
the majority of Free Democrats found in this movement
nothing but matter for congratulation, and joined in it heart and
soul. Giddings, in a letter to Baldwin, of Cleveland, said that
if it was an honest movement, no mere question of names
should hold back the Free Democrats, and added: "If either the
Whigs or Democrats would embrace the truth and maintain the
inalienable rights of all men to liberty I would at once say, Let
the Free Democracy disband. . . . If the movement fails it will
be solely because of bad management or bad faith on the part
of the leaders, not the people."[4] Further to mark his favor,
Giddings advised the Free Democrats of Ashtabula to propose
a "People's" movement, although as an organization they had
absolutely nothing to gain, since they were in a great majority
over both the other parties combined.

The Portage County fusion took place with perfect harmony,
through a full mixed ticket, with a Free Democrat at the head;

---

[1] Quoted in *True Democrat*, June 1, 1853.
[2] *National Era*, June 23, 1853.   [3] Quoted *ibid*.
[4] *Ibid.*, Sept. 1, 1853.

and the same success was attained in Ashtabula, as well as in the Huron and Erie senatorial district, where a Free Soil convention ratified the previous temperance nomination. In two places, however, friction resulted from the suspicions entertained by Free Democrats with regard to Whig desire for union. In Columbiana County, after a Free Soil ticket had been nominated, a "People's" convention met and selected a Maine Law ticket, which included only one of the Free Democrats; nothing was said about slavery in the platform. Thereupon the Free Democratic candidates, by advice of the local papers, the *New Lisbon Aurora*, and the Garrisonian *Anti-Slavery Bugle*, refused to withdraw, and though Giddings and Chase both urged them to abandon this position, the local committee was obdurate.[1] In Cleveland, a "People's" convention, after considerable friction, nominated for Cuyahoga County a joint temperance and anti-slavery ticket, which the *True Democrat* was willing to support; but R. P. Spaulding and some other indignant ex-Democrats induced the Central Committee to call a regular county convention. The result was a meeting with a rather irregular organization, including at least one contested delegation. In a stormy session A. G. Riddle, Edward Wade, and J. C. Vaughn, editor of the *True Democrat*, against the strenuous opposition of Spaulding, succeeded in laying on the table resolutions to run a separate ticket. Spaulding then, as usual, lost his temper completely, refused to let Giddings address the meeting because he was not a delegate, and threatened so loudly to make a party nomination, whether this particular convention agreed or not, that Giddings, Riddle, Wade, Vaughn and the others left in disgust, and let the excited ex-Democrats fulfil their purpose.[2] These events were noticed in the Democratic *Plain Dealer* as follows: " The fusionists taken in and done for — the Whigs sick of the bargain — Vaughn in a towering passion — a free fight all round — the kettle has all boiled over — the fat is in the fire — the ingenious net thrown out to catch the Free Soilers is full of gudgeons." [3]

[1] *National Era*, Sept. 1, 15, 29, 1853; *True Democrat*, Sept. 21, 1853.
[2] *True Democrat*, Sept. 12, 1853.
[3] Quoted *ibid.*, Sept. 28, 1853.

In spite of these local difficulties, the tendency of sentiment in the State at large continued steadily in favor of fusion. The *Columbian*, the central organ of the party, said: " We should deem it our duty to accept any aid which could honorably be obtained in the election of men of the right stamp to the legislature, and should not hesitate . . . to join in any open and fair co-operation with those disposed to join it, or to sustain, for offices not legislative, capable men of other parties." [1] Lewis was the only candidate for Governor of avowed temperance principles; but Allen, the Whig candidate for Lieutenant-Governor, was known to be in favor of the Maine Law. With a desire to further good feeling, Buckingham, the Free Democratic nominee for Lieutenant-Governor, resigned; and his party, after ascertaining that Allen fully indorsed the Pittsburg platform in regard to slavery, gladly supported the latter. [2] The *Holmes County Whig*, by no means a radical paper, asserted that Barrere, the Whig candidate for Governor, had sent to his Central Committee a letter of resignation in favor of Lewis, but that it had been suppressed. [3] Whether or no this assertion were true, the idea became current that the Whigs were to support Lewis.

In these circumstances, the Free Democrats, with memories of 1849, took a prudent middle ground. The *Columbian*, the official mouthpiece, said: " That there are many persons who have heretofore acted with the Whig party, hoping against hope that that party would redeem itself from the domination of slavery, we are well aware. . . . These we would invite to go along with us. Shall our organization be changed or our principles modified? We are not sticklers for forms or party names ; yet we would not abandon them unnecessarily to resort to new ones. . . . Let not the liberal antislavery Whig be alarmed because we call it Democratic. . . . Every true Whig is a democrat. Our principles and our party are making rapid strides toward victory ; let us not be in haste to outrun as a party the tide of our principles." [4]

[1] Quoted *True Democrat*, Sept. 13, 1853.
[2] *Ibid.*, Oct. 4, 1853; *Ohio Columbian*, Sept. 15, 1853.
[3] *Western Reserve Chronicle*, Oct. 6, 1853.
[4] *Ohio Columbian*, July 14, 1853.

Meanwhile, in the midst of complete political stagnation among the old parties, the Free Democratic campaign continued with ever-increasing enthusiasm. County conventions all over the State pressed organization farther than ever before, holding a greater number of meetings than in any other year, except perhaps at the height of the Free Soil revolt of 1848. Lewis gave the country an exhibition of stump-speaking such as is seldom seen: he spoke nearly every secular day for over four months in fifty counties, traversing not only the Western Reserve, but regions such as Scioto, Lawrence, and Gallia in the south, and Stark, Holmes, Tuscarawas, and Coshocton in the centre, places where the Free Democracy was hardly known. In the midst of these tremendous efforts he also found time to make an excursion into Indiana, and to preside over the Fourth Annual Christian Anti-Slavery Convention at Cincinnati in May, at which William Lloyd Garrison strongly urged his views. Wherever Lewis went, his eloquence made a profound impression. Of his visit to Darke County, an ultra-Hunker region, an enthusiastic hearer wrote: "When Mr. Lewis was portraying the working of the fugitive slave act you could see the tear of sympathy fall down the cheeks of some of the old veterans of the Whig and Democratic parties." In Warren County he "completely electrified his audience and frequently moved them to tears"; and — still more noteworthy — in Montgomery County, at a place where there had never been an anti-slavery speaker, his eloquence led numbers of the Old Line to subscribe for the *Columbian*.[1]

By September, Chase, Giddings, Smith, Hamlin, Root, Brisbane, Julian of Indiana, and others were in the field.[2] Wade, Spelman, Riddle, and Vaughn, for example, went to every town in Cuyahoga County. "The movement goes bravely on," said the *Western Reserve Chronicle;* "in no year except in a Presi-

---

[1] *Ohio Columbian*, April 14, 1853.

[2] It is interesting to note that during the canvass Chase found time to write a letter to Edgerton, — a Democratic member of Congress from Ohio, who had spoken of Chase as no Democrat, — reiterating his familiar arguments as to the Democratic character of the third party. See *National Era*, Dec. 22, 1853.

dential campaign has there been anything like it." [1]   When
finally election day came, the vote revealed a new order of
things.[2] The Democrats had carried the State by a large majority, but the total vote polled was 70,000 less than that of the year
before. The local Whig party had fallen to 85,000, the smallest
vote since the party was organized.   Not even the national
Whig party could show greater demoralization.   The Free
Democrats, on the contrary, had raised their vote on minor
offices to almost the exact Van Buren vote of 1848, and, still
better, Lewis had succeeded in polling over 50,000.   In five
Western Reserve counties and in Clinton County the Free
Democrats were ahead of both Whigs and Democrats.   The
Whigs were first in thirteen counties only.   In sixteen other
counties the Free Democrats were ahead of the Whigs; they
had thirteen members of the legislature to the Whigs' twenty;
and the difference between Barrere and Lewis was so slight
that the Free Democrats felt themselves within striking distance of the beaten party.

All were jubilant. Said the *True Democrat*, in comment on
the election: "The Old Line Democracy had no foe to meet
outside of the Free Soil sections.   They walked over the track
elsewhere carrying even undisputed Whig districts.   But the tug
of conflict was felt wherever a Free Soil basis existed, and there
even when the odds were against us the pro-slavery Democrats
were laid low." [3]   "This is a glorious result indeed," said the
Columbian, "and one which will tell upon the future growth of
our party in other states as well as Ohio. . . . It is generally
believed by all parties that the old triangular war is at an end in
Ohio. . . . The anti-slavery men of Ohio have accomplished the
great work over which we all so much rejoice by pursuing

[1] Oct. 6, 1853.
[2] It stood as follows: —

Democratic.	Whig.	Free Democratic.
Medill 147,663	Barrere 85,820	Lewis 50,346
Myers 148,981	Allen 127,272	
Bartley 149,582	Backus 96,689	Hitchcock 35,373

See *Whig Almanac*, 1854.

[3] Oct. 14, 1853.

a practical policy. They have run after no abstractions or phantasms. Definite objects and a probable mode of accomplishing them have been kept constantly before the people."[1] "Thousands of Liberal Whigs," said the *National Era*, "separated from their party in 1848 and have since acted with the Independent Democrats. Thousands have this year followed their example; thousands more are now ready to join the new party. What a prospect opens to the friends of Liberty in Ohio!"[2] The Whig press, chastened by its severe defeat, showed a milder attitude than ever toward the Free Democrats; even the *Cleveland Herald*, "Silver Gray" at all times, while cautioning people not to think that the fusion in Cuyahoga and in other counties was permanent, went so far as to say: "We admit that there are and ever have been reasons which should induce all considerate anti-slavery men to act together."[3] Still more significant, the Whig *Forest City* proceeded after the campaign to unite with the *True Democrat*. The abuse of such "postmaster" papers as the *Ohio Patriot* and the *Geauga Republic*,[4] counted for little in the face of the general feeling in favor of a new movement. "This is the spirit now abroad in Ohio," said the *True Democrat;* "and they who overlook it know not the stuff whereof it is made nor the solidity of its purpose; for those who war against that spirit shall be as dry stubble wherewith the People shall kindle their fires of independence and with their blaze consume them forever."[5]

Exhausted from his labors, but jubilant, Samuel Lewis wrote a parting word to the "Friends of Freedom" in Ohio, urging them not to abate their exertions, but rather to increase them. "My last year of hard service is probably performed," he said; "my health has been providentially preserved this year, but here such labors must end. . . . I am not before you a candidate for any office, probably never shall be again; so you must allow me to press this matter upon you. Yes, you must now lay out your

---

[1] Quoted in *Racine Advocate*, Nov. 8, 1853.

[2] Dec. 1, 1853.　　　　　　　　　[3] Oct. 11, 1853.

[4] *Daily Forest City Democrat* (successor to the *True Democrat* and the *Forest City*). Nov. 1, 1853.

[5] *Ibid.*

work for success; the country and public sentiment expect such a result and everything is ripe for it.   Great moral and political reforms do not grow spontaneously; hard work and much hard work must be performed, but you no longer need labor without expecting success. . . . And, thank God," ended the veteran joyously, "that he enables you to aid in such a glorious work."[1]

In December there came from the State Free Democratic Committee a prophetic address.   It furnished a complete plan for organization, with forms of petitions, projects for local associations, and provisions for four paid lecturers to be constantly in the field throughout 1854.   "The Independent Democracy," it said, "has a great work before them for the next two years. . . . With efficient organization we may possibly secure the State ticket next fall.   We certainly can elect four to five [Representatives] and perhaps a majority of the members of Congress.   We can in 1855 elect our Governor and Legislature, which will not only effect the State reforms which we desire, but also give us a Senator. . . . Be courageous.   The enemy is strong, but God, the people, and truth are stronger; the day of small things is past."[2]

[1] *National Era*, Dec. 1, 1853.
[2] *Ibid.*, Jan. 26, 1854.

CHAPTER XVIII.

WHIGS AND FREE DEMOCRATS IN WISCONSIN.

1853.

WHILE Ohio was carrying on a triumphant campaign, Wisconsin had been undergoing a different but an equally significant experience. The election of 1852 had inspired the Free Democrats of that State with the same enthusiasm as it had aroused elsewhere in the Northwest, and also with a serious determination, the general purpose of which is well expressed by the following extract: "It seems to me that the next four years will be decisive as to the existence of the Free Democratic party as such. Unless we can step into the rank of one of the first parties as to numbers we can hardly in my opinion maintain our organization. . . . We must receive large accessions from the liberal Democrats, and must absorb the liberal Whigs unless that party adopts our principles. Are we not a little severe toward them when we call them without any exception a defeated faction? The term faction, too, is hardly in good taste. . . . A more perfect and thorough State organization is what we now need, with an increase of Free Soil papers, especially German. A great and systematic and prolonged effort must be put forth."[1]

Such sentiments as the foregoing clearly animated the State Free Democratic Convention which met on January 21, 1853. In a very full session, presided over by General J. H. Paine, and comprising most of the leading anti-slavery men of the State, a platform was adopted and a full organization urged. As the foregoing letter indicated, the main interest of Wiscon-

---

[1] From a letter to the *National Era*, dated Racine, Dec. 1, 1852: *Ibid.*, Jan. 6, 1853.

sin Free Democrats lay in their relation to the Whigs; but
with great good sense their convention forbore to suggest the
question of coalition, trusting to time to settle the matter.
During the winter, Whig papers, while insisting on the life and
vigor of their party, began to discuss the possibility of a
"People's" ticket in the coming contest for the Governorship.
Much was said as to the identity of principle between anti-
slavery Whigs and Free Democrats, and no pains were spared
by Whigs to cultivate a friendly feeling between the two bodies,
— a novel sentiment in Wisconsin, for up to this time soft words
between Whigs and abolitionists were the exception, and abuse
or indifference the rule. Some of the Free Democrats received
the unaccustomed courtesy rather ungraciously; and Booth, in
the Milwaukee *Free Democrat*, took care to inform the Whigs
that there were just two methods by which they could effect a
union with the Free Democracy, — either by adopting the Pittsburg platform or by dissolving the Whig party.[1] Neither of
these conditions was likely to be agreeable to a Whig. The
natural candidate in case of fusion was the popular Governor
Farwell, elected in 1851 by Whig and Free Soil votes. During
the discussion, the *Free Democrat* made the mistake of claiming
him as a third-party man, an utterance which irritated the Whigs
to no purpose, and brought out the following protest from the
more practical *Kenosha Telegraph*: "It is folly, or something
worse, to insist on calling Governor Farwell a Free Democrat.
He is not so distinctively any more than thousands of other
Whigs in the State; but he is a very good Governor, and for
that reason should be supported."[2]

In the face of a great Democratic clamor, the two parties
appointed their conventions on successive days of June, three
months earlier than usual; and the general understanding seems
to have been that Governor Farwell was to be renominated by
both.[3] This step would probably have been taken with entire
unanimity, but for the unfortunate fact that Farwell absolutely

[1] *Wisconsin State Journal*, May 21, 1853.
[2] Quoted in *Milwaukee Sentinel*, April 25, 1853.
[3] *Wisconsin State Journal*, April 29, May 30, 1853; *Racine Advocate*,
April 20, May 18, 1853.

refused to run. Having in its programme no provision for this emergency, the Whig convention lost its head and adjourned without nominating. The Free Soil convention the next day finding all plans for union destroyed, proceeded to nominate a full ticket of its own, headed by E. D. Holton. Although no resolution in favor of prohibition was adopted, the candidates were all avowed temperance men, a useful fact in view of the Maine Law agitation then overrunning the country.[1]

Since the Whigs had failed to nominate, and Greeley in the *New York Tribune* distinctly advised the Whigs of Wisconsin to coalesce with the Free Democrats on the Maine Law issue, many of the latter hoped that they would have the field to themselves. "They [the Whigs] may rally this fall," wrote one enthusiastic correspondent of the *National Era*, "but it is doubtful. Farwell told some of our folks that the Whigs ought not to have called a convention or even talked of nominating."[2] Although many Whigs would without doubt have been willing to support Holton, such a stretch of self-abnegation was more than could be expected of the majority of Wisconsin politicians of that party; consequently, to the disappointment of the Free Soilers, a second Whig convention in September nominated a party ticket headed by H. S. Baird. A month before the election, coalition seemed as far off as it had been in the previous year; but at the State Fair at Watertown another effort was made, chiefly by certain anti-slavery Whigs, who called a "People's" convention.[3] This meeting nominated a ticket selected from the candidates already in the field, with Farwell at the head; but again Farwell's modesty wrecked the scheme, for he positively refused to run, and Baird would not withdraw. The "People," however, were not to be balked; and on October 21, scarcely two weeks before the election, the Whig managers agreed to place Holton's name at the head of their ticket. All the Whig and Free Soil candidates not on the ticket then withdrew, and thus after much tribulation the fusion was completed.

[1] *National Era*, June 23, 1853; *Wisconsin State Journal*, June 9, 1853.
[2] *National Era*, July 7, 1853.
[3] *Watertown Chronicle*, Oct. 12, 1853.

With so short a time for a canvass, and weighted down by the incubus of Baird's persistence in running, it is not surprising that the " People's " ticket was decisively beaten.[1]   The Democratic vote was remarkably full, considering the fact that it was an " off " year; but the " People's " vote and that for Baird fell nearly 6,000 short of the combined Free Democratic and Whig votes of 1852.   One reason was that the Free Democrats made the Maine Law the principal issue in the campaign.   Indeed, one of them, who was on the " People's " ticket, has since said that at the time he forgot all about his own candidacy in his work for prohibition.[2]   This agitation so alarmed the Germans in the eastern counties that they cast a heavy vote for the Democratic ticket.

Notwithstanding the difficulty of bringing about this coalition owing to Farwell's inconvenient lack of ambition, there was little real opposition on either side : only one Whig paper objected, and that not on grounds of principle.   From the first, everybody felt the desirability of coalition, and the only difficulties arose as to the method of obtaining it.   In these negotiations and nominations we find a curiously close parallel to the Free Soil and Whig fusion in Michigan in 1849, and the result is apparently similar.   In Wisconsin, however, the motives underlying the coalition were essentially different.   The Whigs in both cases wanted primarily to overthrow the Democratic rule in the State ; but in Michigan they had the prestige of members of a victorious national party, whereas the Wisconsin Whigs were in 1853 in the depths of prostration after an overwhelming State and national defeat.   In Michigan there was no demand for a new anti-slavery party in 1849, whereas in Wisconsin this sentiment appears constantly in 1853.   " The Whig party of this state," said the *State Journal* in May, " as a general thing are just as much opposed to slavery and are doing and will do just as much toward ridding the country of this

---

[1] The vote stood : —

Democratic.	Independent.	Scattering.
Barstow 30,405	Holton 21,886	Baird 3,304
Lewis 32,176	Pinckney 23,378	Dougherty 270

[2] Communicated to the writer by S. D. Hastings in 1895.

evil as the Free Soil party." [1] The Whigs in their State Convention repudiated the national platform by resolving against the extension of slavery and by denying the authority of any convention to decree the finality of any law.[2] Even the *Janesville Gazette*, the only strong Whig opponent of fusion, admitted: "To a great extent the principles of the Free Soil and Whig parties are identical." [3]

In the autumn the Whig papers spoke still more plainly. The *State Journal*, in speaking of the Whig party, said: "There are higher motives than mere political aggrandizement. . . . We have no blind allegiance to that party as a party." [4] The *Milwaukee Sentinel* went still farther: "It is certainly true, that the Whigs and the Free Soilers . . . think alike . . . and it is highly desirable that they should act together. . . . Parties have indeed lost much of their prescriptive authority in this state." [5] After the election the Free Democratic *Kenosha Telegraph* remarked: "The mission of the Free Democracy as an independent party is nearly fulfilled." It described how the slave power was aiming to control the country, and concluded: "When the people come to see this fact clearly a third party has no mission. This is the condition to which people are now rapidly turning." [6] The language of the *State Journal*, in commenting on the foregoing paragraphs, indicates strikingly the difference between Michigan Whigs of 1849 and Wisconsin Whigs of 1853. "Such," it said, "is the language of the *Telegraph*, one of the ablest of the organs of the Free Soil party in the State. It must be admitted that there are numerous indications in the present condition of parties pointing to such a state of things in the future. The ostensible issues have become matters of fancy. . . . That this state of things cannot last long is tolerably certain. A great majority of the people are opposed to the extension of slavery; the humbug of ' saving the Union' is beginning to be appreciated in all quarters. If slavery

---

[1] *Wisconsin State Journal*, May 30, 1853.

[2] *Milwaukee Sentinel*, Sept. 19, 1853.

[3] Oct. 15, 1853.   [4] *Wisconsin State Journal*, Oct. 20, 1853.

[5] Sept. 28, 1853.

[6] Quoted in *Wisconsin State Journal*, Nov. 29, 1853.

can be restricted within its present limits it must inevitably decline." [1]

The year 1853, then, saw the Free Democrats of the Northwest at the height of their activity. In every State their organization was improving, and in three States, — Ohio, Indiana, and Wisconsin, — their vote had largely increased. Throughout the Northwest, Whigs were beginning to regard the Free Democratic party with more interest and toleration, and even when not outright in favor of coalition they seemed inclined to emphasize their anti-slavery position and to repudiate the national Whig platform. In the other States it would be easy to find many sentiments similar to those quoted in Ohio and Wisconsin. The *Indiana State Journal*, though not in the slightest degree sympathizing with the Free Soil organization, said in commenting on the State Convention: "We claim to be as heartily opposed to slavery as any man who may participate in the proceedings of the meeting on Thursday." [2] Later the *Journal*, being charged with "abolitionism," defined its position, calling "Union saving" a hobby. It considered the position of the South with regard to slavery in the Territories as "one which will eventually destroy the Union if it ever is destroyed," adding: "As to the future, should any question arise involving the extension of slavery over territory now free, we shall be found in the opposition to the utmost of our feeble efforts. If these views are 'abolitionism' they can make the most of it." [3]

In Illinois another Old Line Whig paper used similar language. "We have become heartily tired," said the *Chicago Journal*, "of this eternal clamor of a dissolution of the Union. When the area [of slavery] is sought to be extended over freedom's broad and happy domain . . . then its defenders will ever find in us a willing hand to strike a blow for the down-trodden and oppressed." [4] When the *Journal* was charged, like its Indianapolis namesake, with being abolitionist, it replied: "Is it abolitionism to sympathize with the oppressed? So far then we

---

[1] *Wisconsin State Journal*, Nov. 29, 1853.
[2] *Indiana State Journal*, May 24, 1853.
[3] *Ibid.*, Aug. 21, 1853.
[4] *Chicago Journal*, Jan. 4, 1853.

plead guilty to the charge of being abolitionist. We do not by word or thought seek to interfere with slavery in the states, . . . but when its blighting influence is spread in the heretofore glorious state of our adoption we cannot be silenced." [1] This last phrase refers to a law enacted in this year forbidding negroes to come into the State under penalty of imprisonment, fine, or, in default of payment, of sale at auction for a term of years.[2] This law, which practically enacted slavery, met with condemnation by Whig and Democratic papers alike in the northern counties. The *Journal* called it "a dishonor to our State, a deep wrong to our nation, a foul stain upon the character and intelligence of our people," [3] — language with which the *Western Citizen*, the *Journal's* anti-slavery neighbor, could find no fault.

The signs of dissolution, not rapid or willing, but still inevitable, had appeared in the Whig ranks. What profit the cause of anti-slavery should derive from this crisis depended upon the events of 1854; and in full realization of their opportunity the Free Democrats were, at the opening of that year, prepared in every Northwestern State for a prodigious effort. That effort was never expended, or rather it received a direction never anticipated in the wildest dreams of third-party men; for in 1854 came the Kansas-Nebraska excitement, and with it anti-slavery action in the United States entered upon a new, a more serious, and an eventually triumphant career.

[1] March 11, 1853.
[2] See Appendix D, p. 332.
[3] *Chicago Journal*, Feb. 22, 1853.

CHAPTER XIX.

THE FREE DEMOCRATIC PARTY ATTAINS NIRVANA IN THE ANTI-NEBRASKA MOVEMENT.

1854.

ONE may be permitted to surmise what would have been the fate of the Free Democratic party in the Northwest had the situation in regard to slavery been allowed to remain as it was at the end of the campaigns of 1853. The Whig party was slipping away from its platform of 1852, and disintegration was so inevitable in the immediate future that many Free Democrats hoped that their own party might step into its place. The great gains just made in Ohio and Wisconsin seemed to point in that direction, and, as we have seen, encouraged the Ohio Central Committee to make bold prophecies; but so rose-colored a view has no justification when we consider the position of the third party outside of Ohio and Wisconsin. In no one of the other Northwestern States did it, in 1853, seriously threaten the Whigs; in fact, so far as numbers went, it was scarcely more important than the Liberty party had been.

The Whigs were, to be sure, ready for anti-slavery action, and their party name was beginning to lose its magic; but it is hardly conceivable that in the Northwest they would have entered *en masse* into the Free Democratic ranks, as the *National Era* hoped. In spite of the close approximation in principle between Northwestern Whigs and Free Democrats, union must come not through direct absorption, but rather through the medium of some new organization. The truth is, that after 1850 the Free Democracy was somewhat too familiar and commonplace to be attractive to anti-slavery Whigs or Democrats, however anxious for a change they might be. Its doctrines, though true, were trite; its leaders had said their say; and the odor of bargaining and coalition still hanging over from 1849 discredited it widely. The Free Soil party had "shot its bolt," and in the nature of things was less interesting than would be a fresh organization with the same principles, but under a new name.

That this was the case none knew better than the leading Free Democrats. In 1853 a wide correspondence, started by Mr. William Medill, of the Cleveland *Forest City*, between leading Whig politicians and editors and Free Democrats, brought out the fact that the latter were ready and eager to sink their organization in a new one, if only the substitute would take a right attitude on slavery extension; the Whigs, on their side, though more cautious, evidently were gravitating in the same direction.[1] What was now needed was a centre of irritation around which a new party could be crystallized; and in default of the Nebraska Bill something else would have served. The whole narrative up to this point proves that, whatever might come up in Congress, the course of party history in 1854 could not have been very different from what it actually turned out. From the existing chaos of parties a new anti-slavery party sooner or later must have taken form. Already in 1852–53 the Maine Law agitation had been sweeping the country; and when in 1854 the signal for dissolution came in the form of the Kansas-Nebraska Bill, all party lines seemed to vanish in a wilderness of faction. In the elections of 1853–54, tickets were actually put into the field by the Democrats ("Hard" and "Soft"), Temperance Democrats, Maine Law men, Whigs, Know-Nothings, Free Democrats, Anti-Nebraska men, and Republicans.

In 1854 in the Eastern States the Know-Nothing movement carried nearly all before it. In New York and Pennsylvania the Whigs, profiting by Democratic faction and by the absence of any strong third party, maintained their organization; but in the Northwest the event toward which, for long weary years, abolitionists, Liberty men, and Free Democrats had been working, took place in the creation of a new Northern anti-slavery

[1] See letter in *Chicago Tribune*, April 25, 1895.

party. One obvious reason for such radical action by Northwestern Whigs was that their party had been for years losing
ground, and by 1854 was in so hopeless a minority that the
party name retained few attractions; but another reason was to
be found in the greater looseness of party ties in the Northwest.
The Northwestern Whigs and anti-slavery Democrats, not a
whit more earnest in their convictions than their brethren in
the Central and Eastern States, showed greater magnanimity
and much less partisanship throughout the year; they worked
side by side with each other, and with hated " abolitionists " at
a time when Eastern Whigs and Democrats were clinging to
their old organizations, or were rushing into the secrecy and
the futility of the Know-Nothing movement.

Of the general aspects of the Anti-Nebraska movement, from
the first mutterings of alarm in January to the wild outburst
in June and the triumphant campaign in the summer, this
is not the place to speak; but we cannot dismiss the third-party
movement without tracing among the confusion of the popular
uprising the course of the Free Democratic party in the several
States.

The only national Free Democratic action in this year was the
issuing of the " Address of the Independent Democrats in Congress," written by Chase, and signed by him, and by Edward
Wade and Giddings of Ohio, Sumner and DeWitt of Massachusetts, and Gerrit Smith of New York. This last public utterance of the party was a powerful one, a clarion cry producing
a great effect in all quarters and marking the real beginning of
the Republican movement.

In Ohio, when public meetings began to protest against the
Nebraska Bill, the Free Democrats from the outset co-operated
with other protestors. Without claiming anything for party
advantage, without even referring to the past, Root, Vaughn,
Spaulding, Brinckerhoff, and the rest with rare tact fell in with
the current of popular feeling, striving only to aid without
seeming to try to lead. From the beginning, Whigs of all
stripes were, on their part, inclined to co-operate. On the Western Reserve, party lines vanished. The fusion of the Cleveland
True Democrat and *Forest City* was followed by the union of

the Elyria *Courier* and *Independent Democrat*, and by that of
the Ravenna *Star* and *Whig*.[1] Still more significant was the
attitude of the Columbus *State Journal*, the central organ of
the " Silver Gray" Whigs. This paper feared at first that the
question "would be complicated by the over-zealous action of
the extreme anti-slavery partisans in the free States"; but,
when the address of the independent Democrats appeared,
approved it as "fair and reasonably moderate."[2] The *Cleveland Herald*, equally conservative, could not even in this hour
forgive Chase. "We are no political friends of Mr. Chase," it
said; "he obtained his seat in a manner entirely subversive of
political integrity; we hope never again to fall upon such
political times as disgraced Ohio under the reign of the balance of power." When, however, Chase's speech on the bill
was reported, it could not deny that "looking merely at this
one question we know that the Senator speaks the voice of
Ohio."[3]

During the winter and spring, even before the old party leaders were quite ready to talk about a new organization, local
bodies began to fuse together. In many places the Central
Committees of all three parties united to call anti-Nebraska
conventions. A committee of three men was appointed by a
mass meeting at Columbus to issue a call and collect signatures
for a State anti-Nebraska Convention, the Free Soil representative being Dr. J. H. Coulter, formerly on the Free Democratic
State Committee. By the middle of the spring grudging approval gave place to the loud demands for a new party. The
Columbus *State Journal*, *Cleveland Herald*, *Cincinnati Gazette*,
dozens of other Whig papers, and many Democratic journals,
joined in calling for a non-partisan union of "all who hate or
dislike slavery, against its encroachments." The name "Republican" had already been suggested by the private correspondence of Greeley, A. E. Bovay, of Ripon, Wisconsin, and others,
besides Whig and Free Democratic editors. By June it began
to be heard in public. "Let us unite on a common principle,"

1 *Daily Forest City Democrat*, Jan. 27, April 1, 1854.
2 *Ohio State Journal*, Jan. 14, 26, 1854.
3 *Cleveland Herald*, March 7, 1854.

said the *State Journal;* "we shall soon find a common name in the pure Republicanism of our object."[1]

As the day for the assembling of the State Convention drew near, the Free Democrats were afraid that the meeting might be led to take a timid attitude through fear of losing Democratic support. "We are grieved," said the *Cleveland Leader* (formerly *True Democrat*), "to see the effort making in some quarters to whittle down the anti-slavery platform of Ohio to the single issue of the repeal of the Nebraska Bill." It stated that the aim of Northern efforts should be to denationalize slavery, and added: "In this state there are 35,000 Free Soilers and 25,000 German radicals who will surrender their organization to no party whose principles contemplate less than the foregoing."[2] The convention, however, though not so radical in its utterances as many desired, satisfied the Free Democrats by adopting resolutions pledging its members to resist the spread of slavery, and demanding the repeal of the Kansas-Nebraska Act. "True," the *Leader* said, "the resolutions were not up to the spirit of the Convention, but the members of the Convention know, as the people of Ohio know, that the set of the current is right. . . . We have learned to labor and to wait."[3] The *Ohio State Journal* clinched matters as follows: "Whatever errors in policy our Free Soil friends may have committed (and we believe they are many), it is clear that on the issue now tendered by the South *they are right;* and being right, shall Whigs and Democrats refuse their association? We certainly cannot. . . . Men must stand aside, prejudices should be forgotten."[4]

But from the group of Ohio anti-slavery leaders who now, with the stern joy of men who see the promised land, were fighting in the thick of the anti-Nebraska struggle, one eloquent voice was missing. On July 29 died Sam Lewis, the man most beloved by Ohio abolitionists, not even excepting Giddings. He was prematurely worn out by his superhuman exertions in 1852–53. Throughout his career he had com-

[1] *Ohio State Journal*, June 5, 1854.
[2] *Cleveland Leader*, July 6, 1854.
[3] *Ibid.*, July 17, 1854.　　　　[4] July 17, 1854.

bined the rare qualities of a good-tempered radical, a practical philanthropist, an unselfish politician, and a popular leader of an unpopular cause.[1]

With the State Convention of July the separate existence of the Free Democratic party in Ohio ceased, except in a few localities. By a curious coincidence, Geauga County, which in 1839 had run a separate anti-slavery ticket, nominated a Free Democratic ticket in 1854. The first to enter the field, the Geauga third-party men were the last to leave it.

In Indiana, in 1854, the Free Democrats, in sharp contrast to their Ohio brethren, played comparatively little part in the Republican movement. Their State Convention on May 29 showed a conciliatory spirit, and, with the advice of all its leading men, resolved, after condemning the Kansas-Nebraska Bill, "That we have no idolatrous attachment for mere party names, but seek the triumph of principles, and we recommend in the present crisis a co-operation of all persons who are opposed to said measure with a view to its repeal. Therefore we recommend the calling of a State Convention for the purpose of combining all elements of opposition to said measure."[2] To signalize its non-partisan feeling, the convention also resolved to nominate no candidates; but, although Indiana Whigs and many Democrats were genuinely anxious for a new party, the popular prejudice against "abolitionism" was so great that they dared not show much consideration for the Free Democratic leaders. The most they would concede was that S. S. Harding might speak at anti-Nebraska meetings. At the Indiana State anti-Nebraska Convention, held on the same day as that of Ohio, resolutions were offered favoring slavery restriction and the repeal of the Kansas-Nebraska Act. Unlike the Ohio Free Democrats, Julian did not acquiesce, and brought in a minority report demanding the denationalization of slavery. Although the temper of the convention was probably such that his resolutions might have been adopted, the leaders here as in Ohio, preferred a more cautious course, in the hope o

---

[1] W. G. W. Lewis, *Biography of Samuel Lewis*, Cincinnati, 1857.
[2] *National Era*, June 15, 1854; *Ohio Columbian*, Aug. 9, 1854.

drawing the Democratic vote; and the majority report was declared adopted.[1]

Notwithstanding this timid beginning, the Anti-Nebraska triumph in the following campaign was almost as glorious as in Ohio: and the Free Democrats played their part in advocating the success of the anti-Nebraska ticket; nevertheless, as a writer in the *National Era* said, the movement in Indiana was far from radical. " The leaders," he wrote, " are not anti-slavery men, but some of them even pro-slavery Democrats, who merely regret that equilibrium has been disturbed. They recoil from the charge of abolitionism and do their best to keep Free Soil men in the background. . . . The danger is that the anti-Nebraska movement will fritter out, leaving the anti-slavery cause just where it was in 1852." [2] The despondency of the Indiana Free Democrats was not justified by events; for, although Indiana proved a backward State, and although the Republican party formed in this year was never, except in the first election, the strong, courageous organization of Ohio, it continued to oppose slavery extension. More radical doctrine could scarcely have been expected of a State with so large a Southern element in its population.

The Michigan Free Democracy had an interesting experience in 1854. The Whigs of that State, after thirteen years of defeat, had become thoroughly ready for a change. In the early months of 1854, as soon as the Kansas-Nebraska Bill was introduced into Congress, leading Whigs participated in the non-partisan meetings held to protest. The spring found them heartily in favor of a new party; and when Congress finally passed the bill, the *Detroit Tribune* said in its indignation: " The man of whatever party who refuses to sacrifice every personal and party consideration . . . in order to aid in concentrating public sentiment against this great outrage . . . will deserve to be damned to everlasting infamy"; [3] and Jacob M. Howard, hitherto strictest Whig of the strict, said in a speech: " There must be union among men who are opposed to this surrender of

---

[1] *Indiana State Journal,* July 18, 24, 1854.
[2] *National Era,* Oct. 5, 1854.
[3] Quoted in *Racine Advocate,* June 5, 1854.

every principle. That union must be lasting. There is no use standing on punctilios any longer." [1]

The Free Democrats held their State Convention on February 22, at a time when it was still by no means certain that the Kansas-Nebraska Bill would pass. Obviously, whatever might be the result, an opportunity offered itself for the Free Democracy by a judicious campaign to profit largely from the anti-slavery excitement. With this object in view, the three hundred and nineteen delegates present made provision for vigorous local organization, passed resolutions favoring "prohibition" and condemning the Kansas-Nebraska Bill, and nominated a State ticket headed by K. S. Bingham and containing four other Free Soilers, one Democrat, and three Whigs.[2] The purpose of this step was evidently to draw voters from the other two parties; but the action, although commended at the convention by H. H. Emmons, a Whig leader, grated on the majority of his party fellows. The ticket was approved by several party newspapers on each side[3]; but the *Battle Creek Journal* said: "However much we may sympathize with the principles put forth by the Free Soilers we cannot but condemn this haste — this disposition to forestall other parties. How can they expect Whigs and Democrats will dissolve their political connections to aid in electing Free Soil partisans?"[4] There was much force in this complaint; but the Free Democrats continued with great vigor to perfect their organization. Eaton, Clinton, St Joseph, Kalamazoo, Oakland, and Kent counties formed local associations, and local tickets were run in scores of places. In the town elections Whigs and Free Democrats prospered; but from every side came in reports of Free Democratic success "In Burr Oak," said one correspondent, "where eleven year ago there were only three poor despised abolitionists, ever township officer but one was elected."[5] In a few places i

[1] *Detroit Democrat*, June 8, 1854.   [2] *Ibid.*, Feb. 23, 1854.
[3] The *Grand River Eagle* said that it was willing to support Bingham and the *Branch County Journal*, *Jonesville Telegraph*, and *Monroe Commercial* — the two last-named, Democratic papers — commended the ticket.
[4] Quoted *Detroit Democrat*, March 4, 1854.
[5] *Ibid.*, May 13, 1854.

which non-partisan anti-Nebraska tickets were run, the same or even greater success was attained.[1]

By May the desire for an entirely new party was growing so obvious that the Free Democratic leaders found themselves in an awkward position, and I. P. Christiancy at once set to work to get their candidates to withdraw; but they showed a natural reluctance. They seemed at last to have the chance of building up their party out of the ruins of the Whigs and Democrats, and for them to resign both personal advantage and prospective party gain called for much real self-surrender.[2] While the outcome hung in the balance, on May 25 the Independent Democratic Central Committee issued a call for a State Mass Convention at Kalamazoo to oppose the slave power, with the idea, apparently, of using the anti-Nebraska excitement for their own advantage. This was a false move; for the Whigs, who wanted to have a hand in any party-building, took offence. The *Detroit Democrat* worked hard for harmony, saying: "We feel confident that an honorable and satisfactory union can be effected in our State,"[3] and at length the Kalamazoo Convention, though composed principally of Free Soilers, showed a conciliatory spirit. "While asserting the true principles of anti-slavery action, it generously pledged the party to surrender its name and its candidates, provided the people without distinction of party would take the right ground and organize for efficient operations."[4] A committee was appointed, with Christiancy at the head, to withdraw the candidates in case such a step proved advisable. This action met at once with Whig approval, especially among the country editors, who were anxious for a union, and who now said, in the words of the *Cass County Tribune:* "This is magnanimous and right."[5]

On June 23 a call for a State Convention appeared, signed by men of all parties; and on July 6, at Jackson, the "People" met and organized a new party, the "Republican." Strange

---

[1] *Grand River Eagle*, Dec. 13, 1890.

[2] Letter of I. P. Christiancy, in F. A. Flower, *History of the Republican Party*, 172.

[3] June 14, 1854.   [4] *National Era*, July 6, 1854.

[5] Quoted in *Detroit Democrat*, July 1, 1854.

sights were seen in this Convention, men who had been prominent in circulating the Birney forgery serving on committees
side by side with original Liberty abolitionists. The Committee on Resolutions reported through Jacob M. Howard
a ringing series embodying, in great contrast to the meagre
platforms of Indiana and Ohio, all the anti-slavery doctrine that
the most ardent Free Democrat could desire; then came the
most dramatic episode of the day, when I. P. Christiancy,
stepping forward, announced the withdrawal of the Free Democratic ticket and the dissolution of the Free Democratic party.
Loud and prolonged applause followed. The Free Democratic
party of Michigan thus gracefully and definitely withdrew from
the field and turned into the service of the Republican movement that activity which had been so effective in 1852–53.

The Illinois Free Democrats shared to some extent the fate
of their Indiana brethren. In spite of the popular revolt against
Douglas and his bill, the local Whig party with amazing conservatism refused to abandon its name and organization. There
was, however, a general union of anti-Nebraska sentiment, and
in the two northern districts the Republican party was successfully formed. As in 1848, the principal interest lay in the revolt
of the Chicago Democrats, which in its violence led to an actual
mobbing of the author of the obnoxious Nebraska Bill when,
in September, he visited the city. A tendency toward anti-
Nebraska fusion began to appear in the increasing numbers
of non-partisan meetings. Said the *Chicago Tribune* in May:
"The signs of the times seem to us to indicate an affiliation of
those better and more progressive elements without regard to
party as it now exists." [1] When the Nebraska Bill was passed,
the *Chicago Courant* (Democratic) declared: "The political
landmarks can no longer be Whig or Democrat, Free Soil or
Abolitionist, but must be merged into the two great parties,
South and North;" [2] and on August 2 a non-partisan convention for Lake County, the focus of anti-slavery sentiment,
adopted the "Republican" platform and name, and went to
work. In the Second Congressional District a fusion conven-

[1] Quoted in *Racine Advocate*, May 22, 1854.
[2] Quoted *ibid.*, June 5, 1854.

tion met, and after uncompromising speeches in favor of a new party, — one of them by ex-Governor Bebb of Ohio, — adopted the Republican platform of Wisconsin, and with great enthusiasm nominated E. B. Washburne.[1] In the Chicago district a " People's " convention nominated a Republican candidate, but the Whigs refused to coalesce and ran a separate ticket.

While in these movements the Free Democrats were ready cheerfully to merge their identity, the initiative for a State anti-Nebraska organization came from certain of their number who issued a call for a convention at Springfield on October 5. Abraham Lincoln, an old Whig, was just then beginning his anti-slavery career, and efforts were made to engage him in the movement; but his friends dissuaded him from appearing at the convention.[2] The meeting was disapproved by the leading Whig papers, and therefore turned out a Free Democratic affair, led by Codding and Lovejoy. To show its conciliatory spirit, it nominated for State treasurer E. McClure, " a Henry Clay Whig," as the *Chicago Journal* called him.[3] The Whig Central Committee ratified this nomination; but as McClure had declined the Republican nomination, difficulties resulted, which, after some correspondence, were straightened out by the co-operation of the Republican and Whig committees in the selection of Miller. In this campaign, therefore, the Illinois Free Democrats lost their identity as a party. The anti-Nebraska sentiment of the State, in spite of Whig reluctance, was soon to solidify into a Republican party of the Indiana type.

In Wisconsin, as in Ohio, the tale of Free Democratic action in 1854 is soon told. The " People's " movement of 1853 has already been described; it resulted in the temporary coalition of Whigs and Free Democrats; but for all practical purposes the two parties ceased their separate existence in October, 1853. Thereafter the old party machinery was lifeless. Here and there in the state, local organizations ran separate tickets in the spring elections of 1854, but even in such cases fusion was common. On the question of the Kansas-Nebraska Bill, Wisconsin seemed

---

[1] *National Era*, Sept. 14, 1854; *Milwaukee Sentinel*, Sept. 4, 1854.

[2] J. T. Morse, *Abraham Lincoln*, I., 95.

[3] *Chicago Journal*, Oct. 7-10, 1854.

to move as one man. Early in February began frequent non-partisan meetings, in which the foremost Free Democrats and Whigs participated. Probably the earliest of these meetings in the whole country expressly to propose a new party was that called at Ripon, Winnebago County; it has become famous as the starting-point of the Republican party.[1]

When the Nebraska Bill passed, in May, 1854, the organs of both parties with few exceptions, together with a good many individual Democrats, heartily joined in the call for a State Mass Convention. Whig papers, in marked contrast to their Illinois neighbors, spoke kindly of the Free Democrats. "We wish to leave off platforms," said the *Grant County Herald,* "and turn to men. Anybody can ride on a platform. Measures not men elected Pierce, nominated Scott, and both on *identical platforms.* Does any sane man believe that J. P. Hale had not merit enough of his own to shine? He was the only statesman of the lot. We oppose unions or compacts between parties merely for the sake of gaining a majority over a third party."[2] Said the Madison *Journal:* "The Whig and Free Soil parties stand this day, though in the minority, in a position infinitely more proud than the dishonored pro-slavery Democratic party."[3] The Free Democrats, on their part, abandoned their organization without a moment's hesitation, and in the convention at Madison, on July 13, all anti-slavery elements, with enthusiasm and harmony unsurpassed elsewhere, adopted the Republican platform and name. So thoroughly had the fusion of 1853 paved the way for a new party that in 1854 there was hardly the slightest friction in passing from the old to the new dispensation.

In Iowa, as in Michigan, the gallant little band of anti-slavery heroes made a self-denying ordinance, when they saw that the time had come to unite the opponents of the Nebraska Bill. The Whigs of that State had been consistently opposed to the extension of slavery; and, although the party had a full share of "Silver Grays," the more anti-slavery wing was in control in 1854. The Free Democrats early put into the field Simeon

[1] See A. E. Bovay's description, in F. A. Flower, *History of the Republican Party,* 50 *seq.*

[2] Quoted in *Milwaukee Sentinel,* May 27, 1854.   [3] Quoted *ibid.*

Waters as their candidate for Governor. The Whig State Convention, which met February 22, nominated J. W. Grimes for Governor and adopted a plank condemning the Nebraska Bill. Since it was known, from the election of 1852, that the Free Democrats very nearly held the balance of power, the Whig leaders, especially Grimes, were anxious to bring about a concentration of anti-Nebraska sentiment; [1] and by March it had become evident that the Northern States were about to unite against the principle of non-intervention. Hence the Free Democratic leaders, at Whig suggestion, called a State Convention at Crawfordsville to decide on the proper course to pursue under the circumstances. On March 28, after long deliberation, it was resolved that the best way to rebuke the Nebraska swindle was to vote for Grimes. "The standing of Mr. Grimes," said the *Iowa True Democrat*, "was known by many of the oldest and most faithful members of the convention . . . they were ready to vouch for his soundness. We therefore in conjunction with every independent in the State go in, heart and hand, to make J. W. Grimes Governor of Iowa." [2] This indorsement of Grimes had the effect of driving from his support most of the Hunker Whigs; [3] but after the coalition had gained a hard-earned triumph in the August election, it was unencumbered by incongruous elements. The Free Democrats by their action lost nothing and gained everything; and Iowa, hitherto the most pro-slavery of the free States, sprang at a bound ahead of Indiana and Illinois, to stand beside Wisconsin, Michigan, and Ohio in the anti-slavery column.

With the exception of Illinois, every Northwestern State had gone over to the new organization, and tne end for which the Liberty and Free Soil parties had been laboring for fourteen years had at last been attained, — the formation of a powerful and well-organized party absolutely opposed to the influence of slavery.

[1] W. Salter, *Life of J. W. Grimes*, 115.
[2] Quoted in *Chicago Journal*, June 13, 1854.
[3] W. Salter, *Life of J. W. Grimes*, 54.

CHAPTER XX.

THE RESULT OF TWENTY YEARS' EFFORT.

1834–1854.

THE anti-slavery societies of 1834, the Liberty party of 1841, the Free Soil party of 1848, and its other form the Free Democracy of 1851, all set before themselves the same end, — to bring the North to realize its relation to slavery and to exercise its constitutional rights to repress and discourage the institution in every possible way. In 1854 their hopes began to be realized by the birth in the Northwest of a new national party, which accomplished the tremendous task of destroying slavery. The question which tests the real worth of all these anti-slavery organizations is simply this: How much did they contribute to this final result? To those who consider that the history of the United States is prepared in Congress and settled by national elections, and who consequently disregard all unsuccessful third parties as unworthy of study, this question is of little moment. But no history is more one-sided than mere parliamentary or legislative annals. Especially is it a mistake to disregard local political history in the United States; for, as a matter of fact, half the political battles of the period before the Civil War were fought out in State legislatures and State elections, and Congress did little more than ratify the results.

As an outgrowth of conscientious scruples, warm sympathies, keen political foresight, and habits of thought inherited from a New England ancestry, the anti-slavery movement as a moral force in the Northwest deserves a fuller treatment than can be given in a work which deals with it as a political engine. In

two ways, one direct and one indirect, the third-party movement was effective. The direct method was agitation, persistent
dwelling on the sinfulness of slavery, on the duty of the North
to rid the national government of all contact with it, and on the
absolute necessity of resisting all its encroachments. To the
unceasing activity of the abolitionists, of the Liberty men, and
later of the Free Democrats, must in no small degree be ascribed the change in public sentiment which took place between
1830 and 1854. When all due credit has been given to Congressional struggles, to industrial and physiographical reasons
for conflict between the sections, it remains true that, without
vigorous, untiring, often town-to-town and house-to-house work,
the publishing of newspapers, the distribution of documents,
and the incessant reiteration of the incompatibility between
slavery and freedom, Northwestern sentiment could not have
been prepared to alter with such a mighty force and unanimity
as it showed in the year 1854.

Indirectly, the anti-slavery agitators affected public opinion
through politics. They demanded anti-slavery political action,
and from the first threatened not to vote for such candidates
as did not satisfy them. They soon showed that they were
"a vote" which might be attracted or repelled; and hence
members of the old parties, otherwise indifferent, began with
increasing frequency to seek by protestations of some sort to
enlist their support. In the years after 1843 this practice became a potent means of anti-slavery education. Every Whig
or Democratic candidate in a region where abolitionists were
numerous felt obliged to define his position on slavery. Whig
papers that vituperated the Liberty men usually based their
arguments on the claim that they were themselves equally
anti-slavery with the "Birney party," and at the same time
were far more efficient in their action. These two ways in
which anti-slavery agitation affected the public in the Northwest, without discussing other factors, are sufficiently important to account, in large measure, for the prevailing sentiment
of 1854.

As between the various successive forms assumed by the
agitation, the greatest credit is of course due to the earliest.

It was the non-partisan, purely moral action of the anti-slavery societies that laid the foundations for anti-slavery action not only in the third party, but within the old parties as well; it was this action that produced Seward, B. F. Wade, and Greeley, as well as Chase, Lewis, Lovejoy, and Birney, and that provided a medium in which they could act.

With the advent of the Liberty party anti-slavery action assumed a narrower form. Without abandoning their original object of converting the North, the Liberty leaders from this time onward phrased their purpose differently: they now aimed, as did the Free Soilers, to build up a Northern party. In this direct purpose no one will assert that any third-party organization approached success. It is true that there was no year in which, unassisted, it elected more than three Congressmen in the Northwest, or more than twenty or thirty members of the legislatures in all six States together. In fact, the Liberty party in the Northwest never carried any electoral district, larger than a township, by a plurality of its own votes. In this matter, however, we must discriminate between the methods of the two organizations. The Liberty party stuck to the creed of entirely separate action, indifferent alike to Whig and Democrat, and relying upon the spread of its principles among the people for an increase of its vote; the Free Soil party, on the other hand, was perfectly willing to help elect men of other parties if they professed its ideas, or to gain the help of other parties in electing its own candidates. The result was that although, unaided, the Free Soil party was practically little stronger in the Northwest than its predecessor, it was able, by means of coalitions of various kinds, to place in office a very considerable number of anti-slavery men. Beside helping to elect legislative or local officers in several States, the Free Soilers sent to one or the other House of Congress Chase, Edward Wade, Giddings, Root, Townshend, Newton, and Campbell, from Ohio; Julian from Indiana; Sprague, Conger, and Penniman, from Michigan; Durkee and Doty from Wisconsin; and several others, whose success was probably due to Free Democratic votes. Immediately after the Free Soil revolt of 1848, while

the Wilmot Proviso was for the time common political property in the Northwest, several Senators and Representatives
were chosen by the old parties, very largely on account of
their anti-slavery professions, — notably Whitcomb of Indiana, and Doty and Walker of Wisconsin; the nomination
and election of such men were indirectly due to anti-slavery
organization.

The presence of some of these men in Congress proved of
very great benefit to the anti-slavery cause; but, as has been
pointed out above, the very system of coalition which elected
them quickly disintegrated the Free Soil party, and thus nul-
lified the purpose expressed in the Buffalo platform, — to found
a permanent Northern party. The coalitions, moreover, almost
invariably caused suspicion, and exposed the Free Democrats to
the charges of "office-seeking" and "greed for spoils," faults
which, to the virtuous sensibilities of the party not included in
the coalition, were extremely painful, and to the scrupulous of
all parties were distasteful. In contrast with the Liberty party,
which from 1840 to 1846 showed a steady increase in its vote,
the Free Soil party, after its beginning in 1848, went from bad
to worse, and in 1851 had entirely lost State organization in
the Northwest, except in Iowa, Ohio, and Wisconsin. As a
means for building up a party, indiscriminate coalition was
proved to be even worse than absolute refusal to vote for or
with the regular parties. It should be borne in mind, however, that the period from 1848 to 1850 was one of crisis: the
Congressional struggle over slavery in the Territories was at
its height, and did not end until the summer of 1850 brought
the Compromise. In such times it seemed more important to
have anti-slavery men in office, especially in Congress, than to
devote time to separate party-building.

An obvious difficulty encountered by the Liberty and Free
Soil parties was that their policy was national and had no necessary reference to State issues. Belief in the necessity of abolition in the District of Columbia, or in the advisability of the
Wilmot Proviso, or in the unconstitutionality of the Fugitive
Slave Law, was appropriate in a Congressional or a Presidential
candidate, but was not especially pertinent in an aspirant for the

legislature, and seemed wholly unnecessary in district judges, sheriffs, and minor municipal officers. Political organization in the Northwest at that period was not so thorough as entirely to subordinate State elections to national issues; and the anti-slavery parties suffered from this cause. Nevertheless, the disturbing effect of State and local issues must not be exaggerated; for politics, after 1845, were so permeated by the slavery question that the Free Soilers had plenty of reason to keep up their agitation in years when there was no national election.

After 1850, the Free Democratic party renewed its youth, and in 1853 showed that it had reached the true policy for a third party, — namely, the middle course between absolute separation and unreserved coalition. Hence, in 1854, when the signs of the times showed that the longed-for day had come, its members were willing to abandon their organization and to join the new party.

In the boldness of its political manœuvres, its great alternations of fortune, and its strong revival at the end of its career, the Free Soil party of the Northwestern States was far more remarkable than its sister party in the East. Nevertheless, between the individual Northwestern States, alike as they are in these general characteristics, great and not entirely explicable differences exist. Ohio offers the greatest interest; not from the size of its anti-slavery vote, for Liberty men and Free Democrats alike were throughout in a hopeless minority; nor from occasional successes, which were significant only in the senatorial elections of 1849 and 1851; nor from its campaigns, for in none of them except that of 1853 do we find any very marked effect on public sentiment outside the party; but from the personal character of the leaders. From the time of Theodore Weld's great tour, to the foundation of the Republican party, we find in the anti-slavery ranks a greater number of able men than ever worked before in such a cause: Weld, Birney, Bailey, Morris, Lewis, Chase, King, Root, Wade, Giddings, Spaulding, Brinckerhoff, and the rest, were a group without a parallel in any other Northwestern State, or in any State, except, perhaps, Massachusetts. It was the pre-eminent ability and devotion of these men which gave the third party of Ohio its vigor, its persistence, and its oratorical influence; and which kept it alive at the lowest ebb of party fortunes.

In Indiana, on the contrary, both the Liberty and Free Democratic parties show fewer points of interest. The State was so largely under the domination of Southern ideas that anti-slavery work of any kind was a hard, up-hill struggle; and Indiana produced no men, except Julian and Harding, of the real calibre of leaders. Judge Stevens, Vaile, Robinson, Cravens, and Hull were earnest, devoted men; but they were not of the same quality as the Ohio group. Had Bailey, Birney, Lewis, Wade, Chase, and the rest, looked to Indianapolis instead of to Columbus in the years after 1840, the anti-slavery cause of Indiana might have had a different story.

In Michigan, the third-party movement was an alternation of crescendo and diminuendo. The Liberty party of that State, which from 1840 to 1844 was stronger in proportion to its rivals than in any other Northwestern State, soon fell off to a low point; the Free Soil party after a similarly strong beginning, fell even more rapidly and to a lower level. The reason was that, in spite of the amount of strong anti-slavery sentiment in the State, there was no one man with enough of the qualities of a leader to hold the party together. Birney was a Michigan man only by adoption; and his activity ceased after his accident in 1845. Besides him no Liberty or Free Soil man of Michigan attained a national reputation in those days, or even any very wide notice in anti-slavery circles. Holmes, Stewart, Clarke, Bingham, Blair, and Christiancy were strong, able men; but no one of them had enough of the spirit or the force of Giddings or Lewis to keep a third party alive in the face of defeat.

In Illinois the brilliant promise of the Liberty party in the northern district resulted in little but discouragement, after the Free Soil outburst had died away and the anti-Cass Democrats had returned to their old party. Lovejoy and Codding were strong, radical speakers, active and devoted; but, like Julian, they were unable single-handed to create a party.

In Iowa the leaders were men of character and devotion, and, as the persistence of the party through decline and discouragement shows, they had some of the qualities of leadership; but they were in general philanthropists rather than statesmen, and the State came very late into line on the slavery question.

That Wisconsin failed to surpass Ohio or any of the other Western States in anti-slavery success can be laid only to a deficiency in leadership. Durkee, Holton, Booth, and Hastings were all up to the level of the Liberty and Free Soil leaders in most other States; but there was no one man of the first rank. Durkee in his Congressional district had an opportunity to be a second Giddings; yet with all his popularity he lacked entirely the qualities that made Giddings for twenty years the idol of the Western Reserve; and he failed to retain his seat. With opportunities of extraordinary promise in 1849, the Wisconsin Free Soil leaders allowed themselves to be thoroughly outwitted by the Democrats; whereas a far-sighted party leader would have seen and avoided the danger.

Yet, after all due credit is given to leadership, it should be said that another factor played a great part in giving exceptional anti-slavery success in some States. Nothing is so stimulating to a party as to have some district in which it is generally victorious, to which in any circumstances it may reasonably look for support. When such a region exists, the party is always sure of an official mouthpiece and of the consideration that attaches to a constituency. It was this circumstance that made it so much easier to maintain anti-slavery spirit in Ohio and Wisconsin than in the other States. The Western Reserve, especially the eastern half of it, was overwhelmingly for Free Soil. In the darkest hour the party could be sure of electing Giddings and several Representatives in the legislature. Around the Western Reserve anti-slavery sentiment centred; on it the Liberty and Free Democratic men of all parts of the State relied for support. In Wisconsin, Racine, Kenosha, and Walworth counties were always sure to give a plurality for Free Soil; the party might fade elsewhere, but these counties were firm. Hence, in 1850, in the lowest ebb of Free Soil action, Durkee was returned to Congress.

Illinois came very near having such a centre, as is shown by the vote for President in the Fourth Congressional District in

1848.[1] Had Wentworth, the local Democratic leader, a man of strong Free Soil sympathies, thrown his influence on the side of the third party, the northern counties of Illinois would probably have become as ardent a third-party centre as those of southeastern Wisconsin and the Ohio Western Reserve. When Wentworth turned aside, the Presidential Free Soil vote of 1848 faded away, and his influence kept the district true to the national Democratic party.

In Indiana, Iowa, and Michigan, there was no such region. In these States the only Congressional or legislative success possible was that gained by coalition; for the Free Democratic vote in Indiana and Iowa was too small for separate action, and in Michigan too evenly distributed over the State. Hence the coalitions, and hence the inability of Julian and Christiancy to maintain themselves or to keep up their party.

Upon both Liberty and Free Soil parties criticisms may be passed, criticisms which apply less to the regenerated Free Democracy of 1852–54. In the first place, both parties were liable to charges of too great partisanship. Single-mindedness was, of course, an integral part of the creed of the Liberty party; but it was thoroughly impolitic for a movement which was based on an attempt to draw votes from the old organizations. Over-devotion to one's own organization leads inevitably to the disparagement of others; and both Liberty men and Free Soilers had a habit of wholesale denunciation that overshot the mark. It was necessary to be firm in asserting that Whig and Democrat parties as such were untrustworthy in regard to slavery; but it did not follow that every man of anti-slavery professions who voted the Whig or the Democratic ticket was a liar or a hypocrite, or that every man who voted the third ticket was sin-

---

[1] It was as follows: —

Cass.	Taylor.	Van Buren.
9,820	9,189	9,632

Or, if we take the later first and second districts, comprising the sixteen northern counties, it was as follows: —

	Cass.	Taylor.	Van Buren.
First District	4,466	5,829	4,100
Second District . . .	4,435	4,373	4,805

cere and trustworthy. Such language seemed narrow, bigoted, and sometimes self-righteous and hypocritical. It is preposterous, of course, to expect reformers subjected to floods of billingsgate to keep a cool philosophic temper, and to exhibit the astuteness of practical politicians; but some individuals in the Liberty and Free Soil parties in each of the States did almost as much to delay the triumph of their cause by their uniform harshness and extravagance of language as they did by their courage and devotion to prepare for the overthrow of slavery.

Besides this intense partisanship, the anti-slavery men of the Northwest sometimes exhibited what seems extreme shortsightedness. Their hope, in 1849, that the "United Democracy" would prove the longed-for anti-slavery party; their feeling that the natural allies of the Free Soilers lay in the party of Cass, Buchanan, Polk, Foote, and Davis, is extremely surprising. It has been pointed out, however, that in this matter the influence of the New York Barnburners was strong, and that the warm support received by Taylor in the South, coupled with Cass's success in the Northwest, had obscured the real positions held by Whig and Democratic parties previously to 1848.

A third fault was the undue influence of names and of theoretical considerations upon anti-slavery men. The fact that abolition was a step toward democracy; that the equal political rights for which the opponents of the Black Laws had struggled were characteristic of democracy; that liberality, philanthropy, and reform were democratic; these considerations led the Free Soilers of 1848, even those who were Liberty men or Whigs, to find some necessary affinity between themselves, a "democratic" party, and another party which called itself "Democratic," even though the main strength of that other "Democracy" was and always had been in the hands of slave-holders. So little can radical reformers look beneath the surface!

The results accomplished by the Liberty and Free Democratic parties were mainly educational. They stirred up the Western conscience, kept the subject of slavery constantly before the public, powerfully affected the policy and public expressions of the old parties, and by their spokesmen in Congress played an influential part in national politics. More important

than all, they familiarized the minds of all Northwestern people
with political anti-slavery arguments, furnished them with the
proper constitutional and political vocabulary, and thus be-
queathed to the Republicans, in 1854, a strong practical programme.   Without this heritage of principles, experience, and
determination, the Republican party would have been a failure,
if not an impossibility.   Thus, in spite of mistakes in method
and defeats in elections, the anti-slavery political organizations
played an indispensable part in preparing the way for the Republican movement.   Best of all, they trained in every State a
number of able, devoted men, who in the Republican party
found an opportunity to exercise the talents developed and the
experience gained in the arduous school of the Liberty and
Free Soil parties.

Behind the practical results of a long political struggle, in
the foundation of a new national party, we must not forget that
there was a tremendous moral force.   For a young voter or a
young aspirant for political honors to cast in his lot with the
third party was at almost any time and in almost every State
an act of heroic self-abnegation.   As we read of committees and
nominations, and tickets and campaigns, we forget that nearly
all of these meetings and urgent appeals were the laughing-stock
of both the regular organizations; that the Liberty leaders and
nearly all of the Free Soil leaders were cut off from any hope of
election to any office in the gift of the people.   Mistakes and
miscalculations and intemperance of language were effaced by
the magnificent purpose to arouse the nation to a consciousness
of its own guilt and danger from slavery.   To be sure, the names
of the leaders who lived beyond 1854 are the names of the chief-
tains of the Republican party, of the towers of strength in the
Civil War, — Chase, Giddings, Hale, Bingham, Julian — they had
their reward of responsibility and fame.   But what was there for
Birney and Lewis, and thousands of obscure men, but the simple
consciousness of doing their duty as they saw it, and the approval
of a little band of fellow-workers?   The highest service of Liberty,
Free Soil, and Free Democratic organization, was to accustom
men to a steady adherence to a great principle, in the face of
opposition, contempt, and abuse, — to do right for right's sake.

APPENDICES.

———◆———

APPENDIX A.

BIBLIOGRAPHY.

In the present scattered condition of the materials for western history the writer cannot hope that he has succeeded in discovering all sources for the period under consideration. This, then, must be looked upon as a preliminary attempt at forming a bibliography, and as such is doubtless open to correction in many respects. The author can desire nothing more heartily than the pointing out of any omissions.

The materials from which this paper has been prepared were found in the following places: Harvard University Library; Boston Public Library; Congregational Library, Boston; American Antiquarian Society, Worcester; Ohio State Library, Columbus; Western Reserve Historical Society, Cleveland; the *Cleveland Leader* office; Indiana State Library, Indianapolis; Indianapolis Public Library; Detroit Public Library; Ann Arbor Pioneer Society; the *Chicago Journal* office; and the Wisconsin Historical Society, Madison. Information has also been gathered from collections of newspapers and other material in possession of the following gentlemen: George W. Julian and G. S. Nicholson, Indianapolis; R. M. Zug and G. W. Clark, Detroit; S. D. Hastings, Madison, Wisconsin; W. P. Howe, Mt. Pleasant, Iowa; Edward L. Pierce, Milton, Massachusetts; Albert Bushnell Hart and W. H. Siebert, Cambridge, Massachusetts; and the late Theodore D. Weld, Hyde Park, Massachusetts.

GENERAL HISTORIES.

DYER, OLIVER . . . . . Great Senators of the United States. New York, 1889.

FLOWER, FRANK A. . . . History of the Republican Party. Springfield, Illinois, 1884.

HINSDALE, BURKE A. . . . The Old Northwest. New York, 1888.

LANGELAND, KNUD . . . Nordmaendene i Amerika. Chicago, 1889.

PIKE, JAMES S. . . . . . First Blows of the Civil War. New York, 1879.

WILLEY, AUSTIN . . . . The History of the Anti-Slavery Cause in State and Nation. Portland, Maine, 1886.

WILSON, HENRY . . . . History of the Rise and Fall of the Slave Power in America. 3 vols. Boston, 1872–77.

Of the foregoing, Pike's and Flower's works contain a few documents of minor importance ; Dyer's, Willey's, and to some extent Wilson's, have the value of personal reminiscences.

LOCAL HISTORIES.

OHIO.

ADDISON, H. M. . . . . An Episode of Politics. *Magazine of Western History*, IX. 273 (Jan. 1889).

FAIRCHILD, JAMES H. . . Oberlin: the College and the Colony. Oberlin, 1883.

FORD, HENRY A. and K. B. History of Cincinnati. [Cleveland] 1881.

HOWE, HENRY . . . . . Historical Collections of Ohio. 3 vols. Columbus, 1889–91.

HUTCHINS, JOHN . . . . The Underground Railroad. *Magazine of Western History*, V. 672 (March, 1887).

LEE, ALFRED E. . . . . History of the City of Columbus, Capital of Ohio. 2 vols. New York and Chicago, 1892.

RIDDLE, ALBERT G. . . . History of Geauga and Lake Counties. Philadelphia, 1878.

——— ——— . . . Recollections of the Forty-Seventh General Assembly of Ohio, 1847–48. *Magazine of Western History*, VI. 341 (Aug. 1897).

——— ——— . . . Rise of the Anti-Slavery Sentiment on the Western Reserve. *Magazine of Western History*, VI. 145 (June 1887).

——— ——— . . . The Election of S. P. Chase to the Senate, February, 1849. *Republic*, IV. 179.

RYAN, DANIEL J. . . . . A History of Ohio. Columbus, 1888.

TOWNSHEND, NORTON S. . The Forty-Seventh General Assembly of Ohio. *Magazine of Western History*, VI. 623 (Oct. 1887).

WILLIAMS, H. L. and BRO., publishers. History of Trumbull and Mahoning Counties. 2 vols. Cleveland, 1882.

———   ———   . . . History of Washington County. Cleveland, 1881.

———   ———   . . . History of Lorain County. Philadelphia, 1879.

WILLIAMS, WILLIAM W. . History of Ashtabula County. Philadelphia, 1878.

INDIANA.

CHAPMAN, C. C. and Co., publishers. History of St. Joseph County. Chicago, 1880.

PLEAS, ELWOOD . . . . Henry County : Past and Present. New Castle, 1871.

YOUNG, ANDREW W. . . History of Wayne County. Cincinnati, 1872.

MICHIGAN.

CLARKE, HARVEY K. . . Under the Oaks. *Detroit Tribune*, July 6, 1879.

FARMER, SILAS . . . . The History of Detroit and Michigan. Detroit, 1884.

RUST, E. G. . . . . . . Calhoun County Business Directory for 1869–70, with a History of the County. Battle Creek, 1869.

ILLINOIS.

ANDREAS, ALFRED T. . . History of Chicago. 3 vols. Chicago, 1884–86.

CHAPMAN, C. C., and Co. . History of Knox County. Chicago, 1878.

ERWIN, MILO . . . . . The History of Williamson County. Marion, 1876.

KETT, H. F., and Co., publishers. The Past and Present of La Salle County. Chicago, 1877.

———   ———   . . . History of Winnebago County. Chicago, 1877.

LE BARON, W., and Co., publishers. The Past and Present of Kane County. Chicago, 1878.

———   ———   . . . The Past and Present of Lake County. Chicago, 1877.

MOSES, JOHN . . . . . Illinois, Historical and Statistical. 2 vols. Chicago, 1889–92.

WISCONSIN.

BAKER, FLORENCE E. . . . A Brief History of the Elective Franchise in Wisconsin. Madison, 1894.

BUCK, J. S. . . . . . . Pioneer History of Milwaukee. 4 vols. Milwaukee, 1876–86.

STRONG, MOSES M. . . . History of the Territory of Wisconsin, from 1836 to 1848. Madison, 1885.

WESTERN HISTORICAL COMPANY. History of Rock County. Chicago, 1879

———— ———— . . . History of Waukesha County. Chicago, 1880.

IOWA.

———— ———— . . . History of Henry County. Chicago, 1879

Of the foregoing works, the reminiscences published by Messrs. Riddle, Townshend, and others in the *Magazine of Western History* are of especial value, as are also the articles on anti-slavery matters by H. K. Clarke and J. H. Fairchild. From the county histories little is to be gathered, least of all from those compiled under the direction of the Western Historical Publishing Company of Chicago. Occasionally a chapter written by some anonymous contributor on local political history contains interesting political information ; but in the main the only things to be found are the dates, names, and vicissitudes of local anti-slavery newspapers.

BIOGRAPHIES.

BARTLETT, DAVID W. . . Modern Agitators. New York, 1855.

[BIRNEY, WILLIAM]. . . . James G. Birney and his Times. New York, 1890.

[BRADBURN, MRS. F. N.] . A Memorial of George Bradburn. Boston, 1883.

Chicago Tribune. . . . . Account of the Anti-Slavery Reunion at Chicago, June 10–12, 1874.

FERGUS HISTORICAL SERIES. Reminiscences of Early Chicago and Illinois. Chicago, 1876 *seq.*

FROTHINGHAM, OCTAVIUS B. Gerrit Smith : a biography. New York, 1879.

[GARRISON, W. P. and F. J.] William Lloyd Garrison. 1805–1879. 4 vols. New York, 1885–89.

JULIAN, GEO. W. . . . . The Life of Joshua R. Giddings. Chicago, 1892.

JULIAN, GEO. W. . . . . Political Recollections. 1840 to 1872. Chicago, 1884.

———— ———— . . . . Speeches on Political Questions. New York, 1872.

[LEWIS, WILLIAM G. W.] . Biography of Samuel Lewis. Cincinnati, 1857.

[MORRIS, BENJAMIN F.] . The Life of Thomas Morris. Cincinnati, 1856.

PARRISH, W. D. . . . . The Life, Travels and Opinions of Benjamin Lundy. Philadelphia, 1847.

PIERCE, EDWARD L. . . . Sketch of Dr. G. Bailey, *Boston Traveler*, June 27, 1859.

———— ———— . . . Sketch of J. R. Giddings, *Boston Transcript*, April 8, 1892.

REEMELIN, CHARLES. . . Life. Written by himself. Cincinnati, 1892.

REID, HARVEY. . . . . Biographical Sketch of Enoch Long, Chicago Historical Society's Collection. Vol. II. Chicago, 1884.

RIDDLE, ALBERT G. . . . The Life of Benjamin F. Wade. Cleveland, 1886.

SALTER, WILLIAM. . . . The Life of James W. Grimes. New York, 1876.

SCHUCKERS, JAMES W. . . The Life and Public Services of Salmon P. Chase. New York, 1874.

STANTON HENRY B. . . . Random Recollections. New York, 1886.

[TAPPAN, LEWIS] . . . The Life of Arthur Tappan. New York, 1870.

TOWNSHEND, NORTON S. . Salmon P. Chase. *Ohio Archæological and Historical Quarterly*. September, 1887.

WARDEN, R. B. . . . . An Account of the Private Life and Public Services of Salmon Portland Chase. Cincinnati, 1874.

WOOLLEN, W. W. . . . Biographical and Historical Sketches of Early Indiana. Indianapolis, 1883.

WRIGHT, ELIZUR. . . . Myron Holley, and what he did for Liberty and True Religion. Boston, 1882.

Among these biographies there are many so eulogistic in tendency, owing to filial affection or to other reasons, that comparatively little space is left for the political questions of the time ; others are so meagre as to contain little but the bare facts. There are several, however, written either during the anti-slavery struggle, or later by those who had themselves participated in it, which are of the highest importance, especially the writings of G. W. Julian, William Birney's Life of his father, A. G. Riddle's Life of B. F. Wade, and the Lives of Thomas Morris and Samuel Lewis. The two bulky biographies of Salmon P. Chase are of little value except for the documents which they contain. In cases in which the personal opinions of the subject of the biography have colored the narrative we can fortunately balance opposing tendencies by comparing the Lives of other men. Thus the Life of W. L. Garrison forms a counterpoise to the biographies of J. G. Birney, Myron Holley, and Gerrit Smith.

PAMPHLETS.

Address of the Southern and Western Liberty Convention. [By S. P. Chase. Philadelphia, 1845.]

Address to the Voters of . . . the Second Congressional District of Ohio. [Elkton, 1843.]

American Anti-Slavery Society, Reports. New York, 1834–50.

American and Foreign Anti-Slavery Society, Reports. New York, 1841–54.

Correspondence between the Hon. F. H. Elmore and James G. Birney. (The Anti-Slavery Examiner, No. 8.) New York, 1838.

DYER, OLIVER. Phonographic Report of the Proceedings of the National Free Soil Convention at Buffalo, N. Y. Buffalo, 1848.

GARDINER, O. C. The Great Issue. New York, 1848.

Legion of Liberty, New York. 1847.

Liberty Almanac. Syracuse and New York, 1842–51.

Liberty Bell. Boston, 1846.

Massachusetts Anti-Slavery Society, Reports. Boston, 1834–50.

Politics in Ohio. [A letter to Hon. A. P. Edgerton by S. P. Chase.] Cincinnati, 1853.

Proceedings of the Great Convention of the Friends of Freedom in the Eastern and Middle States, held in Boston, Oct. 1–3, 1845. Lowell, 1845.

Resolutions of the Wisconsin Legislature on the subject of Slavery; with the speech of Samuel D. Hastings. New York, 1849.

Whig Almanac. New York, 1838–55.

Out of the floods of anti-slavery pamphlets poured forth in the years between 1831 and 1855, very few concern themselves with political history. The most important are the *Whig Almanac*, invaluable for the results of elections, the *Liberty Almanac*, S. P. Chase's letter to A. P. Edgerton, and O. C. Gardiner's *Great Issue*, a campaign pamphlet of 1848 which relates the previous history of the Free Soil movement.

NEWSPAPERS.

The writer knows of no important collection of Western newspapers which he has failed to examine, except that of the Chicago Historical Society. This, owing to the fact that the new building of the Society was unfinished, proved to be entirely inaccessible. The following list contains those journals used in the preparation of this essay, Abolitionist, Liberty, or Free Soil papers being marked with a star.

OHIO.

Cincinnati Gazette. Cincinnati, 1844–47.
Cleveland Herald. Cleveland, 1853–54.
*Liberty Herald. Warren, 1843–46.
*Ohio American. Cleveland, 1844–47.
*Ohio Columbian. Columbus, 1853–54.
*Ohio Standard. Columbus, 1848–49.
Ohio State Journal. Columbus, 1844–54.
*Palladium of Liberty. Columbus, 1844–45.
*Philanthropist, etc. Cincinnati, 1836–49.
*True Democrat. Cleveland, 1847–54.
*Western Reserve Chronicle. Warren, 1848–54.

INDIANA.

*Free Labor Advocate. New Garden, 1842, 1846.
*Free Territory Sentinel. Centreville, 1848–49.
Indiana State Journal. Indianapolis, 1842–54.
*Indiana True Democrat. Centreville, 1850–52.
Indianapolis Sentinel. Indianapolis, 1844–53.

MICHIGAN.

*Daily Democrat. Detroit, 1854.
Detroit Advertiser. Detroit, 1842–54.
Detroit Free Press. Detroit, 1843–49.
Michigan Argus. Ann Arbor, 1843–49.
*Signal of Liberty. Ann Arbor, 1844.
*True Democrat. Ann Arbor, 1847–48.

ILLINOIS.

Chicago Journal. Chicago, 1844–54.
*Western Citizen. Chicago, 1844.

WISCONSIN.

*American Freeman. Waukesha, 1845–48.
Janesville Gazette. Janesville, 1853.
*Kenosha Telegraph. Kenosha, 1849–51.
Madison Express. Madison, 1845–48.

Milwaukee Courier. Milwaukee, 1842–44.
Milwaukee Sentinel. Milwaukee, 1843–54.
*Racine Advocate. Racine, 1851–54.
True Democrat. Oshkosh, 1849.
Watertown Chronicle. Watertown, 1853.
Wisconsin. Milwaukee, 1848–53.
Wisconsin Argus. Madison, 1849.
Wisconsin Democrat. Madison, 1842–44.
Wisconsin State Journal. Madison, 1849–54.

IOWA.

*Iowa Free Democrat. Mt. Pleasant, 1849–50.
*Iowa True Democrat. Mt. Pleasant, 1850–52.

MISCELLANEOUS.

*Emancipator. New York and Boston, 1834–48.
*Liberator. Boston, 1831–41.
*National Anti-Slavery Standard. New York, 1845.
*Nationai Era. Washington, 1847–54.
New York Tribune. New York, 1844–54.
*Tocsin of Liberty, later *Albany Patriot.* Albany, 1843–44.
Volumes of miscellaneous Western papers, 1831–54.

The newspapers form the principal source of information for party history. The anti-slavery organs, of course, furnish us with the most direct information, but the Whig or Democratic journals are a necessary check to them. If any one paper can be singled out as the most important, it is undoubtedly the *National Era*, from whose wide information, excellent breadth of view, and remarkable fairness of judgment one may gain a good understanding of the whole field of western politics.

MANUSCRIPT MATERIAL.

The author has unfortunately been able to find little in the shape of old letters, diaries, or similar material. The anti-slavery agitators and politicians of the Northwest, in spite of their firm conviction — if we may judge from their oft-repeated assertions — that they were making history, seem to have neglected to preserve any records of their actions. A diligent search in the States of Michigan, Wisconsin, Illinois, and Iowa has revealed nothing of this character. Very important manuscripts, however, remain in the papers of Salmon P. Chase, almost entirely inedited,

in the letters of Charles Sumner, and in the papers of George W. Julian.
From the hand of Chase we have diaries extending from 1830 to 1854, a
series of letters to Sumner, another to E. S. Hamlin, and a miscellaneous
letter-book. Among the Sumner papers are to be found a set of letters
from Joshua R. Giddings and many miscellaneous letters from Western
men. Among the papers of George W. Julian are diaries, an autobio-
graphical memoir and letter-books. Interesting and often important
material has also been found in the scrap-books of Salmon P. Chase,
George W. Julian, Samuel D. Hastings, George W. Clark, Albert G.
Turner, and others.

PERSONAL RECOLLECTIONS.

Though relying mainly on contemporary documents, the author has
not failed to get what light he could from the memories of living men who
were actors in the events of fifty years ago. Correspondence has been
held with a number of gentlemen, particularly Messrs. William Birney,
Sherman M. Booth, A. E. Bovay, John N. Bryant, George W. Clark,
William B. Fyffe, Samuel D. Hastings, George Hoadly, Daniel Huff,
Isaac H. Julian, Albert G. Riddle, and Norton S. Townshend. Moreover, several hundred letters, now in possession of Wilbur H. Siebert, of
Cambridge, Massachusetts, from persons formerly connected with the
Underground Railroad, have been placed at the author's disposal. He
has also had access to notes of conversations held by William B. Shaw
with A. E. Bovay and by Albert B. Hart with Edward S. Hamlin; and he
has conversed personally with Messrs. George W. Julian, Samuel D. Hastings, James D. Ligget, James F. Joy, J. F. Conover, George W. Clark,
Francis Raymond, Seymour Finney, ex-Senator James Harlan, and very
many others.

APPENDIX B.

1836–1854.

In the Bibliography (Appendix A) are mentioned the newspapers actually consulted for the preparation of this work. The following is a list of the permanent and more important Northwestern Liberty and Free Soil papers, including all about which the writer could get definite information. The tables show, in respective order, the years during which the paper was issued, the place of publication, the name of the paper, and the name of the editor, if known.

The years given are only those during which the paper in question was published as a Liberty or Free Soil organ. Some journals, accordingly, appear in the list for a short time only, although they may have existed much longer as Democratic or Whig organs; and all papers are considered as ceasing in 1854 when the Free Democratic Party disappeared.

OHIO.

1836–38.	Cincinnati	*Philanthropist*	J. G. Birney.
1838–46.		(Continued as *Herald*	Dr. G. Bailey.
1847–48.		*National Press*	Stanley Mathews.
1848–49.		*Globe*)	J. W. Taylor.
1843–46.	Warren	*Liberty Herald*	L. L. Rice.
1845–46.	Cadiz	*Liberty Advocate*	R. B. Dennis.
1845–48.	Cleveland	*Ohio American.*	
1848–54.	Cleveland	*True Democrat*	E. S. Hamlin, J. A. Briggs, G. Bradburn, J. C. Vaughn.
1848–54.	Ashtabula	*Sentinel*	J. A. Giddings, W. C. Howells.
1848–54.	Painesville	*Telegraph*	H. C. Gray.
1848–54.	Warren	*Western Reserve Chronicle.*	E. O. Howard.
1848–54.	Mt. Vernon	*Ohio Times.*	B. Chapman.

1848–54.	Ravenna . .	*Ohio Star*	L. W. Hall.
1848–49.	Columbus .	*Ohio Standard*	E. S. Hamlin,
		(Revived in 1850–51, and edited by I. Garrard.)	
1848-50.	Elyria . . .	*Courier*	J. Cotton.
1848-50.	Toledo . .	*Republican*	C. R. Miller.
1848–49.	Sandusky .	*Daily Mirror.*	
1849–54.	Chardon . .	*Free Democrat*	J. F. Asper.
1850.	Medina . .	*Free Democrat.*	
1851–53.	Cleveland .	*Commercial*	H. M. Addison.
1852–54.	Elyria . . .	*Independent Democrat* . .	P. Bliss.
1852–54.	Wellington .	*Journal*	G. Brewster.
1853–54.	Columbus .	*Columbian*	L. L. Rice.
1853–54.	Youngstown	*Mahoning Free Democrat* .	M. Cullotson.
1853.	Wilmington .	*Herald of Freedom* . . .	J. W. Chaffin.
1853.	Greenfield .	*True Republican*	J. H. Rothrock.
1853.	West Unity .	*Williams Democrat* . . .	W. A. Hunter.

In addition to the above, there were a number of ephemeral and campaign papers about which little more than the title is known. Such were the Cleveland *Agitator*, 1840; Columbus *Palladium of Liberty*, 1844; Akron *Free Soil Platform*, 1848, and *Free Democrat*, 1849; Cleveland *Ohio State Tribune*, 1848; Bryan *Spirit of the Age*, 1848; Massillon *Wilmot Proviso and Freeman's Herald*, 1848. There were also several which, though not party papers, were strongly Free Soil in tendency, such as the New Lisbon *Aurora*, the Salem *Homestead Journal*, and two German papers, — the Cincinnati *Treue Demokrat*, 1848, and *Der Unabhängige*, 1853. The greatest number in existence at any one time was probably during the campaign of 1848, immediately after which, it is stated, there were six dailies and twenty weeklies. Probably from first to last between forty and fifty anti-slavery papers were published in the State.

INDIANA.

1841.	Newport . .	*Protectionist*	A. Buffum.
1842–48.	New Garden	*Free Labor Advocate* . .	B. Stanton.
1844–47.	Indianapolis .	*Indiana Freeman*	H. W. De Puy.
1848–49.	Centreville .	*Free Territory Sentinel* . .	R. Vaile.
1850–52.		(Name changed to *True Democrat*.)	
1848.	Lafayette .	*Tippecanoe Journal* . . .	J. B. Seamans.
1848.	South Bend .	*Free Democrat*	E. W. H. Lewis.
1848.	Independence	*Free Soil Banner*	L. Wallace.
1853–54.	Indianapolis .	*Indiana Free Democrat* . .	R. Vaile.

There were also several papers of which only the names are known : The *Liberty Herald* of Union County ; the Jonesboro *Barnburner*, 1848 ; the Madison *Free Soil Democrat*, 1848 ; the New London *Pioneer*, 1848 ; and the Marion *Herald of Freedom*, 1847. The largest number at any one time was seven, in 1848.

MICHIGAN.

1839–40.	Jackson . .	*Michigan Freeman* . . .	S. B. Treadwell.
1842–48.	Ann Arbor .	*Signal of Liberty*	T. Foster,
			G. Beckly.
1848–49.	Battle Creek	*Liberty Press*	Erastus Hussey.
1848–49.	Ann Arbor .	*True Democrat*	O. Arnold.
1849–51.	Detroit . .	*Peninsular Freeman* . . .	R. McBratney,
			J. D. Ligget.
1852–54.	Detroit . .	*Free Democrat*	S. A. Baker,
			J. F. Conover.

Other anti-slavery papers of less persistence were the Detroit *Times*, 1842 ; the *American Citizen*, 1845 ; the Adrian *Free Soil Advocate*, the Hillsdale *Banner*, and the Jackson *Gazette*, all in 1848.

ILLINOIS.

1837.	Alton . . .	*Observer*	E. P. Lovejoy.
1838–39.	Lowell . .	*Genius of Universal Eman-*	B. Lundy.
		cipation.	
1840–42.	Lowell . .	*Genius of Liberty*	Z. Eastman.
1842–54.	Chicago . .	*Western Citizen*	Z. Eastman.
		(With a daily edition, the	
1845.		*Daily News ;* and an-	
1852.		other, the *Daily Times*.)	
1848.	Chicago . .	*Tribune*	T. Stewart.
1848.	Waukegan .	*Lake County Chronicle* . .	A. B. Tobey.
1848–50.	Rockford .	*Free Press*	H. W. De Puy.
1849.	Waukegan .	*Free Democrat*	N. W. Fuller.
1850–54.	Sparta . .	*Freeman* (later, *Journal*) .	I. S. Coulter.
1853–54.	Galesburg .	*Western Freeman* . . .	W. J. Lane.

Other names are those of the Alton *Monitor*, Geneva *Western Mercury*, Princeton *Bureau Advocate*, Quincy *Tribune*, and Peru *Telegraph*, all in 1848. There was one German paper, the Chicago *Staats Zeitung*, 1848, and one Norwegian, *Frihets Banneret*, 1852. There were probably many other ephemeral Free Soil sheets in 1848 ; but their activity was so brief that they sank at once into oblivion, along with the pledges of the Illinois " Barnburners."

WISCONSIN.

1844.	Racine . .	*Wisconsin Aegis*	N. W. Fuller, L. W. Hall.
1844–48.	Waukesha .	*American Freeman* . . .	C. C. Sholes, C. C. Olin, I. Codding.
1848–54.	Milwaukee .	*Free Democrat* . . . . . (Continuation of the preceding.)	S. M. Booth.
1848–54.	Racine . .	*Advocate*	J. C. Bunner, C. Clement.
1848–54.	Kenosha . .	*Telegraph*	C. Clement, C. L. Sholes.
1848.	Janesville .	*Rock County Democrat* . .	G. W. Crabb.
1848–49. 1850.	Norway . .	*Nordlyset* (Norwegian) . . (This was removed to Racine and the name changed to *Demokraten*; edited by .	E. Heg. K. Langeland.
1848–49.	Elkhorn . .	*Western Star*	G. Gale.
1849, 1853.	Oshkosh . .	*True Democrat*	J. C. Densmore.
1853.	Janesville .	*Free Press*	J. Baker.

In addition to these, there were two German campaign papers, one in Kenosha in 1852, the other, the *Volksfreund*, edited by J. Bielfeld, in Milwaukee in 1848 ; and two or three other campaign papers : the Janesville *Battering Ram*, 1848 ; and the Sheboygan Falls *Free Press*, 1853.

IOWA.

1848–49.	Ft. Madison	*Iowa Freeman*	A. St. Clair.
1849–50.	Mt. Pleasant	*Iowa Free Democrat* . . .	D. M. Kelsey.
1850–54.	Mt. Pleasant	*Iowa True Democrat* . .	S. L. Howe.
1853.	Davenport	*Der Demokrat* (German) .	T. Gulich.

It is probable that there were other Free Soil papers in 1848, but the names of none are known.

In the years from 1840 to 1848 there were about twenty Liberty papers, of which only six lived long enough to enter the Free Soil ranks.

With the Free Soil revolt in 1848 sprang up sixty or more anti-slavery papers; but in two years the number had fallen to fifteen or sixteen, of which six were on the Western Reserve. On the eve of the Kansas-Nebraska outbreak, after the Free Democratic revival of 1852–3, there were thirty-one, of which sixteen were in Ohio, one in Indiana, one in Michigan, four in Illinois, seven in Wisconsin, and two in Iowa.

The most noteworthy of the foregoing papers may be mentioned in particular. The *Philanthropist*, founded by J. G. Birney in 1836, and after his departure from Cincinnati in 1838 edited by Dr. Gamaliel Bailey until 1846, was during this period one of the leading anti-slavery papers of the country. Bailey's business ability enabled him to start a daily edition under the name of *Cincinnati Herald*, and his success as well as his political sagacity led to his selection, in 1847, as the one man in the country fitted to edit the Washington *National Era*. After his departure, the *Philanthropist* was edited by Stanley Mathews and J. W. Taylor, and its name was changed successively to *National Press, Globe*, and *Herald* again, until, with the decay of the Free Soil party in Cincinnati, it ceased to exist in 1849. On the Western Reserve the leading paper was the Cleveland daily *True Democrat*, founded in 1846 as a radical anti-slavery Whig paper, and after 1848 the strongest Free Soil organ in northern Ohio. Edited by Hamlin, Briggs, Bradburn, Vaughn, and others, it generally had a Whig bias quite as marked as the Democratic prepossessions of the *Cincinnati Herald;* and it was at times excessively pugnacious, especially under Vaughn's management. The *Ashtabula Sentinel* also deserves mention. It was edited for some years by a son of Giddings, and afterwards by W. C. Howells, and was in some measure a representative and organ of Giddings. Its utterances were always in the line of harmony and common sense, and served in trying times like those of 1849, when the *True Democrat* and *Cincinnati Herald* were at swords' points, to calm anger and to steady excited heads.

In Indiana the *Free Territory Sentinel*, later the *True Democrat* of Centreville, and still later the *Free Democrat* of Indianapolis, was edited by Rawson Vaile. Although in the most backward of all the Northwestern States except Iowa, and constantly involved in bitter controversy with its neighbors, it managed, through the support of Wayne and Henry Counties, to survive when the Michigan *Peninsular Freeman*, ruined by Whig and Free Soil fusion, fell by the wayside.

Another paper which deserves special mention on account of the devotion of its editor was the *Iowa Freeman*, later the *True Democrat* of

Mt. Pleasant, published for years out of the pocket of its editor, S. L. Howe, an anti-slavery prophet crying in the wilderness of a pro-slavery State.

The leading paper west of Ohio was undoubtedly the *Western Citizen*, published at Chicago by Zebina Eastman from 1842 to 1854. It was for many years the central organ of Illinois, northern Indiana, Wisconsin, and Iowa, until the Free Soil revolt standing practically alone. Published under great difficulties, often at a loss to its editor, it was a powerful agency in keeping up the Liberty and Free Soil parties in the Northwest. Had Eastman, besides being a tireless philanthropist, possessed as many of the qualities of a statesman as did Birney or Bailey, he might have made for himself a position of unique importance in the northeastern counties of Illinois. One of the most interesting Free Soil papers in the country was the *Sparta Freeman*, later *Journal*, published in Randolph County, in the very midst of pro-slavery " Egypt." This county and the neighboring one of Madison had been largely settled by Scotch immigrants from Virginia, who had come north to avoid contact with slavery, and who still in 1850, although separated by scores of miles from any sympathizers, kept up a strong anti-slavery feeling.

In Wisconsin the leading paper was the *American Freeman*, published first at Prairieville (now Waukesha), and later removed to Milwaukee. At the time of the Free Soil revolt it took the name of *Free Democrat*, and had a prosperous career free from the hardships of its counterparts in Illinois and Iowa. Edited for the greater part of its course by S. M. Booth, it was one of the most radical of the Western third-party papers, and pugnacious to a degeee unequalled by any other paper, except at times by the Cleveland *True Democrat*. Besides this, the *Kenosha Telegraph* and *Racine Advocate*, papers of the stamp of the *Painesville Telegraph* or the *Elyria Independent Democrat*, lasted through the Free Soil period and kept Free Soil feeling active in the southeastern counties.

If one may generalize on the political anti-slavery press of the Northwest, it was in point of ability superior to the regular party papers. Something more than ordinary strength and courage was required to undertake the task of running a third-party paper, especially in Indiana, Iowa, and Michigan. No higher devotion to a purely moral idea can be imagined than that of S. L. Howe of the *Iowa True Democrat*, who never drew a profit from his paper, nor dreamed of so doing, during seven weary years of third-party action. The very nature of the cause kept Liberty and Free Soil papers free from some features that disfigure " regular" papers. In spite of the denunciations of Whigs, no valid suspicion of venality could attach to them, and, owing to the absence of party discipline, they were never under the necessity of swallowing statements or of changing front on political questions. The nearest approach to such a step was the action of some papers like the Wisconsin *Freeman* and the Indiana *Free Territory Sentinel* in 1848.

The anti-slavery country weeklies, as compared with their neighbors, often showed a refreshing independence of spirit; but their absorption in one idea led very often to an honest bigotry almost as irritating as the partisan character of the old party press. There was a strong tendency for Liberty and Free Soil papers, struggling with continuous disappointment, to become mere vehicles of condemnation. After 1847 the *National Era*, under Dr. Bailey's able editorship, had great influence in humanizing local papers, leading them, by the introduction of local notes and literary matter, to avoid too great devotion to one topic. By 1854 the Free Democratic press had a distinctly saner, more elevated, tone than heretofore; and in the events that led to the formation of a new party, it took, with few exceptions, an extremely well-judged and temperate attitude. It avoided irritating controversy with the Whigs, was willing to drop all past party names and let bygones be bygones, and stood ready to rejoice in the triumph of Anti-Nebraska, whatever became of the Free Soil party.

APPENDIX C.

TABLE OF TOTAL VOTES.

1840–1853.

The following table shows the fluctuations of the third-party vote in the Northwestern States : — [1]

		Ohio.	Indiana.	Michigan.	Illinois.	Wisconsin.	Iowa.
1840	. . .	903	——	318	157	——	——
1841	. . .	(2,800)	599*	1,214	527	——	——
1842	. . .	5,405	(900)	(1,665)	909	——	——
1843	. . .	6,552*	1,684	2,775	1,954*	152	——
1844	State .	8,411	?	——	1,408*	450*	——
	Federal	8,050	2,106	3,632	3,570	——	——
1845	. . .	(8,691)	1,755*	(3,363)	——	790	(60)
1846	. . .	10,799	2,278	2,885	5,147	(215)	——
1847	. . .	(4,379)	——	?	——	973	——
1848	State .	——	——	——	4,748	1,134	——
	Federal	35,354	8,100	10,389	15,774	10,418	1,126
1849	. . .	12,811*	3,018	23,540	——	3,761	564
1850	. . .	13,802	——	2,228	1,073*	——	574
1851	. . .	16,914	——	——	——	2,904	——
1852	State .	22,167	?	6,273	8,809	——	——
	Federal	31,682	6,929	7,237	9,966	8,814	1,604
1853	. . .	50,346	8,000	——	——	21,886	——

This table of total votes does not, however, tell the whole story ; for within each State the anti-slavery vote was distributed among strong and weak localities, and in the Ohio River States there was a distinctly sectional arrangement. The following maps indicate the proportional distribution of the third-party vote in the three elections of 1844, 1848, and 1852, representing respectively the Liberty party, the Free Soil revolt, and the rejuvenated Free Democracy.

[1] The starred figures indicate incomplete returns ; those in parentheses show contemporary estimates. There are numerous varying figures found in newspapers, but those above appear to be the most authentic.

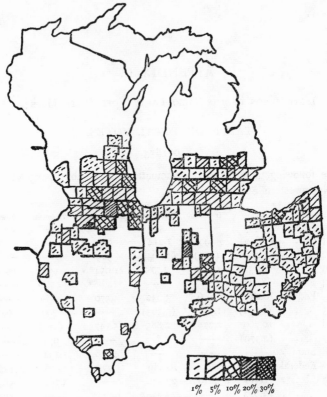

MAP OF THE FREE SOIL VOTE OF 1844.

[NOTE.] In this and the following maps the shading indicates the proportion of the third-party vote to the total vote in each county, according to the scheme of gradation shown above.]

In 1844 those regions that were destined to be centres of anti-slavery action for twenty years, and later to become strongholds of the Republican party, had become marked. In nearly every case the political complexion of a county may be accounted for by two circumstances, — by the ancestry of its settlers and by the presence or the absence of agitation. In Ohio, as the map indicates, the Western Reserve forms a well-marked district where the New England Puritan blood of the inhabitants had been fired by the words of Weld, King, Wade, Paine, and others. In the southeastern counties near Virginia were some New England inhabitants, some Quakers, and many Southerners who had moved North to escape from contact with slavery. This Muskingum region was a net-work of underground railway lines. In the counties around Cincinnati we find another region originally settled from New England, but by 1844 much overlaid by new elements, largely Southern. This is the section in which the influence of Birney, Bailey, Morris, and the *Philanthropist* was strong.

In Indiana the anti-slavery counties are those in which Quakers lived, especially Randolph, Wayne, Union, and Henry counties. There were New Englanders in the State, but they were as yet not waked up. The map shows well the weak and scattered nature of Indiana anti-slavery sentiment.

Michigan, very largely settled from New York, shows a feature which characterizes it throughout its anti-slavery career, in the very general and even distribution of its third-party vote. This in 1844 was quite strong, nearly twice as strong proportionately as that of any other Northwestern State ; but there were no such centres as Ohio, Illinois, and even Indiana possessed.

Illinois shows in its northern counties the effect of large immigration from New York and New England ; but it also indicates the result of vigorous agitation. Lovejoy, Cross, and Codding were doing for Illinois what Birney had done for Michigan ; and in 1844 the northern counties of the State were the strongest centre of third-party action in the North-west, and perhaps in the country. Scattered along the western edge of the State are traces of Liberty votes in places where New England people and Quakers had settled, and down in the heart of " Egypt " we find several counties which give evidence of a population composed of Southern anti-slavery Scotchmen from North Carolina and Virginia.

Wisconsin (for which the vote of 1845 is taken) is practically an appendage of Illinois. Its southeastern counties are contiguous with those worked over by Lovejoy, and are anti-slavery for the same reasons.

The vacant spaces on the map, indicating places where no Liberty votes were cast, may be explained in similar fashion. Since a frontier is never consciously philanthropic, anti slavery sentiment is not likely to flourish there. Hence northern Michigan, Wisconsin, and Iowa furnished no abolitionists. For a like reason the northwestern corner of Ohio, which had been but recently opened to settlement, contained few inhabitants and no abolitionists, although just across the border were Lenawee and Hillsdale counties, both full of anti-slavery men. Extending up into Ohio, in a sort of irregular wedge from the Ohio River, were the Vir-ginia Military Lands. These, settled from Virginia and the South, produced no abolitionists and remained hard ground for fugitive slaves to travel.

The southern halves of Indiana and Illinois, the western half of Wisconsin, and almost the whole of Iowa were settled from the South, and as the foregoing paper abundantly shows, were entirely pro-slavery in sentiment, except where a few Quakers formed occasional oases.

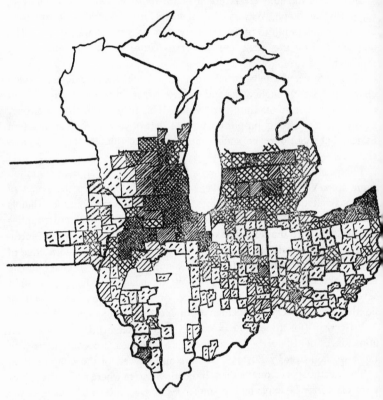

MAP OF THE FREE SOIL VOTE OF 1848.

The above map shows the vote of the Free Soilers of 1848, its most noticeable difference from the map of four years before consisting in the deepening and strengthening of the proportions. No county in 1844 cast over 30 per cent., and only three, all in Illinois, over 20 per cent. Now twenty-five counties cast over 30 per cent., and as many more 20 per cent. In Ohio the Whig revolt has made the Western Reserve solid for the third party and much stronger than the rest of the State, far stronger than in 1844. The Miami and Muskingum regions have spread out, and even the Virginia Military Lands are invaded by a scattering Van Buren vote, while in Williams County, in the extreme northwest, a third-party vote appears where all was blank four years earlier.

In Indiana the Quaker counties in the east are now much reinforced by a Whig bolt of New England-born men in the central and northern counties, so that the State is no longer merely dotted with anti-slavery counties, but is crossed by a broad band.

Michigan remains much the same. There is no alteration of the distribution of the third-party vote, and the increase results merely in increasing the proportion. Two counties cast over 30 per cent, but they are not contiguous, and there is still no centre.

In Illinois the Democratic revolt in the northern counties swings this section over into the Free Soil ranks, causing it to outdo the Western Reserve and to become the strongest anti-slavery district in the country. Down the western side of the State the Van Buren vote gains, and even encroaches on " Egypt's " boundaries ; but in the main the latter section is intact.

Wisconsin follows Illinois ; and, since it is encumbered with no " Egypt," the new State has the honor of being the strongest Free Soil State in the Northwest. According to the original plans subdividing the Northwestern Territory, the southern boundary of Wisconsin would come so far south as to include the two northern tiers of Illinois counties. Had such been the case in 1848, the State might well have gone for Van Buren, and would certainly have had two or three Free Soil congressional districts.

Iowa now appears on the scene with a small Free Soil vote, showing the influence of a contiguity with Illinois, and separated from the northern anti-slavery counties of that State and from Wisconsin by a region occupied by persons who had come up the Mississippi, and were therefore pro-slavery. The counties of Iowa where Free Soil votes are found contain both of the anti-slavery elements, New England men and Quakers.

The vote of the Free Democracy for Hale in 1852 shows us a substratum of the old Liberty party, with a few Free Soil relics left behind by the retiring tide of 1849–50. In Ohio there is less change than in some of the other States ; for in the main the Free Soil Whigs of the Western Reserve have held firm, and we find five counties casting a vote nearly as heavy as that of 1848. In the Muskingum region the proportion is a

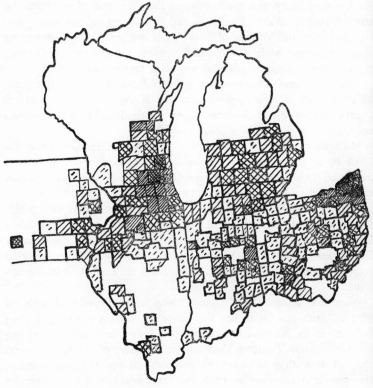

MAP OF THE FREE SOIL VOTE OF 1852.

little better than in 1848, but the Miami district has fallen off, and the traces of anti-slavery sentiment in the Virginia Military Lands due to Democratic bolters have died out.

In Indiana the Quaker counties stand much as they did before; but the New Englanders of the central counties, lacking the stubbornness of those of the Western Reserve, have fallen away.

Michigan has fallen back to almost precisely the situation of 1844; but Illinois shows an even worse drop. Not one of the thirteen counties that cast over 30 per cent. for Van Buren does the same for Hale, and the region which in 1848 surpassed the Western Reserve now is inferior to it. The scattered invaders of "Egypt" have drawn back, and things are not very much better proportionately than they were eight years before. The paralysis into which the return of the Chicago "Barnburners" in 1850 had cast the anti-slavery sentiment of the State is well illustrated by the map.

Wisconsin loses ground since 1848; but there are enough "Barnburners" of sterner stuff than their Illinois neighbors to keep three counties with over 30 per cent. for Hale, and to place Wisconsin second only to the Western Reserve.

In Iowa there is little change, except that Clark County, thinly settled with Eastern men, gives Hale over 20 per cent.

If the reader wishes to see a further proof of heredity and an additional indication of the influence of the Liberty and Free Soil parties, let him turn to Scribner's *Statistical Atlas*. There, in the Presidential vote of 1880, he will find the same counties Republican which in 1844 voted for Birney and Morris.

APPENDIX D.

CONSTITUTIONAL CONVENTIONS AND DIRECT POPULAR VOTES UPON NEGRO DISABILITIES.

1845–1851.

DURING the period under consideration each of the Northwestern States adopted a new constitution ; and in so doing it inevitably was led to take action in regard to negro suffrage and negro rights in general. Although this does not come strictly under the head of anti-slavery party politics, it offers too many valuable illustrations of local popular sentiment to be dismissed without some consideration.

IOWA.

Iowa was first in the field with a Constitutional Convention in the year 1845–46, the proceedings of which, unfortunately, the writer has been unable to find. It is not likely that at that time the question of negro rights aroused much interest. There was little active anti-slavery sentiment in the State ; there were few anti-slavery societies, no organized Liberty Party, and no anti-slavery newspapers. The only disability laid on negroes by the constitution was their exclusion from the suffrage and the militia, and this provision seems to have been adopted without any submission to popular vote.[1]

WISCONSIN.

Wisconsin came next in 1846. Here the limitation of the suffrage to white men was adopted in the convention without much opposition, although several anti-slavery petitions for equal rights were received. The friends of the negro, however, by a vote of 53 to 46, succeeded in having the question of negro suffrage submitted separately to the people.[2]

[1] See the correct text of the constitution of 1846 in *Debates of the Constitutional Convention of the State of Iowa* (Davenport, 1857), II., 1067. Article 12 in B : P. Poore, *Charters and Constitutions*, is wholly incorrect.

[2] *Journal of the Convention to form a Constitution for the State of Wisconsin*, Madison, 1847.

Accordingly in March, 1847, occurred the first referendum relating to negro rights in the Northwest, resulting in a decisive defeat of equal suffrage by a vote of 14,615 to 7,664. In the eastern counties the Germans and Scandinavians voted the Democratic ticket and were anti-negro; and in the western counties the population had come up the Mississippi River and was therefore Southern in character. In the central region, on the other hand, settled by people from New England and New York, eight counties gave favorable majorities.[1]

This constitution having been rejected by the people, another convention, meeting in 1847–48, at a time when the Wilmot Proviso excitement was rising, paid more attention to the negroes. Rufus King, editor of the *Milwaukee Sentinel*, introduced a resolution instructing the judiciary committee to consider the advisability of having an article in the constitution prohibiting all State or local magistrates from rendering assistance in catching fugitive slaves. Nothing came of this attempt; but when it was moved to amend the article defining suffrage qualifications by striking out the word "white," a hot debate arose, and the motion was defeated, 45–22. Another amendment, to the effect that the Legislature be allowed at any time to adopt negro suffrage, was carried, 35–34; but on reconsideration it was struck out by the change of one vote. Charges of abolitionism were made and denied, and the whole slavery question was brought into the discussion. Finally an amendment was carried, 37–29, allowing the Legislature at any time to submit the question of negro suffrage to popular vote; and in this form white suffrage was incorporated in the constitution.[2] The Legislature did not act on this matter until 1849, when it ordered another referendum, with the proviso that "a majority of the votes cast at the election" must favor negro suffrage in other to make an affirmative vote valid. Singularly enough, this referendum aroused scarcely any interest. Free Soilers were quarrelling so violently with Old Line Democrats that no campaign on the subject was made; and at the election the vote on this amendment was absurdly light. It stood as follows: *yes,* 5,265; *no,* 4,075; with no returns from a dozen counties.[3] As the total vote for Governor was 31,727, the majority in favor of negro suffrage was supposed by the terms of the submission to be insufficient; but in 1861 the Supreme Court, taking advantage of the ambiguous wording of the terms, held that the vote had been effective.

[1] F. E. Baker, *The Elective Franchise in Wisconsin,* 8.

[2] *Journal of the Convention to form a Constitution for the State of Wisconsin, with a Sketch of the Debates,* Madison, 1848.

[3] Returns in the office of the Secretary of State, Madison, Wisconsin.

ILLINOIS.

Illinois was the next State to adopt a new constitution, in May, 1848. In the convention the strong anti-slavery men of the northern counties met the pro-slavery delegates from " Egypt," and sharp contests ensued, ending in nearly every case in the total defeat of the friends of equal rights. Early in the session many petitions were handed in from both sections, one class demanding stringent anti-negro provisions of all descriptions, the other calling for equal suffrage and equal rights. The petitions were followed by resolutions to the same purport, most of which were defeated. A resolution that the Legislature have no power to pass laws oppressive to men of color was laid on the table, 92–46 ; and a motion to strike out the word " white " from the constitution was defeated, 137–8. On the other hand, a proviso that the Legislature should never extend the right of suffrage to colored persons was laid on the table, 60–91 ; and an article prohibiting intermarriage and declaring that no colored person should ever under any pretext hold any office was defeated, 65–64.

But though these extreme anti-negro propositions were rejected, others of great severity were adopted. White suffrage was taken as a matter of course, and no attempt was made to have the question submitted to the people. In response to numerous petitions a section was adopted by a vote of 87 to 56, directing the Legislature to pass laws prohibiting the immigration of colored persons ; and this matter was submitted separately to popular vote.[1] Illinois, then, was the second State to have a referendum on the subject of negro rights, not, as in Wisconsin, on the matter of suffrage, but on the proposal to prohibit immigration by constitutional law. The result was an overwhelming defeat for negro rights by a vote of 49,063 to 20,884 ; but although in so great a minority, the anti-slavery men carried fourteen counties in the northern part of the State.[2]

The Illinois Legislature did not act on the section thus adopted until 1853, when it passed a law unequalled for the anti-negro sentiment displayed. It punished by fine and imprisonment any person bringing a slave into the State, and fined every negro, bond or free, who entered the State fifty dollars for the first offence, one hundred dollars for the second, and so on. In default of payment either by himself or by his master,

---

[1] *Journal of the Convention assembled at Springfield, June* 7, 1847, Springfield, 1847.

[2] *Chicago Journal*, May 30, 1848.

the negro was to be sold for his fines and costs, at public auction, to the person bidding the shortest term of service. The prosecutor or informer was to have one half of the money, the remainder was to be used for *the deserving poor*. This bill was vigorously opposed by members from the northern counties, but it passed the House without difficulty. A vote to strike out the enacting clause was lost, 58–7 ; and on the final passage the vote was 48 to 23. The only success won by the friends of the negro was the securing of jury trial, by a vote of 39 to 26. In the Senate the majority in favor of the bill was smaller ; the vote on the final passage being 13–9. Mr. Judd, Senator from Cook and Lake Counties, represented anti-slavery opinion very well when he moved to amend the title to read, " An Act to establish Slavery in this State." [1]

MICHIGAN.

Indiana, Michigan, and Ohio held constitutional conventions in 1850. In the Michigan body, in spite of the fact that there were three Free Soil members, anti-slavery sentiment seems not to have been very strong. When the article on suffrage was reported to the convention, with negroes excluded, a motion was made to strike out the word " white." Some debate resulted, led by Mr. Leach in favor of the negro ; but, when the motion was put to vote, it was lost, and no one called for the yeas and nays. Later the motion to submit negro suffrage to the people was carried, 59–21, and in November the third Northwestern referendum took place.[2] It resulted, as had the other two, in a decisive defeat of equal suffrage by a vote of 30,026 to 12,846, almost exactly the same proportions as that in Illinois. Complete returns are not at hand ; but the friends of equal suffrage seem not to have carried a single county, being distributed quite evenly over the State, as the Liberty men and Free Soilers had been.[3]

INDIANA.

In the Indiana convention of 1850–51, the opponents of negroes showed greater determination than had been displayed in any of the preceding conventions ; for, although there was but one third-party Free Democrat in the body, there was a compact minority of anti-slavery Whigs who, under the lead of Schuyler Colfax, fought the pro-slavery

[1] *Journal of the House of Representatives* (Springfield, 1853), 271, 364, 443–44; *Journal of the Senate*, 475–76.

[2] *Report of the Debates and Proceedings in the Convention*, etc., Lansing, 1850.

[3] *Detroit Advertiser*, November, 1850.

men inch by inch. The question first to be settled was that of suffrage. When it was moved to instruct the Committee on the Franchise to provide that the people might by a direct vote extend the right of suffrage, an amendment to add the words " except to negroes, mulattoes, and Indians " was carried by a vote of 105 to 36. A motion " that negroes vote at all elections " was rejected, 122 to 1, receiving only the support of the one Free Soiler. Finally, when Colfax endeavored to get the subject of negro suffrage submitted separately to the people, he was defeated, 62 to 60.

Having carried this point, the Southern-born members of the convention pushed forward the subject of negro exclusion. Not willing to wait as their Illinois neighbors had done for legislative action, they determined to incorporate the rules of exclusion and penalties for their infringement in the Constitution itself. Accordingly, a stringent article was forced through in spite of Whig resistance. An attempt to strike out the clause at its introduction was defeated, 76 to 39 ; a motion to allow the General Assembly to enact negro exclusion whenever public interest demanded it, was rejected, 81 to 35 ; and after long debate and the steady rejection of all amendments, the subject was referred to a select committee. The committee's report to the convention passed the third reading, 94 to 36 ; amendments were rejected by the same vote ; and the article was adopted in substance as follows : —

1. No negro or mulatto was to come into or settle in the State after the adoption of this constitution.

2. All contracts with such negro or mulatto were to be void, and any person encouraging such to remain was to be fined not over $500.

3. Fines were to be applied to colonization purposes.

4. The General Assembly was to pass laws to carry out these provisions.[1]

This article was submitted separately to the people ; and Indiana in the autumn of 1851 signalized itself by decreeing negro exclusion by an enormous majority, greater in fact than that which the constitution itself received, the vote standing 108,513 to 20,951. The friends of the negro carried only two counties, Randolph and La Grange.[2]

OHIO.

In Ohio, the State where anti-slavery men might have been expected to make a good fight, there was surprisingly little struggle in the conven-

[1] *Report of the Debates and Proceedings of the Convention,* etc., Indianapolis, 1850.
[2] *Indiana Statesman,* Sept. 3, 1851.

tion of 1850–51. Seven Free Soilers were members, if we include Dr. Norton Townshend, for the time being a Democrat. Among them were J. W. Taylor, editor of the *Cincinnati Globe,* J. R. Swan, a Van Buren elector, and L. Swift, a Free Soil Senator in 1849. Some slight debate arose early in the session over the introduction of anti-slavery petitions; but the main, and in fact the only effort of the Free Soilers to do anything in favor of equal rights was made when the article on the franchise was reported, with the restriction contained in the use of the word " white." A motion, supported by Townshend and others, to strike out this word was lost, 12 to 66. A motion to allow the Legislature to extend the right of suffrage was lost, 11 to 68; and with this action the matter dropped. Negro suffrage was not submitted separately to the people ; and thus Ohio, like Iowa, remained without any referendum or plebiscite on questions relating to negroes.[1]

SUMMARY.

In these constitutions we find clear evidence of the state of popular opinion. Even the most anti-slavery of the Northwestern States, Wisconsin, acquiesced in negro exclusion from the suffrage, the apparent majority in favor in 1849 being only one-sixth of the total vote cast for Governor at the same election. Of the three Ohio River States we find Ohio most free from anti-negro feeling, as is shown by the fact that it did not include Black laws in its new constitution. In the distribution of votes the same facts are brought out as are shown in the Liberty and Free Soil elections; and in the total votes friendly to the negro — in the case of Indiana only much larger than the Free Soil maximum figures — we see how very little expectation the third party could have had of increasing its vote on anti-slavery grounds alone.[2] Philanthropy could not hope, unaided, to build up a party.

[1] *Report of the Debates and Proceedings of the Convention,* etc., Columbus, 1851.

[2] This conclusion is rendered more obvious by the following table, in which both votes are shown : —

Free Soil Vote, 1848.		Vote for Negro Privileges.	
Indiana	8,100	20,956	1851
Michigan	10,389	12,046	1850
Illinois	15,774	20,884	1848
Wisconsin	10,418	{ 7,664	1847
		{ 5,265	1849

INDEX.

———